MASTER
VISUALLY®

By Elaine Marmel

Visual

Quickbooks® 2005

Wiley Publishing, Inc.

Master VISUALLY® QuickBooks® 2005

Published by
Wiley Publishing, Inc.
111 River Street
Hoboken, NJ 07030-5774

Published simultaneously in Canada

Library of Congress Control Number: 2004117448

ISBN: 0-7645-7727-1

Manufactured in the United States of America

10 9 8 7 6 5 4 3 2 1

1K/TR/QR/QV/IN

Trademark Acknowledgments

Contact Us

For general information on our other products and services please contact our Customer Care Department within the U.S. at 800-762-2974, outside the U.S. at 317-572-3993 or fax 317-572-4002.

For technical support please visit www.wiley.com/techsupport.

WILEY

U.S. Sales

Contact Wiley
at (800) 762-2974 or
fax (317) 572-4002.

Praise for Visual Books...

"If you have to see it to believe it, this is the book for you!"

—PC World

"A master tutorial/reference — from the leaders in visual learning!"

—Infoworld

"A publishing concept whose time has come!"

—The Globe and Mail

"Just wanted to say THANK YOU to your company for providing books which make learning fast, easy, and exciting! I learn visually so your books have helped me greatly – from Windows instruction to Web development. Best wishes for continued success."

—Angela J. Barker (Springfield, MO)

"I have over the last 10-15 years purchased thousands of dollars worth of computer books but find your books the most easily read, best set out, and most helpful and easily understood books on software and computers I have ever read. Please keep up the good work."

—John Gatt (Adamstown Heights, Australia)

"You're marvelous! I am greatly in your debt."

—Patrick Baird (Lacey, WA)

"I am an avid fan of your Visual books. If I need to learn anything, I just buy one of your books and learn the topic it in no time. Wonders! I have even trained my friends to give me Visual books as gifts."

—Illona Bergstrom (Aventura, FL)

"I have quite a few of your Visual books and have been very pleased with all of them. I love the way the lessons are presented!"

—Mary Jane Newman (Yorba Linda, CA)

"Like a lot of other people, I understand things best when I see them visually. Your books really make learning easy and life more fun."

—John T. Frey (Cadillac, MI)

"Your Visual books have been a great help to me. I now have a number of your books and they are all great. My friends always ask to borrow my Visual books - trouble is, I always have to ask for them back!"

—John Robson
(Brampton, Ontario, Canada)

"I write to extend my thanks and appreciation for your books. They are clear, easy to follow, and straight to the point. Keep up the good work! I bought several of your books and they are just right! No regrets! I will always buy your books because they are the best."

—Seward Kollie (Dakar, Senegal)

"What fantastic teaching books you have produced! Congratulations to you and your staff."

—Bruno Tonon (Melbourne, Australia)

"Thank you for the wonderful books you produce. It wasn't until I was an adult that I discovered how I learn—visually. Although a few publishers claim to present the materially visually, nothing compares to Visual books. I love the simple layout. Everything is easy to follow. I can just grab a book and use it at my computer, lesson by lesson. And I understand the material! You really know the way I think and learn. Thanks so much!"

—Stacey Han (Avondale, AZ)

"The Greatest. This whole series is the best computer-learning tool of any kind I've ever seen."

—Joe Orr (Brooklyn, NY)

Credits

Project Editor
Maureen Spears

Acquisitions Editor
Jody Lefevere

Product Development Manager
Lindsay Sandman

Copy Editors
Kim Heusel
Scott Tullis

Technical Editor
Daniel Hodge

Editorial Manager
Robyn Siesky

Manufacturing
Allan Conley
Linda Cook
Paul Gilchrist
Jennifer Guynn

Book Design
Kathie Rickard

Project Coordinator
Nancee Reeves

Layout
Jennifer Heleine
Amanda Spagnuolo

Screen Artist
Jill A. Proll

Illustrator
Ronda David-Burroughs

Proofreader
Laura Bowman

Quality Control
Brian H. Walls

Indexer
Steve Rath

**Vice President and
Executive Group Publisher**
Richard Swadley

Vice President and Publisher
Barry Pruett

Composition Director
Debbie Stailey

About the Author

Elaine Marmel is president of Marmel Enterprises, Inc., an organization that specializes in technical writing and software training. Elaine has an MBA from Cornell University and worked on projects to build financial management systems from New York City and Washington, D.C. Elaine currently spends most of her time writing; she has been a contributing editor since 1994 to *Peachtree Extra* and *QuickBooks Extra* monthly magazines. She wrote *Peachtree For Dummies*, *Microsoft Project Bible*, and *Master VISUALLY Project 2003*. She has also authored and co-authored more than 25 books about Windows, Word for Windows, 1-2-3 for Windows, digital photography, and Lotus Notes.

Although a native of Chicago, Elaine has seen much of the world, including Cincinnati, Ohio; Jerusalem, Israel; Ithaca, NY; and Washington, D.C. At this writing, she is leaving the warmer climes of Florida for excitement and adventure in Arizona. In Arizona, she intends to live in a perfect house, built to her exact specifications, with her purrrfect cats, Cato, Watson, and Buddy (who seem to be made of velcro when she starts writing), and her doting and loving dog, Josh (who watches the door for visitors and might lick you to death while performing the job of general welcoming committee).

Author's Acknowledgments

Where should I begin? Every book is the combined efforts of many people, and this book is no exception. First, thanks goes to Maureen Spears for her unflagging dedication in making this a good book and keeping me sane while doing it. You made this a fun project, Maureen. Thanks to Jody Lefevere for the opportunity to write the book — I hope you are enjoying your time with your newborn baby girl, Libby, and I hope to speak with you when you return. Thanks to Daniel Hodge, Technical Editor Extraordinaire, who continues to keep me accurate when I write about QuickBooks. Thanks to the copy editors, Kim Heusel and Scott Tullis, for helping me maintain the book's style; your work does not go unnoticed. Thanks to the folks in graphics for all those mystical graphics things you do. Last, on a personal note, thanks to my brother and sister-in-law, Jim and Mariann Marmel, for being you and being there for me. I'm looking forward to the times ahead in AZ.

PART I

Set Up Background Information

1) Get Started with QuickBooks

2) Set Up General Background Information

3) Prepare to Invoice

4) Set Up Payroll Background Information

5) Set Up Customer Background Information

6) Set Up Vendor Background Information

7) Set Up Goods or Services

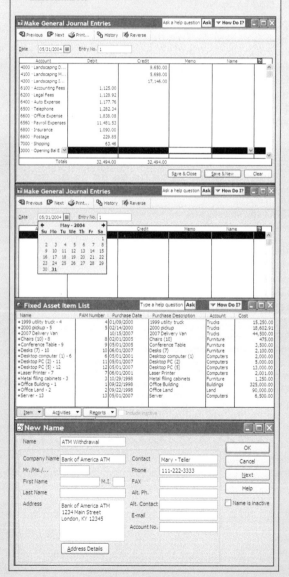

PART II

Payroll Activities

8) Pay Employees

9) Handle Payroll Tax Reporting

10) Track Time

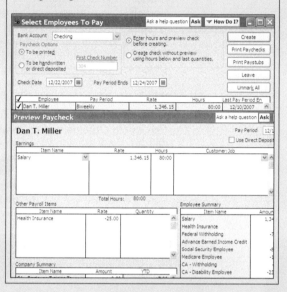

PART III

Customer and Job Activities

11) Invoice Customers

12) Work with Estimates

13) Record Customer Payments

WHAT'S INSIDE

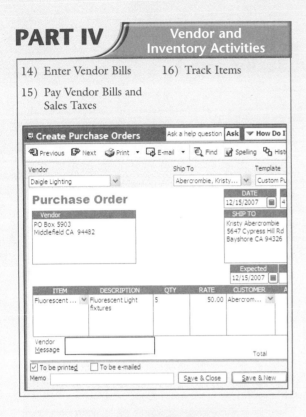

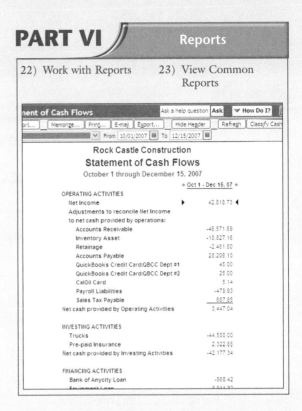

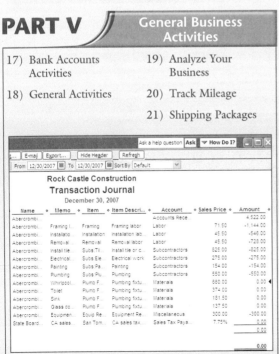

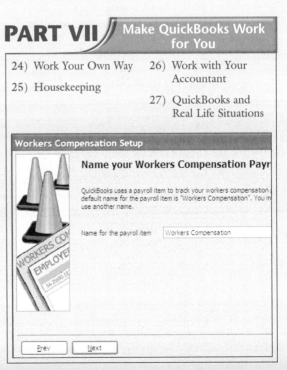

PART I

Set Up Background Information

1 **Get Started with QuickBooks**

2 **Set Up General Background Information**

3 **Prepare to Invoice**

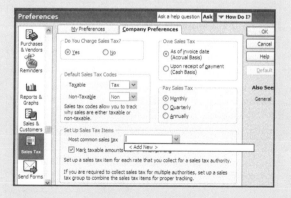

TABLE OF CONTENTS

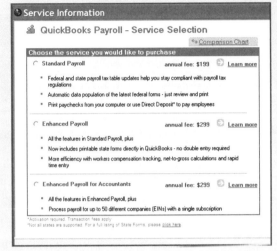

PART II

Payroll Activities

PART III

Customer and Job Activities

TABLE OF CONTENTS

PART IV — Vendor and Inventory Activities

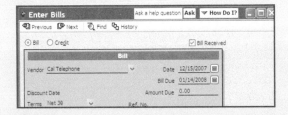

⑯ Track Items

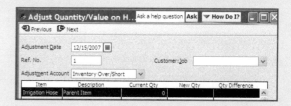

PART V   General Business Activities

⑰ Bank Accounts Activities

⑱ General Activities

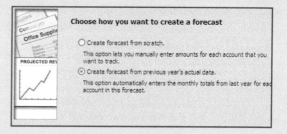

⑲ Analyze Your Business

TABLE OF CONTENTS

PART VI — Reports

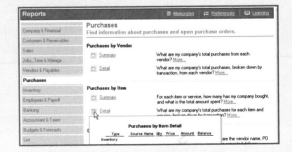

㉓ View Common Reports

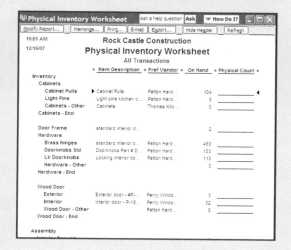

PART VII

Make Quickbooks Work for You

㉔ Work Your Own Way

TABLE OF CONTENTS

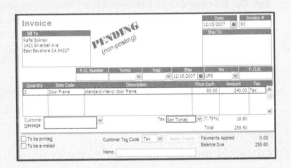

Do you look at the pictures in a book or newspaper before anything else on a page? Would you rather see an image than read how to do something? Search no further. This book is for you. Opening *Master VISUALLY QuickBooks 2005* allows you to read less and learn more about the QuickBooks programs.

Who Needs This Book

This book is for a reader who has never used QuickBooks. It is also for more computer literate individuals who want to expand their knowledge of the different features that QuickBooks has to offer.

Book Organization

Master VISUALLY QuickBooks 2005 has 27 chapters and is divided into seven parts.

Set Up Background Information, Part I, tells you all you need to know to begin using QuickBooks. When you follow the instructions in Chapters 1 to 7, you enter invoice, customer, payroll, vendor, and product background information so you can start benefiting from QuickBooks' many features.

Payroll Activities, Part II, shows you how to use QuickBooks in payroll related tasks, including paying employees, tracking an employee's time and setting up tax deductions from the employee's paycheck.

Customer and Job Activities, Part III, discusses how to invoice customers, work with estimates, and record customer payments.

Vendor and Inventory Activities, Part IV, shows you how to track your company's products as well as how to enter and pay vendor bills.

General Business Activities, Part V, covers how to reconcile bank accounts, how to analyze your business, how to track mileage and how to ship packages.

Reports, Part VI, shows you how to use QuickBooks to produce and review reports about your business.

Make QuickBooks Work for You, Part VII, shows you how to customize QuickBooks to work efficiently and includes information on housekeeping techniques like backing up, working with your accountant, and using QuickBooks in real life situations.

Chapter Organization

This book consists of sections, all listed in the book's table of contents. A *section* is a set of steps that show you how to complete a specific computer task.

Each section, usually contained on two facing pages, has an introduction to the task at hand, a set of full-color screen shots and steps that walk you through the task, and a set of tips. This format allows you to quickly look at a topic of interest and learn it instantly.

Chapters group together three or more sections with a common theme. A chapter may also contain pages that give you the background information needed to understand the sections in a chapter.

What You Need to Use This Book

To use QuickBooks, Intuit recommends at least 500 MHz Intel Pentium II (or equivalent) with 256 MB of RAM. At a minimum, you should have:

- 1,350 MHz Intel Pentium (or equivalent) with 96 MB of RAM
- Windows 98 (SE)/2000/XP
- 450 MB of disk space for QuickBooks installation
- Internet Explorer 6.0 (6.0 provided on CD. Requires an additional 70 MB of disk space)
- Microsoft .NET Framework CLR 1.1 (Provided on CD. Requires an additional 23 MB of disk space)
- At least 256 color SVGA video, 800x600 resolution with small fonts, 2x CD-ROM
- All online features/services require Internet access with at least a 56 Kbps modem
- Word and Excel integration requires MS Word and Excel 2000, 2002, or 2003

HOW TO USE THIS MASTER VISUALLY BOOK

Using the Mouse

This book uses the following conventions to describe the actions you perform when using the mouse:

Click

Press your left mouse button once. You generally click your mouse on something to select something on the screen.

Double-click

Press your left mouse button twice. Double-clicking something on the computer screen generally opens whatever item you have double-clicked.

Right-click

Press your right mouse button. When you right-click anything on the computer screen, the program displays a shortcut menu containing commands specific to the selected item.

Click and Drag, and Release the Mouse

Move your mouse pointer and hover it over an item on the screen. Press and hold down the left mouse button. Now, move the mouse to where you want to place the item and then release the button. You use this method to move an item from one area of the computer screen to another.

The Conventions in This Book

A number of typographic and layout styles have been used throughout *Master Visually QuickBooks 2005* to distinguish different types of information.

Bold

Bold type represents the names of commands and options that you interact with. Bold type also indicates text and numbers that you must type into a dialog box or window.

Italics

Italic words introduce a new term and are followed by a definition.

Numbered Steps

You must perform the instructions in numbered steps in order to successfully complete a section and achieve the final results.

Bulleted Steps

These steps point out various optional features. You do not have to perform these steps; they simply give additional information about a feature.

Indented Text

Indented text tells you what the program does in response to you following a numbered step. For example, if you click a certain menu command, a dialog box may appear, or a window may open. Indented text may also tell you what the final result is when you follow a set of numbered steps.

Notes

Notes give additional information. They may describe special conditions that may occur during an operation. They may warn you of a situation that you want to avoid, for example, the loss of data. A note may also cross reference a related area of the book. A cross reference may guide you to another chapter, or another section within the current chapter.

Icons and Buttons

Icons and buttons are graphical representations within the text. They show you exactly what you need to click to perform a step.

You can easily identify the tips in any section by looking for the Master It icon. Master It offer additional information, including tips, hints, and tricks. You can use the Master It information to go beyond what you have learn learned in the steps.

1
Get Started with QuickBooks

2
Set Up General Background Information

3
Prepare to Invoice

4
Set Up Payroll Background Information

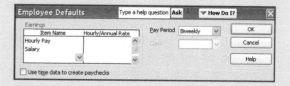

5 — Set Up Customer Background Information

6 — Set Up Vendor Background Information

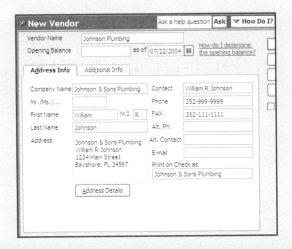

7 — Set Up Goods or Services

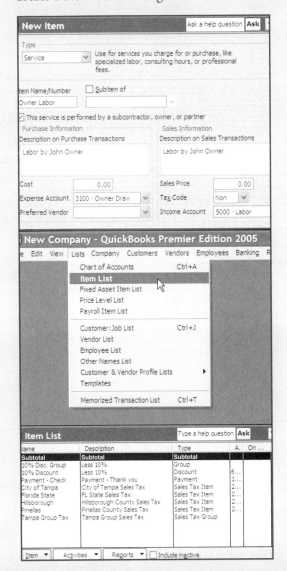

Set Up Chart of Accounts and Start Dates

The chances are excellent that your company will have been operating, if only for a short time, prior to the time you start using QuickBooks. To produce accurate financial information, you must type historical information into QuickBooks to account for the activities of your business up to the point when you start using QuickBooks. For this reason, you need your company's most recent Chart of Accounts. After you obtain this, you must decide on what date to start using QuickBooks.

After QuickBooks is in place, you need to gather the history of your company's finances. For more on gathering this information, see the section "Gather Historical Information."

Chart of Accounts

Every business has a Chart of Accounts that helps organize accounting information so that you can track it effectively. Each account has a name and usually a number. When creating the Chart of Accounts, accountants often use a numbering scheme that makes identifying the type of account easy. For example, accounts with numbers starting with 10000 may represent assets, accounts with numbers starting with 20000 may represent liabilities, accounts with numbers starting with 30000 may represent equity, accounts with numbers starting with 40000 may represent income, accounts with numbers starting with 50000 may represent cost of goods sold, and accounts with numbers starting with 60000 or higher may represent expenses.

You need a copy of your company's Chart of Accounts as well as the balances in each asset, liability, equity, income, cost of goods sold, and expense account as of the day *before* you start using QuickBooks.

Select a Starting Date

For most of your accounts, you can type one number that represents your historical balance in that account on the day you start using QuickBooks. For some accounts, however, you need to supply more detail. For example, the Accounts Receivable account balance represents the total of all invoices that your customers have not yet paid. When you receive a customer payment, you apply it to an open invoice to close that invoice and reduce the Accounts Receivable balance. So, to start using QuickBooks, collect all unpaid customer invoices as of the day you start using QuickBooks.

Before you start gathering information, decide on the first date you intend to use QuickBooks to account for your company's transactions. The date you choose determines the "as of" date of the information you need to collect. You should try to start using QuickBooks on the first day of an accounting period — either on the first day of your company's fiscal year or on the first day of a month. If you start using QuickBooks on January 1, you do not need to supply any historical payroll information.

Gather Historical Information

After you have a Chart of Accounts and have determined when to start QuickBooks per the section "Set Up Chart of Accounts and Start Dates," you must then gather some critical information. Collect the following information as of the day before you start using QuickBooks:

Chart of Accounts Balances
First, you need the balances of all the accounts listed on your Chart of Accounts. Ask your accountant for a Trial Balance report as of the day before you intend to start using QuickBooks.

Employee Information
You need the names, addresses, and background information found on the W-4 form for your employees. You also need to make a list of the various payroll benefits offered and the payroll taxes paid by your company. See Chapter 4 for details on setting up payroll background information.

Vendor Information
Obtain the names, addresses, and background information, such as payment terms, for your customers and vendors. Also have available the sales tax information that your municipality requires you charge your customers. See Chapter 3 for information about setting up sales taxes and other items you need to prepare invoices in QuickBooks. See Chapter 5 for details on setting up customers and Chapter 6 for details on setting up vendors.

Inventory and Product Lists
You need a list of the items that you sell. See Chapter 7 for information on setting up inventory, noninventory, service, and other items.

Reconciled and Unreconciled Items
Obtain the reconciled balance of each checking account and a list of all unreconciled checks and deposits. See Chapter 2 for details on setting up an existing checking account.

Outstanding Customer Balances
Obtain the most recent list of outstanding customer balances along with the invoices that comprise those balances. You type those invoices in QuickBooks the same way that you type new invoices. See Chapter 11 for details on entering invoices.

Vendor Balances
You need the outstanding vendor balances along with the bills that comprise those balances. You enter those bills in QuickBooks the same way that you enter new bills. See Chapter 14 for details on entering bills.

Select the Correct Edition of QuickBooks

Because QuickBooks is available in five different editions, selecting the edition that best supports your needs is important. You can purchase QuickBooks Basic, QuickBooks Pro, QuickBooks Premier, QuickBooks Enterprise Solutions, and QuickBooks Online Edition. QuickBooks Basic, QuickBooks Pro, and QuickBooks Premier are all aimed at small- to medium-sized businesses with 20 employees or less. QuickBooks Basic is a good product to use if you have been tracking your company's business activities either on paper or using a spreadsheet and are just getting started with electronic accounting. QuickBooks Pro contains more tools than QuickBooks Basic and, for example, enables you to customize and e-mail forms and reports. QuickBooks Premier contains all the features in QuickBooks Basic and QuickBooks Pro, along with budgeting, forecasting, and business planning features and stronger inventory tracking capabilities. QuickBooks Enterprise has the same features you find in QuickBooks Premier, but QuickBooks Enterprise works best for businesses with more than 20 employees. QuickBooks Online works well when several people across several locations need access to your accounting data.

In addition, during installation, you have the choice of installing one of the industry-specific editions for accountants, construction, manufacturing, nonprofit, professional services, retailers, and wholesalers. Most people use QuickBooks Basic, QuickBooks Pro, or QuickBooks Premier; this book is based primarily on the non-industry-specific edition of QuickBooks Premier, which contains features not found in QuickBooks Basic or QuickBooks Pro. You can use this book with editions other than QuickBooks Premier, but the screens may differ or features may not be available.

The table below provides you with a general comparison of some of the features in the products.

Feature	QuickBooks Basic	QuickBooks Pro	QuickBooks Premier	QuickBooks Enterprise	QuickBooks Online
Network-capable	No	Yes	Yes	Yes	Internet-based
Connects multiple locations	No	No	No	Yes	Yes
Acounts Payable functions (print checks, pay bills)	Yes	Yes	Yes	Yes	Yes
Accounts Receivable functions (invoice customers, track payments, track sales taxes)	Yes	Yes	Yes	Yes	Yes
Inventory tracking	Yes	Yes	Yes	Yes	No
Payroll functions	Yes	Yes	Yes	Yes	Yes
Account Reconciliation	Yes	Yes	Yes	Yes	No
Job Costing and Estimates	No	Yes	Yes	Yes	No
Time Tracking	No	Yes	Yes	Yes	Yes
Track Fixed Assets, Loans, and Vehicle Mileage	No	Yes	Yes	Yes	No
Supports shipping via UPS or FedEx	No	Yes	Yes	Yes	No
Reporting	Yes	Yes	Yes	Yes	Yes
Customize Forms	No	Yes	Yes	Yes	Yes

QuickBooks Basic

Using QuickBooks Basic, you can print checks, pay bills, track expenses, invoice customers and track their payments, create purchase orders and track inventory, process payroll, and generate reports and graphs. However, QuickBooks Basic does not contain many of the features that you find in the other editions of QuickBooks. QuickBooks Basic is also the only edition of QuickBooks that you cannot use in a network environment or in multiple locations.

QuickBooks Pro

QuickBooks Pro contains all the features you find in QuickBooks Basic along with, for example, the features necessary for job costing and estimating, time tracking, customizing forms, printing shipping labels and packing slips, interfacing with applications such as Microsoft Excel, Word, and Outlook, and e-mailing forms. Although you can use QuickBooks Pro in a network, you cannot use it in multiple locations.

QuickBooks Premier

QuickBooks Premier contains all the features you find in QuickBooks Basic and QuickBooks Pro. In addition, you can use QuickBooks Premier to build and track inventory assemblies, generate purchase orders from sales orders, set price levels for each item, track comprehensive employee information, analyze your business, and access your data in an internal network or remotely over the Internet.

QuickBooks Enterprise Solutions

QuickBooks Enterprise Solutions contains all the features found in QuickBooks Premier, adds some new features, and then expands on other features. For example, you can use QuickBooks Enterprise Solutions to connect not only through an internal network but also across multiple locations; and simultaneous user performance is better in QuickBooks Enterprise Solutions than in the other network-enabled editions. In QuickBooks Enterprise Solutions, you can filter and search customer lists and combine reports from multiple company files through an automatic export to Microsoft Excel. You also can store up to 29,000 customers, vendors, and products; in the other editions of QuickBooks, you can only store up to 10,000.

QuickBooks Online Edition

QuickBooks Online Edition, a subscription service, is a Web-based application that works like the desktop editions of QuickBooks. Instead of buying and installing QuickBooks on an individual computer, users purchase a subscription and then access QuickBooks through the Internet. QuickBooks Online Edition contains many of the features you find in QuickBooks Pro, along with the ability to connect multiple geographic locations.

Start QuickBooks

You can start QuickBooks in several ways. You can use the Start menu, a desktop shortcut, or even the Windows Run command. When you open QuickBooks for the first time, you see the Welcome to QuickBooks window. When you work in QuickBooks, you create a data file, which QuickBooks calls a *company file*, in which you store the information specific to your business. From the Welcome to QuickBooks window, you can open an existing company, create a new company, convert a Quicken file, or open a sample company. If you have not previously used QuickBooks, you must create a new company. See the section "Create a New Company" for details.

I have previously used QuickBooks, but have installed it on a new computer. How do I access my company?

▼ On your old computer, back up your QuickBooks company to either floppy disk, CD, zip disk, or a network hard drive. On your new computer, open QuickBooks. When you see the Welcome to QuickBooks window, click File and then click Restore. See Chapter 25 for details on backing up and restoring.

① Click Start.

② Click All Programs.

③ Click QuickBooks.

④ Click QuickBooks Premier Edition 2005.

Note: If you are using a different edition, click the name of that edition.

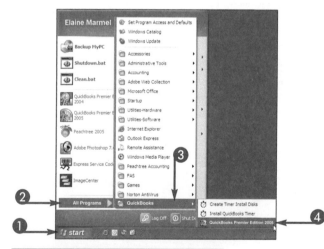

QuickBooks opens.

The Automatic Update screen appears, explaining that the Automatic Update feature is turned on.

⑤ Click OK.

The Welcome to QuickBooks window appears.

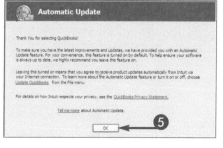

Create a New Company

To use QuickBooks, you must create a company data file to store information about your business. QuickBooks attempts to simplify this process with the EasyStep Interview Wizard, which walks you through the process of creating everything you need to use QuickBooks — a chart of accounts, all of your customers, vendors, employees, payroll information, inventory items, sales tax codes — and sets up opening balances for everything. In addition, you set preferences for all areas of QuickBooks in the EasyStep Interview Wizard.

Although being prompted for this information can ensure that you do not miss anything, you rarely have time to enter all of that information at one time. Although you

can leave and restart the wizard, most people find it easiest to manually create a company file and set up QuickBooks at their leisure. In this section, you create a company data file manually.

If I do not have time to complete the EasyStep Interview Wizard in one sitting, how can I restart the Wizard?

▼ Click File and then click EasyStep Interview.

Create a New Company

① Open QuickBooks.

Note: See the section "Start QuickBooks" to open QuickBooks.

② Click the Create a new company file icon.

The EasyStep Interview Wizard starts.

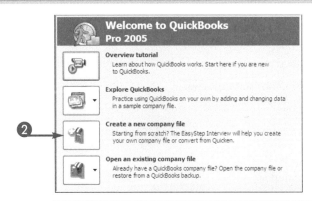

③ Click Next three times to walk through the wizard until you see the Setting up a new QuickBooks company page.

④ Click Skip Interview.

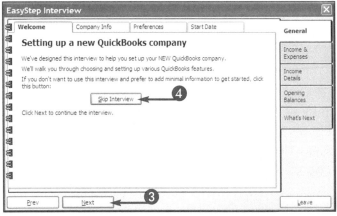

continued

Create a New Company *(Continued)*

To create a company data file, QuickBooks requires only two pieces of information: your company name and a business type. QuickBooks uses the other information you supply — legal name, address, phone numbers, and e-mail address — on reports and forms that you print and send to customers and vendors.

A *fiscal year* is an accounting period of 12 months. For most small businesses, the fiscal year runs from January 1 to December 31 — the calendar year. However, a fiscal year may be any 12-month period.

QuickBooks uses the fiscal year you supply to set the default date range for year-to-date reports that you print. Similarly, QuickBooks uses the tax year you supply to set the default date range for income tax summary and detail reports. You can, of course, change the date range on any report at any time.

If you select a tax form while creating your company, QuickBooks associates accounts listed on your Chart of Accounts with the appropriate lines on the tax form you select. This feature is most useful if you use Turbo Tax — a tax preparation software package sold by Intuit, the makers of QuickBooks — to prepare your business taxes.

Create a New Company *(continued)*

The first page of the Creating New Company Wizard appears.

5 Type your Company Name.

● The rest of the information is optional.

6 Click Next.

The second page of the Creating New Company Wizard appears.

7 Select your type of business.

● The proposed accounts for your Chart of Accounts appear.

Note: *Select your business type carefully; you cannot change it later.*

8 Click Next.

The Filename for New Company dialog box appears.

9 Type a filename for your company.

10 Click Save.

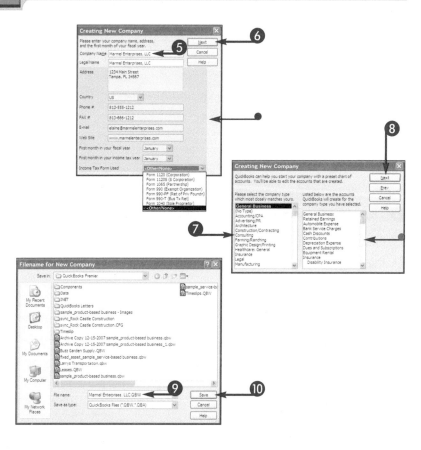

QuickBooks displays the QuickBooks Learning Center window.

- If you do not want to view the QuickBooks Learning Center each time you open your company file, deselect the Show this window at startup option (☑ changes to ☐).

⑪ Click Begin Using QuickBooks.

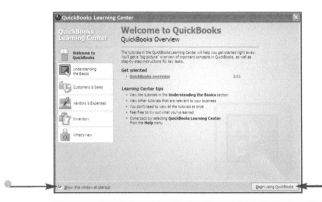

QuickBooks creates your company file and displays your company onscreen.

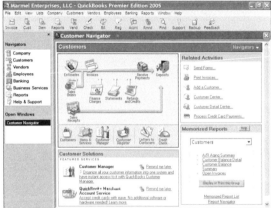

If I create my company file manually, do I need to follow a specific order to set up customers, vendors, and so on?

▼ QuickBooks does not require you to perform setup activities in any order, but the order you follow affects efficiency. First, create your Chart of Accounts. If you intend to use payroll features, set up payroll items — which are items you assign to employees — next and then create employees. You can assign sales representatives to customers, so, if employees do not act as sales representatives, set up sales representatives and then set up customers. Follow Chapters 1 to 7 sequentially to efficiently set up QuickBooks.

Can I create a new company file without any accounts in the Chart of Accounts?

▼ Yes. On the second page of the Creating New Company Wizard, select (No Type) from the list on the left.

Do you have any advice for the filename I supply?

▼ Yes. Using a filename that reflects your company name is a good idea. That way, if you start another business, you can easily distinguish one company file from another.

Understanding the QuickBooks Window

The QuickBooks window contains several features that help you work efficiently while creating and editing projects.

A Title Bar

Displays the name of the program and the current company.

B Menu Bar

Lists the menu names.

C Icon Bar

Contains buttons to help you select common commands, such as creating an invoice or opening the Item List window.

D Open Windows List

Provides an easy way to display a navigator or switch between open windows. Just click an entry in either list.

E Main Work Area

Open windows in QuickBooks appear in this area. If you change preferences to display multiple windows, you can move windows to any part of the screen.

Introducing QuickBooks Navigators

Q uickBooks contains six Navigators that you can use as an alternative to menu commands and the Icon bar to find your way around the program: The Company Navigator, the Customer Navigator, the Vendor Navigator, the Employee Navigator, the Banking Navigator, and the Business Services Navigator. The Business Services Navigator contains links to services and solutions that can help you manage your business. The other Navigators are divided into four areas.

Ⓐ **Process Area**

This area displays an interactive graphic representation of the tasks you commonly perform and how they relate to each other. You can click any icon to display the associated window.

Ⓑ **Related Activities**

This area displays links to additional tasks associated with an accounting area.

Ⓒ **Memorized Reports**

Using this area, you can print or display memorized reports or groups of reports, open the Memorized Report List, or use the Report Finder. For more information on memorized reports and the Report Finder feature, see Chapter 22.

Ⓓ **Customer Solutions**

This area displays links to add-on services that can help you manage your business.

Set Accounting Preferences

Y ou can control several facets of QuickBooks' behavior related to accounting. For example, you can use only names or a combination of names and numbers on the Chart of Accounts. And, if you use account numbers, you can control whether QuickBooks displays a complete account name or simply the lowest subaccount name. You can also use class tracking, a QuickBooks feature that helps you further delineate income and expenses. See Chapter 2 for information about accounts, subaccounts, and class tracking.

If you intend to use the audit trail feature in QuickBooks, you should also set up security to identify both the changes that were made and who made them. See Chapter 25 for

information on security. Using the audit trail feature can slow down QuickBooks and make your company data file larger, because QuickBooks records all changes instead of writing over transactions when you change them.

In the Preferences dialog box, two tabs appear for each set of available preferences: My Preferences and Company Preferences. My Preferences are those settings that you can customize for your own use without affecting other QuickBooks users. The options that appear on the Company Preferences tab affect everyone who uses QuickBooks.

Set Accounting Preferences

① Click Edit.

② Click Preferences.

The Preferences dialog box appears.

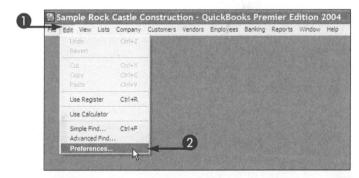

③ Click the Accounting icon.

- You can click the "Autofill memo in general journal entry" option (☐ changes to ☑) to automatically display memo information from the first line of a journal entry on all subsequent lines.

④ Click the Company Preferences tab.

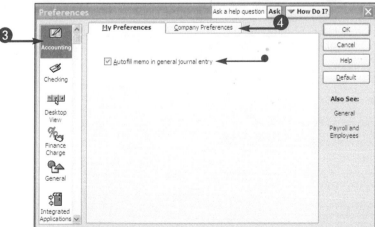

5 Click the options you want to activate
(☐ changes to ☑).

- The first two options control account numbers.

- The Require accounts option ensures that you assign all transactions to an account.

- Click here to use class tracking.

- The audit trail option monitors changes to transactions.

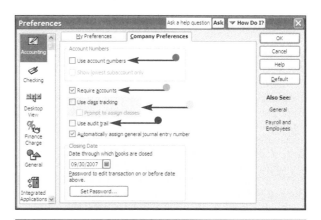

- You can also control the assignment of journal entry numbers.

- You can click the calendar button (▦) to set a closing date for your accounting data.

- You can click Set Password to set a password that users can type to modify closed transactions.

6 Click OK.

QuickBooks saves your Accounting preferences.

What is a closing date?

▼ QuickBooks uses the closing date to identify transactions that you can or cannot edit. You set a closing date to avoid changes to account balances prior to that date. Typically, you set the closing date to the last day of the preceding fiscal year, but you can set the closing date to any date you want.

What does Set Password do?

▼ Clicking this button opens the Set Closing Date Password dialog box in which you type a password twice — once to create the password and once to confirm it. Click OK to save the password.

How does the closing date password work?

▼ If you set a closing date without setting a password, QuickBooks warns you when you try to change transactions dated prior to the closing date, but still lets you make the change. To better protect closed account balances, you can also set a password that a user must supply to change a closed transaction.

What happens if I do not select the Require accounts option (☐ changes to ☑) and I do not assign a transaction to an account?

▼ QuickBooks assigns the transaction to an Uncategorized Income account or an Uncategorized Expense account.

Set Checking Account Preferences

You can control how QuickBooks behaves in relation to checking accounts and transactions affected by them. For example, you can select default checking accounts to use whenever you open any window from which you write a check, pay a bill, or make a bank deposit.

In addition to the payee name, the date, the total amount, the first 16 lines of the information in the memo field, and the amount field, which all print by default, you also can print the first 16 lines of the account name. On payroll checks, QuickBooks prints payroll item names instead of account names. On checks that pay for inventory items,

QuickBooks prints inventory item names. If you store account numbers for payees, QuickBooks can insert those account numbers automatically in the check memo field.

In the Preferences dialog box, two tabs appear for each set of available preferences: My Preferences and Company Preferences. My Preferences are those settings that you can customize for your own use without affecting other QuickBooks users. The options that appear on the Company Preferences tab affect everyone who uses QuickBooks. If you enabled security options, only the administrator can change the options on the Company Preferences tab.

Set Checking Account Preferences

① Click Edit.

② Click Preferences.

The Preferences dialog box appears.

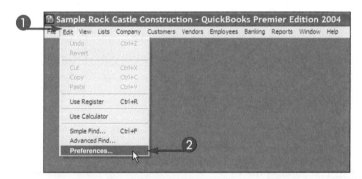

③ Click the Checking icon.

● Click these boxes (☐ changes to ☑) to select default checking accounts to use with each form.

④ Click the Company Preferences tab.

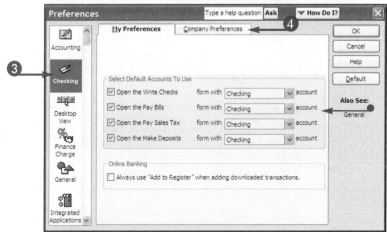

5 Click the options you want to activate
(☐ changes to ☑).

- The Print account names on voucher option controls the information that prints on check stubs.

- Click this option to change a check's date to the date that you print the check.

  The Start with payee field on check option positions the insertion point in the name field on checks, bills, and credit card charges.

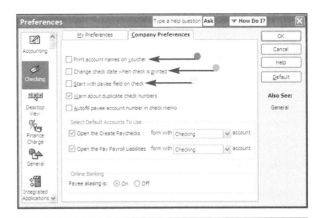

- You can click the Autofill option to automatically enter, in the Check Memo field, the account number stored with the payee's record.

- You can click these options to select default checking accounts for payroll-related transactions.

6 Click OK.

QuickBooks saves your Checking preferences.

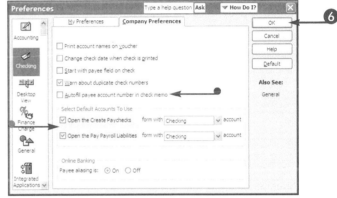

What information prints on the check stub if I do not select the "Print account names on voucher" check box?

▼ QuickBooks does not print the account name, payroll item name, or inventory item name, but still prints the payee name, date, the total amount, and the first 16 lines of the information in the Memo field and the Amount field. On stubs of checks that pay bills, QuickBooks prints the vendor's invoice number, date, and amount.

I do not see all my accounts when I select a default account. Why not?

▼ QuickBooks displays only bank accounts because only bank accounts are appropriate.

What happens if I do not select the "Change check date when check is printed" check box?

▼ Quickbooks prints the check with the date that is on the check form, even if it's several days before or after the current date.

Why would I not want to select the "Warn about duplicate check numbers" check box?

▼ QuickBooks takes longer to record a check because it must search your company data file for other occurrences of the check number. If you have a large company data file, enabling this option significantly affects performance.

Set General Preferences

Setting General Preferences enables you to control features that affect the QuickBooks program as a whole. For example, you can set the default date displayed for new transactions to either the current date or the last date you entered. You can also let QuickBooks automatically fill in transaction information from the last bill, check, or credit card charge you created for a particular name from a particular account.

You can also control the way QuickBooks displays time entries. If you select Decimal as the time entry format and type four-and-a-half hours as 4:30, QuickBooks displays 4.5 hours. Similarly, if you select Minutes and type 4.5, QuickBooks displays 4:30.

You can display two-digit or four-digit years; if you display four-digit years, you can type a two-digit year and QuickBooks displays four digits.

In the Preferences dialog box, two tabs appear for each set of available preferences: My Preferences and Company Preferences. My Preferences are those settings that you can customize for your own use without affecting other QuickBooks users. The options that appear on the Company Preferences tab affect everyone who uses QuickBooks. If you enabled security options, only the administrator can change the options on the Company Preferences tab.

Set General Preferences

1 Click Edit.

2 Click Preferences.

The Preferences dialog box appears.

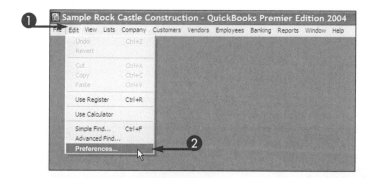

3 Click the General icon.

4 Click the options you want to activate (☐ changes to ☑).

- The first option enables you to use Enter to move from field to field on transactions.

- The second option activates an audible confirmation when saving transactions.

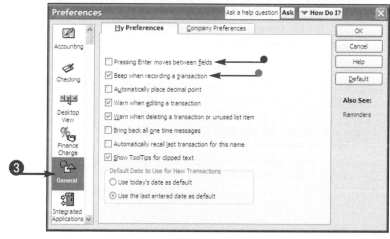

● Click the fourth and fifth options to display a warning when you try to edit or delete a transaction or delete an unused list item.

Click the sixth option to have QuickBooks redisplay one-time messages.

● This option automatically fills bills, checks, and credit card transactions with data from the last transaction you entered for that name.

5 Click the Company Preferences tab.

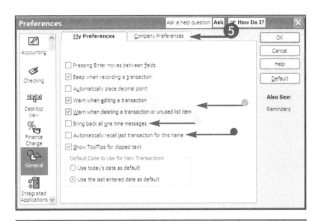

6 Click the options you want to activate (☐ changes to ☑ or ○ changes to ◉).

● The Time Format options enable you to select either a decimal or minutes format when recording time entries.

● This option displays four-digit years.

The last option enables you to avoid updating name list entries if you change information associated with that name on a transaction.

7 Click OK.

● QuickBooks saves your preferences.

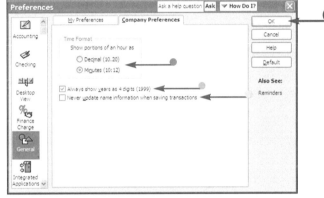

What happens if I do not select the Pressing Enter moves between fields option?

▼ If you do not select this option (☑ changes to ☐), you can use the Tab key or the mouse to move from field to field and press the Enter key to save transactions.

How do I save a transaction if the Enter key moves the insertion point from field to field.

▼ In the transaction window where you create the transaction, click Save & Close, or press Ctrl+A. You can also click Save & New, or press Ctrl+S.

What does the Show ToolTips for clipped text option on the My Preferences tab do?

▼ Some fields are not wide enough to automatically display all the information they contain. When you select this option (☐ changes to ☑) and move the mouse pointer over one of these fields, the entire content of the field appears in a ToolTip.

How does the Automatically place decimal point option work?

▼ When you select this option (☐ changes to ☑) and type a number with no decimal point, QuickBooks inserts a decimal between the second and third digits from the right end of the number. For example, 2995 becomes 29.95. When you do not select this option, 2995 becomes 2995.00.

Open an Existing Company

I f you set up more than one company in QuickBooks, or you want to test something in one of the sample company data files that ships with QuickBooks, you need to open an existing company. You may set up more than one company in QuickBooks because you run more than one business, or because you want separate QuickBooks data files for each division of your business.

The name of the currently open company appears in the QuickBooks title bar along with the edition of QuickBooks you are using. During the process of switching companies, QuickBooks automatically closes the current company for

you without any special action on your part. The company name disappears from the title bar, leaving only the name of the program. After you open another company, that company's name appears in the title bar.

This section presents two methods to open an existing company. In one method, you select a QuickBooks company using a dialog box. You can identify QuickBooks companies by the icon that appears next to the name and by the data filename's extension; QuickBooks company names end in *.qbw*, and an Accountant's copy of a QuickBooks company ends in *.qba*.

Open an Existing Company

Select any Company

① Click File.

② Click Open Company.

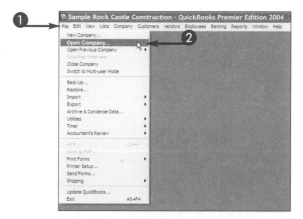

QuickBooks closes the current company and displays the Open a Company dialog box.

③ Click a QuickBooks company.

● The company name appears in the File name box.

④ Click Open.

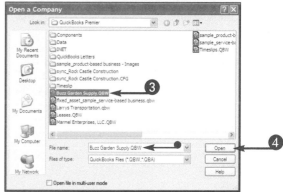

The company opens.

● The company's name appears in the title bar.

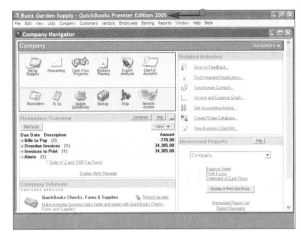

Open a Recently Opened Company

1 Click File.

2 Click Open Previous Company.

A list of the last four companies you opened appears.

3 Click the company you want to open.

QuickBooks opens the company, and the company name appears in the title bar.

How many previously opened companies can I display?

▼ Anywhere from 1 to 20. To change the number of previously opened companies that appears in the list, perform steps 1 to 2 in the subsection "Open a Recently Opened Company." At the bottom of the menu that lists the previously opened companies, click Set number of previous companies. QuickBooks displays a dialog box where you type a number between 1 and 20.

Can I control the order of the companies listed when I open a previously opened company?

▼ Not really. QuickBooks lists the companies from most recently opened to least recently opened.

What is an Accountant's Copy of a QuickBooks company?

▼ You and your accountant can share your QuickBooks data file so that both of you can work on the file simultaneously. As part of the process, you create an Accountant's copy of your company data file that you give to your accountant, who works on it and then gives it back to you. You ultimately merge the accountant's changes into your regular QuickBooks data file. For more information, see Chapter 26.

Create a
New Account

Although QuickBooks can create basic accounts when you create a company, rarely are these accounts sufficient or totally accurate for your business. You need to add or change the default QuickBooks accounts. Every business has assets, liabilities, equity, income, costs of selling, and expenses, and some of these categories break down even further. You create accounts in these categories and then post transactions to appropriate accounts to produce reports that accurately reflect the activity in your business.

Each account has a name and usually a number: Most people use a numbering scheme to easily identify the type of account. Typically, accounts with numbers starting with

10000 represent assets, accounts with numbers starting with 20000 represent liabilities, accounts with numbers starting with 30000 represent equity, accounts with numbers starting with 40000 represent income, accounts with numbers starting with 50000 represent cost of goods sold, and accounts with numbers starting with 60000 or higher represent expenses.

You also can use subaccounts to break down an account. Suppose that you pay telephone bills for landline service and several cellphones. To separately track phone service expenses, you may set up a Telephone expense account with subaccounts — one for Landline Service and separate subaccounts for each cellphone number.

Create a New Account

① Click Lists.

② Click Chart of Accounts.

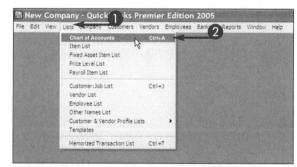

The Chart of Accounts window appears.

③ Click Account.

④ Click New.

The New Account window appears.

5 Click here and select an account type.

The fields change based on the account type.

6 Click in the Name field and type a name for the account.

● All other fields are optional.

Note: *If you see an Opening Balance field, leave it blank.*

7 Click OK.

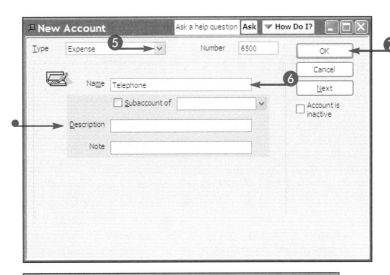

● The account appears in the Chart of Accounts window.

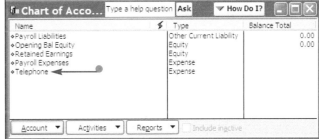

How do I enter opening balances for my accounts if I start QuickBooks midyear?

▼ Using the Trial Balance you received from your accountant, make two journal entries: one for all income and expense accounts and one for balance sheet accounts *except* bank accounts, Accounts Receivable, Accounts Payable, and Payroll Liabilities. For these remaining accounts, enter outstanding transactions. See Chapters 11 and 14 to enter open invoices and bills. For details on the journal entries and to establish opening balances for bank accounts, see the sections "Enter Opening Account Balances" and "Set Up an Existing Bank Account."

How do I edit an account?

▼ Follow steps 1 to 2 in this section and then click the account you want to edit. Follow step 3. For step 4, click Edit instead of New.

How do I delete an account?

▼ Follow steps 1 to 2. Click the account you want to delete and follow step 3. For step 4, click Delete instead of New. Note that you can delete an account only if your company data file contains no transactions associated with it. If you want to stop using an account, deactivate it using the same steps, but select Make Inactive in step 4.

Enter Opening Account Balances

Setting up opening balances for each account produces accurate reports and financial statements. For accuracy, first establish the date you intend to start using QuickBooks, and get a Trial Balance report from your accountant as of the day before you intend to start using QuickBooks. That is, if you intend to start using QuickBooks on June 1, get a Trial Balance report as of May 31.

Most people use two journal entries to set up opening balances. The first should include all income and expense accounts; post the amount not assigned to an account — the amount needed to balance the entry — to the Opening Bal Equity account. Use the same technique for the second journal entry, but include all Balance Sheet accounts *except* bank accounts, credit cards for which you record every transaction, Accounts Receivable, Accounts Payable, and Payroll Liabilities.

To create opening balances for Accounts Receivable and Accounts Payable, enter outstanding invoices and bills to retain aging detail and make posting payments easy; see Chapters 11 and 14. To create opening balances for checking accounts and credit cards for which you record transaction details, see the section "Set Up an Existing Bank Account." For payroll beginning balances, see Chapter 4.

Enter Opening Account Balances

① Click Company.

② Click Make General Journal Entries.

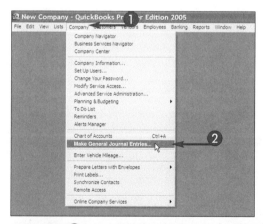

The Make General Journal Entries window appears.

Note: You may see a one-time message about numbering journal entries.

③ Click the calendar button (▦) to select the date for the entry.

Select the day before your QuickBooks starting date.

④ Click here to type a number for the entry.

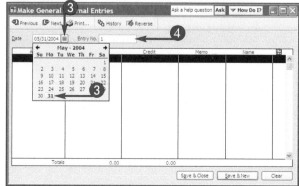

⑤ Click here to select an account.

⑥ Type an amount.

Most income account balances are credits; follow your Trial Balance report.

● QuickBooks displays the unassigned amount needed to balance the entry as you work.

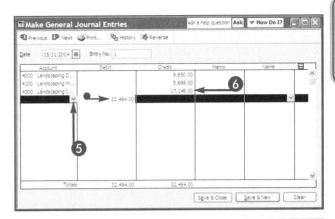

⑦ Repeat steps 5 to 6 for each income and expense account.

⑧ Assign the last line to Opening Bal Equity to balance the entry.

⑨ Click Save & New.

⑩ Repeat these steps for all balance sheet accounts except cash accounts, Accounts Receivable, Accounts Payable, and Payroll Liabilities.

⑪ Click Save & Close.

QuickBooks saves your opening account balances.

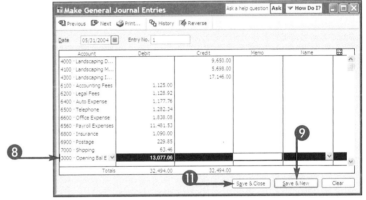

How can I check my work to ensure that I set up opening balances correctly?

▼ After entering opening balances for all accounts, including bank accounts, Accounts Receivable, Accounts Payable, and Payroll Liabilities, print the Trial Balance report. The Opening Bal Equity account should *not* appear on it.

What does the Reverse button do?

▼ Available only in Premier and Enterprise Solutions editions, the Reverse button creates a journal entry — dated the first day of the following month — that uses the same accounts but switches the debits and credits.

How do I handle credit cards if I pay them off in full each month?

▼ You have no opening balances for your credit card accounts and do not need accounts for them. When the credit card bill arrives, enter a bill in QuickBooks, assigning each credit card charge to an expense account.

How do I handle credit cards if I do not pay them off in full each month, nor do I want to enter every credit card transaction?

▼ Your credit cards have balances, so set up accounts for them and include their balances in the journal entry for Balance Sheet accounts.

Set Up an Existing Bank Account

Having an accurate checking account balance is the top item on the priority list of most business owners. But accurately reconciling the account each month is equally important; and, because bank reconciliation gets most people's vote for being their least favorite accounting task, making reconciliation easy should also be a high priority. You can easily reconcile a bank account in QuickBooks if you enter the correct opening balance for the account along with all transactions that have not yet cleared the bank. For more information on reconciling bank accounts in QuickBooks, see Chapter 17.

The opening balance number for a bank account should be the ending balance that appears on your last bank statement. If you did not reconcile your last bank statement, you must do so before you can really get started in QuickBooks; otherwise, you may find it difficult to reconcile the account later.

In this section, you set up a checking account that you have already been using. This section assumes that you have created a bank account with a zero balance in QuickBooks. For help creating the account, see the section "Create a New Account."

Set Up an Existing Bank Account

① Click Lists.

② Click Chart of Accounts.

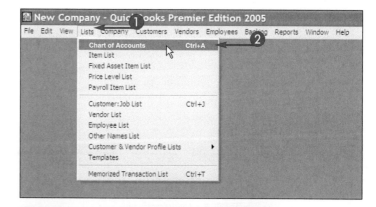

The Chart of Accounts window appears.

③ Click the bank account you want to set up.

④ Click Activities.

⑤ Click Use Register.

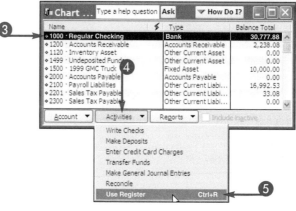

The register for the account appears.

6 Click 🔲 to select a date.

The date should precede your QuickBooks starting date.

7 Click here and type the ending balance on your last bank statement.

8 Click here and select Opening Bal Equity.

9 Click Record.

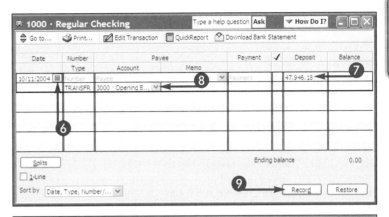

10 Click 🔲 and select a date.

11 Click here and type an outstanding check number.

12 Click here and type an outstanding check amount.

13 Click here and select Opening Bal Equity.

14 Click Record.

15 Repeat steps 10 to 14 for all outstanding transactions.

QuickBooks sets up your checking account.

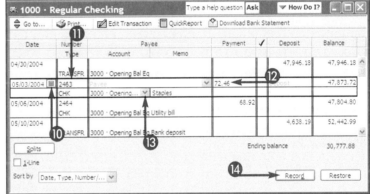

Is there a way that I can identify the purpose of these transactions?

▼ If you type anything in the Payee field, QuickBooks wants to add what you type to a list. Instead, type the descriptions for these opening balance transactions in the Memo column, which is next to the Account column where you select Opening Bal Equity.

How do I enter outstanding deposits?

▼ Follow steps 10 to 14 except for step 11; and, in Step 12, enter the amount in the Deposit column as you did when you entered the ending balance on your last bank statement in step 7.

How can I view more lines in the window?

▼ You can drag the bottom border of the window down or the top border of the window up to enlarge the window. You can also click the 1-Line option (☐ changes to ☑) to display only one line per transaction in the register. In 1-Line view, however, the Memo column does not appear.

What does the Splits button do?

▼ The Splits button enables you to assign portions of an amount to different accounts. Do not click Splits while entering opening balance information.

Create Classes

C lass tracking is a QuickBooks feature that helps you further delineate income and expenses. To determine the classes to use, think about the way that you want to report on income and expenses. For example, if you operate in several locations, set up a class for each location. You can also use classes to track income and expenses for different lines of business; attorneys may set up classes for litigation, real estate, estate planning, and family law. Although you can use accounts and subaccounts for this type of tracking, you risk making your Profit and Loss statement lengthy and difficult to read.

You use classes for only one purpose. To see your income and expenses in more than one way, consider using either accounts or items along with classes. Also, be aware that classes are available only for income and expense accounts.

After you establish classes, you assign the classes to each transaction. You can then print the Profit & Loss by Class report for a breakdown of income and expenses by class. See Chapters 22 and 23 for information on reporting.

To create classes, you must turn on the preference for class tracking. For more on setting accounting preferences, see Chapter 1.

Create Classes

① Click Lists.

② Click Class List.

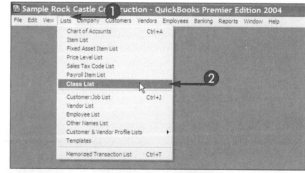

The Class List window appears.

③ Click Class.

④ Click New.

The New Class dialog box appears.

⑤ Click in the Class Name field and type a name.

● You can click here (☐ changes to ☑) to assign a subclass and then click ☑ to select the parent class.

⑥ Click OK.

● The new class appears in the Class List window.

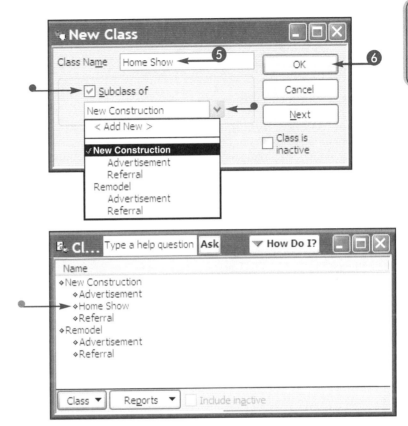

What should I do if I know that I cannot classify all transactions?

▼ If you do not classify a transaction, the Profit & Loss by Class report displays a column called Unclassified. To avoid this situation, set up a class called Other for transactions you cannot classify.

Am I required to assign a class to every transaction?

▼ When you turn on class tracking, you can set an option that prompts you to assign a class as you save the transaction. However, the prompt is not a requirement; you can save the transaction without a class.

Must I assign an entire transaction to one class?

▼ You can classify both income and expense transactions on a line by line basis. On income transactions, you have the choice of classifying according to line or transaction; but on expense transactions, you can classify only according to line.

How do I easily identify and classify unclassified transactions?

▼ Display the Profit & Loss Unclassified report and double-click any amount to see a list of the transactions that comprise the amount. Double-click a transaction to open it in the window in which it was created and assign the transaction to a class. For more on accessing the Profit & Loss Unclassified report, see Chapters 22 and 23.

Create a New Fixed Asset Item

Fixed assets are things that you own and use in a way that benefits your business for longer than one year and generates revenue, either directly or indirectly, for your business. If you own the printing presses you use, those presses are fixed assets. The ovens used to prepare food in a restaurant are fixed assets. Buildings, office furniture, computers, cash registers, and vehicles are all considered fixed assets.

Because fixed assets last longer than one year, generally accepted accounting principles require you to allocate the expense of a fixed asset purchase over the asset's useful life, rather than recognizing the entire expense in the year you

make the purchase. This process of spreading an expense over the life of the asset is called *depreciation*.

As you depreciate fixed assets, their value on your financial statements declines, affecting both the value of your business and the amount of taxes you pay. Several methods of depreciating assets exist; you should consult your accountant to select the most appropriate method.

To accurately calculate depreciation, you need to track information about your fixed assets. In QuickBooks, you use fixed asset items to track the life of fixed assets for tax and depreciation purposes.

Create a New Fixed Asset Item

① Click Lists.

② Click Fixed Asset Item List.

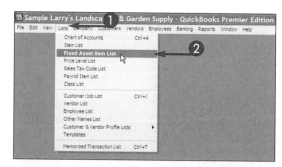

The Fixed Asset Item List window appears.

③ Click Item.

④ Click New.

The New Item window appears.

5 Type a name for the new item.

6 Click here and select an account.

7 Type purchase information in this section.

● Optionally, you can type information that describes the asset.

8 Click OK.

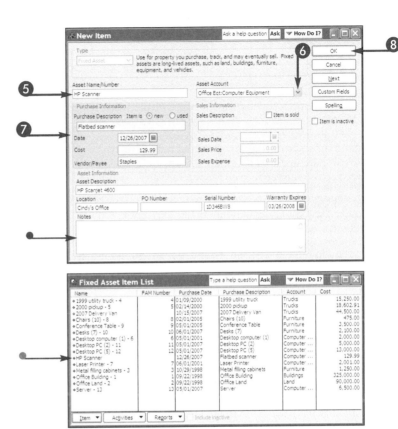

● The new fixed asset item appears in the Fixed Asset Item List.

What fixed asset information do I need to track to calculate depreciation?

▼ Typically, you need the asset's purchase date, purchase price, sale date, and sale price. It is also useful to track where you bought the asset, its current location, and, if appropriate, its serial number and warranty information.

Should I assign each fixed asset to its own account on the Chart of Accounts?

▼ Only if you do not intend to use fixed asset items. Prior to the introduction of fixed asset items in QuickBooks, using separate accounts was the best way to track purchase and sale price information.

How do I record the purchase of a fixed asset?

▼ You enter a bill or write a check using a fixed asset item. If you purchase two laser printers at the same time, create separate fixed asset items for each printer and list the printers on two line items on the bill or check. See Chapter 14 for information on bills and checks.

How can my accountant use this information?

▼ Using the QuickBooks Fixed Asset Manager, your accountant can calculate depreciation and enter it in your company data file. Otherwise, using the Fixed Asset Listing, your accountant can provide you with depreciation information.

Set Up Loans

When you borrow money, the amount of the loan becomes a liability for your company, and you need to track loan payments. You can use the Loan Manager in QuickBooks to view payment schedules, set up loan payments, and analyze different loan scenarios.

Set up a liability account to track a loan (most loans are long-term liabilities). Also set up the vendor to whom you make loan payments; see Chapter 6 for details. Each loan payment is comprised of both interest and principal. Because the interest you pay is deductible on your taxes, track it separately from your loan payment using an interest expense account.

If your loan requires that you make escrow payments, you also need to set up an Other Current Asset account for escrow. *Escrow* is a portion of the loan held in an account by a third party until the conditions of the loan are met. Home loans often require escrow payments for property taxes and homeowner's insurance. To use the Loan Manager, you also need a bank charges expense account.

When you add the loan to the Loan Manager, have your loan papers available so that you can supply the necessary information.

Set Up Loans

① Click Banking.

② Click Loan Manager.

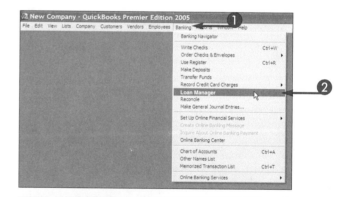

The Loan Manager window appears.

③ Click Add a Loan.

The Add Loan Wizard begins.

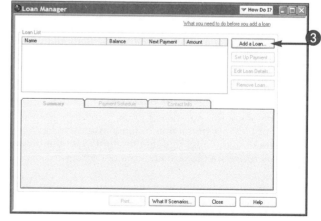

④ Click here and select a loan.

⑤ Click here and select the lender.

⑥ Click ▤ to select the origination date.

⑦ Type the original loan amount as well as the number of weeks, months, or years.

⑧ Click Next.

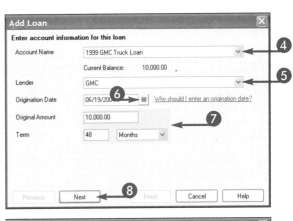

The next page of the wizard appears.

⑨ Click ▤ to select the due date of the next payment.

⑩ Type the payment amount here, including principal and interest.

⑪ Click here to select a payment period.

⑫ Click an option for escrow payments (○ changes to ◉).

⑬ Click Next.

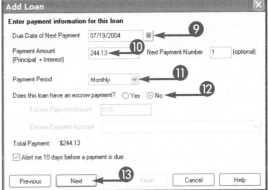

How do I set up the loan amount?

▼ If the lender gives the money directly to you, record a deposit to your checking account and assign the deposit to the loan's liability account. If the lender gives the money to a third party on your behalf — for, say, a truck — set up an asset account for the truck and a liability account for the loan. Then record a journal entry that debits the asset account and credits the liability account. Assign the lender to the credit line of the journal entry.

If my loan requires an escrow payment, what do I do?

▼ Click Yes (○ changes to ◉) next to Does this loan have an escrow payment? Then type the escrow payment amount listed in your loan documents and select an escrow account for the escrow portion of the loan payment.

How does QuickBooks alert me that a payment is due?

▼ QuickBooks sets up an alert in your Reminders list that reminds you of the loan payment ten days before the due date. For more information on reminders, see Chapter 24.

continued

Set Up
Loans *(Continued)*

The documents that lenders give you include the loan origination date and amount, the term, the payment amount and period, the interest rate, and the compounding period.

The compounding period, which is the frequency used to compound interest on the loan, affects the amount of interest you owe. The more frequently interest is calculated, the more interest you pay over the life of the loan. For the compounding period, the Loan Manager can use either exact days or the same time frame as your payment period.

If your lender uses exact days to compound interest, daily interest charges are calculated on either a 360- or a 365-day year — check your loan documents for the value.

The Loan Manager can also help you evaluate the effects of making changes to your loan. For example, if you increase your loan repayment amount, you pay off the loan sooner and pay less interest, dropping the total cost of borrowing. You can calculate the effects of various loan payment amounts on the total you pay and the loan's maturity date. You can also test the effects of different interest rates, a new loan, refinancing an existing loan, or comparing two possible loans.

Set Up Loans *(continued)*

The last page of the Add Loan Wizard appears.

⑭ Type the interest rate of the loan.

⑮ Click here to select a compounding period.

● If necessary, select a Compute Period.

⑯ Select accounts from which you write loan checks, post interest, and post bank charges.

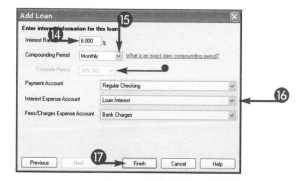

⑰ Click Finish.

The loan appears in the Loan Manager window.

⑱ Click the Payment Schedule tab.

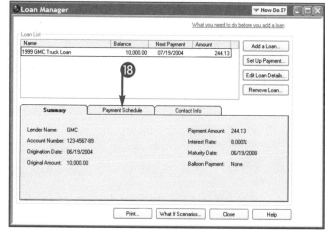

- The Loan Manager displays an amortization schedule showing each payment's principal and interest amounts and the loan balance after each payment.

19 Click What If Scenarios.

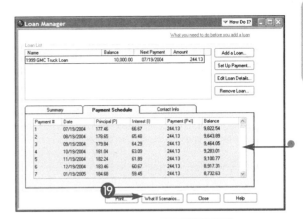

The What If Scenarios dialog box appears.

20 Click here to select a scenario.

21 Click ⊡ and select a loan.

22 Click Calculate.

The Loan Manager recalculates the loan information.

What does the Loan Manager do with the loan origination date?

▼ The Loan Manager uses it to calculate the loan maturity date and the number of remaining payments you see in the amortization schedule on the Payment Schedule tab.

What choices are available for the payment period?

▼ The Loan Manager can manage loans with weekly, biweekly, semimonthly, monthly, bimonthly, quarterly, semiannual, or annual payment periods.

What happens if I click Edit Loan Details in the Loan Manager?

▼ For the loan selected in the Loan List, the Loan Manager starts the wizard you used to set up the loan, displaying details you entered previously. You can make changes as needed.

What happens if I click the Contact Info tab on the Loan Manager?

▼ The Loan Manager displays the details associated with your lender. You store those details when setting up the lender in one of QuickBooks' lists — either the Vendor List or the Other Names List.

Create Other Names

You can use the Other Names List to store information that does not fit into any other QuickBooks list. Lists serve as the backbone of QuickBooks because they store all the information that you use repeatedly. You must set up, in the appropriate list, every customer, vendor, employee, item, payroll item, and so on, that you use in QuickBooks. Among other details in the Customer:Job List, you store name and address information, the terms for each customer, the sales rep responsible for each customer, and, if appropriate, the various jobs you perform for your customers. The Vendor List serves the same purpose for vendors, and the Employee List serves the same purpose for employees. See Chapters 4, 5, and 6 for information on creating list entries for employees, customers, and vendors.

Occasionally, you may have to record cash transactions for people who do not really fit in the Customer:Job List, the Vendor List, or the Employee List. For example, sole proprietorships write checks to owners for the owners' draw. Owners are not customers, jobs, vendors, or employees. You record ATM withdrawals by writing a check, but no payee really exists. In these situations, use the Other Names List to record cash transactions; if you want to enter a bill, set up a vendor.

Create Other Names

① Click Lists.

② Click Other Names List.

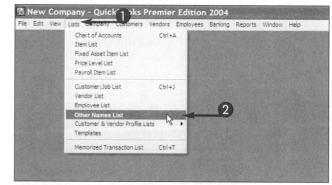

The Other Names window appears.

③ Click Other Names.

④ Click New.

The New Name dialog box appears.

5 Click in the Name field and type a name for the list.

● All other fields are optional.

6 Click OK.

● The new name appears in the Other Names window.

● If a note exists for an entry, you see this icon (☑).

You can double-click ☑ to view the note.

What are notes and how do I create a note for an entry in the Other Names List?

▼ You can store miscellaneous information that does not fit elsewhere in a note. Double-click in the Notes column next to the name for whom you want to create a note. QuickBooks opens the Notepad dialog box for the selected name. The information you stored about the Other Name entry appears in the top portion of the dialog box — you cannot edit that information here — and a large text box appears at the bottom of the dialog box. Type your note and click OK.

How do I edit an Other Names entry?

▼ Double-click the entry in the Name column. QuickBooks displays the Edit Name dialog box, which looks exactly like the Add Name dialog box in this section, except that the Edit Name dialog box contains a Notes button (☑) on the right side (and the Notes button opens the Notes dialog box).

What does the Next button in the New Name dialog box do?

▼ It saves the currently displayed information and presents an empty version of the box so that you can add another name without closing and reopening the dialog box.

Define
Custom Fields

QuickBooks provides custom fields so that you can store information for which no fields exist in QuickBooks pertaining to customers, vendors, employees, and certain items. For example, if your business operates from two locations, you may want a custom field for customers that identifies the office that services them. You can use the same custom field for employees to identify the office from which each employee works. Essentially, you create labels that appear in the records of customers, vendors, employees, and items. Then, in customer, vendor, employee, and item records, you supply the information indicated by the label.

After you define custom fields, you can include them on transactions on-screen in QuickBooks, when you print the transaction form, or both if you activate the custom fields in the forms you use. See Chapter 24 for details. You also can list the contents of custom field information on reports.

In this section, you set up custom fields for customers, vendors, and employees by pretending to create a new vendor; you can pretend to create a new customer or employee to set up custom fields. The process for setting up custom fields for items is essentially the same.

Define Custom Fields

① Click Lists.

② Click Vendor List.

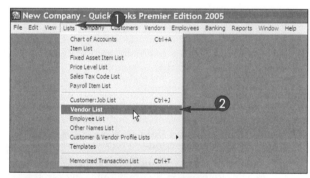

The Vendor List window appears.

③ Click Vendor.

④ Click New.

The New Vendor dialog box appears.

5 Click the Additional Info tab.

6 Click Define Fields.

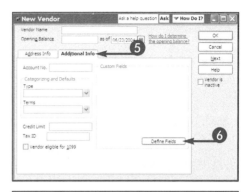

The Define Fields dialog box appears.

7 Type field labels and click options
(☐ changes to ☑) to activate the fields.

8 Click OK to save the custom fields.

A message appears describing how to use custom fields in transactions. Click OK.

9 Click Cancel to avoid saving the vendor.

For what types of items can I set up custom fields?

▼ You can set up custom fields for Service, Inventory, Non-Inventory, Inventory Assembly, Other Charge, Group, Discount, and Payment items.

Are custom fields available on reports?

▼ Yes. You can sort and filter most list and detail reports on which you include custom fields according to one custom field.

What kinds of custom fields can I store for items?

▼ If you sell clothing, you may want to store color and fabric information. If you store items in bins, you can use a custom field to identify the bin number. If your business has more than one warehouse, you can use a custom field to indicate the warehouse where you store the item.

Can I edit an existing list entry instead of creating a new one to define custom fields?

▼ Yes. In place of steps 3 and 4, double-click an existing entry.

Create a New Subtotal Item

W hen you create a sales or purchasing transaction, such as an invoice or a purchase order, you place items on the invoice or purchase order. QuickBooks automatically subtotals the items that appear on the transaction, applies taxes if appropriate, and then totals the transaction. However, you may want to subtotal the transaction before applying taxes; for example, you may want to give a discount to a customer or apply a special handling charge. In cases like these, you use a Subtotal item.

The *Subtotal item*, which you can place anywhere on the transaction, adds all items above it until another Subtotal item appears. By strategically placing Subtotal items on a

transaction, you can subtotal different sets of items. For example, you can subtotal the first three items on the invoice and apply a 10 percent discount to them and then subtotal all subsequent items and apply a 5 percent discount to them.

Subtotal items work not only on invoices, but also on all QuickBooks transactions that use items, and the same principles apply when you use a Subtotal item on another QuickBooks transaction.

For more about setting up items to use on transactions, see Chapter 7. For more on preparing sales transactions, see Chapter 11. For more on entering a purchasing transaction, see Chapter 14.

Create a New Subtotal Item

① Click Lists.

② Click Item List.

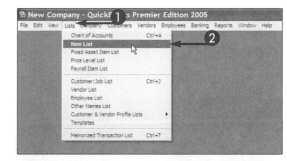

The Item List window appears.

③ Click Item.

④ Click New.

The New Item dialog box appears.

5 Click here and select Subtotal.

6 Type a name for the Subtotal item.

You can use both numbers and letters.

7 Type a description of the item.

8 Click OK.

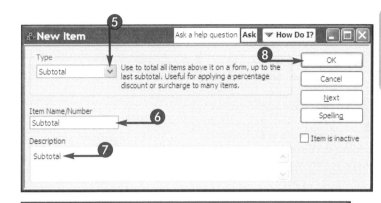

● The new Subtotal item appears in the Item List window.

Is there a difference between the Item Name and the Description?

▼ Yes. On the various QuickBooks form windows, you select the item's name from a list. After you select the item, QuickBooks displays the item's description in the Description column of the form. Typically, whatever you see in the Description column on the form also prints when you print the form.

What does the Activities button in the Item List window do?

▼ When you click Activities, QuickBooks displays commands you commonly perform when using items. In particular, you can open the Create Invoices window, the Enter Sales Receipts window, or the Change Item Prices window from the list that appears when you click Activities.

What does the Next button do?

▼ If you want to continue creating items, click Next to redisplay an empty New Item window. You can create any kind of item, not just a Subtotal item.

How do I give the customer a discount?

▼ You use a Discount item; see the section "Create a New Discount Item" for more information.

Create a New Discount Item

To give your customers discounts, you must set up a Discount item to use when entering sales transactions in QuickBooks. See Chapter 7 for more on setting up the items you sell or buy, and see Chapter 11 to prepare sales transactions.

You can apply dollar-amount discounts or percentage discounts. You can discount an entire document, a portion of a document, or a single item on a document. QuickBooks calculates a discount for the item that precedes the Discount item on the document. If the preceding item is a subtotal, QuickBooks applies the discount percentage to that subtotal. So, to discount the entire document, place a subtotal followed by the Discount item at the bottom of the transaction. To discount part of a document, place a subtotal after the discounted items, followed by the Discount item and then the remaining, nondiscounted items. To discount a single item, enter the Discount item immediately after the item you want to discount.

Do not confuse the Discount item with the timely payment discount you give to customers or receive from vendors. Timely payment discounts are based on terms, and QuickBooks calculates them automatically once you assign terms to customers and vendors. For more on setting up terms, see Chapter 5.

Create a New Discount Item

① Click Lists.

② Click Item List.

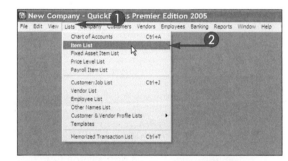

The Item List window appears.

③ Click Item.

④ Click New.

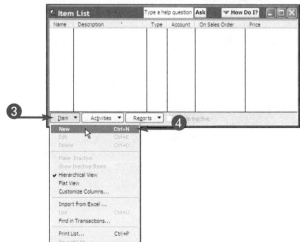

The New Item dialog box appears.

5 Click here and select Discount.

6 Type a name, a description, and the discount amount or percentage.

● You can click the Subitem of option (☐ changes to ☑) and select an item.

7 Click here and select an account.

8 Click OK.

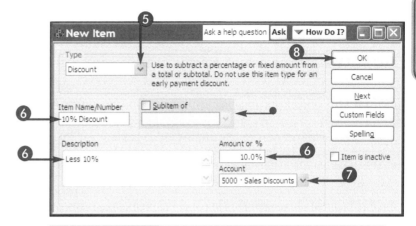

The new Discount item appears in the Item List window.

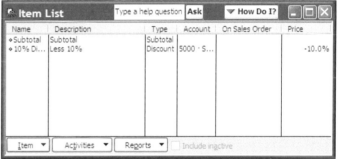

I offer some customers a bigger discount than other customers. How should I handle these cases?

▼ For each discount you offer, create a Discount item. That is, if you offer a 10% discount and a 5% discount, each to different customers, set up a 10% Discount item and a 5% Discount item. The Discount item is not tied directly to a customer. The discount you apply and its position on the transaction determine how QuickBooks calculates the discount and for whom.

How do I indicate that I want to discount a dollar amount?

▼ When you type the discount amount or percentage, type only the amount; do not type a dollar sign or a percent sign (%). QuickBooks determines whether to calculate a dollar amount discount or a percentage discount based on whether you include or exclude the percent sign.

What is a subitem?

▼ You can use subitems to create a hierarchy of items as a matter of convenience. Subitems help you group items together on reports and do not appear any differently than items when you use them on forms. To use subitems, first create the parent item — the item under which you want to group the subitems. Then, create the subitems. Subitems must use the same item Type that the parent item uses, and you must assign accounts to both parent items and subitems.

Create a New Group Item

Y ou can create a Group item to quickly enter a collection of items on a sales or purchasing document. For example, if you give discounts only on subtotals, you can create a Group item that includes the Subtotal item and the Discount item. When you enter the Group item, QuickBooks automatically enters two items for you in the order they appear in the Group item.

You use a Group item if you always sell or buy certain items together, as a group. If you always buy or sell chairs and printer stands whenever you buy or sell desks, save time

while entering purchasing or selling documents by using a group that consists of a desk, a chair, and a printer stand. When you enter the Group item on a sales or purchasing document, QuickBooks enters three items simultaneously.

You can include both taxable and nontaxable items in a group; similarly, you can include inventory and other types of items in a group. If the group includes taxable items, QuickBooks calculates sales tax for the individual items in the group. If the groups include inventory parts, QuickBooks updates the quantity on hand at the time you sell or buy the group.

Create a New Group Item

1 Click Lists.

2 Click Item List.

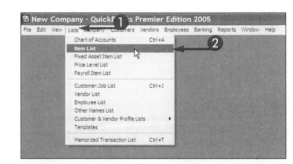

The Item List window appears.

3 Click Item.

4 Click New.

The New Item dialog box appears.

⑤ Select Group.

⑥ Type a name and description.

● You can click this option (☐ changes to ☑) to print individual items.

⑦ Click here and select the items to include in the group.

⑧ Click OK.

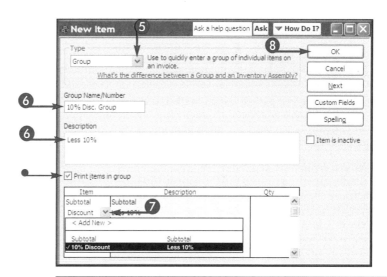

The new Group item appears in the Item List window.

What does the Print items in group option do?

▼ On-screen, you see no difference, regardless of whether this option is selected. However, when you select this option (☐ changes to ☑) and print a form that includes a Group item, individual lines print for each item in the group. If you do not select this option, QuickBooks does not print the individual items that are part of the group. By deselecting the option, you can present your customers with a simple, uncluttered invoice and simultaneously keep track of the details of each sale in QuickBooks.

Should I enter a quantity?

▼ For some types of items, you can, but you do not need to enter a quantity. You can include or change an item's quantity when you use the item on a transaction.

Can I include a group inside a group?

▼ No. You cannot include one Group item as part of another Group item. For example, you cannot create a group that includes several inventory items and then another group that discounts the group of inventory items.

Create a New Payment Item

I f a customer pays you part of the amount due at the time you make a sale, you need to record the payment, and you can use a Payment item to do so. A Payment item reduces the customer's outstanding balance.

When you create a Payment item, you can group payments with other undeposited funds or place the money directly in a bank account. Base your selection on the way your bank handles deposits on your bank statement. Suppose that you deposit a group of five checks in your bank. If those five items will appear individually on your bank

statement, you can set up your Payment item to place the money directly in a bank account. However, if your bank prints only one line on your bank statement — the sum of the five checks — then you should set up your Payment item to group payments with other undeposited funds. By grouping payments with other undeposited funds, you can select the items that appear on each deposit and make your deposits in QuickBooks match the deposits on your bank statement. Balancing your bank statement is easier if your QuickBooks deposits match your bank statement deposits.

Create a New Payment Item

① Click Lists.

② Click Item List.

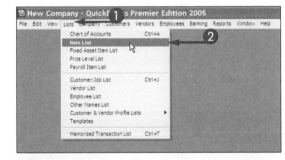

The Item List window appears.

③ Click Item.

④ Click New.

The New Item dialog box appears.

5 Click here and select Payment.

6 Type a name and a description.

7 Click here and select a Payment Method.

8 Click a deposit option (○ changes to ◉).

9 Click OK.

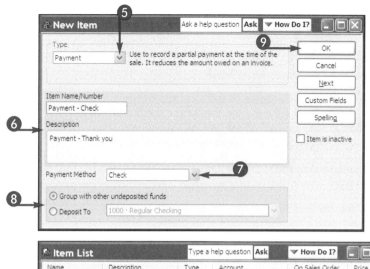

● The new Payment item appears in the Item List window.

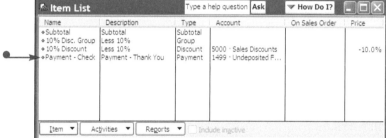

What are the Payment Methods, and what does QuickBooks do with them?

▼ You can select American Express, Cash, Check, Discover, Mastercard, or Visa or create other payment methods. You group your deposits by Payment Method so that you deposit all checks in one deposit, all American Express charges in another deposit, all Mastercard charges in another deposit, and so on. Besides helping you balance your bank statement, grouping deposits can help you match your charge card receipts to the credit card company's deposits into your bank account, because most credit card companies make one deposit into your account for each day's receipts.

What should I do if I receive money using more than one Payment Method?

▼ Set up separate Payment items in QuickBooks for each Payment Method your company accepts. For ease of use, give your Payment items unique, easily identifiable names.

Can I use a Payment item on an invoice if the customer pays me in full?

▼ Yes, you can, but the Sales Receipt form in QuickBooks eliminates your need to use a Payment item for a paid-in-full sale, because QuickBooks automatically pays off the entire sale when you record it using the Sales Receipt window. See Chapter 11 for more information.

Set Up
Sales Taxes

Most companies must collect sales tax on the items they sell and then remit the sales tax to the sales tax authorities. In QuickBooks, you set preferences to enable sales taxes. You identify whether you owe sales tax as of the date of the sale or the date you collect payment, along with the frequency with which you pay sales taxes — monthly, quarterly, or annually.

As part of setting sales tax preferences, you must create the sales tax item that you expect to use most often. A Sales Tax item stores the rate you must charge your customers for a particular sales tax authority's jurisdiction. If you

collect sales tax for more than one sales tax authority, set up additional sales tax items using the steps in the subsection "Create a Sales Tax Item."

As part of the process of creating the Sales Tax item, you must create a vendor for the sales tax authority to whom you pay sales tax.

After you create sales tax items, you assign them to customers so that, on sales documents, QuickBooks automatically calculates the sales tax amount to charge using the customer's sales tax item. See Chapter 5 for details on assigning a sales tax item to a customer.

Set Up Sales Taxes

Sales Tax Preferences

1 Click Edit.

2 Click Preferences.

The Preferences dialog box appears.

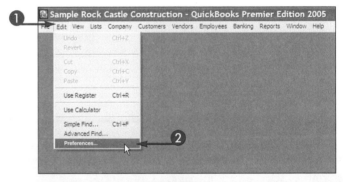

3 Click the Sales Tax icon.

4 Click the Company Preferences tab.

5 Under the Do You Charge Sales Tax? section, click Yes (○ changes to ◉).

6 Click an option to select the basis on which you owe sales tax (○ changes to ◉).

7 Click a payment frequency (○ changes to ◉).

8 Click here to add the sales tax item you use most often.

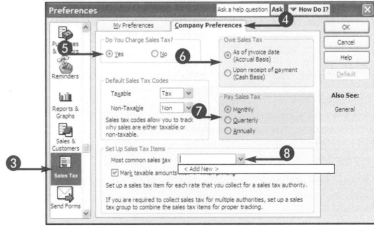

PART I

Create a Sales Tax Item

The New Item dialog box appears.

9 Click here and select Sales Tax Item.

10 Type a name.

11 Type a description.

12 Type the rate charged by the jurisdiction.

13 Click here to add the sales tax authority.

Create the Sales Tax Authority

The New Vendor dialog box appears.

14 Type a Vendor Name, Company Name, and Address.

15 Click OK three times.

16 Click OK when QuickBooks asks if you want to make all existing customers, inventory, and noninventory items taxable.

QuickBooks saves the vendor, the sales tax item, and your sales tax preferences.

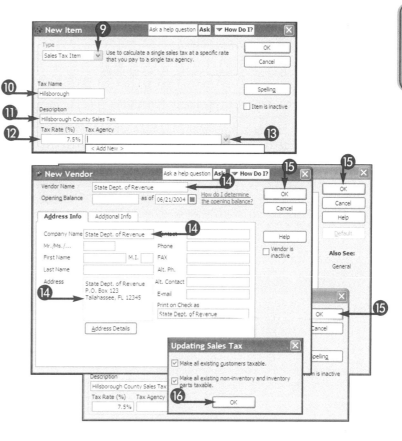

What do I do if some customers and things I sell are not subject to sales tax?

▼ You can use sales tax codes to separate taxable from nontaxable customers and items. You can set up sales tax codes to match your sales tax reporting needs. For details, see the section "Create a New Sales Tax Code."

Is there a place that I can store my state sales tax account number so that it prints on checks to the sales tax authority?

▼ Yes. While setting up the taxing authority vendor, click the Additional Info tab and type the number in the Account Number field.

What do I do if some or most of my customers, inventory, and noninventory items are not taxable?

▼ Step 16 assumes that most of your customers and items are taxable. If most of your customers and items are *not* taxable, then, in step 16, deselect both options (☑ changes to ☐) before you click OK. If most, but not all, of your customers and items are taxable, leave the boxes selected in step 16 and then edit the affected customers and items and mark them nontaxable.

Create a New Sales Tax Group Item

I n many states, you must charge your customers a combination of sales taxes, and sales tax group items help you simplify this task. Your state may have a base sales tax rate, while individual counties and cities may have separate, additional rates, and you must charge the customer sales tax based on the rate for a customer's location.

When you sell to customers in different counties and cities, each with its own sales tax rate on top of the state's base rate, you create individual sales tax items for each jurisdiction; see the section "Set Up Sales Taxes" for more

information. While you can assign any sales tax item to a customer as the default item and, when you make a sale, add other appropriate sales tax items, this technique is time-consuming and error-prone.

Instead, you can create sales tax groups that consist of the required sales tax items for each location in which you have customers. Then, you can assign the appropriate sales tax group to each customer instead of assigning an individual sales tax item. Using this technique, you charge the correct amount of sales tax and your customers see one entry for sales tax on their invoices.

Create a New Sales Tax Group Item

① Click Lists.

② Click Item List.

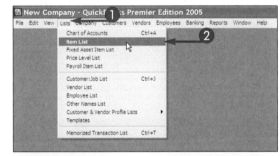

The Item List window appears.

③ Click Item.

④ Click New.

The New Item dialog box appears.

⑤ Click here and select Sales Tax Group.

⑥ Type a name and a description.

⑦ Click here and select a sales tax item.

⑧ Repeat step 7 for each sales tax item in the group.

⑨ Click OK.

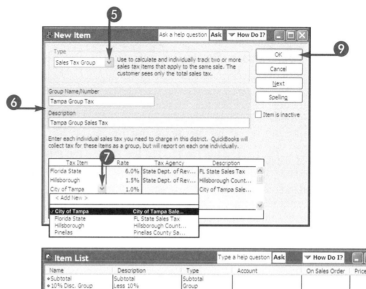

● The sales tax group appears in the Item List window.

If all my sales are in my city and I collect 5 percent for my state, 1 percent for the county, and 1.5 percent for the city, how many sales tax items should I set up and what rates should they contain?

▼ Set up three sales tax items — one for the state, one for the county, and one for the city — and one sales tax group. You should make the state item's rate 5 percent, the county item's rate 1 percent, and the city item's rate 1.5 percent.

Why not set up individual sales tax items that combine the rates for all jurisdictions?

▼ Sales tax reporting requires that you break down the sales taxes you collect on behalf of each jurisdiction. In most states, you pay the total to one state agency and that agency distributes the money to each jurisdiction, and the state uses your sales tax report to determine how much to give to each jurisdiction. If you set up sales tax items that combine rates, you will not have the breakdown information that you need to report.

Create a New
Sales Tax Code

Sales tax codes enable you to specify the tax liability of a customer, inventory, inventory assembly, noninventory, service, or other charge item. QuickBooks automatically creates two sales tax codes for you — Tax and Non — but you may need others to help you categorize sales for sales tax return reporting purposes. For example, your sales tax authority may require that you report why nontaxable customers are not taxable. You may not need to collect sales tax from a customer because the customer is a nonprofit organization, a government agency, or a wholesaler. For taxable, out-of-state customers, you

may need to remit sales tax to another state's sales tax authority. Or you may not need to collect sales tax on certain things you sell; for example, in some states, services and necessities of life, such as food, are not taxable.

If your state requires that you report sales tax collections for more than just taxable and nontaxable customers, you need to set up additional sales tax codes. In Chapters 5 and 7, you learn how to assign sales tax codes so that when you sell an item to a customer, QuickBooks can determine whether to charge sales tax and categorize the sale properly.

Create a New Sales Tax Code

① Click Lists.

② Click Sales Tax Code List.

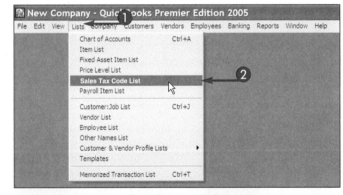

The Sales Tax Code List window appears.

③ Click Sales Tax Code.

④ Click New.

The New Sales Tax Code dialog box appears.

5 Type a code.

You can use no more than three characters.

6 Type a description.

7 Click either the Taxable or Non-Taxable option (○ changes to ◉).

8 Click OK.

● The new sales tax code appears in the Sales Tax Code List window.

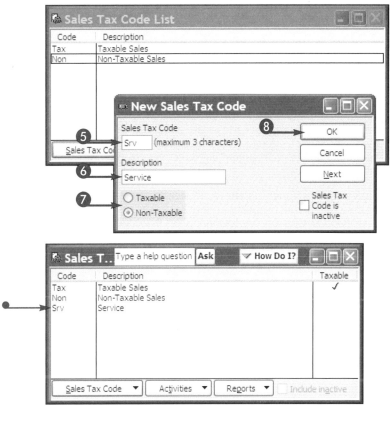

Can you recommend a naming scheme for sales tax codes?

▼ Try to match the names that your sales tax authority uses. If those names exceed three letters, try to use a variation of the name, such as the first three letters or the first two letters and the last letter. Be sure to use the complete name in the Description box. When you assign the code to a customer or item, the list from which you select displays both the name and description of the sales tax code.

Can I view how much I have sold broken down by sales tax code?

▼ Yes. QuickBooks contains two reports. The Sales Tax Revenue Summary shows, for each sales tax item, the amount of revenue tied to each sales tax code, along with totals by sales tax item and sales tax code for a particular period. The Sales Tax Liability report shows the same information, along with the tax rate, the tax collected, and the tax payable for the period. You can print these reports by clicking Reports in the Sales Tax Code List window.

Create Customer Messages

Occasionally, you want or need to include a message to a customer on a sales transaction. QuickBooks creates a series of standard messages automatically, but you may need to create a message of your own. For example, during the holiday season, you may want to include a "Happy Holidays" message on customer invoices and sales receipts.

Customer messages appear on sales transactions on-screen and on the printed sales transaction form. To assign a customer message to a sales transaction, open the sales

transaction window, complete the transaction as usual, and select the appropriate message from the Customer Message field. For help completing a sales document, see Chapter 11.

You can edit existing customer messages to tailor them for your needs. If you have never used a message — that is, if you did not include the message on any sales transaction — you can delete the message. If you previously included a message on a sales transaction, but you no longer want to use the message on future transactions, you can hide the message in the list by making it inactive; when you hide a message, it no longer appears as an available choice when you select a message to include on a sales transaction.

Create Customer Messages

① Click Lists.

② Click Customer & Vendor Profile Lists.

③ Click Customer Message List.

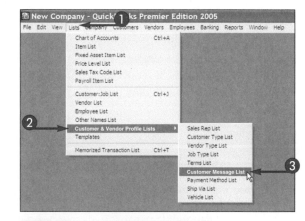

The Customer Message List window appears.

④ Click Customer Message.

⑤ Click New.

The New Customer Message dialog box appears.

6 Type a message.

7 Click OK.

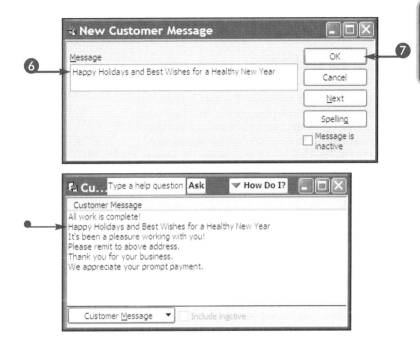

● The new message appears in the Customer Message List window.

What does the Spelling button in the New Customer Message dialog box do?

▼ Click Spelling to check spelling in the Description field of the New Customer Message window. If QuickBooks finds spelling mistakes, the Check Spelling on Form window appears, giving you the opportunity to correct the mistake.

How do I edit an existing customer message?

▼ Double-click the existing message in the Customer Message List window. The Edit Customer Message dialog box appears; it looks just like the New Customer Message dialog box except for the title bar of the box. Change the message as needed and click OK.

Can I print the Customer Message List?

▼ Yes. Follow steps 1 to 4 in this section to display the Customer Message List window. At the bottom of the menu that appears when you complete step 4, click Print List.

What should I do when I no longer want to use a message?

▼ If you do not use the message on any transactions, you can delete it. Otherwise, you can hide it so that it no longer appears as a choice to include on a sales transaction. Follow steps 1 to 4 in this section to display the Customer Message List window. Click Delete or Make Inactive.

Create Payment Methods

Payment methods represent the different ways you receive money from your customers. QuickBooks automatically populates the list with the most common payment methods: Cash, Check, American Express, MasterCard, Visa, and Discover. You may need to add a payment method to this list.

You use payment methods when you record a receipt from a customer; you can assign a payment method to the receipt. QuickBooks does not require you to assign a payment method to a customer receipt, but, if you assign payment methods, you may find it easier to make bank

deposits and reconcile your bank statement. By assigning payment methods, you can create bank deposits for each payment method. Recording deposits by payment method is particularly useful if you accept credit cards. Most credit card companies deposit the amount due to you as one lump sum for a given day. If you assign payment methods, you benefit twice. First, you can match your daily receipts for each credit card to the deposits that each of the credit card companies makes. Second, your deposits will match the deposits reported on your bank statement, making bank reconciliation easy.

Create Payment Methods

① Click Lists.

② Click Customer & Vendor Profile Lists.

③ Click Payment Method List.

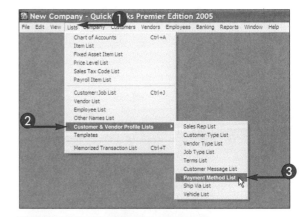

The Payment Method List window appears.

④ Click Payment Method.

⑤ Click New.

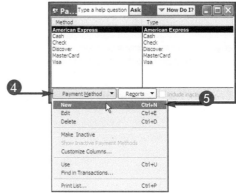

The New Payment Method dialog box appears.

⑥ Type a name for the Payment Method.

⑦ Click here and select a Payment Type.

⑧ Click OK.

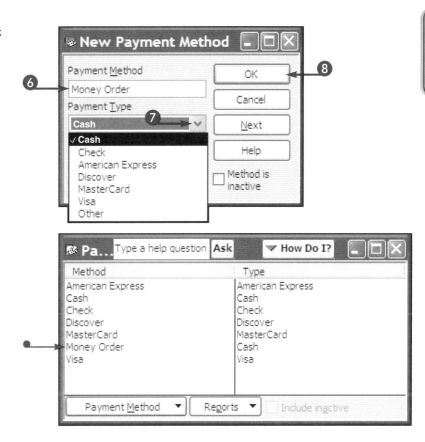

● The new payment method appears in the Payment Method List window.

Can I rename a payment method?

▼ Yes. You edit the payment method by double-clicking the entry in the Payment Method List window to display the entry in the Edit Payment Method dialog box. Change the Payment Method field and click OK.

Can I view all the transactions assigned to the various payment methods?

▼ Yes. You can create QuickReports for each Payment Method. Follow steps 1 to 3 to display the Payment Method List window. Click the first payment method for which you want to view transactions. Click Reports, and then click Quick Report. QuickBooks displays all transactions for the fiscal year to date.

How do I select only one payment method for a deposit?

▼ The Payments to Deposit dialog box lists all payments you received but have not yet deposited to a bank account. In the dialog box, QuickBooks also lists the Payment Method for each receipt. To create a deposit, you select the receipts you want to include in the deposit; by selecting receipts of the same payment method, you group receipts by Payment Method. For detailed information on creating a bank deposit, see Chapter 13.

Create Shipping Methods

Shipping methods represent the different ways you ship products to your customers. The shipping method appears on product-based sales documents, and you select the shipping method as you fill out the document. For more information on completing sales documents in QuickBooks, see Chapter 11.

By using shipping methods, you can produce reports that show you sales dollars by shipping method, which you can use in conjunction with shipping rates for each method to help determine if you are shipping too many sales dollars by more expensive shipping methods than necessary.

QuickBooks automatically populates the list with the most common shipping methods: DHL, Federal Express, UPS, and U.S. Mail. You may need to add a shipping method to this list. For example, you may have your own trucks or use a local delivery service to make local deliveries.

If you use one shipping method more often than any other, you can select that shipping method as the default method to appear on sales transactions automatically — you can change the default method as necessary. If you charge your customers for shipping, you also can specify a default markup for shipping costs at the same time that you select a default shipping method.

Create Shipping Methods

1 Click Lists.

2 Click Customer & Vendor Profile Lists.

3 Click Ship Via List.

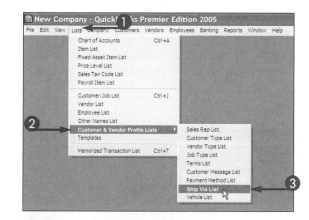

The Ship Via List window appears.

4 Click Shipping Method.

5 Click New.

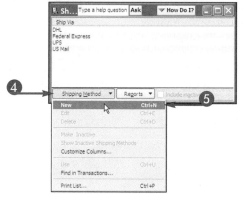

The New Shipping Method dialog box appears.

6 Type a name for the Shipping Method.

7 Click OK.

● The new shipping method appears in the Ship Via List window.

How can I print a report of sales dollars by shipping method?

▼ Open the Reports menu and click Custom Summary Report. In the Modify Report box that appears, select Shipping Method from the Display rows by list.

What other reports can I print about shipping methods?

▼ You can print the list of shipping methods and a QuickReport for a particular shipping method that shows you the transactions using that shipping method. To print the list, follow steps 1 to 4 and click Print List. To print a QuickReport, select the shipping method, click Reports, and click QuickReport.

How do I set a default shipping method and set a markup for shipping costs?

▼ Click Edit, and then click Preferences. In the Preferences dialog box, click the Sales & Customers icon on the left side of the dialog box. Click the Company Preferences tab. To set the default shipping method, select the shipping method you want to use from the Usual Shipping Method list. To set a markup for shipping costs, type the percentage you want to mark up shipping costs in the Default Markup Percentage box.

Sign Up for a Payroll Tax Service

To use payroll, you must select a payroll option. Most people opt to use a fee-based payroll service to make payroll processing easier. If you have only a few employees and can enter payroll tax amounts manually on every check each pay period, you do not need to sign up for a payroll service.

You can select from four fee-based payroll options. Both the Standard and Enhanced Payroll options enable you to prepare and print paychecks, the 941 and 940 payroll tax returns, W-2s, and 1099s from QuickBooks. The Enhanced Payroll option also enables you to track workers' compensation information, print state payroll tax forms automatically, prepare bonus checks automatically, and

rapidly enter hours worked for multiple employees. Using the Assisted Payroll option, you prepare and print paychecks using QuickBooks, but an outside service prepares payroll tax returns and W-2s for you. Using the Complete Payroll option, all payroll tasks are handled for you by an outside service.

Each option provides you a year's worth of service. Because most QuickBooks users select the Standard Payroll option, this section describes how to sign up for that payroll option and download a payroll tax table update. The process involves selecting a payroll option — to use a service or prepare payroll manually — and then signing up and paying for a payroll service, which includes downloading a payroll tax table.

Sign Up for a Payroll Tax Service

Select a Payroll Option

1 Connect to the Internet if necessary.

2 Click Lists.

3 Click Payroll Item List.

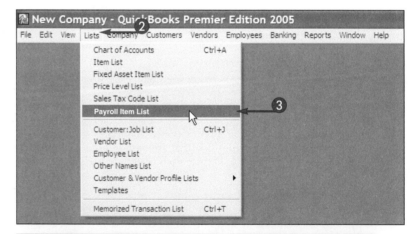

A message appears, indicating that you have not signed up for a payroll service.

4 Click Yes to start the wizard that helps you sign up.

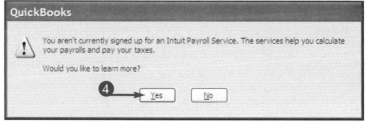

The Payroll Setup Steps screen of the wizard lists the steps you must take to set up payroll.

⑤ Click Continue.

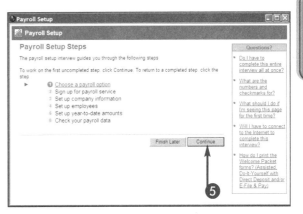

The Choose a Payroll Option screen appears.

⑥ Click an option (○ changes to ⊙).

⑦ Click Continue.

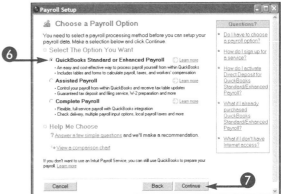

I want to enter payroll manually, but QuickBooks keeps prompting me to sign up for a payroll tax service. How do I get around this problem?

▼ Follow steps 1 to 6. On the Choose a Payroll Option screen, click the Learn more link at the bottom of the page. On the page that appears, click the To calculate payroll taxes manually link. The page that appears contains instructions on how to enter payroll manually. Print this page, and then click the I choose to manually calculate payroll taxes button to complete the process of selecting a payroll option.

How much do the various payroll options cost?

▼ At the time of this writing, you pay $199 a year for the Standard Payroll option and $299 for the Enhanced Payroll option. For Assisted Payroll and Complete Payroll, the amount you pay depends on the number of employees, the frequency with which you pay them, the number of states in which you file payroll taxes and the optional features you select (such as 1099 MISC processing), direct deposit of employee paychecks, and next business day delivery of processed payroll. Intuit estimates that the average price paid by a five-employee company for biweekly payroll is $80 per month; for Assisted Payroll; and $84 per month for Enhanced Payroll.

continued

Sign Up for a Payroll
Tax Service *(Continued)*

After selecting your payroll option, a wizard walks you through the process of purchasing a payroll tax table service. As you step through the wizard, screens appear that give you the opportunity to sign up for the Employee Organizer, an add-on that helps you manage employee information. You also get the opportunity to download your payroll tax table update or to receive it via U.S. Mail. If you choose to receive the payroll tax table update by mail, you must wait until the disk arrives to complete the payroll setup process.

You then provide name and address information and use a credit card to purchase a payroll service. After you complete the payment process, your payroll tax table subscription service number appears onscreen; print that screen for your records. QuickBooks then downloads to your computer and installs a payroll tax table update that contains all the latest withholding information. QuickBooks uses this information to calculate payroll taxes when you create paychecks.

A message appears onscreen to let you know when QuickBooks finishes downloading the payroll tax table update. You also have an opportunity to read a description of the changes contained in the payroll tax table update.

Sign Up for a Payroll Tax Service *(continued)*

The Payroll Setup Steps screen reappears, showing that you have completed the first step.

8 Click Continue.

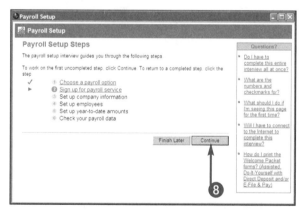

Select a Payroll Service

The QuickBooks Payroll – Service Selection screen appears.

9 Click an option (○ changes to ◉) to select a payroll service.

10 Scroll down to click Continue.

The wizard walks you through screens that ask for your company name, address, EIN, and credit card information.

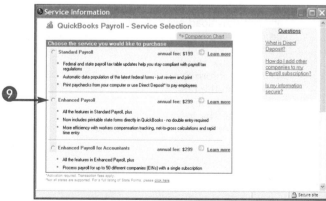

Once your credit card has been accepted, a screen appears indicating that your order is being processed.

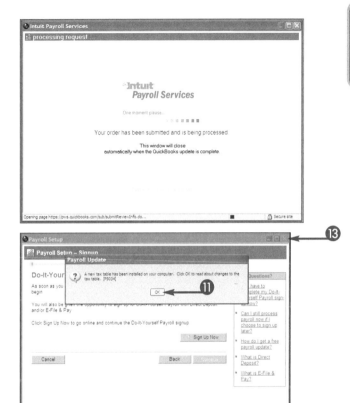

When order processing finishes, QuickBooks downloads and installs the payroll update, adding federal payroll tax items to the Payroll Item List.

When the installation is complete, QuickBooks displays a message.

⑪ Click OK.

The Payroll Update News window appears, containing a summary of payroll update changes.

⑫ Close the Payroll Update News window by clicking the Close button (⊠).

⑬ Close the Payroll Setup window by clicking ⊠.

Can I use the payroll tax service on a trial basis?

▼ You can download one free tax table update, which expires on February 15 of the following year, and try out payroll processing using the Do-It-Yourself option. Follow steps 1 to 11, but do not enter your credit card information to download the payroll tax table. When the table expires, you must choose between manually entering payroll or subscribing to a service. The free tax table is available by download only.

Is Direct Deposit available? If so, how do I sign up for Direct Deposit?

▼ Direct Deposit is available for a fee. When you sign up for a payroll service, you are prompted to add the Direct Deposit service.

Using Do-It-Yourself Payroll, can I file payroll tax returns electronically?

▼ Yes. You can sign up for E-File & Pay, another add-on service. Using E-File & Pay, you can file Federal Forms 940, 941, 941 with Schedule B, and W-2 Copy A electronically, and you can electronically pay FUTA and 941 liabilities.

Create a Wage Payroll Item

QuickBooks does not set up the wage payroll items you need to pay employees even if you sign up for a payroll service using the steps in "Sign Up for a Payroll Tax Service." When you select a payroll option in that section, QuickBooks creates federal payroll tax items — Federal Withholding, Federal Unemployment, Medicare and Social Security items for both your company and employees, and an Advance Earned Income Credit item. You still need to add other payroll items, like wage payroll items.

You can create wage items to pay salaries, hourly wages, commissions, and bonuses, and you assign wage items to your payroll expense account. You also use wage items to track sick and vacation pay.

QuickBooks offers two wizards to set up payroll items: the Easy Setup Wizard and the Custom Setup Wizard. You have more control over the options of payroll items using the Custom Setup Wizard, so, this section shows you how to set up wage items using the Custom Setup Wizard.

After you set up wage items and any other deductions or additions you need to include on employee paychecks, you assign payroll items to each employee so that QuickBooks can accurately calculate paychecks.

Create a Wage Payroll Item

① Click Lists.

② Click Payroll Item List.

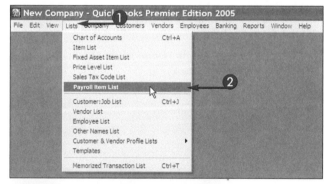

The Payroll Item List appears.

③ Click Payroll Item.

④ Click New.

The Add new payroll item Wizard begins.

5 On the Select setup method screen, click the Custom Setup option (◯ changes to ◉).

6 Click Next.

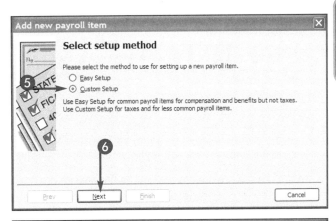

The Payroll item type screen appears.

7 Click the Wage option (◯ changes to ◉).

8 Click Next.

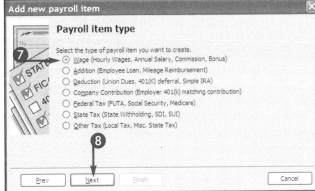

How does the Easy Setup Wizard differ from the Custom Setup Wizard?

▼ The Easy Setup Wizard displays four pages that list common payroll items. You select the ones you want (☐ changes to ☑) and click Finish. QuickBooks creates the items, but you have no way of knowing what options QuickBooks selected when creating the items unless you edit them. When you edit them, the Custom Setup Wizard walks you through the same screens you see in this section, showing you the choices QuickBooks made. On occasion, QuickBooks makes incorrect choices.

How do I establish the amount of wages?

▼ You can fill in a wage rate when you pay an employee or, when you create employees, you can assign at least one wage item to each employee and specify the employee's wage rate when you assign the wage item. Most companies use the second approach of assigning a wage item to each employee and specifying the wage rate. See the section "Create an Employee" for details on assigning payroll items and establishing their rates. See Chapter 8 for details on paying employees.

continued

Create a Wage
Payroll Item *(Continued)*

In this section, you see how to set up an hourly wage payroll item. If you pay some of your employees a salary, you also need to set up a salary wage item. And, if you pay commissions or bonuses, you need to set up a commission wage item and a bonus wage item.

The Custom Setup Wizard offers you the same choices you see when you set up a salary payroll wage item as you see when you set up an hourly wage payroll item. When you set up commission or bonus payroll items, the Custom

Setup Wizard does not ask you if these are regular, vacation, or sick leave wage items because vacation and leave pay are associated only with hourly or salaried wages.

When you set up commission payroll items, you see one additional screen not shown in this section — it asks you to supply a commission rate. If most of the employees who receive commissions receive the same commission rate, enter a commission rate and QuickBooks suggests this rate each time you assign the commission wage item to an employee. If commission rates vary greatly, do not assign a commission rate to the wage item.

Create a Wage Payroll Item *(continued)*

The Wages screen appears.

⑨ Click the Hourly Wages option (○ changes to ◉).

⑩ Click Next.

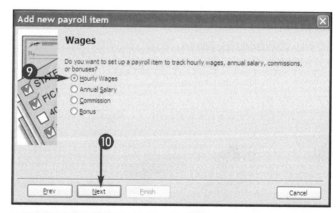

The second Wages screen appears.

⑪ Click the Regular Pay option (○ changes to ◉).

⑫ Click Next.

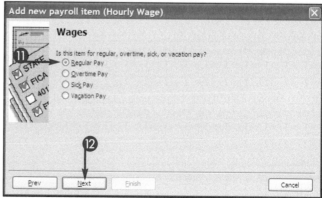

The Name used in paychecks and payroll reports screen appears.

⑬ Type a name for the item.

⑭ Click Next.

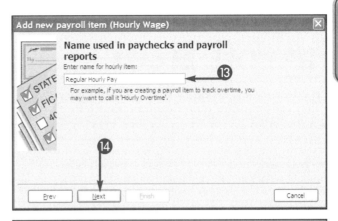

The Expense account screen appears.

⑮ Click here and select the account to which you assign payroll expenses.

Note: Many companies segregate wages from payroll taxes by assigning all wages to a wage expense account and all payroll taxes to a payroll tax expense account.

⑯ Click Finish.

The new item appears in the Payroll Item List window.

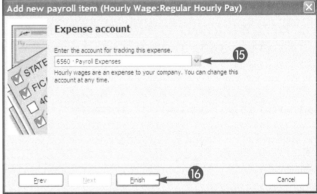

How do I set up a wage payroll item for employees to whom I pay a salary plus commission?

▼ You do not set up one wage payroll item to accommodate salary plus commission. Instead, you set up two wage payroll items: one for the salary portion and one for the commission portion. You add both the wage and the commission payroll item to the records of employees who receive both types of wages. See the section "Create an Employee" for details.

When I set up a commission wage payroll item, can I express the commission as dollars?

▼ You can express the commission as dollars or a percentage of an amount or quantity. Establish a percentage commission rate by typing the percent sign along with the rate. If you pay more than one commission rate, set up separate commission payroll items for each rate and assign the rate on the Default rate screen.

Should I set up wage payroll items for each employee because I pay them different wage rates?

▼ No. You need to set up wage payroll items for each different type of pay you offer — hourly and salary are two different types of pay. Vacation pay is another type of pay. By setting up wage payroll items for each type of pay your business offers to its employees, you have all the necessary wage items available to assign to employees when you create them.

Create an Overtime Payroll Item

If your company has hourly employees to whom you pay overtime when they work more hours than a typical work week contains — usually 40 hours — you can set up an overtime payroll item so that you can include overtime pay on paychecks. QuickBooks enables you to create two predefined overtime payroll item calculations — one payroll item calculates time-and-a-half pay and the other payroll item calculates double-time pay. If your company uses a different calculation for overtime pay, you can create an overtime payroll item that uses a custom calculation. QuickBooks calculates the overtime pay rate by multiplying the value of the overtime payroll item by the regular pay rate.

To pay overtime, you include the overtime payroll item on an employee's paycheck in the Earnings section; for more information on paying employees, see Chapter 8. If you do not pay overtime frequently, simply add the overtime item to the payroll check whenever you need to pay overtime. You supply the number of overtime hours on the paycheck, and QuickBooks calculates the amount of overtime pay. If you pay overtime fairly often, assign the overtime payroll item to the records of employees. Whenever you pay these employees, the overtime payroll item will automatically appear and you supply the number of overtime hours. See "Create an Employee" for more information about including the overtime payroll item on an employee's record.

Create an Overtime Payroll Item

① Follow steps 1 to 10 in the section "Create a Wage Payroll Item" to open the Custom Setup Wizard.

② Click the Overtime Pay option (○ changes to ◉).

③ Click Next.

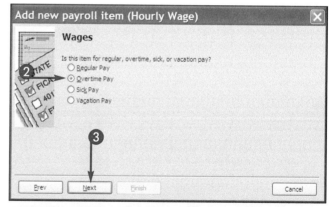

The Name used in paychecks and payroll reports screen appears.

④ Type a name for the overtime payroll item.

⑤ Click Next.

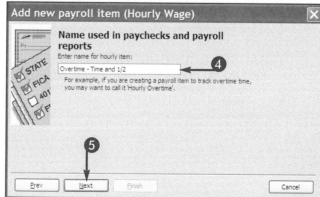

The Define Overtime screen appears.

6 Click an option to describe the method QuickBooks should use to calculate overtime pay (○ changes to ●).

7 Click Next.

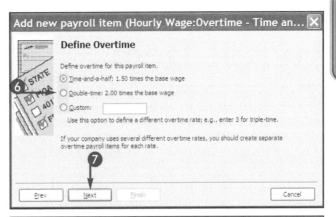

The Expense account screen appears.

8 Click here and select your payroll expense account.

9 Click Finish.

The overtime payroll item appears in the Payroll Items List.

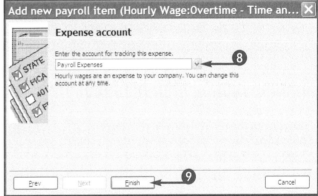

Can I pay overtime to salaried employees?

▼ Most organizations do not pay overtime to salaried employees. If you select Annual Salary on the first Wages screen of the Payroll Setup Wizard, the Overtime Pay option will not be available on the second Wages screen. If your company pays overtime to a salaried employee, you can add the overtime payroll item to the paycheck, supply the number of overtime hours and an overtime rate, and QuickBooks calculates the amount of overtime pay and adds it to the employee's paycheck.

How do I create an overtime payroll item that calculates time and one quarter?

▼ Follow steps 1 to 6; in step 6, select the Custom option (○ changes to ●). In the box next to the Custom option, type **1.25.** When you pay the employee and use this overtime payroll item, you supply the number of overtime hours. QuickBooks multiplies the regular pay rate for the employee by the number you type in the box beside the Custom option to calculate the overtime pay rate. QuickBooks then multiplies the number of hours you supply by the overtime rate to calculate overtime pay.

Create an Addition Payroll Item

You need addition payroll items if you pay employees additional money that is not part of hourly or salary wages. For example, you need addition payroll items if you pay tips, mileage reimbursements, moving expenses, or travel advances. You easily add this information using the wizard discussed in the section "Create a Payroll Wage Item."

You should assign a name to the addition payroll item to describe its purpose, and then assign it to your Payroll Expense account. You should also classify the payroll expense so that it is reported properly on payroll tax forms,

such as Federal Form W-2 and Federal Form 941, which report the payroll taxes you collect based on the wages you paid for a quarter. When you select a tax tracking type to classify the addition payroll item, you also determine some of the rest of the screens that appear as you walk through the wizard.

To set up a mileage expense reimbursement, use your automobile expense account instead of the payroll expense account on the Expense account screen. The mileage expense also is not subject to taxes, so you do not need to track taxes. You can calculate the expense based on a quantity — the number of miles driven by the employee.

Create aN Addition Payroll Item

① Follow steps 1 to 8 in the section "Create a Wage Payroll Item" to open the Custom Setup Wizard, but in step 7, click Addition.

② Type a name for the item.

● You can click here (☐ changes to ☑) to track payroll expenses by job, class, and service item.

③ Click Next.

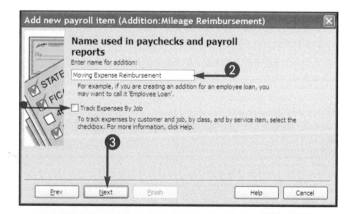

The Expense account screen appears.

④ Click here and select the account to which you assign payroll expenses.

⑤ Click Next.

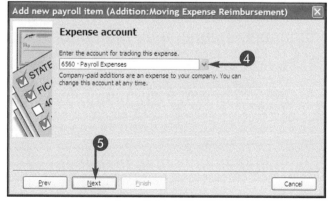

The Tax tracking type screen appears.

6 Click here and select a tax tracking type.

7 Click Next.

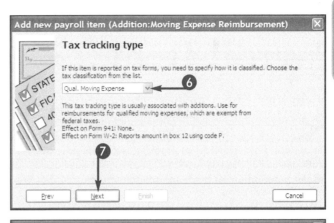

The Taxes screen appears.

8 Click next to each tax (☐ changes to ☑) that is affected by this addition.

● You can click Default to see the taxes that typically are affected by the tax tracking type you selected.

9 Click Next.

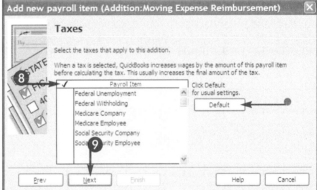

What does the Track Expenses By Job option do?

▼ This option (☐ changes to ☑) works in conjunction with a Payroll preference that you can set if you click Edit and then click Preferences. In the Preferences dialog box that appears, click Payroll & Employees and then click the Company tab. You can then enable an option that tells QuickBooks to break down company-paid payroll taxes, additions, and company contributions by job, service item, or class if you use class tracking, on reports of expenses. If you then click the Track Expenses By Job option while creating an addition, payroll tax, or company contribution payroll item, QuickBooks breaks down this payroll item on reports of expenses.

How does checking a tax on the Taxes screen affect the payroll item?

▼ The effect on any of the taxes depends on the type of payroll item you are creating. For additions, wage items — hourly, salary, commission, or bonus — and company contributions, checking a tax increases the amount of the selected tax that QuickBooks calculates because QuickBooks adds the amount of the addition, wage item, or company contribution to gross wages before calculating the tax amount. Because the gross wage amount is higher, a larger amount is subject to the tax, so the amount of the tax increases.

continued

Create an Addition Payroll Item *(Continued)*

Q uickBooks can calculate addition payroll items or you can manually enter the addition amount on paychecks. If QuickBooks calculates the amount of the addition payroll item, you indicate whether you want QuickBooks to calculate based on a quantity or based on hours. For example, you may calculate a mileage reimbursement expense based on the number of miles, but may make tips or a moving expense reimbursement a flat amount that you enter manually on a paycheck.

If you select the Secondary Local Tax, Local Income Tax, Company Paid Other Tax, or Qualifying Moving Expense Tax tracking type, the Custom Setup Wizard displays an additional screen: the Gross vs. net screen, on which you must identify whether QuickBooks should calculate the addition based on gross or net pay.

At the end of the wizard, you have the opportunity to specify a default rate and annual limit for the addition payroll item. Enter a default rate if the rate applies to most of the employees who receive this additional pay. If the rate varies greatly, do not enter a rate; you can supply it either when you establish payroll information on the employee's record or when you record paychecks.

Create an Addition Payroll Item *(continued)*

The Calculate based on quantity screen appears.

⑩ Click an option to select the method you want QuickBooks to use to calculate the amount of the addition payroll item (○ changes to ⦿).

⑪ Click Next.

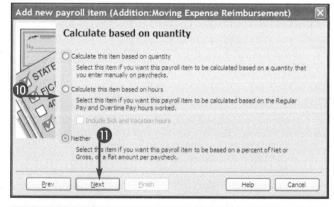

The Gross vs. net screen may appear, depending on the taxes you select in step 8.

⑫ Click an option (○ changes to ⦿) to specify whether QuickBooks should calculate percentage-based payroll additions using gross or net pay.

⑬ Click Next.

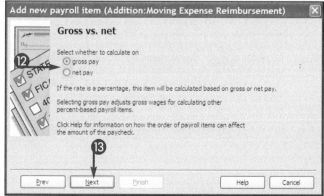

The Default rate and limit screen appears.

● If QuickBooks calculates the payroll addition, you can type a rate here.

● You can type an annual limit for the item here.

⑭ Click Finish.

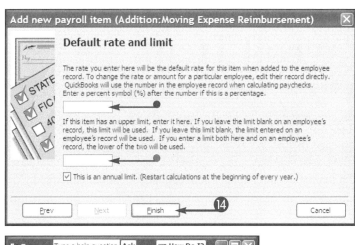

● The new addition payroll item appears in the Payroll Item List window.

How do I indicate that I want to use a percentage calculation?

▼ On the Calculate based on quantity screen, click the last option — Neither (○ changes to ⊙). Then, include a percent sign (%) on the Default rate and limit screen when you fill in the default rate number to have QuickBooks treat the number as a percentage. If the rate changes from employee to employee so that you do not want to supply a rate on the Default rate and limit screen, leave it blank. When you assign the addition payroll item to an employee, include the percent there.

Does the order in which I create payroll items matter?

▼ No, but the order in which you add payroll items to the records of employees can matter. If QuickBooks calculates any of your payroll items based on gross pay, those payroll items may increase gross pay. For example, if you create an addition payroll item that QuickBooks calculates based on gross pay, you increase gross pay. When a payroll item increases gross pay, all taxes increase and affect the net amount of the check. However, if QuickBooks calculates the same addition payroll item based on net pay, gross pay is not affected and therefore taxes are not affected.

Create a Deduction Payroll Item

To account for payroll deductions when preparing a paycheck in QuickBooks, you create deduction payroll items. You create one deduction payroll item for each deduction you use on paychecks, and you assign each deduction payroll item to a liability account and a vendor. See Chapters 2 and 6 to create accounts and vendors.

You may need to create deduction payroll items for employee loan repayments, union dues, employee-paid insurance premiums, or employee contributions to a retirement plan. This section provides an example for setting up an employee-paid health insurance plan, but you handle the other situations similarly.

Deductions reduce an employee's paycheck to provide the money to pay for something else — repay a loan you made to the employee, pay an insurance premium or union dues, or contribute to a pension plan. In each case, you must account for the money you deduct.

You post the employee loan repayment to an asset account you set up to track the employee's loan — see Chapter 27 for details on setting up an employee loan. You post employee-paid insurance deductions, union dues, and contributions to pension plans to liability accounts, because you must pass those amounts along to insurance companies or pension plan funds.

Create a Deduction Payroll Item

① Follow steps 1 to 8 in the section "Create a Wage Payroll Item" to open the Custom Setup Wizard, but in step 7, click Deduction.

② Type a name for the item.

③ Click Next.

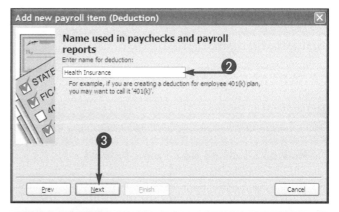

The Agency for employee-paid liability screen appears.

④ Click here and select the name of the vendor to whom you pay the liability.

● You can type a vendor account number that identifies your business.

⑤ Click here and select the account to which you assign the liability.

⑥ Click Next.

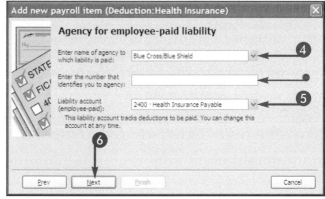

The Tax tracking type screen appears.

7 Click here and select a tax tracking type.

8 Click Next.

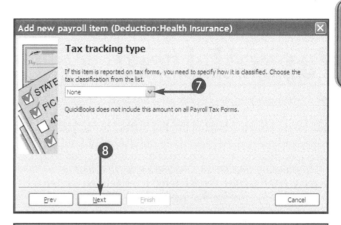

The Taxes screen appears.

9 Click next to each tax (☐ changes to ☑) that is affected by this deduction.

● You can click Default to see the taxes that typically are affected by the tax tracking type you selected.

10 Click Next.

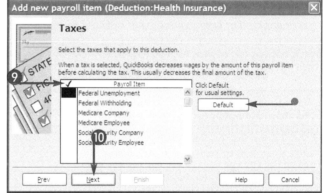

What is a tax tracking type?

▼ QuickBooks uses the tax tracking type to identify amounts that must appear on payroll tax forms like the Federal Form 941, Federal Form 940, or W-2s. For some deductions, such as employee-paid health insurance, you do not report amounts on any of these forms, so you assign a tax tracking type of None to the deduction. The tax tracking type you select impacts other screens in the Custom Setup Wizard. For example, when you select a tax tracking type of None, QuickBooks indicates that no taxes apply to the deduction on the Taxes screen.

What exactly happens to the amounts that QuickBooks deducts from employee paychecks?

▼ QuickBooks posts those amounts to the account you specify on the Agency for employee-paid liability screen and creates liabilities for the vendor you specify. You pay those liabilities using the Pay Payroll Liabilities window. See Chapter 9 for details.

How do I set up a cafeteria plan health insurance deduction?

▼ Follow the steps in this section, but, when you select a tax tracking type in step 7, select Premium Only. Check with your plan administrator to make sure that the taxes QuickBooks suggests are correct for your plan.

continued

Create a Deduction Payroll Item *(Continued)*

401(k) plans often permit an employee to make a contribution and the company to make some form of matching contribution. For 401(k) plans, you may need to set up two payroll items — one deduction for the employee's share and a company contribution payroll item for the company's payment. See the section "Create a Company Contribution Payroll Item" for details on setting up the company contribution payroll item.

You set up the employee's deduction for a 401(k) plan using the steps in this section, but you select 401(k) for the tax tracking type. For taxes, QuickBooks indicates that only

Federal Withholding applies to an employee's 401(k) deduction; check with the 401(k) plan administrator to confirm this setting.

To set up a union dues deduction, set up a liability account for union dues and a vendor to whom you pay the dues. Typically, the union dues payroll item also is not subject to taxes. The method you use to calculate the deduction can vary. For example, you may need to deduct a flat amount each month, an amount equal to a specified number of hours' pay each month, an amount based on hours worked, or a percentage of gross pay.

Create a Deduction Payroll Item *(continued)*

The Calculate based on quantity screen appears.

⑪ Click an option to select the method you want QuickBooks to use to calculate the amount of the deduction payroll item (○ changes to ◉).

⑫ Click Next.

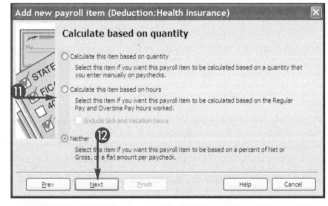

The Gross vs. net screen may appear, depending on the taxes you select in step 9.

⑬ Click an option to specify whether QuickBooks should calculate percentage-based payroll deductions using gross or net pay (○ changes to ◉).

⑭ Click Next.

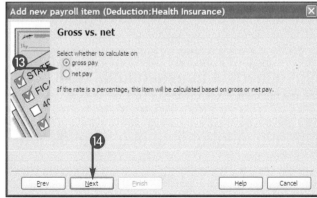

The Default rate and limit screen appears.

● If QuickBooks calculates the payroll deduction, you can type a rate here.

● You can type an annual limit for the item here.

⑮ Click Finish.

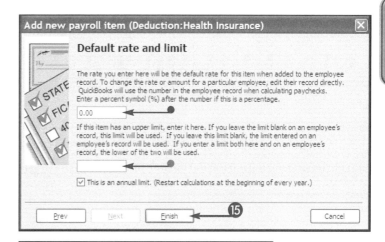

● The new deduction payroll item appears in the Payroll Item List window.

How does a deduction from gross pay affect a paycheck compared to a deduction from net pay?

▼ Neither a deduction from gross pay nor a deduction from net pay has any effect on gross pay. If a deduction affects taxes, net pay will change. A deduction from net pay does not affect taxes. However, a deduction from gross pay typically affects taxes. A deduction from gross pay decreases the taxes you select on the Taxes screen because it reduces the gross wages subject to these taxes. Because a deduction from gross pay reduces taxes, net pay changes to accommodate the tax reduction.

How do I set up a Simple IRA plan to which both the employee and my business contribute?

▼ Set up a deduction for the employee's contribution, making sure that you select a tax tracking type of SIMPLE IRA. On the Taxes screen, QuickBooks indicates that only Federal Withholding applies to an employee's Simple IRA deduction; check with the Simple IRA plan administrator to confirm this setting. If your business also contributes to the Simple IRA on behalf of the employee, you need a company contribution payroll item for the Simple IRA. See the section "Create a Company Contribution Payroll Item" for details on setting up a company contribution.

Create a Company
Contribution Payroll Item

You create a company contribution payroll item whenever your business contributes something on behalf of employees. Most company contributions represent benefits that employers offer to employees. As such, your business pays the calculated amount to a vendor responsible for providing the benefit. For each company contribution that you create, you must create a vendor and a liability account where QuickBooks can store the amounts calculated for the company contributions. See Chapter 6 for help creating a vendor and Chapter 2 for help creating a liability account.

To understand the concept of company contributions, think of Social Security and Medicare. To these federally run retirement plans, each employee contributes a share of gross wages — 6.2 percent for social security and 1.45 percent for Medicare at the time of this writing — and the employer contributes a matching share of both taxes. QuickBooks automatically creates these taxes for you and does not label the company's share as a company contribution payroll item, but the company's shares of both taxes are company contributions.

Most company contributions, as employee benefits, are taxable; you need to check with the agency that provides the benefit to determine the taxes to which the contribution is subject.

Create a Company Contribution Payroll Item

① Follow steps 1 to 6 in the section "Create a Wage Item" to open the Custom Setup Wizard.

The Payroll item type screen appears.

② Click the Company Contribution option (○ changes to ◉).

③ Click Next.

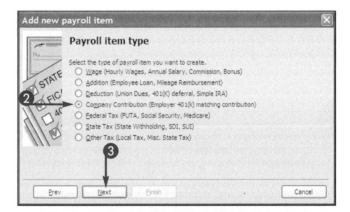

The Name used in paychecks and payroll reports screen appears.

④ Type a name for the item.

⑤ Click Next.

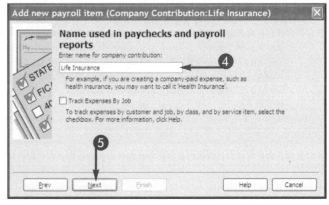

The Agency for company-paid liability screen appears.

6 Click here and select the name of the vendor to whom you pay the liability.

● You can type a vendor account number that identifies your business.

7 Click here and select liability and expense accounts for the payroll item.

8 Click Next.

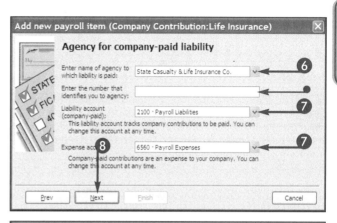

The Tax tracking type screen appears.

9 Click here and select a tax tracking type.

You can select Taxable Grp Trm Life if appropriate; check with the benefits administrator.

10 Click Next.

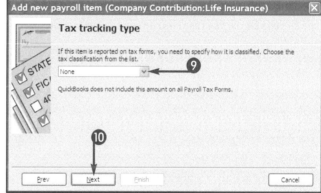

Why do I select both a liability account and an expense account for a company contribution payroll item?

▼ Each time you produce a paycheck for an employee who uses this payroll item, QuickBooks credits the liability account, creating a bill you need to pay, and debits the expense account that you entered on the Agency for company-paid liability screen. The expense side of the transaction represents the cost to your company to offer the benefit. You pay the bill created by the liability side of the transaction like you pay all payroll liabilities using the Pay Payroll Liabilities window. See Chapter 9 for details.

When should I select the Track Expenses By Job option on the Name used in paychecks and payroll reports screen?

▼ You can click this option (☐ changes to ☑) to track expenses by Customer:Job, class, or service item for the payroll item you are creating.

Does clicking Default tell me which taxes to select?

▼ No. The Default button shows you the taxes most often associated with the tax tracking type you select and you should not rely on it. Instead, check with the benefits plan administrator for a list of taxes to which the benefit is subject.

continued

Create a Company Contribution Payroll Item *(Continued)*

4 01(k) plans, 403(b) plans, Simple IRA plans, and SEP plans often include both employee and employer contributions. The employee's contribution is a payroll deduction; see the section "Create a New Deduction Payroll Item" for details on setting up the employee's contribution.

Not all company contribution payroll items involve an employee contribution. For example, suppose that your company offers life insurance to its employees — life insurance for which the employee pays nothing and the company pays all. In this case, you set up only a company contribution payroll item.

You may find that you need to create company contributions for some state or local taxes, and, if your company pays health insurance premiums as a benefit for employees, you need a company contribution payroll item for health insurance.

The process to set up a company contribution does not change for the specific company contribution. The taxes to which the contribution is subject may change, and the need for a deduction payroll item for an employee contribution along with a company contribution for a benefit changes depending on the benefit.

Create a Company Contribution Payroll Item *(continued)*

The Taxes screen appears.

QuickBooks displays the taxes most often associated with the tax tracking type you selected.

⑪ Click next to each tax (☐ changes to ☑) that is affected by this company contribution.

⑫ Click Next.

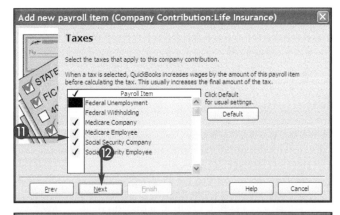

The Calculate based on quantity screen appears.

⑬ Click an option (○ changes to ◉) to select the method you want QuickBooks to use to calculate the amount of the company contribution payroll item.

⑭ Click Next.

The Default rate and limit screen appears.

- If QuickBooks calculates the payroll item, you can type a rate here.

- You can type an annual limit for the item here.

⑮ Click Finish.

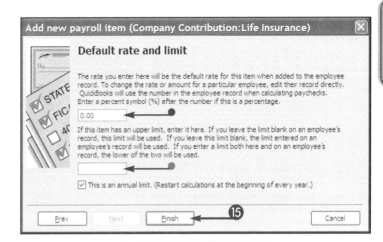

- The new company contribution payroll item appears in the Payroll Item List window.

When should I use Taxable Grp Trm Life as the Tax tracking type?

▼ Select this tax tracking type when you are setting up a payroll item for the taxable amount of a group term life insurance policy that you provide to employees with coverage over $50,000. Using this tax tracking type increases the taxable wages on line 2 of the Federal Form 941. On the W-2, this tax tracking type also increases the taxable wages that appear in Box 1 and reports the amount in Box 12 using IRS code C.

What effect does a company contribution have on gross pay and taxes?

▼ Company contributions have no effect on gross pay. However, company contributions increase the taxes you select when you set up the company contribution item. By selecting those taxes, you indicate that the company contribution benefit is subject to those taxes. When you increase taxes, you affect net pay, because net pay changes to accommodate the taxes.

How does QuickBooks calculate gross pay?

▼ QuickBooks adds together all wage payroll items, taxable company contribution payroll items, and addition payroll items in the order that they appear when you add them to the employee's payroll information either in the employee's record or in the Earnings section of a paycheck. You can see changes to gross pay if you simply reorder the payroll items on an employee's paycheck. Exercise care when you establish the order, because taxes are calculated on gross pay.

Create a State Tax Payroll Item

I f your state has a state income tax, a state unemployment tax, or any other state tax based on payroll, you must create state tax payroll items for each state tax.

To set up state taxes, you need a vendor to whom you pay the tax and a liability account — and possibly an expense account — in which to store the tax you collect until you pay it. See Chapter 6 for details on setting up a vendor and Chapter 2 for details on creating accounts.

When you set up state taxes, include the identification number that your state assigns to you on the Agency for employee-paid liability screen. Doing this allows QuickBooks

to include your identification number on checks you write to remit state taxes and ensures that you will receive proper credit for state tax payments.

The process to set up state income taxes is the same as the process to set up state unemployment taxes with one exception. When you set up an unemployment tax, QuickBooks displays an additional screen with the unemployment rates commonly used in your state. This section shows you how to set up a state unemployment tax payroll item.

Create a State Payroll Tax Item

① Follow steps 1 to 6 in the section "Create a Wage Payroll Item" to open the Custom Setup Wizard.

The Payroll item type screen appears.

② Click the State Tax option (○ changes to ⊙).

③ Click Next.

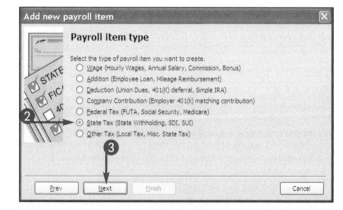

The State tax screen appears.

④ Click here and select a state.

⑤ Click the type of tax you want to set up (○ changes to ⊙).

⑥ Click Next.

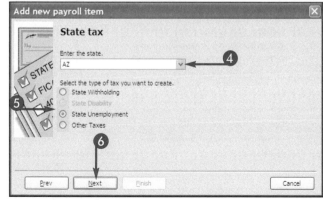

- The Name used in paychecks and payroll reports screen appears.

- QuickBooks suggests a name that you can change if you want.

7 Click Next.

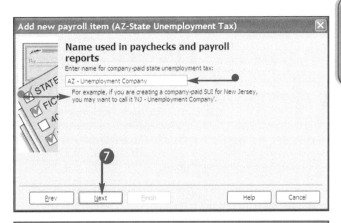

The Agency for company-paid liability screen appears.

8 Click here and select the name of the vendor to whom you pay the liability.

- You can type the ID number assigned to you by your state.

9 Click here and select liability and expense accounts for the payroll item.

10 Click Next.

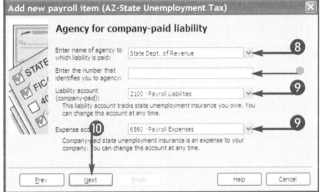

When should I use separate liability accounts for payroll items?

▼ You should set up liability accounts for payroll either by the vendor to whom you pay the liability or by the type of liability. For example, because you pay federal withholding, Social Security, and Medicare to the same vendor, you do not need separate liability accounts for each tax. Similarly, if you pay all state taxes to the same agency, set up one liability account for state taxes. For benefits that you remit on behalf of employees, set up separate accounts for each benefit to make tracking easier for you.

Should I set up separate vendors for each state tax?

▼ If you pay all payroll taxes to the same vendor, set up only one vendor; do not set up different versions of the same vendor for each tax.

Should I use separate payroll liability or expense accounts for each payroll tax item?

▼ No. You can set up separate liability accounts for each *type* of payroll tax or for each vendor to whom you pay tax, but do not set up liability accounts for each payroll item. For example, you can assign all state payroll tax items to the same payroll expense account.

continued

Create a State Tax Payroll Item *(Continued)*

Most states collect unemployment insurance from employers; states use unemployment insurance payments to pay unemployment compensation to eligible workers who lose their jobs. You set up unemployment payroll tax items for each state to which you pay state unemployment taxes.

Your state may require that both your employees and your business pay state unemployment taxes. In these cases, QuickBooks automatically creates both state payroll tax items at the same time when you create your state items. QuickBooks stores your company's share of the

unemployment tax in the expense account you designate and the amount you must remit to the state in the liability account you designate.

If your state limits each employee's taxable annual income, QuickBooks stops calculating the tax when an employee's annual income reaches the specified amount. You cannot control the amount; QuickBooks obtains the amount from the state payroll tax tables included when you select a payroll service. If you do not sign up for a payroll service — either Do-It-Yourself Payroll or one of the assisted payroll plans — QuickBooks does not calculate state taxes. See the section "Sign Up for a Payroll Tax Service" for information on selecting a payroll service.

Create a State Tax Payroll Item *(continued)*

The Company tax rates for current year screen appears.

⑪ As needed, change the rates QuickBooks suggests for any quarter.

⑫ Click Next.

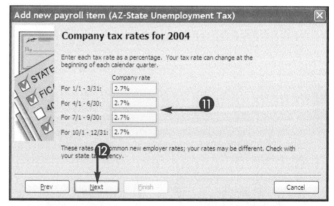

The Taxable compensation screen appears.

QuickBooks displays the payroll items most often subject to the tax you are creating.

⑬ Click next to each tax (☐ changes to ☑) that is affected by this state tax.

⑭ Click Next.

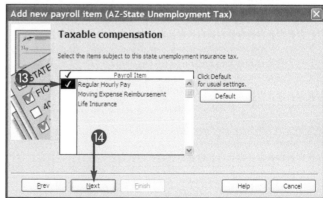

The Pre-tax deductions screen appears.

⑮ Click next to each deduction
(☐ changes to ☑) that reduces gross
wages for the tax you are creating.

⑯ Click Finish.

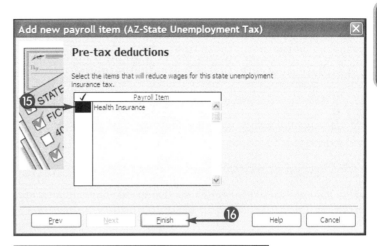

● The new state tax payroll item
appears in the Payroll Item List
window.

How do I know which state taxes to set up?

▼ When you select your state, QuickBooks displays the only options available to you. For example, Florida has no state income tax or state disability tax, so those options are not available, but Florida does have an unemployment tax, so that option is available. Similarly, California and New Jersey both have state income tax, state disability tax, state unemployment tax, and other taxes.

What kinds of "Other Taxes" can I set up as state taxes, as listed on the Other taxes screen?

▼ Other taxes are usually additional taxes you collect on behalf of a municipality within your state or for other reasons decided upon by state and local legislators. Arkansas collects a Stability tax, Hawaii collects an EFT Assessment tax, and Massachusetts collects a Workforce Training tax. The types of Other Taxes vary from state to state; see the section, "Create an Other Tax Payroll Item" for details on creating these taxes.

How do I set up my state's disability tax?

▼ If your state has a disability tax, QuickBooks makes that option available when you select your state on the State tax screen. Select it and walk through the wizard. The same screens appear for disability tax as for unemployment tax, except the tax rate screen changes, based on your state's requirements. For example, in California, only employees pay state disability tax, while in New Jersey, both employers and employees pay state disability tax.

Create an Other Tax Payroll Item

Many states collect additional taxes from businesses, and you can set up these additional taxes using the Other Tax payroll item in QuickBooks.

Your state may collect additional taxes on behalf of a municipality within the state or for other reasons decided upon by state and local legislators. For example, Arizona collects a Job Training Tax, which is similar to a tax in California called an Employment Training Tax. Georgia charges an Administrative Assessment Tax, while Michigan and Indiana both collect payroll taxes based on where employees work and where employees reside.

When you select a payroll service, as described in the section "Sign Up for a Payroll Tax Service," and QuickBooks downloads payroll tax tables, the tax tables include many of the common "other taxes" charged by state and local authorities. You can find the tax you want to set up listed, and you can see an example of setting up a listed "other tax" in this section.

If the tax you need to set up does not appear in the list, you can create a user-defined payroll tax, where you define elements, such as whether the employer or the employee pays the tax, and whether the tax is calculated based on a quantity.

Create an Other Tax Payroll Item

1 Follow steps 1 to 8 in the section "Create a Wage Payroll Item" to open the Custom Setup Wizard, selecting Other Tax in step 7.

The Other tax screen appears.

2 Click here and select a tax.

3 Click Next.

4 On the Name used in paychecks and payroll reports screen that appears, accept the suggested name or type a new name for the tax and click Next.

The Agency for company-paid liability screen appears.

5 Click here and select the vendor to whom you pay the liability.

- You can type the ID number assigned to you by your state.

6 Click here and select liability and expense accounts for the payroll item.

Note: You may not see both a liability and an expense account.

7 Click Next.

The Company tax rate screen appears.

8 Click here and select your company's tax rate.

9 Click Next.

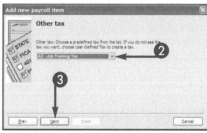

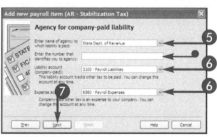

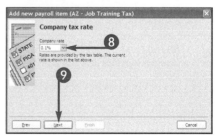

The Taxable compensation screen appears.

QuickBooks displays the payroll items most often subject to the tax you are creating.

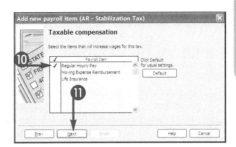

⑩ Click next to each item (☐ changes to ☑) that affects this other tax.

⑪ Click Next.

The Pre-tax deductions screen appears.

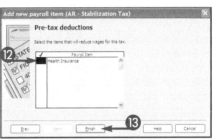

⑫ Click next to each deduction (☐ changes to ☑) that reduces gross wages for the tax you are creating.

⑬ Click Finish.

● The new Other Tax payroll item appears in the Payroll Item List window.

How do I create a tax that does not appear in the list on the Other tax screen?

▼ You can select User-Defined Tax from the list to create the tax. Some of the Custom Setup Wizard screens change and other screens appear that you do not see in this section. For example, on the Other tax screen, you choose to define an employee-paid tax or an employer-paid tax. The Agency screen changes to display a liability account if you select an employee-paid tax or an expense account if you select an employer-paid tax.

What screens appear when I select User-Defined Tax on the Other tax screen?

▼ In addition to the screens shown in this section, the Custom Setup Wizard also displays the Tax tracking type screen. The Tax tracking type controls the default taxes QuickBooks suggests for the payroll item. The Calculate based on quantity screen also appears, where you can specify if the tax is based on a quantity, hours, or neither. Last, the Default rate and limit screen appears, where you specify a rate and limit for the tax if appropriate. All of these screens appear in the section "Create a Deduction Payroll Item."

Set Payroll &
Employee Preferences

Like other areas in QuickBooks, you can set preferences that affect the way QuickBooks handles certain payroll issues. For example, in the Employee List, you can display employees in alphabetical order by either first name or last name. And, you can maintain privacy concerning pay rates by hiding them while you pay employees.

QuickBooks sets default Payroll & Employee preferences when you select a payroll option, as described in the section "Sign Up for a Payroll Tax Service," but you can change those options.

Perhaps the most powerful Payroll & Employee preference enables you to identify and save the payroll items most commonly assigned to employees. After you create all the payroll items your company needs to assign to employees using the sections presented in this chapter, you can establish a list of the most commonly assigned payroll items and, if appropriate, the most common rates for those items. QuickBooks assigns these default payroll items and their settings to each new employee that you create. When you establish default payroll items, you speed up the process of creating employees, because you only need to edit the employee records that do not match the established defaults.

Set Payroll & Employee Preferences

① Click Edit.

② Click Preferences.

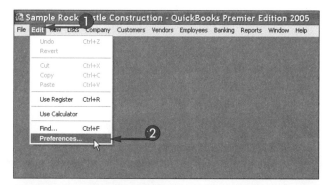

The Preferences dialog box appears.

③ Click the Payroll & Employees icon.

④ Click the Company Preferences tab.

⑤ Click an option (○ changes to ◉) to display employees by first or last name.

⑥ Click here (☐ changes to ☑) to hide employee pay rates.

⑦ Click Employee Defaults.

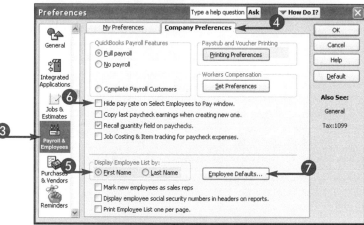

The Employee Defaults window appears.

8 Click here to select the most common pay period.

9 Click here to select wage payroll items.

10 Click here to select additions, deductions, and company contributions.

11 Click here to set up options for taxes and sick and vacation leave.

12 Click OK.

The Preferences dialog box reappears.

13 Click Printing Preferences.

The Payroll Printing Preferences dialog box appears.

14 Click these options (☑ changes to ☐) to avoid printing elements on paycheck vouchers or paystubs.

15 Click OK twice.

Your choices are saved.

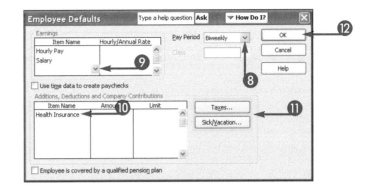

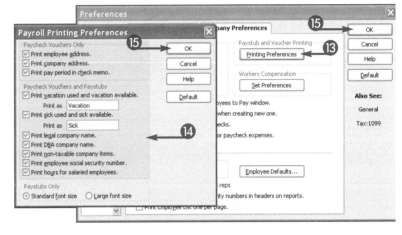

What does the Print Employee List one per page option do?

▼ By default, when you print the Employee List, QuickBooks prints one employee per line on the report. However, if you select this option (☐ changes to ☑), located in the Preferences dialog box, and you print the Employee List, QuickBooks prints each employee on a separate page. This feature is handy for producing a report of the information you want for placement in an employee's file.

What does the Report all payroll taxes by Customer:Job and Service Item option do?

▼ Located in the Preferences dialog box, this option (☐ changes to ☑) works in conjunction with company-paid payroll taxes, addition, and company contribution payroll items. When you enable this option in Payroll preferences, you can tell QuickBooks to break down these payroll items by job, service item, or class, if you use class tracking, on reports of expenses.

If I sort my employees alphabetically by last name, does that affect names on paychecks?

▼ No. QuickBooks still prints paychecks in first name, last name order.

In the Preferences dialog box, what does the Mark new employees as sales reps option do?

▼ When you click this option (☐ changes to ☑), QuickBooks automatically creates sales reps whenever you create an employee. You can assign sales reps to customers and to invoices to track sales by person. For more information on creating sales reps, see Chapter 3.

Create an Employee

After you create the wage, addition, deduction, company contribution, and state and local tax payroll items that you need to assign to employees and set payroll options, you are ready to create new employees.

When you create an employee, you store a wide variety of information about the employee. Most of the information you supply appears on paychecks and reports, helping you quickly and easily complete everyday payroll tasks.

The New Employee dialog box contains three sets of different types of payroll information: personal information, compensation and tax information, and employment information. Within each type of information, you may see one or more tabs on which you fill in or select the appropriate data.

For personal information, you supply the employee's name, social security number, gender, date of birth, address, phone number, e-mail address, and pager information. You also have the opportunity to create an employee ID for each employee and to fill in information stored in employee custom fields. For more information on custom fields, see Chapter 2.

Create an Employee

① Click Lists.

② Click Employee List.

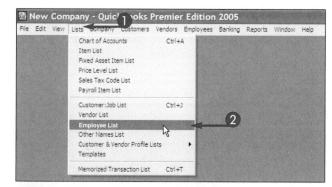

The Employee List window appears.

③ Click Employee.

④ Click New.

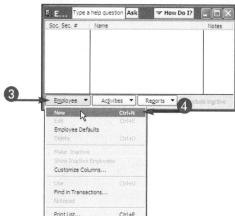

The New Employee dialog box appears.

⑤ Type the employee's name.

● QuickBooks fills in this box.

⑥ Type the employee's social security number.

⑦ Select the employee's gender and date of birth.

⑧ Click the Address and Contact tab.

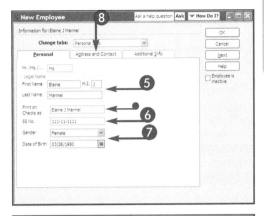

⑨ Type the employee's address information here.

⑩ Type phone numbers here.

⑪ Type e-mail and pager information here.

⑫ Click the Additional Info tab.

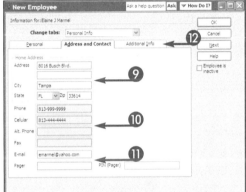

How do I add a payroll item that does not appear on the Payroll Info tab?

▼ Assuming you already set up the item, click Payroll and Compensation Info from the Change tabs list. Then, click in the Earnings or Additions, Deductions, and Company Contributions section, and QuickBooks displays an arrow (▾) that you can click to select the payroll item. QuickBooks displays items appropriate to the section where you click.

What does the Use time data to create paychecks option do?

▼ This option appears on the Payroll Info tab after you select Payroll and Compensation Info from the Change tabs list. When you click this option (☐ changes to ☑), QuickBooks prefills the employee's paychecks with data entered on the weekly timesheet or using individual time entries. For more information, see Chapter 10.

When should I select the Employee is covered by a qualified pension plan option?

▼ This option appears on the Payroll Info tab after you select Payroll and Compensation Info from the Change tabs list. If your company provides a retirement plan — a 401(k), a 403(b), an SEP plan, or a SIMPLE plan — click the option (☐ changes to ☑). All employees are considered covered even if they do not make contributions to the plan.

continued

Create an Employee *(Continued)*

On the Payroll Info tab of the New Employee dialog box, you identify the employee's pay period, add or delete payroll items as necessary, and fill in rates for wage, addition, deduction, and company contribution payroll items applicable to the employee you are creating. You also have access to tax and sick and vacation leave settings for the employee.

When you click the Payroll Info tab, the payroll items that you selected when you set up employee defaults already appear. To read more about setting up employee defaults, see the section "Set Payroll & Employee Preferences."

You supply annual rates for salary wage items and hourly rates for hourly wage items. For commission wage items, supply a commission rate. For deductions, supply a "per pay period" amount. Suppose, for example, that you offer an employee-paid health insurance plan where the plan collects the health insurance premium monthly. If you pay your employees biweekly, calculate the annual amount, divide it by 26 — the number of biweekly pay periods in a calendar year — and enter that amount for the deduction. If you pay an employee biweekly and the employee pays $250.00 per month, the annual amount equals $3000.00 and the biweekly deduction amount should be $115.38.

Create an Employee *(continued)*

● You can type an employee ID number here.

● You can fill in custom field information here.

⑬ Click here and select Payroll and Compensation Info.

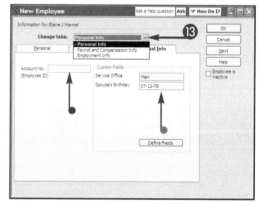

The Payroll Info tab appears.

⑭ If necessary, click here and select a different pay period.

⑮ Type an annual salary or an hourly rate amount here.

⑯ Type pay period amounts for additions, deductions, and company contributions here.

● You can, as needed, add payroll items by clicking the ⊡ that appears on a blank line.

⑰ Click Taxes.

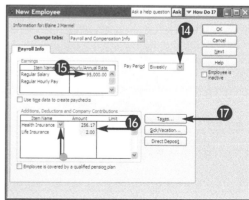

The Federal tab of the Taxes dialog box appears.

18 Click here to select a new filing status.

○ You can type numbers for allowances and extra withholding here.

● You can click these options to change the taxes to which an employee is subject.

19 Click the State tab.

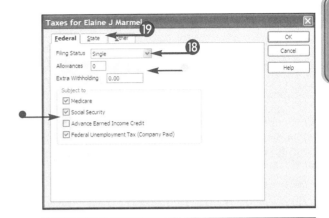

20 Click here to select the employee's work state.

21 Click here to select the employee's state for withholding purposes.

● You can supply state withholding status, amounts, and allowances here.

22 Click the Other tab.

How do I enter amounts for commission wage items and deductions?

▼ Enter the commission rate as a percentage, making sure that you type a percent sign (%) to indicate that QuickBooks should treat the value as a percentage. For deductions, it does not matter if you enter positive or negative numbers. QuickBooks automatically supplies the negative sign because deduction payroll items are subtracted.

How do I know how much extra withholding to enter?

▼ Use the information that the employee supplies on the Federal Form W-4 or on your state's withholding form. These forms also include filing status information and the number of allowances the employee wants to claim. You need to keep Federal Form W-4 on file for each employee, and you should have your employees complete a new one each year.

Is there a limit on the number of allowances an employee can claim?

▼ QuickBooks permits you to enter up to 999 allowances; however, you will rarely enter a number higher than 10.

What choices are available for the sick and vacation leave accrual period?

▼ Your choices are beginning of the year, every paycheck, or every hour on paycheck.

continued

Create an Employee *(Continued)*

From the Payroll Info tab, you have access to the Taxes dialog box, where you can change the employee's options for federal, state, and other taxes. In most cases, you do not need to change federal tax options. If your state has state and local payroll taxes, you must set up both state taxes and other taxes for each employee.

You also have access to vacation and sick leave options for the employee from the Payroll Info tab. For both types of leave, you can enter the hours available as of the date you set up the employee, the hours used in the current calendar year, how often the employee accrues each type of leave, the number of hours accrued each time the employee accrues leave, and the maximum number of hours for each type of leave. You also can specify whether the employee retains all accrued leave indefinitely or loses any unused leave at the end of the year and starts accruing leave again at the beginning of the next year.

On the Employment tab of the New Employee dialog box, you can store the date you hire the employee, the date the employee leaves the company, and the employee's type.

Create an Employee *(continued)*

The Other tab appears.

㉓ Click here to add any other taxes needed.

㉔ Click OK.

The Payroll Info tab of the New Employee dialog box reappears.

㉕ Click the Sick/Vacation button.

The Sick & Vacation dialog box appears.

㉖ Type sick hours available and used here.

㉗ Set sick leave accrual options here.

㉘ Type vacation hours available and used here.

㉙ Set vacation leave accrual options here.

㉚ Click OK.

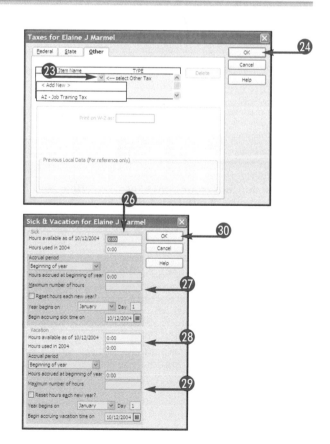

The New Employee dialog box reappears.

31 Click here and select Employment Info.

32 Click the calendar button (▥) and select a hire date.

33 Click ▥ and select a release date if appropriate.

34 Click here and select an employee type.

35 Click OK.

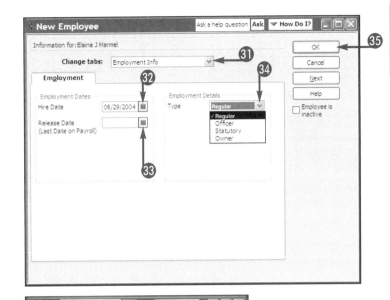

● The new employee appears in the Employee List.

What do the employee types mean?

▼ Basically, most of your employees are regular employees. Regular employees are people who perform services, and you control what is done and how it is done. You have officers if you are incorporated. Set up owners in the Other Names list unless they already appear in your Employee List; then designate them as owners. Statutory employees are very specifically defined by the IRS in Publication 15, Circular E, Employer's Tax Guide, and you should read this document for complete information on this and all other employee types. If you are not certain of an employee's type, check with your accountant.

Why should I set up an owner in the Other Names List?

▼ Because of tax laws, QuickBooks does not allow you to produce paychecks from the Pay Employees window for owners or partners. Instead, you pay owners and partners by writing a check through the Write Checks window. See Chapter 15 for details on using the Write Checks window.

How can I store more information about employees than I see on the Employment tab?

▼ You can purchase the Employee Organizer, which is an add-on product that integrates into QuickBooks and allows you to track and store employee information in one central location.

Enter Employee Beginning Balances

To produce accurate reports and payroll tax returns, you must enter beginning balance information for employees if you are not starting to use payroll in QuickBooks on January 1 and you have previously paid employees during the current calendar year outside QuickBooks.

To enter beginning balances for wages, taxes withheld and accrued, deductions, additions, and benefits, you can summarize the information. But, before you start collecting information, decide the first date on which you prepare payroll in QuickBooks — aim for the first day of a quarter or a month and collect all payroll information prior to that date.

The Payroll Setup Wizard starts out where you left off when you signed up for the payroll service in "Sign Up for a Payroll Tax Service," but, because you have completed most of the steps listed, you skip those steps as you walk through the wizard. In the Company Setup Tasks section, you skip setting up payroll taxes and additional payroll items, but you select a vendor — a bank — to which you make payroll tax deposits; if you have not yet set up the vendor, the Payroll Setup Wizard helps you. You also skip establishing default payroll settings and setting up employees.

Enter Employee Beginning Balances

① Click Employees.

② Click Payroll Services.

③ Click Set Up Payroll.

The Payroll Setup Wizard begins.

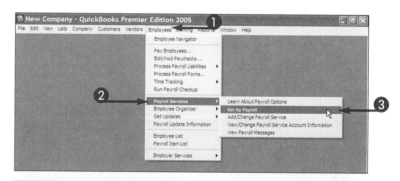

④ Click Continue.

The Payroll Setup Wizard walks you through setting up company information and employees.

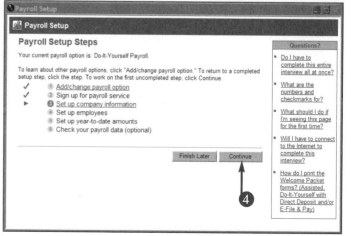

5 Click Continue or Done through all of the Company Setup Tasks until steps 3 and 4 have check marks (☑) beside them on the Payroll Setup Steps screen.

6 Click Continue.

The Enter Year-to-Date Payroll Amounts in QuickBooks screen appears.

7 Click Set Up YTD Amounts.

The Set Up YTD Amounts Wizard begins.

● An informational screen explains that you will enter summary amounts.

8 Click Next.

The When should YTD summaries affect accounts? screen appears.

9 Click ▣ and select the date summaries should affect payroll liability and expense accounts.

10 Click ▣ and select the date summaries should affect your payroll bank account.

11 Click Next.

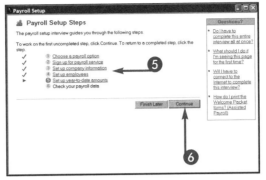

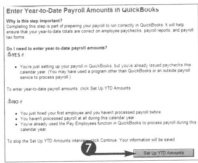

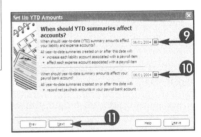

Do I need to enter beginning balances for an employee who no longer works for the company?

▼ If you paid the employee during the current calendar year, you need to supply the employee with a W-2 form for the current calendar year. If you want to produce the W-2 through QuickBooks, you must set up the employee and enter the employee's payroll history at your company by entering beginning balances. You can plan to manually prepare the W-2 at the end of the year when you prepare the other W-2s using QuickBooks, but you will also have to manually calculate your Federal Forms 940 and 941.

Can you suggest a way to summarize information from paycheck stubs?

▼ Create a spreadsheet for each employee, typing the employee's name in an empty cell at the top. Set up a row for each wage, tax, deduction, addition, and benefit you pay. Set up columns for each pay period date. Before you fill in the cells, save the spreadsheet so that it can serve as the foundation for another employee. Then, fill in the cells and then sum the columns. Last, set up rows where you can store the sum of the pay period sums that comprise a summary period.

continued

Enter Employee Beginning Balances *(Continued)*

To enter beginning balances, you summarize information for each quarter prior to the date you plan to start using payroll in QuickBooks. If you start in the middle of a quarter, prepare monthly summaries for that quarter. If you start midmonth, enter summaries for full accounting periods — quarters or months — but enter the payrolls for the beginning of the current month using the Pay Employees window. See Chapter 8 for details.

The Set Up YTD Amounts Wizard asks you to specify the date that summary amounts should affect payroll liability and expense accounts and your payroll checking account, and the date on which you plan to prepare your first payroll

using QuickBooks. Assuming you entered beginning account balances as described in Chapter 2, enter all three dates using the first day of the first month for which you plan to record paychecks in QuickBooks. If you plan to prepare paychecks on June 15 for the pay period May 31 through June 11, use June 1 as the date. Enter summaries for whole quarters and, if necessary, individual months. Using this technique, QuickBooks can accurately prepare all payroll reports, including the 941 report for the quarter you start using payroll. Be aware, however, that you should enter pay period summaries if your company must file Federal Form 941 Schedule B.

Enter Employee Beginning Balances *(continued)*

The Earliest QuickBooks payroll date screen appears.

⑫ Click 🔳 and select the date you will begin using QuickBooks to create paychecks.

⑬ Click Next.

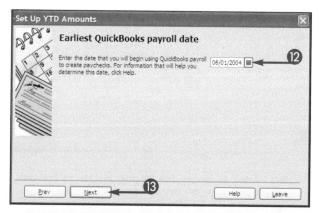

The Employee summary information screen appears.

⑭ Click an employee for whom you want to enter beginning balances.

⑮ Click Enter Summary.

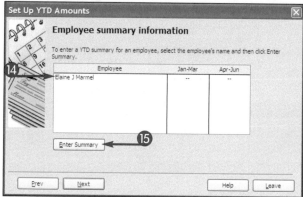

The YTD Adjustment screen for the selected employee appears.

⑯ Click 🔲 and select From and To dates for the summary.

⑰ Type the period totals here.

● You may need to scroll down.

⑱ Click Next Period.

⑲ Repeat steps 16 to 18 for each summary period.

⑳ Click OK.

The Employee summary information screen reappears, showing summaries for the employee.

㉑ Repeat steps 14 to 20 for other employees.

㉒ Click Leave to redisplay the Payroll Setup Wizard.

㉓ Click 🗵 to close the Payroll Setup Wizard.

QuickBooks saves beginning balance information.

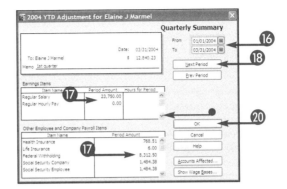

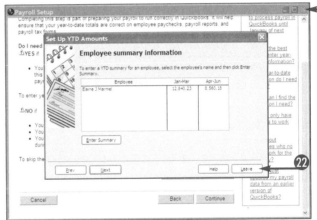

How can I find the necessary payroll information if I did not previously use a payroll service?

▼ You can collect this information from your employees' paycheck stubs or from the outside payroll service you may have used previously. Because most paycheck stubs contain both current pay period and year-to-date information, you can enter beginning balance information for the first quarter using the year-to-date information found on the last paycheck of the quarter. For other quarters or months, you may find it easiest to simply use a spreadsheet to summarize pay period information.

Do I have to enter all beginning balances for all employees while I have the wizard open?

▼ No. You can return to enter an employee's beginning balances as long as you enter the beginning balances before you process payroll for the employee. Perform steps 1 to 4 and then continue with steps 7 to 23.

What happens when I click the Show Wage Bases button?

▼ Click this button to add a Wage Base column to the Other Employee and Company Payroll Items section. QuickBooks displays the wage base for all appropriate payroll items; you can change the wage base if appropriate.

Create
Sales Reps

Many companies assign sales representatives to customers so that customers have a contact person within the company. Sales representatives may be salaried or hourly employees who may also receive commissions. Alternatively, they may be individuals who receive a commission for selling your products, but they are not employees of your company for payroll tax reporting purposes.

QuickBooks allows you to assign an employee, a vendor, or another name as a sales rep to a customer in the Rep field of the customer's record. You can use the Rep field to help track commissions, to identify the employee who is primarily responsible for managing a customer's orders, or to identify the person or business that referred the customer to you.

Before you can create a sales rep, the rep's information must appear either in the Vendor List, the Employee List, or the Other Names List. See Chapters 6 and 4 for details on creating a vendor and employee, respectively. You can set up sales representatives who are not employees or vendors in the Other Names List; see Chapter 2. If you intend to use the Rep field to store referrals, set up the referring entity in the Other Names List.

Create Sales Reps

1 Click Lists.

2 Click Customer & Vendor Profile Lists.

3 Click Sales Rep List.

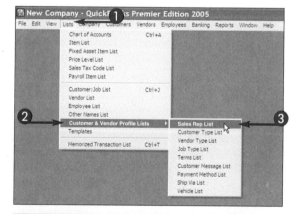

The Sales Rep List window appears.

4 Click Sales Rep.

5 Click New.

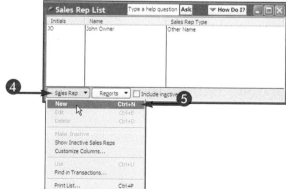

The New Sales Rep dialog box appears.

6 Click here to select a name.

● QuickBooks fills in Sales Rep initials and type.

7 Click OK.

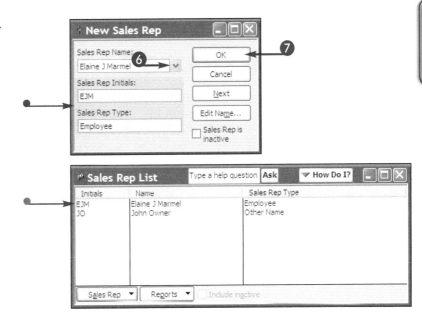

● The new sales rep appears in the Sale Rep List window.

Is there a way to print a list of the sales representatives assigned to each customer?

▼ Yes. After you assign representatives to customers, you can customize a Contact List. See the section "Create a New Customer" for more information. Click Lists and then click Customer:Job List. In the Customer:Job List window that appears, click Reports, and then click Contact List. Click Modify, and on the Display tab that appears, deselect options (☑ changes to ☐) that appear next to all fields except Customer and select the Rep field (☐ changes to ☑). Click OK to redisplay the report of customers and their assigned representatives.

I want to change the Sales Rep Type, but QuickBooks does not let me. Why not?

▼ For the Sales Rep Type field, QuickBooks uses the name of the list in which you stored the person you selected in the Sales Rep Name field. For example, if you select an employee, QuickBooks displays Employee in the Sales Rep Type field. You cannot change the Sales Rep Type unless you add the person you select for the Sales Rep Name field to the Vendor or Other Name List and then select the entry from that list.

Create Customer Types

I n many businesses, it is helpful to categorize customers so that you can better serve them; in QuickBooks, you use the Customer Type List to create categories that you can assign to customers.

Suppose, for example, that you run a lawn service business and you have both commercial and residential customers. And, suppose that your business services three different towns. You can create customer types — and subtypes — to help distinguish between commercial and residential customers in each locality you serve.

A subtype is nothing more than a further breakdown of a customer type. In the example in this section, the customer types are Commercial and Residential, and the subtypes are

the towns in which commercial and residential customers are located. If you serve commercial customers in Tampa and Clearwater, you set up one customer type for commercial customers and two subtypes: Commercial Tampa and Commercial Clearwater. If you service residential customers in the same areas, you set up one customer type for residential customers and two more subtypes for Residential Tampa and Residential Clearwater.

Once you assign customer types to customers, you can sort and filter reports based on customer type and subtype. See Chapter 22 for details on reports.

Create Customer Types

① Click Lists.

② Click Customer & Vendor Profile Lists.

③ Click Customer Type List.

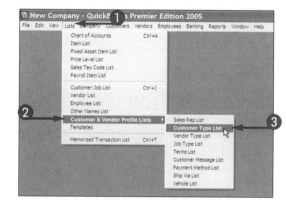

The Customer Type List window appears.

④ Click Customer Type.

⑤ Click New.

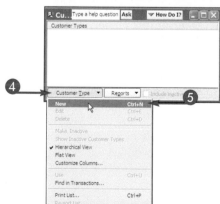

The New Customer Type dialog box appears.

6 Type a name.

- To make the entry a subtype, you can click the Subtype of option (☐ changes to ☑) and select an existing customer type.

7 Click OK.

- The new customer type appears in the Customer Type List window.

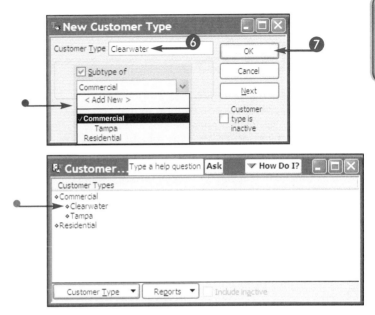

Are there other reports where I can make use of the information stored in the Customer Type field?

▼ Yes. You can filter any number of customer reports by customer type or subtype. For example, you can print an A/R Aging Summary report and filter it by customer type. For details on printing and filtering a report, see Chapter 22. You also can print mailing labels for one or more selected customer types — very useful when you need to communicate with a particular kind of customer; for example, you may want to send a discount coupon to residential customers. For details on printing mailing labels, see Chapter 21.

What reports are available in the Customer Type List window?

▼ You can create a QuickReport on any customer type or subtype. To print a QuickReport, open the Customer Type List window by following steps 1 to 3 in this section. Then, select the customer type or subtype on which you want to report, click Reports, and then QuickReport.

What information appears on a QuickReport for a customer type or subtype?

▼ The report displays transactions related to customers assigned to the selected customer type. You do not see the customer type on any transaction.

Create Job Types

Like its cousin the Customer Type, the Job Type helps you classify jobs you perform so that you can group and subtotal comparable jobs and use the information to help you identify the types of jobs that are most profitable.

Suppose, for example, that you run a lawn service business and you offer mowing services that include mowing; trimming and edging; fertilization services, where your staff feeds lawns and uses chemicals to eliminate bugs and weeds; and installation and removal services, where you remove an existing lawn if necessary and lay sod or plant seed for a new lawn.

You can create job types that you can assign to jobs you perform for customers so that you can produce reports for one or more selected job types. You can further break down each job type into subtypes if you need to further categorize job information. For example, if you need to produce reports that segregate lawn installation services job type information into finer categories, you can break down lawn installation services into lawn removal services, lawn planting services, shrubbery removal services, tree removal services, shrubbery planting services, and tree planting services.

Create Job Types

1. Click Lists.
2. Click Customer & Vendor Profile Lists.
3. Click Job Type List.

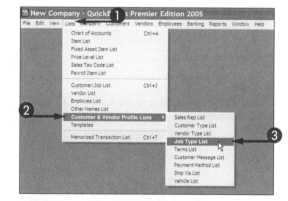

The Job Type List window appears.

4. Click Job Type.
5. Click New.

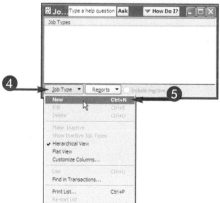

The New Job Type dialog box appears.

6 Type a name.

● To make the entry a subtype, you can click the Subtype of option (☐ changes to ☑) and select an existing job type.

7 Click OK.

● The new job type appears in the Job Type List window.

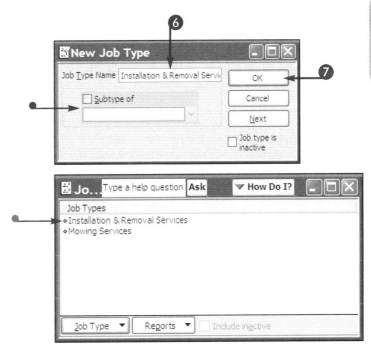

How do I delete a job type?

▼ Follow steps 1 to 4, then click Delete. If you have not assigned the job type to any jobs, QuickBooks deletes the job type. If you have assigned the job type to a job, you cannot delete the job type. Instead, you can hide it from view by making it inactive. To make a job type inactive, complete steps 1 to 3 in this section. Then, select the job type you want to hide, click Job Type, and click Make Inactive.

What do I do if I change my mind and want to start using the job type again?

▼ First, display all list items. Follow steps 1 to 3 in this section, and click the Include Inactive option (☐ changes to ☑). Next, select the hidden list entry, so that an X appears next to its name, and click Job Types. From the menu that appears, click Make Active.

How do I edit a job type?

▼ Follow steps 1 to 3 in this section to display the Job Type List window. Then, double-click the job type you want to edit. QuickBooks displays the Edit Job Type window, which looks exactly like the New Job Type window shown in this section except for the title bar. Make changes and click OK.

Create
Payment Terms

Terms describes when you expect to receive payment from a customer or when a vendor expects to receive payment from you. QuickBooks supports two types of terms: Standard and Date Driven. Standard terms are based on calculations from the issue date of the document, while date-driven terms do not use the issue date of the invoice or bill but rely on specific days of the month.

The names of terms are usually expressed in a shorthand method. Standard terms of 2% 10 Net 30 mean that a customer can discount 2 percent from the invoice or bill if

the customer pays the bill within 10 days of the bill date; otherwise the full amount is due 30 days from the bill date. Similarly, date-driven terms of 2% 10th Net 30th mean that a customer can discount 2 percent from the invoice or bill if the customer pays the bill by the 10th day of the next month; otherwise, the full amount is due on the 30th of the next month.

Date-driven terms work well for companies that send invoices monthly, usually on the last day of the month. If you intend to invoice your customers whenever you complete work, use Standard terms.

Create Payment Terms

1 Click Lists.

2 Click Customer & Vendor Profile Lists.

3 Click Terms List.

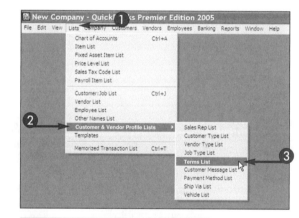

The Terms List window appears.

4 Click Terms.

5 Click New.

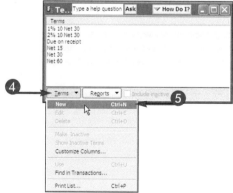

The New Terms dialog box appears.

6 Type a name.

7 Click either the Standard or Date Driven option for the type of terms you want to create (○ changes to ⊙).

8 Type numbers to describe the terms.

9 Click OK.

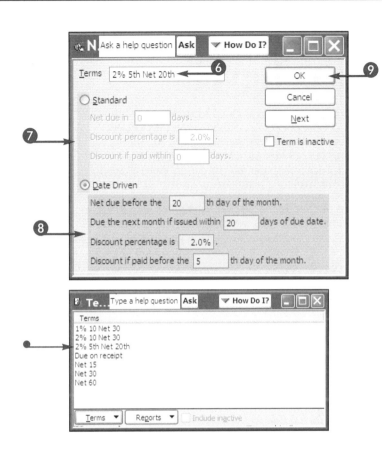

● The new terms appear in the Terms List window.

What does Net Due mean?

▼ Net Due refers to the date that payment of the entire amount of the invoice or bill is due. Using Standard terms, QuickBooks calculates the Net Due date using the entry date of the invoice or bill. For Date Driven terms, the Net Due date is a specific day of the month, regardless of the transaction date of the invoice or bill.

How do discounts work?

▼ If you assign Standard terms to the customer, QuickBooks applies the discount percentage if the customer pays the invoice or bill within a specified number of days. If you assign Date Driven terms to the customer, then QuickBooks applies the discount percentage if the customer pays by a specific day of the month.

How does QuickBooks use the number I type in the Due the next month if issued within X days of due date box?

▼ Suppose that you type 15 in the box. QuickBooks temporarily sets the due date of the invoice or bill to the 15th day of the current month. It then compares the temporary due date to the document's transaction date. If the difference between the dates is less than 15 — the number you type — QuickBooks sets the due date to the following month.

Create a New Price Level

U sing price levels in QuickBooks, you can connect special pricing to customers and jobs or apply one-time markups or markdowns to sales transactions. QuickBooks calculates the new pricing you specify in a price level based on the current price of service, inventory, noninventory, and inventory assembly items.

All versions of QuickBooks support fixed-percentage price level increases or decreases, which enable you to increase or decrease all item prices by a percentage you specify. Once you create a price level, you can apply it to a sales

document or you can assign it to a customer. Applying a price level to a sales document discounts or marks up everything on the document — a one-time action tied to the specific sales transaction. When you assign a price level to a customer, QuickBooks marks up or marks down everything on all future sales transactions for that customer.

QuickBooks Premier and above support per-item price levels that enable you to assign special pricing to selected items, making it easy for you to be very specific about special pricing. Like fixed-percentage price levels, you can apply a per-item price level to a sales transaction or assign it to a customer.

Create a New Price Level

1 Click Lists.

2 Click Price Level List.

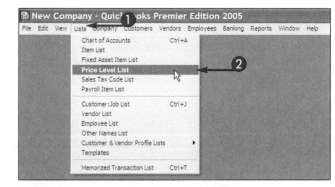

The Price Level List window appears.

3 Click Price Level.

4 Click New.

The New Price Level dialog box appears.

5 Type a name.

6 Click here and select a Price Level Type.

This example uses Fixed %.

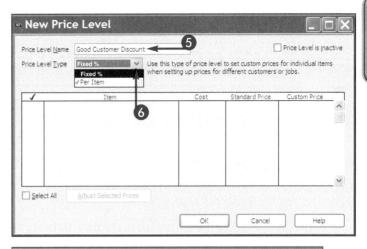

QuickBooks redisplays the New Price Level dialog box with options that you selected either in step 6.

7 In the This price level will box, select either increase or decrease.

8 Type a percentage.

9 Click OK.

The new price level appears in the Price Level List window.

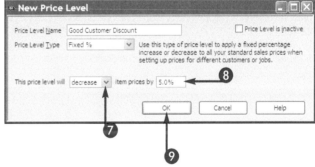

How does a per-item price level help you be more specific about special pricing?

▼ Per-item price levels affect only selected items and you specify a price that does not need to be a percentage of the current price. When you apply a per-item price level to a sales document, QuickBooks discounts or marks up only the items specified in the price level instead of the entire document. When you apply the price level to a customer, QuickBooks discounts or marks up only the selected items sold to the customer instead of all items sold to that customer.

What reports are available on the Reports menu in the Price Level List window?

▼ You can print an Item Price List that shows the prices for all sales items established when you create these items; see Chapter 7 for details on creating these items. Print this report by clicking Reports in the Price Level List window and selecting the report. You also can print a Selected Price Level Report that displays item prices based on the selected price level. Print this report by selecting a price level, clicking Reports, and then selecting the report.

Set Sales and Customer Preferences

Y ou can set defaults that affect sales orders, shipping, reimbursable expenses, and the way that QuickBooks applies customer payments when you set preferences for Sales & Customers.

Some companies have reimbursable expenses — expenses you incur on behalf of customers for which customers repay you. By default, QuickBooks assigns both your expense and the customer's repayment of the expense to one expense account, but you can assign the expense portion of a reimbursable expense to an expense account and the customer's reimbursement to an income account.

You can select a default template for packing slips; for more about templates, see Chapter 24. For more about shipping preferences, see Chapter 21. For more on price level preferences, see the section "Create a New Price Level."

What does the Automatically apply payments option do?

▼ With this option enabled (☐ changes to ☑), QuickBooks automatically applies customer payments to all outstanding invoices. If an outstanding invoice exists for the exact amount of the payment, QuickBooks applies the payment to that invoice, otherwise it applies the payment starting with the oldest open invoice. If you turn off this option, you must manually apply customer payments.

Set Sales and Customer Preferences

① Click Edit.

② Click Preferences.

The Preferences dialog box appears.

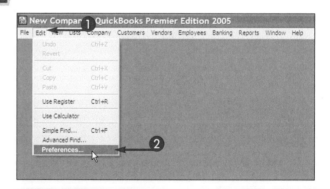

③ Click the Sales & Customers icon.

④ Click the Company Preferences tab.

⑤ Set shipping preferences here.

⑥ Click to select sales order preferences (☐ changes to ☑).

⑦ Click OK.

QuickBooks saves your preferences.

Set Preferences for Jobs and Estimates

If your business breaks down its workload by job or project, you must set preferences for jobs and estimates. In the construction industry, each home or building is a job. For convention planners, each convention is a job. For lawyers, each case is a job. When your business handles many jobs, tracking the status of each job becomes important — and you can create descriptions for your company's job statuses and then assign them to each job.

Customers of businesses that work by job often request estimates to anticipate both the cost and the scope of the job. You can create estimates in QuickBooks that do not affect your books, but provide the necessary information for the customer; if awarded the job, you can convert an estimate to an invoice.

What is Progress Invoicing?

▼ Many businesses bill for jobs as they complete portions of the job. When you do not use progress invoicing, you simply create an invoice for the full amount due using the estimate. When you use progress invoicing, QuickBooks lets you invoice for selected portions of an estimate, for a percentage of the estimate, or for differing percentages on selected lines of an estimate. Progress invoicing also enables you to display, on the invoice, the amount of the estimate that you previously invoiced the customer so that the customer can see how far along the job has progressed.

Set Preferences for Jobs and Estimates

① Click Edit.

② Click Preferences.

The Preferences dialog box appears.

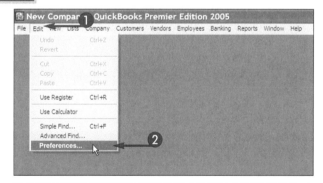

③ Click the Jobs & Estimates icon.

④ Click the Company Preferences tab.

⑤ Type job status descriptions here.

⑥ Click Yes (○ changes to ◉) to enable estimate preparation.

⑦ Click OK.

QuickBooks saves your preferences.

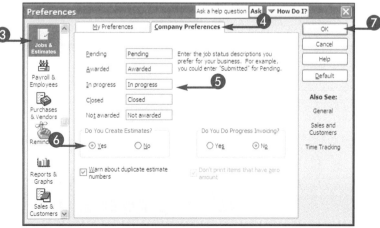

Create a New Customer

You can create customers in QuickBooks for any person or organization with whom you plan to do business on a long-term basis. In particular, you must create customers for those entities to whom you plan to send invoices and statements.

When you create a customer, QuickBooks saves all the pertinent information about the customer that you need to prepare and mail invoices and statements. You enter the name you use to select the customer from lists in QuickBooks windows, the customer's company name, and first and last name. As general background information,

you also supply an address for sending bills and, if different, another address for shipping goods. You can enter contact information for the customer, including two phone numbers, a fax number, an alternate contact name, and an e-mail address.

You can enter existing balance information for the customer, but only as an outstanding lump sum. To better track your receivables and easily record customer payments when you receive them, you should leave the Opening Balance field blank and instead create individual invoices that sum to each customer's outstanding balance. See Chapter 11 for details.

Create a New Customer

① Click Lists.

② Click Customer:Job List.

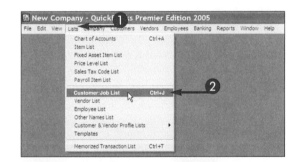

The Customer:Job List window appears.

③ Click Customer:Job.

④ Click New.

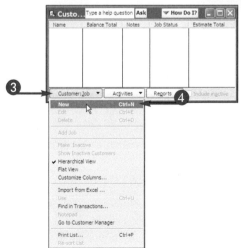

The New Customer dialog box appears.

⑤ Type a name for the new customer.

⑥ Type a company name.

⑦ Type first and last names, address information, and contact information.

⑧ Click the Additional Info tab.

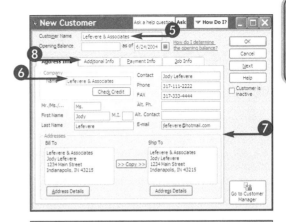

⑨ Click ⌄ and select a customer type, terms, rep, and preferred method to send sales document options.

⑩ Click here and select a sales tax code.

⑪ Click here and select a sales tax item.

How should I enter my customer's currently outstanding balance?

▼ To effectively track invoices that are outstanding when you begin using QuickBooks, you should enter each outstanding invoice using the Create Invoices window. To create beginning balance invoices, first create an item called Beginning Balance, making it an Other Charge item and nontaxable. Then, as you enter invoices, assign the total outstanding invoice amount using the item called Beginning Balance. See Chapters 7 and 11 for details.

What is a Resale Number?

▼ Organizations that buy items to resell later are typically exempt from paying sales taxes on their purchases, and the sales tax authority supplies such organizations with a resale number to identify the organization's sales tax exempt status. If a customer presents a resale number to you, you should enter it for your records and then set the customer up as nontaxable so that QuickBooks does not calculate and charge sales tax when you invoice the customer.

What does the Check Credit button do?

▼ It connects you via the Internet to the QuickBooks Credit Check Service. For free, you can look up a commercial customer address. For a fee, you can receive a credit report.

What options are available to send sales transactions?

▼ You can send sales transactions via regular mail or e-mail, or you can select None, which means that you do not intend to send estimates, invoices, or statements to this customer.

continued

Create a New Customer *(Continued)*

On the Additional Info tab, you can select options for most of the elements you set up earlier in this chapter. For example, you select a customer type, terms, a sales rep, and sales tax information. You also can select a price level to assign to the customer if appropriate and supply information for custom fields.

On the Payment Info tab, you can enter a customer account number and a credit limit for the customer. You also can select the customer's preferred payment method. If you select a credit card and supply a credit card number,

QuickBooks fills in the name on the card, the address, and the ZIP code using the information that appears on the Address Info tab. You can, of course, change that information.

You use the Job Info tab while creating a customer if you plan to perform only one job for the customer. If you plan to perform several jobs for the customer, set up jobs separately. On the Job Info tab, you can store the job's status, start date, projected end date, actual end date, description, and job type. In reports, QuickBooks separates the job name from the customer name using a colon.

Create a New Customer *(continued)*

- ● If appropriate, type a resale number.
- ● You can click here and select a price level to assign to the customer.
- ⑫ Type custom field information here.
- ⑬ Click the Payment Info tab.

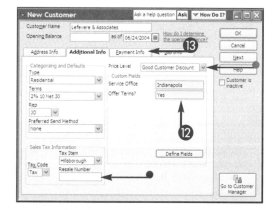

- ● You can type an account number and credit limit.
- ⑭ Click here and select a preferred payment method.
  - ● If appropriate, supply credit card information.

  If you type a credit card number, QuickBooks fills in other information from the Address Info screen.
- ⑮ Click the Job Info tab.

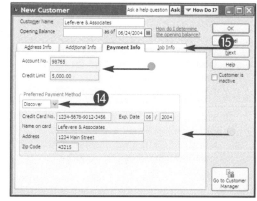

Note: *Fill in this tab if you plan to perform only one job for this customer.*

⑯ Click here and select a job status.

⑰ Click ▦ and select start, projected end, and end dates as appropriate.

⑱ Type a job description.

⑲ Click here and select a job type.

⑳ Click OK.

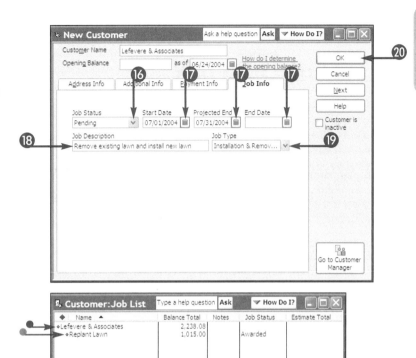

● The new customer appears in the Customer:Job List window.

● Jobs you add separately appear indented under the appropriate customer.

What does the Go to Customer Manager button do?

▼ If you click Go to Customer Manager, you can connect to the Internet to view a tour of the Customer Manager, which is an add-on product that you buy to enhance QuickBooks. The Customer Manager integrates contact information from QuickBooks, Outlook, and Outlook Express, providing, in one central location, access to contact information, recent history including QuickBooks transactions and other linked documents, to-do notes, appointments, related projects, related contacts, and year-to-date revenue. Using Customer Manager, maintaining customer information becomes faster and more accurate, because all the information appears in one location.

If I plan to perform multiple jobs for a customer, how do I set them up?

▼ First, set up the customer. Then, select the customer for whom you want to create a job in the Customer:Job List window. Click the Customer:Job button and, from the menu that appears, select Add a Job. The New Job window that appears looks like the New Customer window. Type a Job Name and complete the Job Info tab using steps 16 to 20. You do not need to fill in the other fields because QuickBooks fills them in for you. The saved job entry appears in the Customer:Job List window under the customer entry and is indented slightly to help you easily identify each customer's jobs.

Create
Vendor Types

Vendors are the companies from which you buy goods or services. You create vendor types to help you organize vendors by whatever means make the most sense in your business. For example, you can create vendor types that identify a vendor's industry or a vendor's location or any other information you want to track about a vendor. After you create vendor types, you can assign a vendor type to each vendor you create. See the section "Create a New Vendor" for more information.

By using vendor types, you can create reports in QuickBooks that identify vendors with the type you specify. For example, suppose that you regularly obtain price quotes for materials

and services from your suppliers. You can create a vendor type called "Supplier" and assign it to vendors who are suppliers. When you need to obtain quotes, you can print a Contact List of only those vendors who are suppliers. If you need written quotes, you can print mailing labels for vendors who are suppliers. See Chapter 21 for details on preparing mailing labels. And, using both the Contact List of suppliers and the Write Letters feature in QuickBooks, you can prepare a letter requesting a written quote. See Chapter 15 for details on the Write Letters feature.

Create Vendor Types

① Click Lists.

② Click Customer & Vendor Profile Lists.

③ Click Vendor Type List.

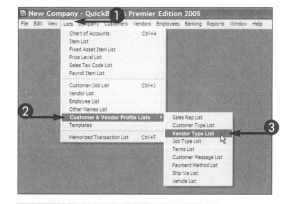

The Vendor Type List window appears.

④ Click Vendor Type.

⑤ Click New.

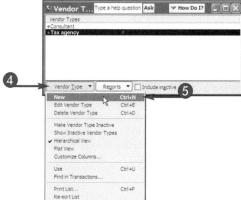

The New Vendor Type dialog box appears.

6 Type a phrase for the new vendor type.

- You can click this option (☐ changes to ☑) to create a subtype of an existing vendor type and then click ▾ to select the existing vendor type.

- You can click Next to create another vendor type.

7 Click OK.

- The vendor type you created appears in the Vendor Type List window.

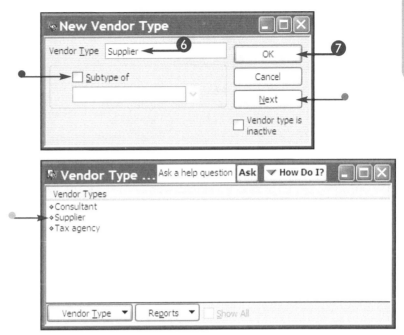

How many characters can I use when I create a vendor type?

▼ You can use 31, including spaces. However, you must avoid using special characters, such as slash (/) or backslash (\).

What is a subtype?

▼ You may create vendor types that encompass broad categories, such as consultant. You can use *subtypes* to organize in a more specific way. For example, under a vendor type of consultant, you may create subtypes of software and hardware. On the Vendor List, QuickBooks displays subtypes underneath and slightly indented from the associated vendor type.

What kinds of reports are available for vendor types?

▼ When you select a vendor type and click Reports, you see only one report — a QuickReport. The QuickReport for a particular vendor type shows you, in chronological order, year-to-date transactions for vendors to whom you have assigned the selected vendor type. You can modify the report to change the date range, eliminate or add columns to the report, or filter the report based on other criteria. You also can display the details of any transaction on the report by double-clicking it.

Create a
New Vendor

Vendors are the companies from which you buy goods or services. In general, vendors fall into two categories. You buy goods or services from some vendors to make products that you sell to customers or to simply resell to customers. Other vendors supply you with goods and services such as telephone service, office space, and electricity that you need to run your business; these vendors are often referred to as *overhead vendors*.

Regardless of what you purchase from a vendor, you need to set up the vendor in QuickBooks. When you set up a vendor, you supply name and address information that

QuickBooks prints on checks you write to the vendor. You also can supply an account number by which the vendor references you and, by setting a particular preference, QuickBooks prints the account number in the Memo field of the check.

You also can assign terms and a credit limit to the vendor, and you can identify if a vendor is a subcontractor and eligible for a Form 1099. If the vendor is eligible, you supply a Tax ID number that QuickBooks prints on the Form 1099. You also can select a vendor type; see the section "Create Vendor Types" for details.

Create a New Vendor

1 Click Lists.

2 Click Vendor List.

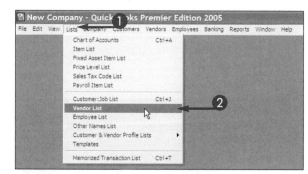

The Vendor List window appears.

3 Click Vendor.

4 Click New.

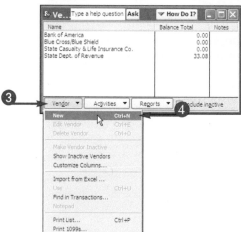

The Address Info tab of the New Vendor window appears by default.

⑤ Type a name.

QuickBooks displays this name in the Vendor List window.

⑥ Type additional name and address information.

● QuickBooks automatically fills this field, but you can change it.

⑦ Click the Additional Info tab.

● You can type an account number here.

◉ You can select a vendor type here.

⑧ Click here to select terms.

You can click here to establish a 1099 vendor and Tax ID.

● You can type custom field information here.

⑨ Click OK.

QuickBooks saves your settings.

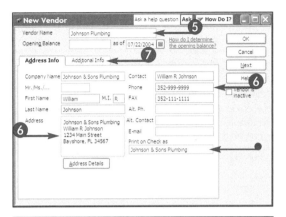

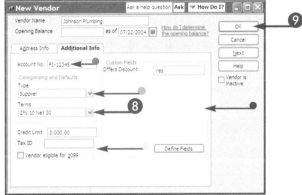

Should I fill in the opening balance for a vendor if I am just setting up QuickBooks for the first time?

▼ You can, but because you enter a total owed to the vendor, you cannot retain information about the individual bills you owe to a particular vendor, and you cannot retain any aging information. Instead of entering an oustanding sum as you create the vendor, enter individual outstanding bills the same way you enter regular bills — see Chapter 14 for details — but enter one line item for the bill using the Beginning Bal Equity account. Make sure that you set the date for each outstanding bill correctly so that QuickBooks ages the bill properly.

What are terms?

▼ *Terms* describe when a vendor expects to receive your payment. They also explain when a late fee will be charged and often include a discount as an incentive to pay early. You can create Standard and Date Driven terms in QuickBooks; see Chapter 5 for details. Terms of 2% 10 Net 30 mean that you can reduce the bill by 2 percent if you pay it within 10 days of the date on the bill; otherwise, you owe the full amount 30 days from the date on the bill. Terms of 2% 10th Net 30th mean that you can discount the bill by 2 percent if you pay it by the 10th day of the month; otherwise, you owe the full amount on the 30th of the month. For more on terms, see Chapter 5.

Set Purchasing and Vendor Preferences

Y ou can establish purchasing and vendor preferences that specify the default behavior for QuickBooks when dealing with inventory and purchase orders and when entering and paying bills.

You can enable the inventory and purchase order features of QuickBooks. When you enable them, you can specify whether you want to be warned about duplicate purchase order numbers, when insufficient inventory exists to make a sale, and, if you are using sales orders, when the item quantity you are selling exceeds the quantity on hand after subtracting the quantity reserved on sales orders.

You also can set up the default number of days that you want QuickBooks to age a bill from the date you supply when you enter the bill, and you can choose to automatically apply available discounts and credits when you pay a bill.

MASTER IT

Why should I allow QuickBooks to warn me about duplicate bill numbers from the same vendor?

▼ This feature can help you to avoid paying the same bill twice. Assume that your vendor assigns a number to the bill and you enter that number when you record the bill — see Chapter 14 for details on entering bills. If you enable this setting and enter a bill number twice for the same vendor, QuickBooks displays a warning about the duplicate numbers. If you do not enable this setting, QuickBooks lets you enter the bill and pay it.

Set Purchasing and Vendor Preferences

① Click Edit.

② Click Preferences.

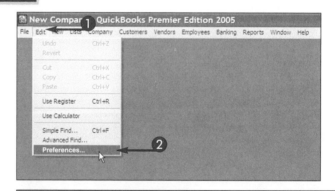

The Preferences dialog box appears.

③ Click the Purchases & Vendors icon.

④ Click the Company Preferences tab.

⑤ Click these options (☐ changes to ☑) to enable inventory and purchase order features and to set inventory and purchase order warnings.

⑥ Type the number of days from the entry date that you want most bills to be due.

⑦ Click this option (☐ changes to ☑) to automatically use discounts and credits.

⑧ Click OK.

QuickBooks saves your preferences.

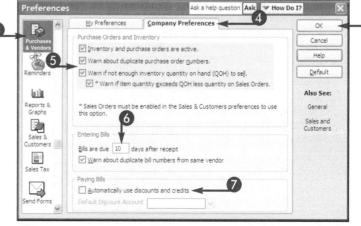

Set 1099 Preferences

I f you use 1099 vendors such as subcontractors in your business, you can set up QuickBooks to track payments to those 1099 vendors. That way, you can print and file 1099-MISC forms when your payments to those 1099 vendors exceed limits established by the Internal Revenue Service.

Most businesses need to track only nonemployee compensation, but the types of payments you must track and report depend on your business. Check with your accountant or local IRS office to determine if you need to track other types of payments to 1099 vendors.

When you set Tax: 1099 preferences in QuickBooks, you identify the accounts that you use when making payments to 1099 vendors. You also can change limits associated with a particular 1099 category if necessary. You can print 1099 forms easily from QuickBooks; see Chapter 15 for details.

How can I select more than one account for a particular 1099 category?

▼ While viewing Company Preferences for Tax: 1099, click ⊡ next to the category and click Selected accounts from the list. From the Select Account dialog box that appears, select Manual on the left. From the list on the right, click each account you want to select. When you finish selecting accounts for a particular 1099 category, click OK. In the Account column on the Company Preferences tab for Tax: 1099 options, QuickBooks displays Selected Accounts.

Set 1099 Preferences

1 Click Edit.

2 Click Preferences.

The Preferences dialog box appears.

3 Click the Tax: 1099 icon.

4 Click the Company Preferences tab.

5 Click here to enable 1099 tracking in QuickBooks (○ changes to ◉).

6 Click here to select an account.

7 Repeat step 6 for each 1099 category.

8 Click OK.

QuickBooks saves your preferences.

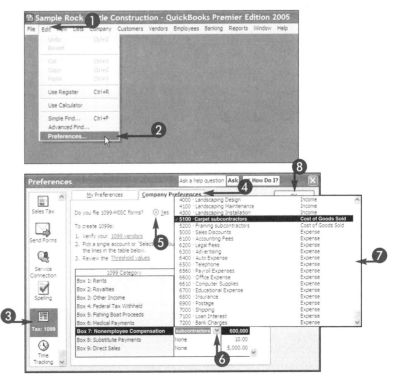

Create a New Service Item

For each service that you sell, you need to create a service item in QuickBooks to assign income to the proper account. Services are generally intangible, such as subcontractor labor, consulting, legal advice, and accounting advice. For example, pest control businesses sell a service where someone sprays chemicals or sets traps to eliminate pests. The business purchases the chemicals and traps, but typically sells a service that covers the cost of the products and the labor needed to apply them.

You can both buy and sell services; for example, attorneys sell their own services and buy the services of accountants. You may also buy and sell the same service. For example,

you may pay subcontractors to perform work for customers; in this case, you buy subcontracted labor and then sell it to customers.

If your business is not a corporation and you pay business owners, partners, or subcontractors for work they perform, set up a separate service item because you need to record the cost of the owner's or partner's work against an equity account and the cost of the subcontractor against an expense account.

Create a New Service Item

Create Regular Services

1 Click Lists.

2 Click Item List.

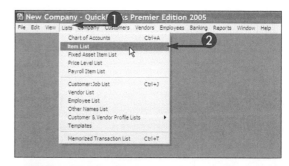

The Item List window appears.

3 Click Item.

4 Click New.

The New Item dialog box appears.

⑤ Select Service and type a name or code.

⑥ Type a description to appear on invoices.

⑦ Click here to select a tax code.

⑧ Click here to select an income account.

⑨ Click OK.

QuickBooks saves your selections.

Create Services Performed by Owners or Subcontractors

① Complete steps 1 to 8 in the "Create Regular Services" subsection.

② Click here to select the subcontractor, owner, or partner option (☐ changes to ☑).

③ Type a description for purchase transactions.

④ Click here and select an equity or expense account.

⑤ Click OK.

QuickBooks saves your selections.

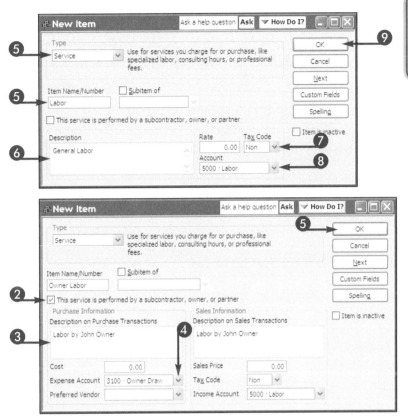

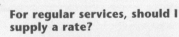

For regular services, should I supply a rate?

▼ You can, but you do not need to supply a rate; QuickBooks displays the rate on invoices and other sales transactions when you select the service item. You can change the rate when you assign the service item to a sales transaction. Follow the general guideline of assigning rates when the rates do not vary each time you use the item.

Do I need to set up service items for services that I purchase, such as legal advice?

▼ You can set up service items for services that you purchase, but QuickBooks does not require you to use items on purchase transactions. Instead, on purchase transactions, you can select an account. Therefore, you can assign bills from your attorney or your accountant directly to an expense account called, for example, Professional Services.

For services performed by subcontractors, what is the value of setting up both an income and an expense account?

▼ By assigning both an income and an expense account to a service item for subcontractors, you can use the item to track both purchases and sales. If you also use the job costing features of QuickBooks, you can assign services you purchase to jobs as reimbursable expenses and then produce reports that help you determine the profitability of jobs.

Create a New Inventory Part Item

I nventory part items are tangible things that you keep on hand — either by buying them or manufacturing them — so that you can sell them to customers. When you place an item in inventory, its value appears in an inventory account as an asset on your balance sheet income statement. When you sell an inventory item, QuickBooks reduces the value of your inventory account and increases the value of your cost of goods sold account, an income account, and either a cash account or an accounts receivable account.

When you create an inventory part item in QuickBooks, you establish the correct inventory, cost of goods sold, and income accounts for QuickBooks to update when you buy or sell the item. You also establish a purchasing and selling description for the item, and identify whether the item is taxable. You also can set up cost and selling prices, a preferred vendor from whom you buy the item, and a quantity at which QuickBooks can remind you to reorder the item.

Create a New Inventory Part Item

① Click Lists.

② Click Item List.

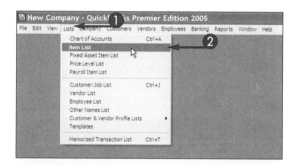

The Item List window appears.

③ Click Item.

④ Click New.

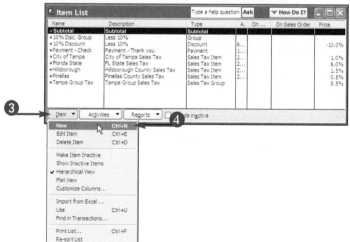

The New Item dialog box appears.

5 Click here and select Inventory Part.

6 Type a name or code for the item.

7 Type a description to appear on bills.

Note: QuickBooks assigns the same description for sales transactions.

8 Click here to assign a purchase account.

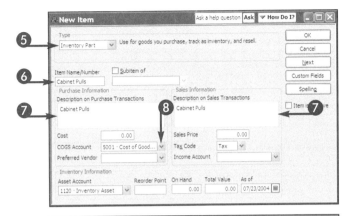

9 Click here to select a tax code.

10 Click here to select an income account.

11 Click here to assign an asset account.

12 Type the minimum available quantity at which QuickBooks reminds you to reorder.

13 Click OK.

QuickBooks saves your selections.

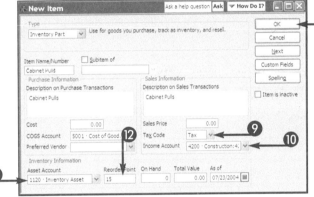

In the Inventory Information section of the New Item dialog box, should I supply quantities in the On Hand and Total Value boxes?

▼ If you are setting up QuickBooks for the first time and using the technique described in Chapter 2, do not type either the quantity you own in the On Hand box or the value in the Total Value box. Instead, record inventory adjustments for each inventory part item to establish the starting quantity and total value of the item. Make sure to select the Value Adjustment option at the bottom of the Adjust Quantity/Value dialog box and use the Opening Balance Equity account as the Adjustment Account. For more information on entering inventory adjustments, see Chapter 16.

Do I need to supply a cost and sale price for the item?

▼ You can assign the cost and the sale price either when you create the item or when you buy or sell the item. Typically, assign a cost and sale price to the item to make purchasing and selling easier for users.

Does typing a reorder quantity automatically make QuickBooks remind me to reorder?

▼ No. You must also set a preference. Click Edit and then Preferences to open the Preferences dialog box. Click the Reminders icon and then click Company Preferences. Select the Show List for the Inventory to Reorder option.

Create a New Inventory Assembly Item

I f you are using QuickBooks Premier or QuickBooks Enterprise, you can create inventory assembly items. Each assembly item consists of several existing inventory part items. QuickBooks calculates the value of an inventory assembly item by summing the value of the component parts of the item. The inventory assembly item is useful for including assembled items that comprise a small number of parts on sales documents and reports. Use the Manufacturing & Wholesale edition of either QuickBooks Premier or QuickBooks Enterprise for more detailed inventory tracking throughout the manufacturing process.

If your business assembles the item, you identify whether the item is taxable, and you set up a cost of goods sold account, an income account, and an optional sales price for the assembly. You also identify the component items of the assembly and the quantity of each component necessary to create the assembled item. For inventory information, you provide an inventory asset account and a quantity at which QuickBooks reminds you to build the assembly item.

If you purchase the assembly from another vendor for the purpose of reselling it, you enter all the information described above along with an optional cost, a purchase description, and a preferred vendor for the item.

Create a New Inventory Assembly Item

① Click Lists.

② Click Item List.

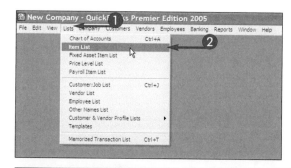

The Item List window appears.

③ Click Item.

④ Click New.

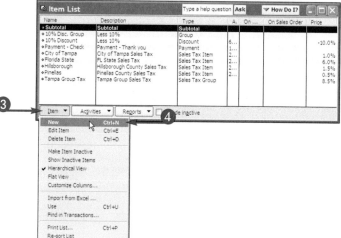

The New Item dialog box appears.

5 Click here to select Inventory Assembly.

6 Type a name or code for the item.

7 Click here to assign a purchase account.

8 Type a description to appear on invoices.

9 Click here to select a tax code.

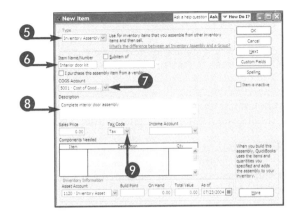

10 Click here to select an income account.

11 Click here to select an assembly component item.

12 Type the quantity of the component.

13 Repeat steps 11 to 12 for each component.

14 Type the build point.

15 Click OK.

QuickBooks saves your selections.

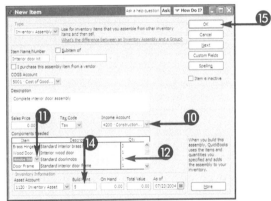

What happens if I click the "I purchase this assembly item from a vendor" option (☐ changes to ☑)?

▼ QuickBooks changes the appearance of the New Item dialog box to include two sections. On the left, a section appears called Purchase Information, where you supply a description for QuickBooks to use on purchase transactions, a cost, a cost of goods sold account, and a preferred vendor. On the right, a section appears called Sales Information, where you supply a description for QuickBooks to use on sales transactions, a selling price, a tax code that identifies whether the assembly is taxable or nontaxable, and an income account. The Components Needed section and the Inventory information section do not change.

How does QuickBooks know how many of the assembly item to build when I create it?

▼ QuickBooks does not actually make any of the assembly item when you create the item. Making assemblies is actually a two-part process. First, you create the item, using the steps in this section. Then, you use the Build Assemblies window to create an assembled item. See Chapter 16 for details.

Can I add components to an inventory part?

▼ You can convert the inventory part to an assembly and then add components. Double-click the item in the Item List and change the Type to Inventory Assembly. QuickBooks displays a message that you cannot reverse this action. Click OK, and QuickBooks changes the Edit Item dialog box so that you can add components. You also can edit the component list of an existing inventory assembly.

Create a New
Noninventory Part Item

You need to create noninventory parts for goods you purchase that do not qualify as inventory. Typically, you can think of noninventory parts as items you purchase but do not resell, such as office supplies. You may also have noninventory items that you sell that you did not purchase. For example, computer support people often receive older equipment, for which they do not pay, from their clients. If the computer support person resells one of these pieces of equipment, he sets up the item as a noninventory part in QuickBooks.

You may also have noninventory items that you purchase and resell that do not qualify as inventory. For example, if a customer asks you to place a special order for an item you do not usually sell, treat that item as a noninventory item.

For regular noninventory items, you set up the selling side of the item's information — an item description, a tax code to indicate whether the item is taxable, and an income account. For noninventory items you use for a job, you also want to track the purchasing side of the item's information so that you can charge the customer for the item and produce job profitability reports.

Create a New Noninventory Part Item

Create Regular Noninventory Items

1. Click Lists.

2. Click Item List.

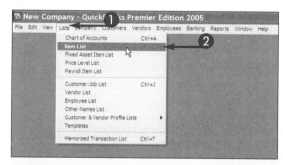

The Item List window appears.

3. Click Item.

4. Click New.

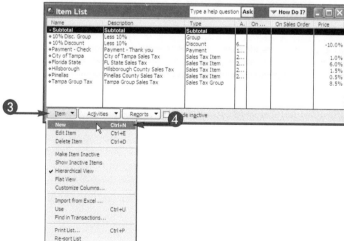

The New Item dialog box appears.

5 Click here to select Non-inventory Part; type a name or code.

6 Type a description to appear on invoices.

7 Click here to select a tax code.

8 Click here to select an income account.

9 Click OK.

QuickBooks saves your selections.

Create Noninventory Parts for Jobs

1 Complete steps 1 to 8 in the subsection "Create Regular Noninventory Items" on the previous page.

2 Click here to select this option (☐ changes to ☑).

3 Type a description for purchase transactions.

4 Click here to select an expense account.

5 Click OK.

QuickBooks saves your selections.

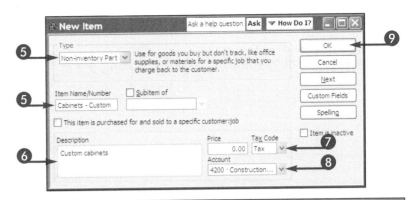

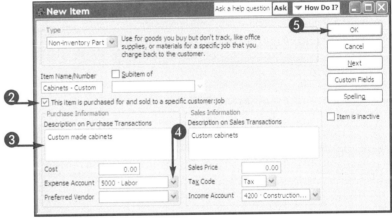

What is a subitem?

▼ You can use *subitems* to help you organize items on the Item List. For example, suppose that you sell doors. You may sell interior wood doors, interior steel doors, exterior wood doors, exterior steel doors, and exterior fiberglass doors. To help you organize these items so that you can find them easily on the Item List, you can create an item — referred to as a *parent item* — called Doors, and subitems for Interior Wood, Interior Steel, Exterior Wood, Exterior Steel, and Exterior Fiberglass. When you create a subitem, the screen you see is no different than the screen for a regular item except that you must identify the parent item.

What happens if I click Custom Fields in the New Item dialog box?

▼ The first time you click this button, QuickBooks displays a message telling you that no custom fields exist. When you click OK, QuickBooks displays a dialog box that contains a Define Fields button. Click Define Fields, and QuickBooks displays the Define Custom Fields for Items dialog box. In it, you type custom field labels and then click the "Use box beside each label you want available when you define an item" option (☐ changes to ☑). The custom field is available for *all* items, not just the item you are currently creating. Use custom fields for items to describe elements such as color or size.

Create a New Other Charge Item

You create Other Charge items for situations that do not fit into any of the item categories described in this chapter and in Chapter 3. For example, if you receive a check that the bank returns to you due to insufficient funds in the issuer's account, you need an Other Charge item to reestablish the client's outstanding balance, and if you charge your customer a returned check fee, you need another Other Charge item for the service charge. You also can use an Other Charge item to create opening balances for outstanding vendor bills and customer invoices.

In the cases described above, you create a regular Other Charge item, setting up a sales transaction description, a tax code to indicate whether the item is taxable, and an income account. You also can use Other Charge items to create reimbursable expenses and establish a purchase transaction description, an expense account, and, if appropriate, a cost and a preferred vendor. If you need to rent equipment to complete a job for a customer, you can set up an Other Charge item for the equipment rental and use it both when you rent the equipment and when you charge the customer for the equipment rental.

Create a New Other Charge Item

Create Regular Other Charge Items

1 Click Lists.

2 Click Item List.

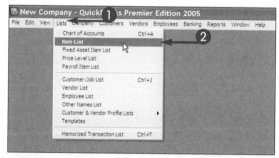

The Item List window appears.

3 Click Item.

4 Click New.

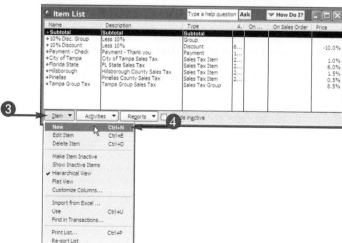

The New Item dialog box appears.

5 Select Other Charge and type a name or code.

6 Type a description to appear on invoices.

7 Click here to select a tax code.

8 Click here to select an account.

9 Click OK.

QuickBooks saves your selections.

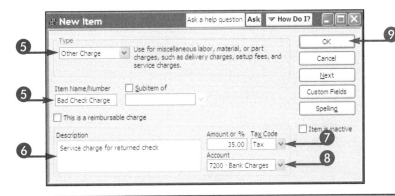

Create Reimbursable Expense Items

1 Complete steps 1 to 8 in the subsection "Create Regular Other Charge Items" on the previous page.

2 Click the "This is a reimbursable charge" option (☐ changes to ☑).

3 Type a description for purchase transactions.

4 Click here to select an expense account.

5 Click OK.

QuickBooks saves your selections.

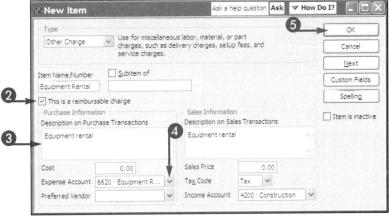

How can I use an Other Charge item to establish outstanding vendor and customer balances?

▼ Assuming that you use the technique described in Chapter 2 to set up opening balances, use steps 1 to 9 in the subsection "Create Regular Other Charge Items" on this page to create an Other Charge item with a name like Opening Balance and assign it to the Beginning Bal Equity account. Make sure that you set this up as a nontaxable item. Then, using the steps in Chapters 11 and 14, prepare individual invoices and bills for each outstanding invoice or bill. On each transaction, use the opening balance Other Charge item in the line item section, and assign the document's full balance, including tax.

What is a reimbursable expense?

▼ A reimbursable expense is a cost you incur on behalf of a customer for which you intend to invoice the customer so that you can recover the cost. QuickBooks enables you to use the same item when you incur the cost and when you assign it to an invoice so that you can track job profitability accurately. You create a reimbursable expense when you enter a bill for a cost you intend to recover; see Chapter 14 for details. When you invoice a customer for a reimbursable expense, you can mark up the expense so that you make a profit on it. See Chapter 11 for details on invoicing a customer for a reimbursable expense.

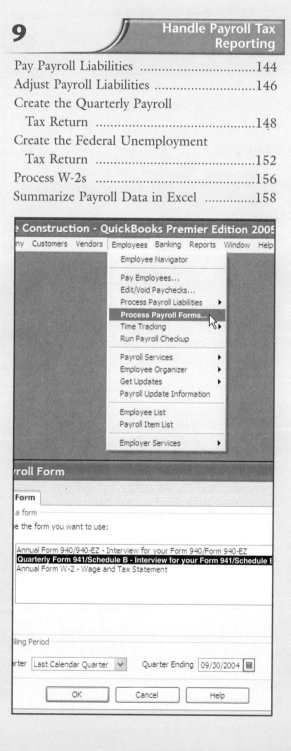

10

Track Time

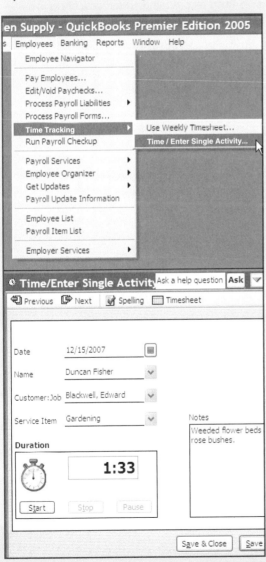

Pay Employees

After you complete all the tasks in Chapter 4, you can pay your employees in QuickBooks. You can set up employees to be paid daily, weekly, biweekly, semimonthly, monthly, quarterly, or annually. You do not need to set up all employees with the same pay period because, when you pay a group of employees, QuickBooks displays a window from which you select the employees that you want to pay.

When you select employees, you also specify the paycheck date as well as the pay period ending date. You should make the paycheck date the date that you want to affect

the bank account; if you are paying employees on January 3 for work performed in December, QuickBooks records the payroll liability — and the employee's income — in the new year.

QuickBooks does not require that you print paychecks; instead, you can record handwritten paychecks in QuickBooks to maintain the accuracy of your company's books. The steps in this section demonstrate printing payroll checks, as well as previewing paychecks before printing them. If the payroll information at the bottom of the Select Employees To Pay window is correct, you can create paychecks without previewing them.

Pay Employees

① Click Employees.

② Click Pay Employees.

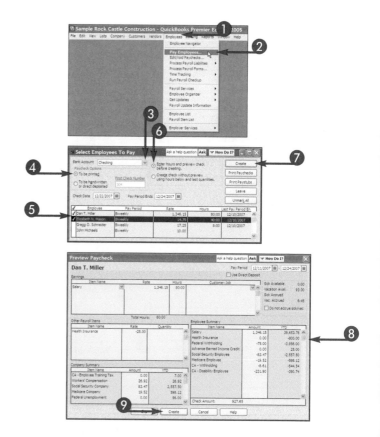

The Select Employees To Pay window appears.

③ Click here and select a bank account.

④ Click the To be printed option to print checks in a batch (○ changes to ◉).

⑤ Click next to each employee you intend to pay (☐ changes to ☑).

⑥ Click the "Enter hours and preview check before creating" option (○ changes to ◉).

⑦ Click Create.

The Preview Paycheck window appears.

⑧ Review the first selected employee's paycheck for accuracy and make changes as needed.

⑨ Click Create.

QuickBooks displays the next employee's paycheck.

⑩ Repeat steps 8 to 9 until the Select Employees To Pay window reappears.

⑪ Click Print Paychecks.

The Select Paychecks to Print dialog box appears.

⑫ Click here and select a bank account, verifying the first check number to print.

⑬ Click OK.

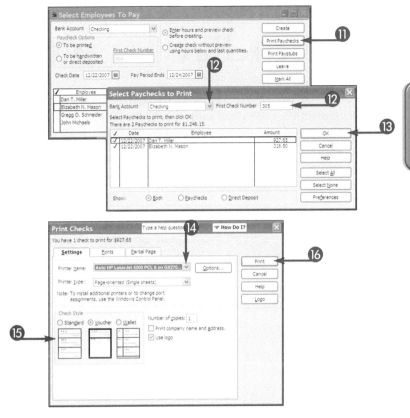

The Print Checks window appears.

⑭ Click here and select the printer.

⑮ Click a check style option (○ changes to ◉).

⑯ Click Print.

QuickBooks prints the paychecks.

What do I do if checks jam in the printer?

▼ After QuickBooks prints the checks, you see a message inquiring if any checks printed incorrectly. Supply the number of the first incorrectly printed check and click OK. QuickBooks assumes that the check you identified and all subsequent checks did not print correctly, so QuickBooks reprints the identified check and all subsequent checks.

Can I change any number while previewing a paycheck?

▼ You cannot change year-to-date amounts, and you *should* not change the amounts QuickBooks calculates for Social Security and Medicare because these amounts are mandated percentages of adjusted gross pay. If you change Social Security or Medicare amounts, you will make your payroll reports inaccurate and you risk paying an incorrect payroll liability amount.

If I do not want to print paychecks and only want to record handwritten or directly deposited paychecks, what should I do differently?

▼ In the Select Employees To Pay window, select the "To be handwritten or direct deposited" option (○ changes to ◉) and click Create. Fill in the Preview Paycheck window with the employee's paycheck information and click Create. You may want to print paycheck stubs for employees who receive handwritten checks. For more information, see the section "Print a Paycheck Stub."

Using Rapid Time Entry to Pay Employees

I f you subscribe to the Enhanced Payroll Service that Intuit offers, you can quickly enter hours for each employee using the Enter Hours window, which speeds up the process of creating paychecks.

In the Enter Hours window, QuickBooks displays a table that lists employees down the side and up to five payroll items across the top. You fill in hours worked by each employee under each appropriate payroll item. You can then preview paychecks before QuickBooks creates them to ensure accuracy and make changes if necessary. Using Rapid Entry, you enter all hours or salaries for all employees at the same time. You then review all paychecks individually. If you use

the technique described in the section "Pay Employees," you enter hours or salaries for employees individually as you create paychecks.

Being able to enter hours rapidly is one of several features available only if you subscribe to the Enhanced Payroll Service; using this service, you also can easily produce bonus checks and you can track workers' compensation wages; see Chapter 27 for details on these features. You also can process state payroll forms if you subscribe to the Enhanced Payroll Service; when you process payroll forms as described in Chapter 9, an option for state forms is available.

Using Rapid Time Entry to Pay Employees

① Click Employees.

② Click Pay Employees.

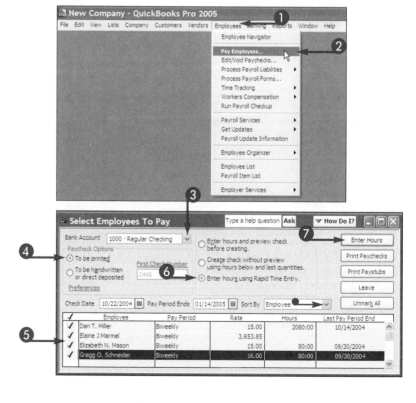

The Select Employees To Pay window appears.

③ Click here and select a bank account.

④ Click the To be printed option to print checks in batches (○ changes to ◉).

⑤ Click next to each employee you intend to pay (☐ changes to ☑).

⑥ Click the "Enter hours using Rapid Time Entry" option (○ changes to ◉).

● You can click here to select a sort order.

⑦ Click Enter Hours.

The Enter Hours window appears.

8 Click ⌄ to select a payroll item.

9 Repeat step 8 for all necessary payroll items.

10 Under the correct payroll item, type the number of hours worked.

11 Repeat step 10 for all employees.

12 Click Preview.

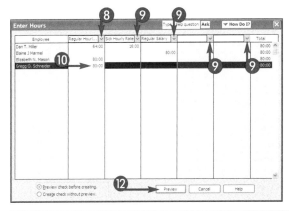

The Preview Paycheck window appears.

13 Review the first selected employee's paycheck for accuracy and make changes as needed.

14 Click Create.

QuickBooks displays the next employee's paycheck.

15 Repeat steps 13 to 14 until the Select Employees To Pay window reappears.

16 Click Print Paychecks.

17 Complete steps 12 to 14 of the section "Pay Employees" earlier in this chapter.

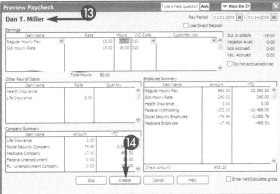

What sort orders are available?

▼ You can sort employees by employee name, pay period, pay rate, hours, or last pay period end date. For example, if you enter the same hours for many employees, you can sort employees by hours and then easily and rapidly enter the same number of hours for all employees. Or, if your timesheet information is organized alphabetically, sort employees by name to quickly enter hours.

What should I do if I accidentally enter sick pay hours where I meant to enter regular pay hours?

▼ Do not close the Enter Hours window or you will lose all the hours you entered. Instead, you can correct the mistake by clicking the ⌄ next to sick pay hours and selecting regular pay hours. QuickBooks does not erase the hours you entered; instead, QuickBooks applies the existing hours to the new payroll item that you select.

What should I do if I get a warning about a pay rate not existing for an employee?

▼ The warning appears when you assign hours to a payroll item that you did not assign to the selected employee. Click OK to clear the warning. If you assigned the hours by accident, delete the hours. Otherwise, leave the hours in the Enter Hours window. When you preview the employee's paycheck, add a rate in the Earnings section so that QuickBooks can calculate the pay.

Print a Paycheck Stub

Y ou can print paycheck stubs on blank paper instead of check stock, which is useful if employees have signed up for direct deposit, or if you do not print paychecks but instead record handwritten paychecks in QuickBooks. Or, you may be using an outside payroll service and entering payroll information into QuickBooks to keep your company data accurate; in this case, you can produce a paycheck stub for each employee.

To print paycheck stubs, you must record paychecks in QuickBooks. See the section "Pay Employees" for details. You do not need to print the paychecks that you record; you simply need to create them.

After you have created paychecks, you can print them from the Select Employees To Pay window. You can select a bank account and a date range for which you want to print paycheck stubs, and QuickBooks displays all paychecks written using the selected bank account during the selected date range.

While you select paycheck stubs to print, you also can control the information that QuickBooks prints on the paycheck stubs.

Print a Paycheck Stub

① Click Employees.

② Click Pay Employees.

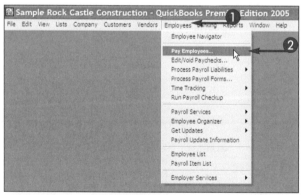

The Select Employees To Pay window appears.

③ Click Print Paystubs.

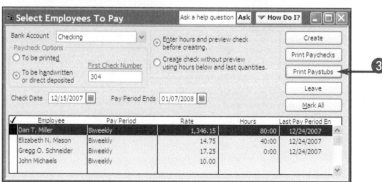

The Select Paystubs to Print window appears.

● You can change the bank account and selected date range to change the paychecks for which you can print paystubs.

④ Click next to each employee for whom you do *not* intend to print a paystub (☑ changes to ☐).

⑤ Click Preview.

A preview of the first selected employee's paystub appears.

⑥ Click Next page to preview the next paystub.

⑦ Repeat step 6 for all paystubs.

⑧ Click Print.

QuickBooks prints the paystubs and redisplays the Select Employees To Pay window.

⑨ Click Leave.

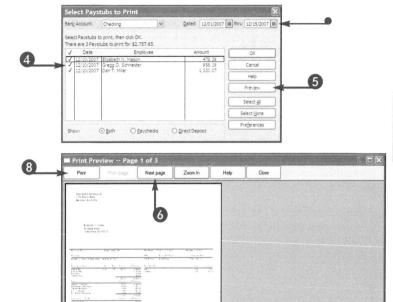

How can I control the information that appears when I print paycheck stubs?

▼ While viewing the Select Paystubs to Print dialog box, click Preferences. QuickBooks displays the Payroll Printing Preferences dialog box. On paystubs, QuickBooks usually prints vacation used and available information, sick time used and available information, your legal company name and your "doing business as" name, nontaxable company payroll items, and the employee's social security number. On paycheck vouchers, QuickBooks usually prints all the same information just listed for paycheck stubs along with the employee's address, the company's address, and the pay period in the check Memo field.

On what kind of forms can I print paychecks or paystubs?

▼ You print both paystubs and paychecks on 8½-by-11-inch sheets. Paystubs print on plain paper. For paychecks, you can use standard, voucher, or wallet checks. All three types of checks use an 8½-by-11-inch page size. Standard checks come three to a page, and each check is as wide as the page. Voucher checks come one to a page; the check at the top is as wide as the page and the bottom two thirds of the page are the voucher. Wallet checks come three to a page, but the check is *not* as wide as the page; the left side of the check serves as the voucher.

Edit/Void Paychecks

I f you create a paycheck that is not correct, you need to either edit or void the paycheck. For example, after you create paychecks, an employee may tell you that he actually did not work the full week; he went home two hours early on the last day of the week because he was sick. If you have not yet printed the paycheck, you can edit it. If you have printed the paycheck but it is still in your possession, you can void it and then create a new, accurate paycheck.

If you have printed and given paychecks to an employee, you can safely edit paychecks as long as the changes you make do not affect net pay. For example, you can switch an

amount on a paycheck to a different payroll item, or you can change the class or job assignment or hours worked.

If the changes you need to make affect net pay and the paycheck is in the employee's possession, you must get the paycheck back from the employee; then you can void the check and issue a new paycheck.

If the employee cashes the check before the mistake appears, you must make adjustments to your company payroll data on the employee's next paycheck.

Void a Paycheck

① Click Employees.

② Click Edit/Void Paychecks.

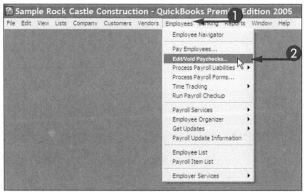

The Edit/Void Paychecks window appears.

③ Click the calendar (▦) to select a date range for paychecks.

④ Click here and select a sorting method.

⑤ Click the check to void.

⑥ Click Void.

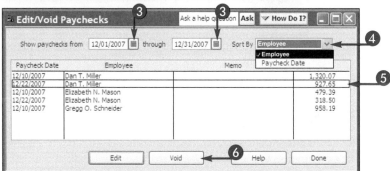

The Warning window appears.

7 Type **yes**.

8 Click Void.

QuickBooks voids the check and redisplays the Edit/Void Paychecks window.

VOID: appears in the Memo column next to the voided check.

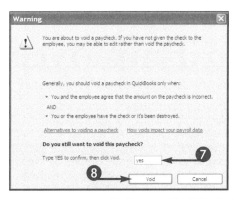

Edit a Paycheck

1 Complete steps 1 to 6 on the previous page but click Edit in step 6.

The Paycheck window appears.

2 Click Paycheck Detail.

3 In the Review Paycheck window that appears, make changes.

Note: *See the Preview Paycheck window in the section "Pay Employees" for a sample.*

4 Click OK to save your edits.

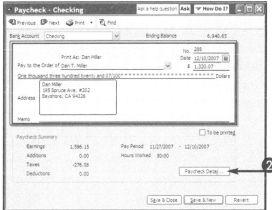

When would I edit a paycheck to change its amount?

▼ After you create the paycheck but before you print it, you can edit it to make changes to the amount. After you print a paycheck, you must not edit the paycheck amount in QuickBooks; the amount the bank pays on the check does not match the amount recorded in QuickBooks, and you may have trouble reconciling your bank statement.

If I need to change a paycheck amount after I print the paycheck, what should I do?

▼ You should void the paycheck and then issue a new paycheck. Although you may be tempted to delete the paycheck, deleting eliminates the trail of the actions you took — called the "audit trail" — and a check number will be missing from QuickBooks. Voiding the check helps your accountant understand the actions you took.

How does QuickBooks save changes I made while editing a paycheck?

▼ After step 4 of the subsection "Edit a Paycheck" on this page, QuickBooks redisplays the Paycheck window. Click Save & Close.

Can I make changes in the Paycheck window or do I have to open the Review Paycheck window?

▼ You must open the Review Paycheck window to make changes that affect the amount of the check. You can make changes to the Address block in the Paycheck window.

Write a Letter to an Employee

QuickBooks makes it easy to correspond with employees on a variety of matters using the Write Letters Wizard and Microsoft Word 97 or higher. QuickBooks comes with its own selection of business letters, already formatted, ready to use, and grouped by the type of recipient to whom you would usually send the letter. You can make temporary changes to a letter after you create it by simply editing the document in Microsoft Word; QuickBooks supplies a special version of the Merge toolbar to help you. If you are using QuickBooks Pro, QuickBooks Premier, or QuickBooks Enterprise, you can make permanent changes to a letter to better suit your business's needs, or add a letter that does not come with QuickBooks. You also can duplicate a letter, delete it, rename it, or move it to another group.

As you walk through the wizard, you select the type of letter you want to send, the specific letter you want to use, and the recipients of the letter. You can choose to send the letter to just one employee, to any selection of employees, or to all employees. You also supply the name and title of the person who will sign the letter.

Write a Letter to an Employee

① Click Company.

② Click Prepare Letters with Envelopes.

③ Click Employee Letters.

The Review and Edit Recipients screen of the Write Letters Wizard opens.

● You can view active, inactive, or both types of employees.

④ Click next to the names of employees to whom you want to write (☐ changes to ☑).

⑤ Click Next.

The Choose a Letter Template screen appears.

⑥ Click a letter.

⑦ Click Next.

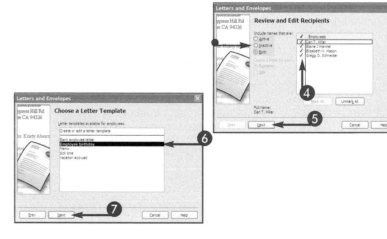

The Enter a Name and Title screen appears.

⑧ Type the name that will appear as a signature of the letter.

⑨ Type the signatory's title.

⑩ Click Next.

QuickBooks begins communicating with Microsoft Word to create the letters.

Note: *If appropriate, the Information Is Missing dialog box appears; click OK.*

The letter(s) appear in Microsoft Word.

If necessary, supply missing information.

⑪ Click the Print button (🖨▾).

⑫ You can click the Close button (✕) to close Word to return to QuickBooks.

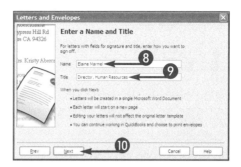

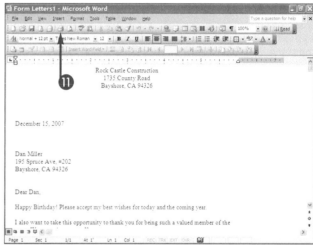

How can I edit an existing letter to customize it to my company's needs?

▼ Follow steps 1 to 2 on this page. On the Choose What You Want to Work on screen, select Customize Letter Template and click Next. On the following screen, select View or Edit Existing Letters and click Next. Select a letter to edit and click Next. The letter appears in Microsoft Word for editing. To save the letter as your own version, click File, and then Save and supply a new name for the letter.

How can I rename an existing QuickBooks letter?

▼ Start the Write Letters Wizard using steps 1 to 2. On the Choose What You Want to Work on screen, select Customize Letter Template and click Next. On the following screen, select Organize Existing Letters and click Next. Then select a letter and click Rename. In the box that appears, type the new name for the letter and click OK.

If I supply missing information in the letter in Word, does Word update my QuickBooks file with that information?

▼ No. To permanently fix the problem, edit the employee's record in QuickBooks and supply the missing information there.

Can I edit an existing letter but make my own version?

▼ Yes. When you save your changes in Microsoft Word, click File and then click Save As and supply a new name for the letter.

Pay Payroll Liabilities

You must deposit the taxes you withhold each payroll by a date specified by the IRS; similarly, you must pay other payroll-related liabilities, such as health insurance premiums, by dates specified by those vendors. You write these checks through the Pay Liabilities window in QuickBooks.

Every business is either a monthly or a semiweekly payroll tax depositor. If the total taxes your company withholds for the previous four quarters — using line 11 of Federal Form 941 — is $50,000 or less, your company is a monthly depositor; otherwise, your company is a semiweekly

depositor. Monthly depositors must deposit payroll taxes by the 15th day of the month after the liability is incurred. Semiweekly depositors must deposit payroll taxes for liabilities incurred on Wednesday, Thursday, or Friday by the following Wednesday. For liabilities incurred on Saturday, Sunday, Monday, or Tuesday, the semiweekly depositor must make the deposit by the following Friday.

In most cases, you make payroll tax deposits by making the payroll tax liability check payable to a local bank, and you complete Federal Form 8109, a coupon that serves as a deposit ticket, to describe your deposit and ensure that your business gets credit for the deposit.

Pay Payroll Liabilities

① Click Employees.

② Click Process Payroll Liabilities.

③ Click Pay Payroll Liabilities.

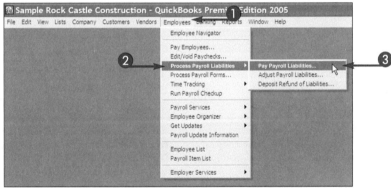

The Select Date Range For Liabilities dialog box appears.

④ Click here to select a time frame.

● You can select specific dates by clicking the calendar icon (▦).

⑤ Click OK.

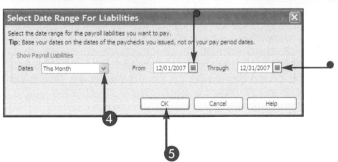

The Pay Liabilities window appears.

6 Click ☑ or ▦ to select a bank account and check date.

7 Click the "Review liability check to enter expenses/penalties" option (○ changes to ◉).

8 Click next to each liability you want to pay (☐ changes to ☑).

9 Click Create.

The payroll liability check appears.

● You can print the check by clicking the Print button, or you can wait to print the check with a group of other checks.

10 Click Save & Close.

QuickBooks saves the check.

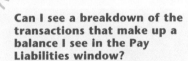

Can I see a breakdown of the transactions that make up a balance I see in the Pay Liabilities window?

▼ Yes. In the Pay Liabilities window, click Payroll Liabilities Report. A report appears for payroll liabilities in the selected time frame. Double-click any number to display a report of the transactions included in the number. Double-click any line on the detail report to see the transaction in the window where you originally created it.

Can I select liabilities due to more than one vendor at the same time?

▼ Yes. QuickBooks creates separate checks for the total owed to each selected vendor; when QuickBooks displays the Liability Check window, you see the first check created. Click Next to view subsequent liability checks to other vendors. However, you should not select both payroll and nonpayroll tax liabilities paid to the same vendor simultaneously because the IRS requires separate deposits for payroll and nonpayroll tax liabilities.

How do I pay benefit providers, such as the company providing health insurance?

▼ You must make payments for all deductions from paychecks — including medical insurance and other benefits — using the Pay Liabilities window if you expect your payroll reports in QuickBooks to be accurate. If you try to pay a payroll liability from the Write Checks window, when you select the Payroll Liabilities account, QuickBooks warns you to use the Pay Liabilities window.

Adjust Payroll Liabilities

On occasion, you may need to adjust the amount in your payroll liabilities account as it appears on the Balance Sheet. For example, suppose that your state unemployment rate changes, but you forget about the change until you see the preprinted rate on your state unemployment tax return.

During the quarter, QuickBooks calculates and accrues state unemployment at the wrong rate and you now need to adjust the balance of the payroll liabilities account before you pay your state unemployment tax.

When you make a liability adjustment, you can adjust the balance of the payroll liabilities account or you can select a particular employee's balance to adjust. You also enter the date you create the liability adjustment and the date the liability adjustment should affect your books; the effective date must be either the same as or earlier than the date you assign to the liability adjustment transaction.

You enter the liability adjustment amount as either a positive or negative number. If you enter a positive number, you increase your payroll liabilities, and if you enter a negative number, you decrease your payroll liabilities. You also can choose whether to affect your payroll liability account balances.

Adjust Payroll Liabilities

1 Click Employees.

2 Click Process Payroll Liabilities.

3 Click Adjust Payroll Liabilities.

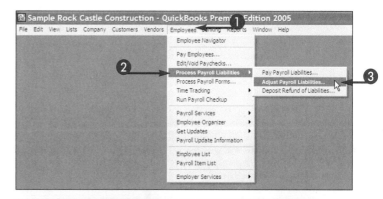

The Liability Adjustment dialog box appears.

4 Click ▦ to select a date for the adjustment.

5 Click ▦ to select an effective date for the transaction.

6 Click an option to adjust the company's or an employee's balance (○ changes to ◉).

7 Click here and select an item to adjust.

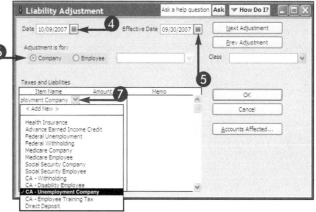

8 Type an amount.

9 Type a description of the reason you are making the adjustment.

10 Repeat steps 7 to 9 as needed.

11 Click Accounts Affected.

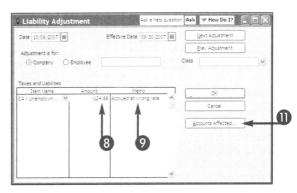

The Affect Accounts? dialog box appears.

12 Click the "Affect liability and expense accounts" option (○ changes to ◉).

13 Click OK.

The Liability Adjustment dialog box reappears.

14 Click OK.

QuickBooks saves the adjustment.

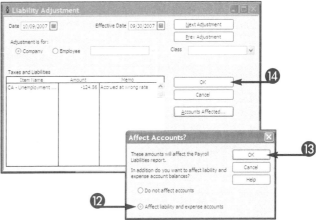

Is there any circumstance under which I should not affect accounts?

▼ Two common mistakes made by users may lead you to not affect accounts with a payroll liability adjustment. First, if you previously entered a journal entry to adjust the payroll liabilities account balance, you should not affect accounts when you record the adjustment to correct your Payroll Liability Balances report. Second, although QuickBooks warns you not to pay liabilities using the Write Checks window, you may have ignored the warning. In this case, do not affect accounts when you record the adjustment.

Can I simply use a journal entry to adjust payoll liabilities?

▼ No. QuickBooks does not update all your payroll reports if you use journal entries. Instead, use the Liabilities Adjustment window and choose to affect account balances in the Affect Accounts? dialog box.

When I affect accounts, how do I know what account to select for the other side of the transaction?

▼ This is only an issue when you select Employee in step 6. When you select Company, the accounts you use are built into the payroll item. Typically, you make payroll liability adjustments for amounts withheld from paychecks. In this case, you select a payroll expense account for the other side of the transaction. If you are not certain, ask your accountant.

Create the Quarterly Payroll Tax Return

E very calendar quarter, you must file the Federal Form 941 Payroll Tax Return to report on employee wages and taxes withheld and tax deposits made, and QuickBooks enables you to complete the form and print it, producing a form that has been approved by the IRS. Both monthly and semiweekly depositors can prepare Federal Form 941 from QuickBooks.

To prepare Federal Form 941, you use a wizard that interviews you, and shows you the information currently recorded for your company name and address; the number

of employees on which you are reporting; and summaries of wages, taxable wages, taxes, and deposits for the quarter. You can adjust any of these numbers for the report without leaving the wizard. If you need to make adjustments other than rounding adjustments, you should correct your data before preparing the report.

At the bottom of Form 941, you see whether you owe additional payroll taxes or whether you have overpaid. If you overpay, you can choose to apply the overpayment to the next Federal Form 941 Payroll Tax Return or receive a refund check from the federal government.

Create the Quarterly Payroll Tax Return

① Click Employees.

② Click Process Payroll Forms.

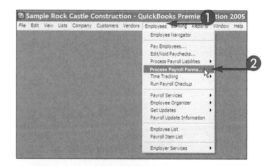

The Select Form Type dialog box appears.

③ Click Federal form (○ changes to ⊙).

④ Click OK.

The Select Payroll Form dialog box appears.

⑤ Click Quarterly Form 941/Schedule B – Interview for your Form 941/Schedule B.

● You can select a different filing period if necessary.

⑥ Click OK.

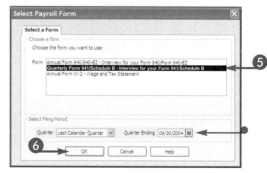

A message appears, explaining why the on-screen form does not look like the form you file.

⑦ Click OK.

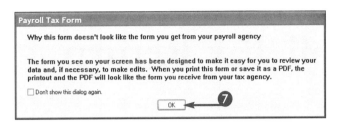

Payroll Tax Form

Why this form doesn't look like the form you get from your payroll agency

The form you see on your screen has been designed to make it easy for you to review your data and, if necessary, to make edits. When you print this form or save it as a PDF, the printout and the PDF will look like the form you receive from your tax agency.

☐ Don't show this dialog again.

[OK] ⑦

The interview page appears.

⑧ Review the questions, clicking in boxes to check them (☐ changes to ☑) as appropriate.

You may need to scroll down to complete the interview page.

⑨ Click Next.

Tax Form for EIN: 80-1234567

Interview for your Form 941/Schedule B
Employer's Quarterly Federal Tax Return

Instructions: Use this interview to help you fill out your Form 941 and Schedule B (if applicable).
* QuickBooks uses your answers to complete your Form 941.

Do you need a Schedule B?

Do you need a **Schedule B**? ⑧ → ☐ Yes ☐ No

To find out if you need a Schedule B, click the "Details about this form" link.

Answer the following questions for Form 941

Enter the **state code** for the state in which taxes were paid, **only if different** from the state of your address
Use the code 'MU' if you made deposits in more than one other state than the state of your company's address. Leave this blank if you only made tax payments in the state of your address.

If your **address is different** from on your prior return, check here ⑧ → ☐

If you **do not have to file** returns in the future, check here ☐
and enter the date that final wages were paid
You would not have to file returns in the future if you went out of business or stopped paying wages

Details about this form   ◀ Prev   Next ▶ ⑨   Filing and Printing Instructions

How does QuickBooks know how much I deposited as my payroll tax liability?

▼ When you pay your liabilities using the steps in the section "Pay Payroll Liabilities," you supply a date through which you want to pay your liabilities. QuickBooks uses that date, which you enter in the Through date field, on liability checks in the quarter for which you prepare a Federal Form 941 to calculate amounts paid and amounts due.

How do I make QuickBooks create the 941 to match my fiscal year?

▼ Payroll tax reporting is mandated by the federal government to operate on a calendar year. You file quarterly payroll tax returns based on the calendar quarters of March 31, June 30, September 30, and December 31, even if your company operates on a fiscal year other than the calendar year. The 941 returns are due on the last day of the month after the quarter ends.

How does QuickBooks calculate the amounts for wages reported on Line 2?

▼ QuickBooks sums the amounts reported on paychecks for wage payroll items and addition payroll items with a tax tracking type of Compensation, Reported Tips, SEC 457 Distribution, Non-qual. Plan Distr, Fringe Benefits, Other Moving Expenses, Taxable Grp Trm Life, and SCorp Pd Med Premium. QuickBooks reduces wages reported on Line 2 by certain deductions such as retirement accounts.

continued

Create the Quarterly Payroll Tax Return *(Continued)*

The wizard also asks if you need to complete Schedule B. If you are a monthly depositor, you do not need to complete Schedule B; instead, you verify total deposits for each of the three months in the quarter for which you are reporting at the bottom of the first page of Form 941. If you need to change any of the monthly total values, you can enter an adjustment on that screen.

If you are a semiweekly depositor, you must complete Schedule B. You complete Lines A, B, and C of Schedule B of Federal Form 941, reporting your payroll tax liability for each day of the first, second, and third months of the quarter. If you need to adjust the amount of any day, you can select that day and type the adjustment. Also on that screen, you see both your total liability for the quarter and your net taxes, which should equal each other.

When you finish the Schedule B screens, the wizard displays a screen that contains filing and printing instructions, including the address to which you must mail Federal Form 941.

Create the Quarterly Payroll Tax Return *(continued)*

The first page of the Form 941 appears.

⑩ Review the information on the page and make changes if necessary.

⑪ Click Next.

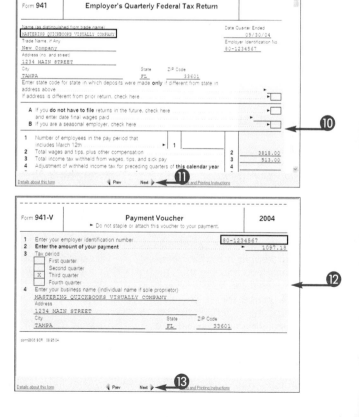

The Payment Voucher portion of the form appears.

⑫ Review the information and make changes if necessary.

⑬ Click Next.

The Filing and Printing Instructions page appears.

Note: *If you indicated on the Interview page that you need a Schedule B, Schedule B appears; review the information, make changes if necessary, and click Next.*

⑭ Click Check Form.

● At the top of the screen, a message appears, indicating if there are errors in the form.

⑮ If errors exist, click Back to form; then, click Next until you find the page on which the errors exist and correct the errors so that QuickBooks can automatically update the error section of the screen.

If there are no errors on your form, skip to step 16.

● You can click Print to print your form.

⑯ Click Done.

The Next Steps dialog box appears, telling you to update QuickBooks with any changes you made to the 941.

⑰ Click OK.

QuickBooks creates your quarterly Payroll Tax Return.

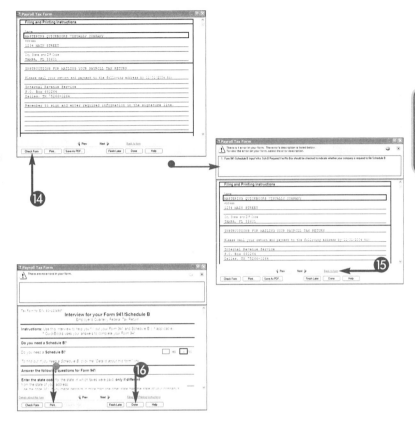

What do I do if Net taxes and the total liability for the quarter are different by just a few cents?

▼ Typically, these amounts do not match because of rounding errors. You do not need to take any action, however, because QuickBooks automatically records the difference for you on Line 9, the Fraction of Cents line.

What happens if I click the Save As PDF option?

▼ QuickBooks displays the Save As dialog box, where you can select a location to save Federal Form 941 as a PDF file for future reference. QuickBooks automatically names the file INWKS941 followed by the quarter ending date in numeric format — for example, 09302004.

What do I do if I printed my form and discovered, before mailing it, that there is an error?

▼ You can correct the data in QuickBooks and then recreate the form. Restart the Payroll Tax Form Wizard using steps 1 to 3. When a Federal Form 941 exists in QuickBooks, QuickBooks lets you either edit it or create a new form. If you made changes in QuickBooks, you should start a new form to force QuickBooks to use the corrected data.

How come the State form option is not available in the Select Form Type dialog box?

▼ The State form option is available only when you subscribe to the Enhanced Payroll Service.

Create the Federal Unemployment Tax Return

Annually, you must prepare and file a Federal Form 940 to report on the unemployment taxes you must pay under the Federal Unemployment Tax Act (FUTA). The Federal Unemployment Tax Act collects funds from employers and uses them to provide unemployment compensation to workers who have lost their jobs and used up any state benefits available to them. Your company makes FUTA payments if your company has paid at least $1,500 of wages in any calendar quarter during the current or the previous year or your company has had one or more employees for at least 20 weeks.

You are required to make FUTA deposits as soon as the amount of unemployment compensation you have accrued reaches $100, but you complete Federal Form 940 or Federal Form 940-EZ only once each year — this section demonstrates completing Federal Form 940-EZ. You make FUTA deposits at a local bank using Federal Form 8109, a coupon that serves as a deposit ticket and describes your deposit to ensure that your business gets credit for the deposit.

The technical rate for FUTA tax is 6.2 percent, but the federal government gives businesses a credit of 5.4 percent for paying state unemployment taxes, making the actual FUTA tax rate .8 percent of the first $7,000 of gross wages for each employee.

Create the Federal Unemployment Tax Return

1 Click Employees.

2 Click Process Payroll Forms.

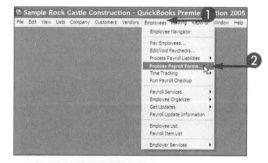

The Select Form Type dialog box appears.

3 Click Federal form.

4 Click OK.

The Select Payroll Form dialog box appears.

5 Click Annual Form 940/940-EZ – Interview for your Form 940/Form 940-EZ.

● You can select a different filing period if necessary.

6 Click OK.

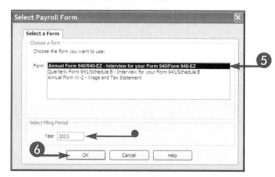

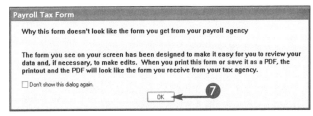

A message box appears, explaining why the on-screen form does not look like the form you file.

7 Click OK.

Payroll Tax Form

Why this form doesn't look like the form you get from your payroll agency

The form you see on your screen has been designed to make it easy for you to review your data and, if necessary, to make edits. When you print this form or save it as a PDF, the printout and the PDF will look like the form you receive from your tax agency.

☐ Don't show this dialog again.

[OK] ← **7**

The interview page appears.

8 Review the questions, clicking in boxes to check them (☐ changes to ☑) as appropriate.

You may need to scroll down to complete the interview page.

9 Click Next.

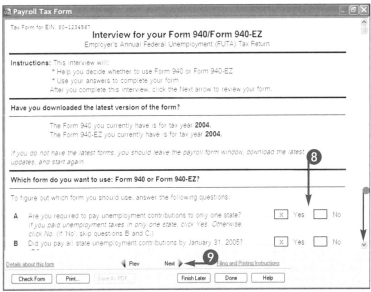

Payroll Tax Form

Tax Form for EIN: 80-1234567

Interview for your Form 940/Form 940-EZ
Employer's Annual Federal Unemployment (FUTA) Tax Return

Instructions: This interview will:
* Help you decide whether to use Form 940 or Form 940-EZ
* Use your answers to complete your form
After you complete this interview, click the Next arrow to review your form.

Have you downloaded the latest version of the form?

The Form 940 you currently have is for tax year **2004**.
The Form 940-EZ you currently have is for tax year **2004**.

If you do not have the latest forms, you should leave the payroll form window, download the latest updates, and start again.

Which form do you want to use: Form 940 or Form 940-EZ?

To figure out which form you should use, answer the following questions:

A   Are you required to pay unemployment contributions to only one state?   ☒ Yes   ☐ No
If you paid unemployment taxes in only one state, click Yes. Otherwise, click No. (If 'No', skip questions B and C.)

B   Did you pay all state unemployment contributions by January 31, 2005?   ☒ Yes   ☐ No

Details about this form   ◀ Prev   Next ▶ ← **9**   Filing and Printing Instructions

[Check Form] [Print...] [Save As PDF...]   [Finish Later] [Done] [Help]

How do I know that QuickBooks is using the right version of the form, because the federal government changes the form periodically?

▼ You receive form updates for the year as part of your subscription to Do-It-Yourself payroll. Through the Automatic Update feature — see Chapter 25 for details — QuickBooks checks for program and payroll form updates, informs you when they exist, and installs them.

If I complete a Federal Form 940 instead of 940-EZ, what differences will I notice?

▼ You also complete Parts II and III of the Federal Form 940. Both Part II and Part III appear below the payment voucher. In Part II, you calculate your FUTA tax, applying any credits due to you, taking into consideration your company's state experience rate and contributions paid to your state. In Part III, you provide a record of your quarterly FUTA liability.

Does QuickBooks calculate my FUTA tax liability using the 6.2 percent rate or the .8 percent rate?

▼ QuickBooks assumes that you are paying state unemployment taxes and want credit for them and therefore calculates your FUTA tax liability at the .8 percent rate.

Is there a maximum FUTA tax liability that I owe?

▼ Using the .8 percent rate, you owe a maximum of $56 for each employee who earns at least $7,000 during the calendar year.

continued

Create the Federal Unemployment Tax Return *(Continued)*

In QuickBooks, you prepare and print the Federal Form 940, the FUTA tax return, using a wizard. The wizard interviews you to determine whether you need to complete Federal Form 940 or 940-EZ. As you walk through the wizard, you confirm your company's name and address and the calendar year on which you are reporting. You also verify information about the FUTA tax deposits you have made throughout the year and you verify the calculation of the total FUTA tax due. You can, if necessary, adjust information

on the report as you walk through the wizard. If you need to make adjustments other than for rounding, you should correct your data before you produce the report.

Toward the end of the form, you can adjust your FUTA tax liability for each quarter of the year, if necessary. When you print the form, use plain paper. Although the format may vary slightly from the format of the preprinted Federal Form 940 that you receive from the federal government, the federal government approved the form that QuickBooks prints.

Create the Federal Unemployment Tax Return *(continued)*

The Form 940 or Form 940-EZ appears, depending on your answers on the interview page.

⑩ Review the information on the page and make changes if necessary.

⑪ Scroll down.

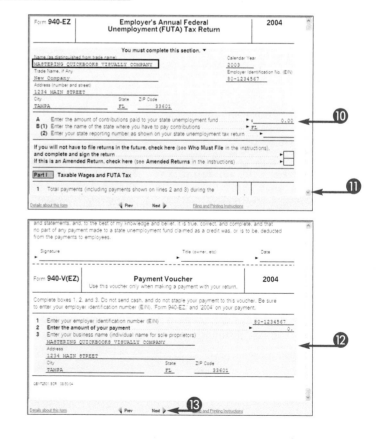

The Payment Voucher portion of the form appears.

⑫ Review the information and make changes if necessary.

⑬ Click Next.

The Filing and Printing Instructions page appears.

⑭ Click Check Form.

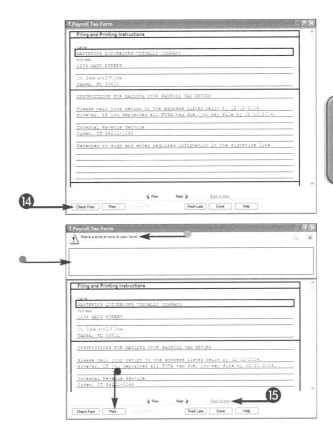

● You can click Print to print your form.

● At the top of the screen, a message appears, indicating if there are errors in the form.

⑮ If errors exist, click Back to form; then, click Next until you find the page on which the errors exist and correct the errors so that QuickBooks can automatically update the error section of the screen.

   ● If there are no errors on your form, skip to step 16.

The Next Steps dialog box appears, telling you to update QuickBooks with any changes you made to the 941.

⑯ Click OK.

The Unemployment Tax Return is created.

Is there a way in QuickBooks to review prior Federal Form 940 Payroll Unemployment Tax Act returns that I filed?

▼ QuickBooks stores only one FUTA tax return at a time. You can restart the Form 940 Wizard using steps 1 to 3. When a Federal Form 940 exists in QuickBooks, QuickBooks lets you choose to edit it or create a new form. You can edit the last form to review it, but, if you create a new form, QuickBooks overwrites the prior form.

How and where do I make Federal Form 940 tax deposits?

▼ Use the steps in the section "Pay Payroll Liabilities" to pay your FUTA tax liability. Make the check payable to a local bank unless otherwise instructed, and fill out a Federal Form 8109 to accompany the deposit. On the Federal Form 8109, be sure to indicate that the deposit is for Form 940.

Can I prepare a Federal Form 940 in QuickBooks, and if so, how?

▼ QuickBooks enables you to prepare both the Federal Form 940 and the Federal Form 940-EZ, and the interview page of the wizard determines which form you need to complete. Based on your responses to the interview questions, QuickBooks automatically displays the appropriate form for you to complete.

Process
W-2s

At the beginning of each calendar year, your business must prepare W-2s that report wages, Social Security wages, Medicare wages, and federal, Social Security, and Medicare taxes withheld for each employee for the preceding calendar year. In some cases, the W-2 also reports certain state information, such as state wages and taxes withheld. QuickBooks can print W-2s for you using the payroll data in your company using the Process W-2s Wizard.

When you use the wizard, you select employees for whom you want to print W-2s, and then you review the W-2s on-screen. You can use the Employee Earnings Summary to help you verify that the amounts on the W-2 are accurate; see Chapters 22 and 23 for details on printing this report.

You can change amounts on W-2s if necessary, but if your company data file contains accurate and complete payroll information, you should not need to make changes. Any changes you make on the W-2 form do not affect the employee's payroll data or paychecks in your company. If you have questions about if or how to report particular benefits, talk to your accountant.

QuickBooks also enables you to print Federal Form W-3, the transmittal form for W-2s, from the same window where you print W-2s.

Process W-2s

① Click Employees.

② Click Process Payroll Forms.

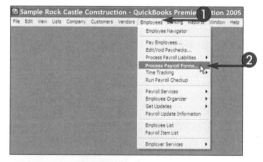

The Select Form Type dialog box appears.

③ Click Federal form.

④ Click OK.

The Select Payroll Form dialog box appears.

⑤ Click the Annual Form W-2 – Wage and Tax Statement option.

⑥ Click OK.

A message appears, explaining that any adjustments you made prior to installing QuickBooks 2005 have been removed and you must manually re-enter the adjustments.

⑦ Click OK.

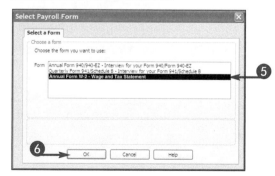

The Process W-2s window appears.

8 Click here and select the year for which you are creating W-2s.

9 Click next to each employee for whom you want to print a W-2 (☐ changes to ☑).

10 Click Review W-2.

The Employee W-2 window appears.

11 Review the information.

You can double-click various fields to change them on the W-2.

12 Click Next to review the next W-2.

13 Repeat steps 11 to 12 for each W-2.

14 Click OK.

The Process W-2s window reappears.

● Check marks (☑) appear next to each employee whose W-2 you have reviewed.

● You can click Print W-2s or Print W-3s to begin the process of printing your W-2s.

15 Click Done.

QuickBooks completes the processing of your W-2s.

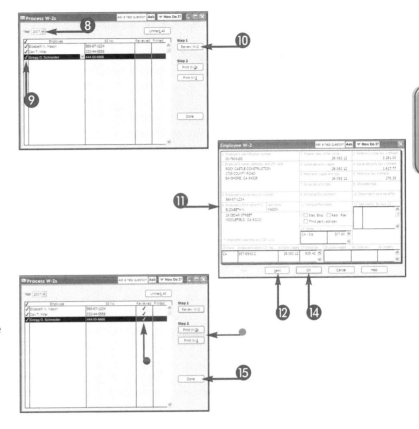

Can I change any field on the W-2?

▼ You can change any field containing information. To change information in some fields, such as Boxes B–F, you must close the W–2 wizard. To change the information in Boxes B and C, use the Company Information window, which you open by clicking Company and then Company Information. To change information in Boxes D, E, and F, use the Edit Employee List to open the employee's record.

If I click the blank paper option, should I click all the options under it in the Print Form W-2 dialog box?

▼ By clicking each option (☐ changes to ☑), you tell QuickBooks to print filing instructions for Forms W-2 and W-3 plus the Social Security Administration copy of the W-2, one copy of Copies B, C, and D, and two copies each of Copy 1 and Copy 2 of the W-2.

Are W-2s on blank paper acceptable to the federal government?

▼ Yes, as long as you print them on white or cream-colored, 11-inch-long, 18-pound paper using printer ink that is black. The same rules apply for W-3s printed on blank paper.

Why can I not print W-2s on blank paper?

▼ QuickBooks enables blank paper as an option only if you subscribe to Do-It-Yourself payroll.

Summarize Payroll Data in Excel

You can view some QuickBooks payroll wage information in a preformatted Excel workbook; you can summarize your company's payroll data in this workbook for a variety of time periods. To use this feature, you must use Excel 97 or higher and you must set security in Excel to permit macros to run.

The workbook contains nine preformatted worksheets, and each contains different payroll information. Some worksheets are formatted using PivotTables, and you can modify the worksheets as needed. A *PivotTable* is an interactive table that enables you to quickly and easily swap rows and columns to summarize data in different ways, and filter the data to display only information that interests you. You use a PivotTable when you have a lot of data that you want to look at in a variety of ways. You can identify the worksheets that use PivotTables by the down arrows that appear next to column or row headings.

This feature exports your company's payroll data to the Excel workbook for you and you select a date range for the information you want to view. QuickBooks updates the workbook based on the date range you select.

You can, but do not need to, save the workbook; when you save it and reopen it, QuickBooks prompts you for a date range to update the workbook's information.

Summarize Payroll Data in Excel

1 Click Reports.

2 Click Employees & Payroll.

3 Click Summarize Payroll Data in Excel.

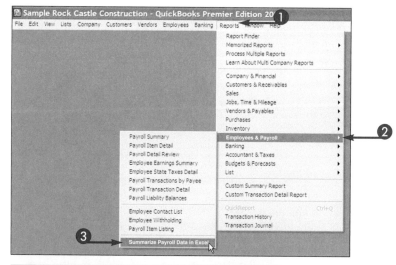

An Excel workbook opens and the Welcome dialog box appears.

4 Click OK.

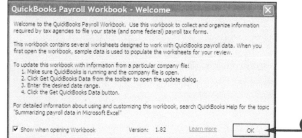

The Date Range window appears.

5 Click Get QuickBooks Data.

QuickBooks exports your company data to the workbook.

A message appears telling you the workbook is updated with your data.

6 Click OK.

The State Wage Listing report appears.

● You can click the various tabs to review the information on them.

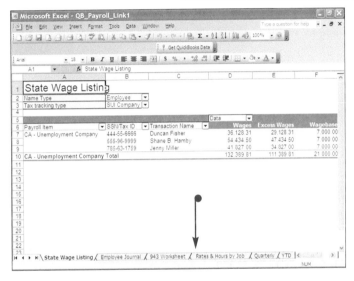

PART II

MASTER IT

Is it safe to enable macros in Excel? I have heard that macros can contain viruses.

▼ When you do not know who wrote the macro or you are not expecting macros to run when you open a workbook, it is not safe to enable macros. However, the macros contained in the workbook that ships with QuickBooks have been tested and do not contain any viruses, so you can safely allow them to run.

How do I set security to permit macros to run in Excel?

▼ In Excel, click Tools and then click Options. When the Options dialog box appears, click the Security tab. In the Macro Security section, click Macro Security. When the Security dialog box appears, click the Security Level tab. Select second-highest setting — High — and try running the macro. Repeat the steps in this tip, selecting a lower security level each time until the macro runs.

If I want to look at a different range of payroll data, must I start over?

▼ While you work in the Excel workbook, the Get QuickBooks Data button is always available to you on the toolbars at the top of the screen. When you click Get QuickBooks Data, you are prompted for a date range for data. Once you supply the date range, your company data is imported into the workbook again, replacing existing information.

Set Time Tracking Preferences

I f you use QuickBooks Pro, Premier, or Enterprise, you can track time that you, your employees, and your vendors work for customers by turning on the Time Tracking feature. You can bill back time spent to customers, and you can pay employees and vendors based on the hours they enter. You do not need to set up anything to track time for owners or partners.

QuickBooks contains a stopwatch that enables you to time an activity as it happens. For users without access to QuickBooks, you can install the stopwatch feature only on their computers so that they can track time; then you can import their time into the main QuickBooks program when you want to bill customers, pay employees or vendors, or produce reports.

How does QuickBooks change when I turn on the time-tracking feature?

▼ A Time Tracking menu, in which you can record time spent using a weekly timesheet or the window that also contains the stopwatch, appears on both the Customers menu and the Employees menu. QuickBooks also adds four reports to the Jobs & Time menu that appears when you click Reports. These reports help you analyze the breakdown of your company's time according to job, employee, or the type of work your company does.

Set Time Tracking Preferences

① Click Edit.

② Click Preferences.

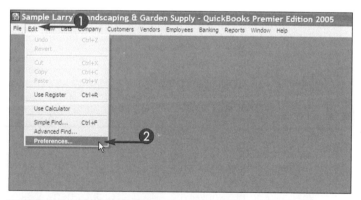

The Preferences dialog box appears.

③ Click the Time Tracking icon.

④ Click the Company Preferences tab.

⑤ Click Yes (○ changes to ◉).

⑥ Click here and select the first day of the work week.

⑦ Click OK.

QuickBooks saves your preferences.

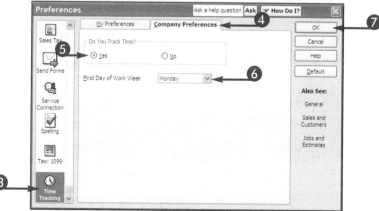

Record Time Single Activity

You can record the time you spend on a task as you perform the task if you use the Time/Enter Single Activity window. Using this window, you record one task for one customer on one date.

You select a service item to identify the work performed on a customer invoice, and QuickBooks records the income associated with the time entry to the income account associated with the selected service item. Any information you type in the Notes box can appear on a customer invoice. You can enter the duration of the task or use the stopwatch to time the activity. If you use the stopwatch, the window must remain open while the timer runs.

Do I do anything differently if I pay my employees for time they enter?

▼ You set up the employee as described in Chapter 4. When you select that employee in the Time/Enter Single Activity window, the Payroll Item list box appears, from which you select the wage payroll item that QuickBooks should use when recording the time activity. When you pay the employee, QuickBooks allocates the time from the activity to the selected payroll item. QuickBooks "remembers" the payroll item that you select for a particular employee and service item in the Time/Enter Single Activity window, automatically selecting the same item the next time you select the same employee.

Record Time Single Activity

1 Click Employees.

2 Click Time Tracking.

3 Click Time/Enter Single Activity.

The Time/Enter Single Activity window appears.

4 Click the calendar icon (▦) to select a date.

5 Click here and select the name of the person recording the time.

6 Click here and select a Customer:Job and a service item.

7 Click here to make the activity billable (☐ changes to ☑).

8 Type a description of the work here.

9 Type a duration here.

10 Click Save & Close.

QuickBooks saves the time entry.

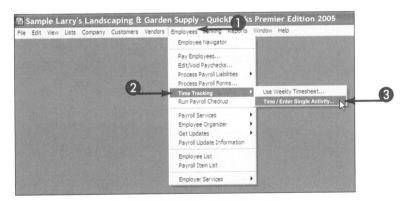

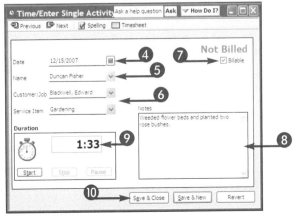

Record
Time Weekly

If you are using QuickBooks Pro, QuickBooks Premier, or QuickBooks Enterprise, you can record time using the Weekly Timesheet window. Entries you record in the Time/Enter Single Activity window also appear in the Weekly Timesheet window; the window you use to enter time is a matter of personal preference. Use the Time/Enter Single Activity window if you need to use the stop watch.

Using the Weekly Timesheet window, you can record all entries for a particular vendor or employee during a given week. You select the person and week for which you want to enter time. Then, on individual lines of the timesheet, you select the customer for whom the work was done and the service item that describes the work, and enter the time spent on the appropriate day. You also can supply a description of the work that can appear on the customer's invoice.

You can print a blank timesheet and distribute it to employees and vendors, who can then fill in the form to provide a written record of time worked. Because the form matches the Weekly Timesheet window, data entry is easy.

Record Time Weekly

① Click Employees.

② Click Time Tracking.

③ Click Use Weekly Timesheet.

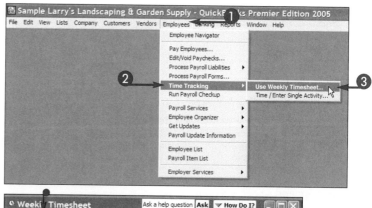

The Weekly Timesheet window appears.

④ Click here and select the name of the person recording time.

⑤ Click Set Date to select the week for which you want to record time.

- You can click Next or Previous to view the timesheet of the next or previous week.

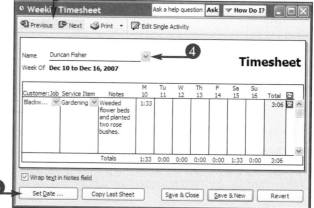

The Set Date dialog box appears.

6 Click ▦ to select a date.

You can select any day in the week for which you want to record time.

7 Click OK.

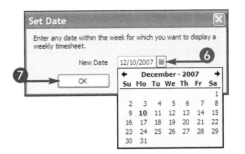

The Weekly Timesheet window for the week you selected appears.

8 Click here to select a customer for whom work was done.

9 Click here to select the service performed.

10 Type here to describe the work done.

11 Click in a day column and type the time worked.

● QuickBooks totals the time for the day.

12 Repeat steps 8 to 11 as needed, or steps 4 to 11 for another person.

13 Click Save & Close.

QuickBooks saves the entry.

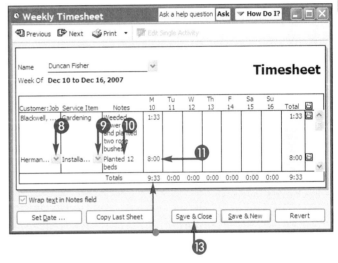

How can I print a blank timesheet form?

▼ Use steps 1 to 3 to display the Weekly Timesheet window. Then, click the ☑ next to the Print button (🖨 ▾). QuickBooks displays a menu; click Prink Blank Timesheet. The Print Timesheets window appears, where you can select a printer. Click Print. You also can print a timesheet of information that appears in QuickBooks using the same technique except, from the menu that appears when you click 🖨 ▾, select Print. The Select Timesheets to Print dialog box appears. Place a check mark next to the name of each person whose timesheet you want to print and click OK. When the Print Timesheets box appears, select a printer and click Print.

Can I use both the Time/Enter Single Activity window and the Weekly Timesheet window?

▼ Yes. You can use either window and then switch to the other window as it suits you.

How do I make hours recorded billable to customers?

▼ By default, all time entries are billable. If you do not want an entry available when you prepare invoices, click the icon that appears in the rightmost column of the Weekly Timesheet window. QuickBooks places an X through the icon, and the entry is not available when you produce an invoice for the selected customer. You do *not* need to mark an entry as not billable to avoid billing it. See the section "Invoicing for Time Charges" for details.

Invoice for Time Charges

Y ou can include time charges you record through QuickBooks on invoices to customers. By default, QuickBooks marks the time charges you enter using either the Time/Enter Single Activity window or the Weekly Timesheet window as billable, enabling you to include them on customer invoices. Essentially, QuickBooks treats these billable time entries as reimbursable expenses.

Although you are not required to bill time charges to customers, you can include time charges on customer invoices. The entries appear as line items on an invoice. For

the description column on the invoice, you can choose to use the description typed in the Notes field of a time entry, or the description you supplied when you created the service item assigned to the time entry. Or, QuickBooks can include both descriptions on the customer's invoice.

If you have many time entries for a particular customer, you also can choose to combine the time entries into one line item entry on the customer's invoice. If you combine entries, QuickBooks prints no information from the Notes fields of the time entries.

Invoice for Time Charges

① Click Customers.

② Click Create Invoices.

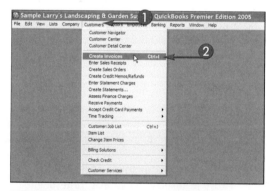

The Create Invoices window appears.

③ Click here and select the Customer:Job.

④ Click Time/Costs.

The Choose Billable Time and Costs dialog box appears.

⑤ Click the Time tab.

⑥ Click in the Use column beside the entry you want to include on the invoice (☐ changes to ☑).

⑦ Click Options.

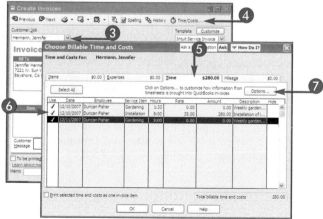

The Options for Transferring Billable Time dialog box appears.

⑧ Click an option (○ changes to ◉) to identify how the description should appear on the invoice.

⑨ Click OK.

The Choose Billable Time and Costs dialog box reappears.

⑩ Click OK.

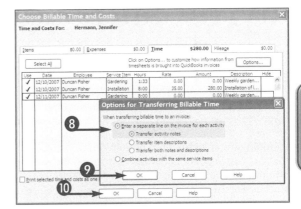

● The entries appear on the invoice using the description you selected.

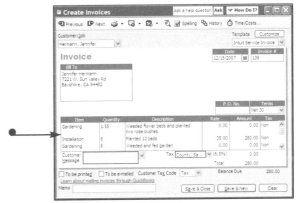

What do the options mean in the Options for Transferring Billable Time dialog box?

▼ First, you can include each time entry as a separate line on the invoice, or you can print one line for all time entries with the same service item. If you choose to print one line for all time entries that use the same service item, QuickBooks prints the service item description on the invoice. If you choose to include separate lines for each time entry, then you can print, as the Description on the invoice, the information stored in the Notes field of the entry, the service item description, or both.

Why did the time entries that I included on a customer invoice appear separately when I clicked the "Print selected time and costs as one invoice item" option (☐ changes to ☑)?

▼ On-screen, the entries appear separately; but, when you print the invoice, one line with a description of "Total Reimbursable Expenses" appears. Descriptions from time entries do not appear.

Is there a report that I can print to view unbilled time charges?

▼ Yes. You can print the Time by Job Detail report. Click Reports, click Jobs, click Time & Mileage, and then click Time by Job Detail.

Payroll and Time Tracking

I f you are tracking in QuickBooks the time that employees work, you can choose to pay employees for the hours recorded on time entries in QuickBooks. In this case, you need to set up the employee so that QuickBooks knows to use time entries when calculating paychecks. You indicate that you want to pay an employee based on time entries by editing the information that appears on the Payroll Info tab for the employee.

After you establish that QuickBooks should use time entries to calculate pay, you do not need to change any procedures. You still pay employees as described in

Chapter 8. When you select an employee whose pay is based on time entries, QuickBooks automatically supplies the hours recorded on time entries for the pay period; but QuickBooks still calculates the employee's pay based on the rates you enter in the Earnings section of the Payroll Info tab.

Hours from time entries can, but do not necessarily, affect gross wages. Employees paid by the hour are paid for the hours recorded as time entries. Salaried employees are paid based on their salary, but QuickBooks allocates their salary based on the time entries.

Payroll and Time Tracking

① Click Lists.

② Click Employee List.

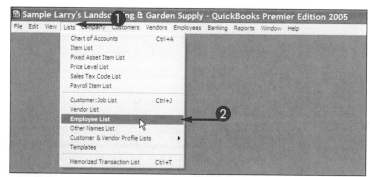

The Employee List window appears.

③ Click the employee you want to pay based on time recorded.

④ Click Employee.

⑤ Click Edit.

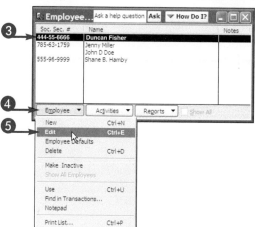

The Personal Info tab of the Edit Employee dialog box appears.

⑥ Click here and then click Payroll and Compensation Info.

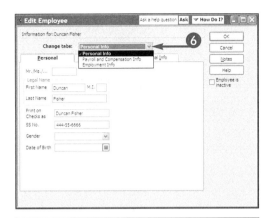

The Payroll and Compensation Info tab appears.

⑦ Click the "Use time data to create paychecks" option (☐ changes to ☑).

⑧ Click OK.

QuickBooks saves the change.

When you pay the employee, QuickBooks automatically displays hours recorded for the pay period.

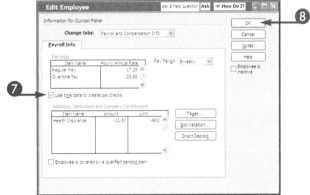

I understand how paying based on time entries affects hourly employees, but can you explain how it affects salaried employees?

▼ When you pay based on time entries, QuickBooks prefills the hours worked on the paycheck. For salaried employees, QuickBooks allocates their salary based on the customer for whom they worked and the service item stored on the time entry. When you pay a salaried employee *without* using time entries, only one line appears for gross wages in the Earnings section of the paycheck. When you pay a salaried employee using time entries, multiple lines appear, but the pay remains the same. Using this technique, the employee's time is automatically allocated to jobs for you.

If an employee does work that I do not want to allocate to a job, what should I do?

▼ If a time entry was recorded, delete the customer information from the paycheck. If no time entry was recorded, simply add a line to the paycheck and do not assign the line to a Customer:Job.

Do I have to pay an employee for time recorded on time entries if I use time tracking in QuickBooks?

▼ No. You can use time tracking in QuickBooks so that you can bill customers for time worked, but you do not need to tie an employee's pay to the time entries.

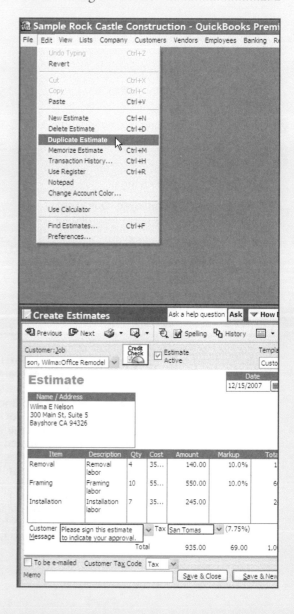

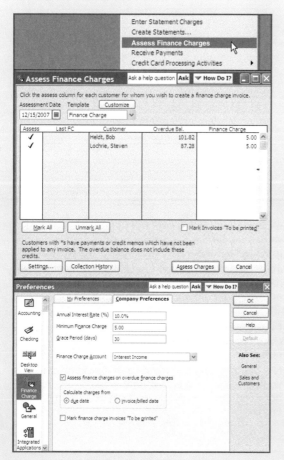

13 Record Customer Payments

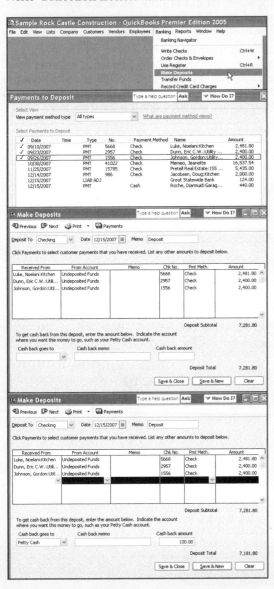

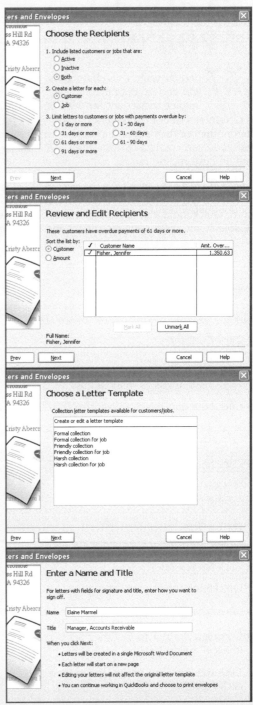

Create an Invoice

When customers purchase items or services from you and do not pay immediately, you record an invoice to account for the income and record the customer's debt to you. QuickBooks comes with several different invoice formats, and if none of them meets your needs, you can create a custom form. See Chapter 24 for more on customizing forms.

When you create the invoice, you select a customer and QuickBooks fills in address information from the customer's record. QuickBooks also fills in today's date and the next available invoice number; you can change these fields as

necessary. You can select items and fill in the quantity, and QuickBooks calculates the amount due, including sales tax if the customer and item are taxable. If you select an out-of-stock item, QuickBooks warns you; you may use sales orders to track orders for out-of-stock items. See the section "Create a Sales Order" for details. You can also assign a message to the invoice as discussed in see Chapter 3.

You can print the invoice when you create it, or you can print it later as part of a batch of invoices. And you can preview it before you print it. QuickBooks also provides a service for e-mailing invoices; QuickBooks requires you to register to e-mail invoices, but the service is free.

Create an Invoice

Set Up the Invoice

1 Click Customers.

2 Click Create Invoices.

The Create Invoices window appears.

3 Click here and select a Customer:Job.

● You can click here to select a different invoice form.

4 Click here to select an item.

● QuickBooks fills in the description and rate.

5 Type a quantity.

6 Repeat steps 4 to 5 for additional items.

7 Click Save & New.

QuickBooks saves your settings

Preview the Invoice

1 Complete steps 1 to 6 of the "Set Up the Invoice" subsection.

2 Click the Print button (🖨 ▾) and then click Preview.

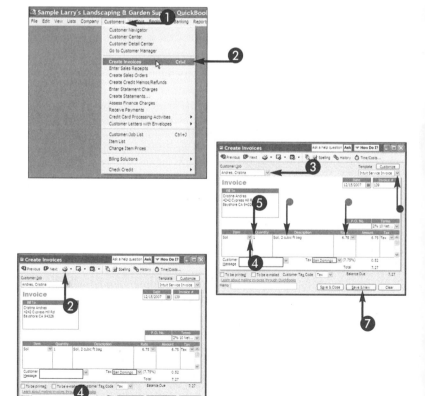

A preview of the invoice appears.

- You can click here to enlarge the preview.

  You can click Print to print the invoice now.

③ Click Close.

④ Click Save & Close in the Create Invoice window.

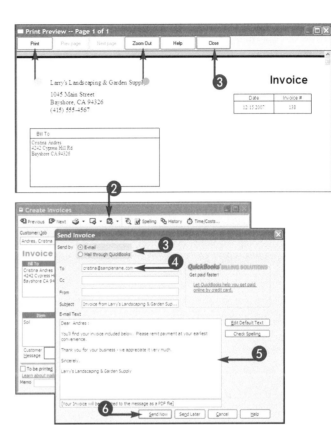

E-mail an Invoice

① Set up an invoice by completing steps 1 to 6 in the subsection "Set Up the Invoice."

② Click the Send button () and then click E-Mail Invoice.

QuickBooks saves the invoice and the Send Invoice window appears.

③ Click a Send by option (○ changes to ◉).

④ Verify the e-mail addresses.

⑤ Verify the message text.

⑥ Click Send Now.

QuickBooks e-mails the invoice.

How do I fill out an invoice if the customer pays cash?

▼ You should not use the Create Invoice window when the customer pays cash; although you can enter a Payment item to record the payment, this method is considered less favorable. Instead, for cash sales, use the Sales Receipt window. See Chapter 13 for details on entering a sales receipt.

How can I print invoices in a batch?

▼ Click the To be printed option (☐ changes to ☑) at the bottom of the Create Invoices window when you are ready to print a batch of invoices. See the section "Print Invoices in Batch" for details.

How can I preview an invoice I already saved?

▼ Using steps 1 to 2 in the subsection "Set Up the Invoice," open the Create Invoices window. Then, use the Next and Previous buttons in the Create Invoices window to find the invoice; see Chapter 18 for details on finding a transaction. Once the invoice appears in the Create Invoices window, follow the steps in the subsection "Preview the Invoice."

What is Mail through QuickBooks?

▼ Intuit offers a fee-based service that prints, folds, and mails invoices. You simply prepare and send your invoices to the QuickBooks Billing Solutions service via e-mail and the service does the rest.

Invoice for Reimbursable Expenses

Your company may make purchases from vendors that you need to bill to customers; these purchases are reimbursable expenses. You can include reimbursable expenses on a regular invoice along with other charges.

By default, QuickBooks marks items you purchase and expenses you incur as reimbursable expenses if you assign a customer to the line on the bill. While you are not required to bill these charges to customers, you can include the charges on customer invoices. If you bill customers for items you purchase, you can choose to display the details of

the items or to print one line on the invoice for all the items. If you print items individually, QuickBooks prints the description associated with the item, but you can change the description by simply editing it on the invoice. If you combine entries, QuickBooks prints no detailed description information; instead, a line called Total reimbursable expenses appears on the invoice.

If you bill customers for expenses you incur, you can mark up the expenses by a percentage or a flat amount. Markups will appear on invoices unless you choose to print one entry for all expenses.

Invoice for Reimbursable Expenses

1 Click Customers.

2 Click Create Invoices.

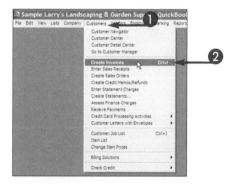

The Create Invoices window appears.

3 Click here and select a Customer:Job.

4 Click Time/Costs.

The Choose Billable Time and Costs dialog box appears.

5 Click the Items tab.

6 Click beside the entries you want to include on the invoice (☐ changes to ☑).

7 Click the Expenses tab.

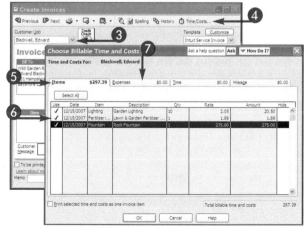

8 Click beside the entries you want to include on the invoice (☐ changes to ☑).

9 Type a markup amount or percentage here.

● You can click this option to print all costs as one entry on the invoice (☐ changes to ☑).

● You can click this option to mark the expenses as taxable (☐ changes to ☑).

10 Click OK.

● The entries appear on the invoice using the description you selected.

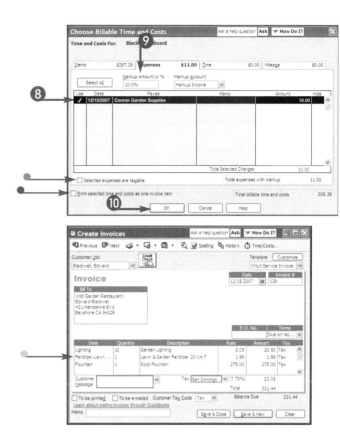

Is there a way to print the individual expenses but hide the markup?

▼ To hide the markup, you must print expenses as one line on the invoice. To work around the problem, perform the steps in this section twice. To place items individually on the invoice, perform steps 1 to 6 and click OK. Then, perform steps 1 to 10, skipping steps 5 and 6 and clicking the "Print selected time and costs as one invoice item" option (☐ changes to ☑). QuickBooks then prints item reimbursable expense entries individually, but groups expense reimbursable expense entries into one line on the invoice. The markup does not appear, but is calculated as part of the expense entry.

Why do the entries I include on a customer invoice appear separately when I click the "Print selected time and costs as one invoice item" option (☐ changes to ☑)?

▼ On-screen, the entries appear separately, but when you print the invoice, one line with a description of "Total Reimbursable Expenses" appears. You can change this description if you prefer. Descriptions from the entries do not appear.

Is there a report that I can print to view unbilled reimbursable expenses?

▼ Yes. You can print the Unbilled Costs by Job report. Click Reports, then click Jobs, Time & Mileage, and then Unbilled Costs by Job.

Statement Charges: Another Way to Invoice

If you accumulate transactions for a customer before preparing an invoice — similar to the way lawyers, accountants, and consultants work — you may prefer to record statement charges as you work instead of creating invoices. Then, on some regular basis, such as once each month, you can prepare a customer statement that includes the statement charges you enter.

QuickBooks keeps track of each customer's balance in an accounts receivable register for the customer. When you enter statement charges, you record an entry to a customer's accounts receivable register. Be aware, however,

that you cannot record taxable transactions in a customer's register. This approach works well if you sell primarily nontaxable items.

For details on creating statements to bill your customers, see the section "Create Customer Statements."

Can I print a customer's register?

▼ Yes. Display the customer register that you want to print using steps 1 to 3. Then, click File and click Print Register. From the Print Register dialog box that appears, select a date range, click OK, and then click Print.

Statement Charges: Another Way to Invoice

1 Click Customers.

2 Click Enter Statement Charges.

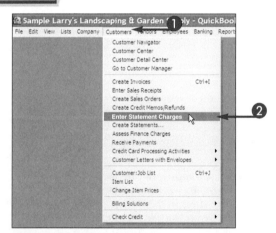

The Accounts Receivable window appears.

3 Click here to select a Customer:Job.

4 Click the calendar button (▦) to select a date.

5 Click here to select an item.

- QuickBooks fills in the description and rate.

6 Type a quantity.

7 Click Record.

8 Repeat steps 4 to 7 for additional items.

- QuickBooks calculates the customer's balance.

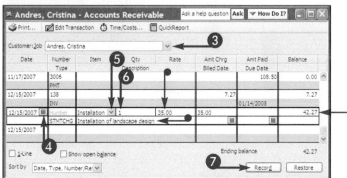

Create a Sales Order

I f you are using QuickBooks Premier or QuickBooks Enterprise, you can use sales orders to help you track out-of-stock items that customers order. Suppose that a customer places an order and you have everything the customer needs except one item. You can fill the entire order by creating an invoice and then enter a sales order for the out-of-stock item. When you receive the out-of-stock item and want to ship it and invoice the customer, you can convert the sales order to an invoice. See the section "Create an Invoice from a Sales Order" for details on converting a sales order to an invoice.

You can e-mail a sales order to the customer placing the order. See the subsection "E-mail an Invoice" in the section "Create an Invoice" for more information.

Does QuickBooks tell me when inventory arrives that can fill a back-ordered item?

▼ No, but you can print the Open Sales Orders by Customer report or the Open Sales Orders by Item report each time you receive inventory. To open these reports, click Reports, Sales, and then click Open Sales Orders by Customer or Open Sales Orders by Item.

PART III

Create a Sales Order

① Click Customers.

② Click Create Sales Orders.

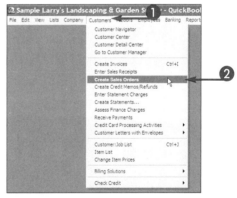

The Create Sales Orders window appears.

③ Click here to select a Customer:Job.

 ● You can click here to select a different sales order form.

④ Click here to select an item.

 ● QuickBooks fills in the description and rate.

⑤ Type a quantity.

⑥ Repeat steps 4 to 5 for additional items.

⑦ Click Save & New.

Your sales order is created.

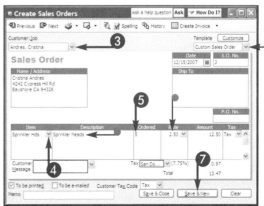

Create an Invoice
from a Sales Order

I f you use QuickBooks Premier or QuickBooks Enterprise and you have enabled sales orders, you can create invoices from sales orders as back-ordered merchandise arrives.

QuickBooks enables you to use the information stored on sales orders to create invoices so that you do not need to enter the same information more than once. You can create an invoice from a sales order starting from either the Create Invoices window, as demonstrated in this section, or from the Create Sales Order window. Starting in either window

yields the same results; you create an invoice for whatever portion of a sales order you choose. If you start from the Create Invoices window, QuickBooks displays a dialog box that lets you know sales orders exist when you select the customer and lets you select the sales order that you want to fill.

While you can create an invoice for all items on a sales order, you do not need to invoice an entire sales order all at the same time. Instead, you can invoice only some items on the sales order, or you can invoice part of the total quantity of an item on a sales order.

Create an Invoice from a Sales Order

① Click Customers.

② Click Create Invoices.

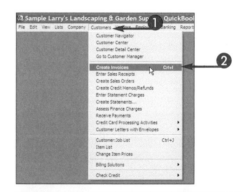

The Create Invoices window appears.

③ Click here to select the Customer:Job.

The Available Sales Orders dialog box appears.

④ Click the order you want to fill.

⑤ Click OK.

The Create Invoice Based On Sales Order dialog box appears.

⑥ Click an option for creating the invoice (○ changes to ◉).

⑦ Click OK.

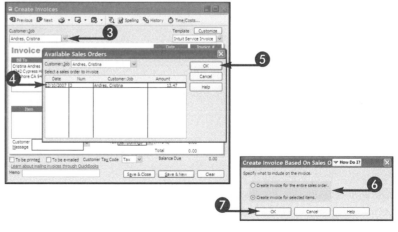

If you invoice the entire sales order, the Create Invoices window appears; otherwise, the Specify Invoice Quantities for Items on Sales Order dialog box appears.

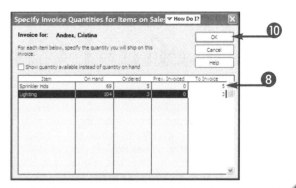

8 Type the number of items to invoice.

9 Repeat step 8 as needed.

10 Click OK.

● QuickBooks places the items on the invoice.

11 Click Save & Close.

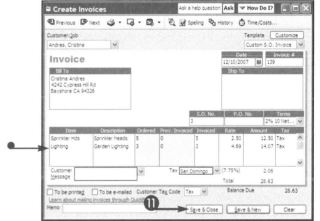

PART III

How can I figure out what sales orders to fill?

▼ You can use the Stock Status by Item report, which shows the items on sales orders. Click Reports, Inventory, and then click Stock Status by Item. You can double-click the item to display an Inventory Item QuickReport for the selected item. On the QuickReport, a list of sales orders for the item appears. Double-click any entry in that list, and QuickBooks displays the sales order in the Create Sales Orders window. You can then fill all or part of the order using the steps in this section.

What should I do if I only want to invoice for part of a sales order?

▼ In the Specify Invoice Quantities for Items on Sales Order dialog box, type 0 in the To Invoice column next to each item you do not want to invoice.

Is there a way to create an invoice while viewing the sales order?

▼ Yes. Display the sales order in the Create Sales Order window and then click the Create Invoice button. Then, follow steps 6 to 11. To display the Create Sales Order window, see the section "Create a Sales Order."

Create Credit Memos and Refund Checks

Occasionally, you must give money back to a customer. Suppose that one of your best customers purchases two locking interior doorknob kits and then decides to return the merchandise for a refund. If the customer has not yet paid you, you can issue a credit memo that reverses the sale on your books and reduces the customer's outstanding balance by the amount of the sale. If, however, the customer has paid you in full, you need to record both a credit memo and a refund check.

If your customer returns the merchandise to you, select the items on the credit memo to return the merchandise to inventory and adjust accounts properly. If the customer does not return the merchandise — perhaps it was defective and you cannot resell it — you can create an item called Returns and Allowances, make the item taxable, and assign the item to an appropriate income account or a Sales Returns and Allowances account. Then, use the Returns and Allowances item on the credit memo instead of the inventory item that the customer did not return. By making the Returns and Allowances item taxable, the credit memo adjusts your sales tax liability as well as your sales and receivables.

Create Credit Memos and Refund Checks

Create a Credit Memo

① Click Customers.

② Click Create Credit Memos/Refunds.

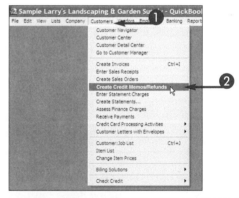

The Create Credit Memos/Refunds window appears.

③ Click here to select a Customer:Job.

- You can click here to select a different credit memo form.

- You can click ▥ to change the date.

- You can click here to change the credit memo number.

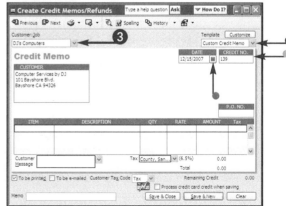

178

④ Click here to select an item.

　QuickBooks fills in the description and rate.

⑤ Type a quantity.

⑥ Repeat steps 4 to 5 for additional items.

⑦ Click Save & Close.

　The credit memo is created.

Create a Refund Check

① Complete steps 1 to 6 in the subsection "Create a Credit Memo."

② Click the Use Credit to button (⊞).

③ Click Give refund.

　The Issue a Refund window appears.

④ Confirm the information in the window.

● To print the check, select the To be printed option (☐ changes to ☑).

⑤ Click OK to save the check.

⑥ Click Save & Close.

　QuickBooks creates the credit memo and applies the refund check to it.

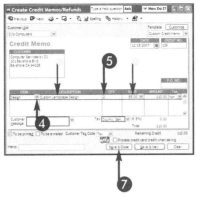

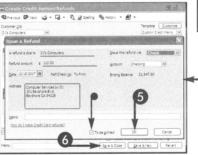

PART III

What should I do if a customer overpays me and wants a refund?

▼ When you record the payment, QuickBooks automatically creates a credit for the customer, as shown on the A/R Aging Detail report. To issue the refund check and match it to the credit, in the Banking menu, click Write Checks. In the Write Checks window, click the Pay to the order ☑ to select the customer. Type the amount of the refund check. On the Expenses tab, select Accounts Receivable in the Account column. Select the customer's name in the Customer:Job column. Save the transaction.

What should I do if the customer does not want a refund check, but instead wants me to apply the overpayment to the next invoice?

▼ Record a credit memo as described in the subsection "Create a Credit Memo." Then, after you record the next invoice, you see both a positive and a negative amount on the customer's A/R Aging Detail report. At that point, click Customers and then Receive Payments. Select the customer and highlight the invoice to which you want to apply the credit. Click the Set Credits button. QuickBooks applies the credit to the invoice and cleans up the A/R Aging Detail report.

Print Invoices in Batch

I n your business, you may find it most efficient to print all invoices at the same time — in a batch — instead of printing them as you create them. This approach works particularly well if you take orders over the phone; toward the end of the day, you can print the day's invoices and mail them.

To print a batch of invoices, you need to make sure that you select the To be printed option as you create your invoices. QuickBooks marks these invoices for printing and displays them as available for printing when you print the batch.

After QuickBooks finishes printing a batch of invoices, you have the opportunity to identify the first invoice that did not print correctly, perhaps because the paper jammed in the printer. If necessary, supply the number of the first invoice that did not print correctly, and QuickBooks does not mark that invoice and the ones that follow as printed, enabling you to reprint the batch. If all invoices print correctly and you do not supply an invoice number, QuickBooks marks the invoices as printed so that they do not appear again when you print the next batch of invoices.

Print Invoices in Batch

① Click File.

② Click Print Forms.

③ Click Invoices.

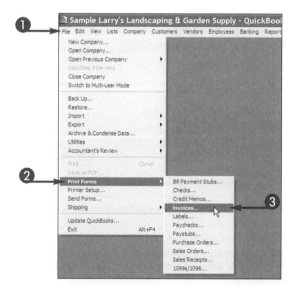

The Select Invoices to Print dialog box appears.

④ Click next to each invoice you want to print (☐ changes to ☑).

⑤ Click OK.

The Print Invoices dialog box appears.

● You can click here to select a different printer.

6 Click a form option (○ changes to ◉).

7 Type the number of copies you want to print of each invoice.

8 Click Print or Preview.

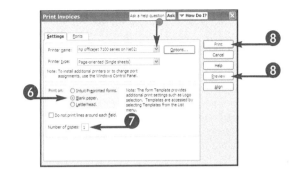

If you click Print, QuickBooks prints the invoices.

If you click Preview, QuickBooks displays the invoices on-screen.

● You can click here to enlarge the print and read the invoice.

9 Click Prev page or Next page to navigate between invoices.

10 Click Print.

QuickBooks prints the invoices.

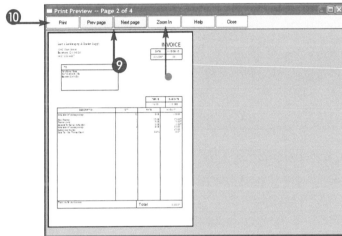

Is there a way that I can reprint an invoice after clicking OK when the message appears asking if any invoices printed incorrectly?

▼ You can reprint an invoice if you display it in the Create Invoices window. Use the Next page and Prev page buttons in the window, or see Chapter 18 for details on finding a transaction. Then, click the To be printed option again (□ changes to ☑).

What options appear on the Fonts tab?

▼ None, actually. For forms, all font settings appear on the form template, and, on this tab, QuickBooks refers you to the form template to change font settings. If you want to change the fonts for the title, company name, company address, item information, or the column, subtotal, or total labels, you must edit the form template. See Chapter 24 for details.

What happens if I click the "Do not print lines around each field" option in the Print Invoice dialog box?

▼ The lines that separate the fields on the form shown in this section do not appear if you click this option. You should click this option (□ changes to ☑) if you select Intuit Preprinted forms as the type of form you are using. The lines make the invoice easier to read, however, if you print invoices on blank paper or letterhead.

Assess Finance Charges

Y ou may find it necessary to charge a late fee called a finance charge when customers do not pay on time. If your customers pay slowly for goods or services you already provided, you may not have the cash you need to purchase inventory or pay your operating expenses.

QuickBooks enables you to specify an annual percentage to charge that QuickBooks calculates on the unpaid balance. QuickBooks also lets you specify a grace period before charging a finance charge. You can calculate finance charge amounts for the unpaid balance from the due date or from

the invoice date. You also can specify a minimum finance charge amount; if the calculated percentage finance charge is less than the minimum finance charge amount, QuickBooks charges the minimum amount. And, while you can impose finance charges on past-due finance charge assessments, this practice is not legal in all states, so check with your accountant before you enable this feature.

You can assess finance charges as you create statements or separately. See the section "Create Customer Statements" for details on assessing finance charges as you create statements.

Assess Finance Charges

① Click Customers.

② Click Assess Finance Charges.

The Assess Finance Charges window appears.

③ Click here to select a date for the finance charge.

④ Click next to each customer for whom you want to assess finance charges (☐ changes to ☑).

● You can change the amount of the finance charge by typing here.

⑤ Click Settings.

The Company Preferences tab for Finance Charges appears.

● You can change the finance charge rate here.

● You can change the minimum finance charge or grace period.

⑥ Click an option to determine the date from which QuickBooks calculates finance charges (○ changes to ⊙).

⑦ Click OK.

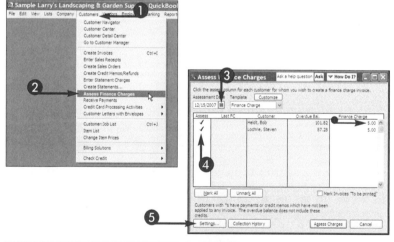

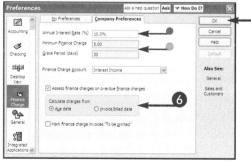

The Assess Finance Charges window reappears.

8 Click a customer (☐ changes to ☑).

9 Click Collection History.

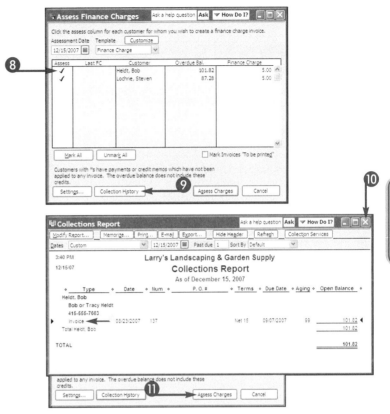

The Collections Report for the selected customer appears.

- You can double-click a transaction to view it in the window where it was created.

10 Click the Close button (☒) to redisplay the Assess Finance Charges window.

11 Click Assess Charges.

QuickBooks assigns the charges to the customers.

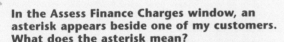

In the Assess Finance Charges window, an asterisk appears beside one of my customers. What does the asterisk mean?

▼ An asterisk (*) beside one or more customers indicates that the customer has unapplied credits. When the customer's credits are not applied, the customer's invoices appear to be unpaid, even though they may actually be paid in full. Because you do not want to accidentally assess finance charges for customers who may not owe you money, close the Assess Finance Charges window without assessing charges. Then, open the Receive Payments window, select the customer, select an open invoice, and click the Set Credits button. QuickBooks adjusts the customer's balance. After you apply all credits, you can perform the steps in this section.

Does QuickBooks permit me to assess finance charges more than once on the same day?

▼ Yes, but QuickBooks first warns you if you have already assessed finance charges today. You can, however, assess them again.

What does the Mark Invoices "To be printed" option on the Preferences dialog box do?

▼ If you click this option (☐ changes to ☑), QuickBooks creates invoices containing only the finance charges that you can print and send to customers. If you intend to send statements as described in the section "Create Customer Statements," do not click this option; QuickBooks includes the finance charge on the statement.

Create Customer Statements

If you issue many invoices to customers, you may find it useful to periodically send a statement; a statement lists all the invoices issued during the specified statement period. Most businesses send statements monthly to recap the invoice activity during the preceding month.

For companies that primarily provide services instead of selling inventory; statement charges may be a more effective way of tracking the work you perform, and you can print statements to provide your customers with a list of statement charges you enter. You enter statement charges each time you provide a service for a customer, and then, monthly or on some other regular basis, print a statement to summarize your work and present it to your customer as a bill for services rendered. For details on entering statement charges, see the section "Statement Charges: Another Way to Invoice." Note that you can use statement charges and statements in lieu of invoices if your company sells inventory; most companies that sell inventory find invoices more practical than statement charges.

When you print statements, you assign a date to the statement and then specify a time frame — a set of dates — for the statement. You also can select customers by name, by type, or by the preferred send method.

Create Customer Statements

1 Click Customers.

2 Click Create Statements.

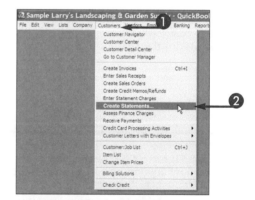

The Create Statements window appears.

3 Click ▦ to select a statement date.

4 Click ▦ to select the period the statement covers.

5 Click these options to select customers (○ changes to ◉).

● To view the customers for whom QuickBooks will print statements, click View Selected Customers.

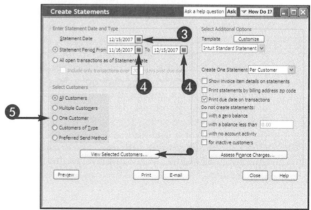

- You can click here to select a statement form.

6 Click here to select whether to create statements per customer or per job.

7 Click this option to print details from invoices on statements (☐ changes to ☑).

8 Click this option to print statements sorted in ZIP code order (☐ changes to ☑).

9 Click this option to include invoice due dates (☐ changes to ☑).

10 Click Print or Preview.

If you click Print, QuickBooks prints the statements; otherwise, statements appear on-screen.

- You can click here to enlarge the print and read the statement.

11 Click Prev page or Next page to navigate between statements.

12 Click Print.

QuickBooks prints the statements and asks if they printed properly.

13 Click Yes or No.

If you click Yes, QuickBooks sets the beginning date for the next set of statements to the day after the ending date of the statements you just printed.

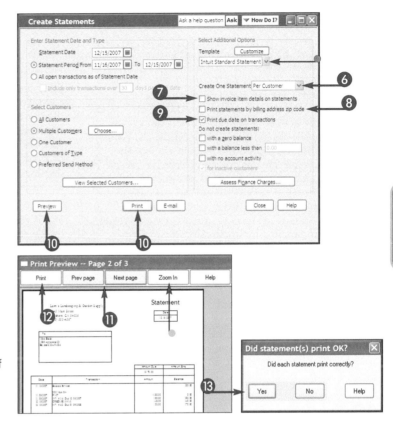

What happens if I click the Preferred Send Method option when I select customers?

▼ When you click this option (○ changes to ⊙), QuickBooks displays a list box from which you can select e-mail, mail, or none. You may want to create statements for all customers to whom you e-mail statements in one batch and then create statements for customers to whom you mail statements in a second batch. QuickBooks uses the information stored in the setting of each customer's information on the Additional Info tab of the Edit Customer dialog box to select customers. To see the list of customers selected, click View Selected Customers.

Why do I not see the options to avoid printing statements for customers who meet certain criteria?

▼ These options are available only in QuickBooks Premier or QuickBooks Enterprise.

Can I print a statement that shows only unpaid invoices?

▼ Some people feel that showing all activity is confusing, particularly if some of the activity is paid and some is unpaid. You can print a statement that shows only unpaid invoices as of the date of the statement if you click the "All open transactions as of Statement Date" option (○ changes to ⊙).

Create a Job Estimate

I f your business requires that you produce a description of proposed work or products you intend to sell before actually selling them, you can create estimates in QuickBooks to handle these proposals. When you create an estimate, you do not actually update the account or item values in your company because no accounting transactions have occurred. If a customer accepts your estimate, you can convert the estimate to an invoice in a couple of different ways; see the sections "Convert an Estimate to an Invoice" and "Create a Progress Invoice" for more details.

Estimates can be very lengthy documents, and the work can take a long time to complete, depending on the nature of your business. Often, businesses that use estimates agree with their customers to invoice for part of the job at specified periods of time. This partial invoicing is called *progress invoicing*, and if you intend to progress invoice, consider creating your estimates in sections with subtotals at the breaking points.

You can create more than one estimate for a particular job, and if you make relatively the same bids over and over, you may want to use the memorize feature to record an estimate so that the estimate is easier to create later.

Create a Job Estimate

① Click Customers.

② Click Create Estimates.

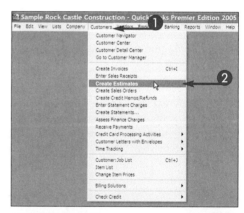

The Create Estimates window appears.

③ Click here and select a Customer:Job.

④ Click here to make the estimate inactive (☑ changes to ☐).

⑤ Click here to select a different estimate form.

⑥ Click the calendar button (▦) to select a date for the estimate.

⑦ Click here to change the estimate number.

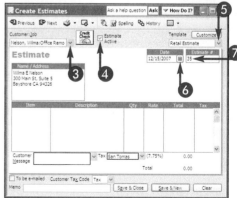

8 Click here to select an item.

- QuickBooks fills in the description and rate.

9 Type a quantity.

- You can type a markup percentage or amount for the line here.

10 Repeat steps 8 to 9 for additional items.

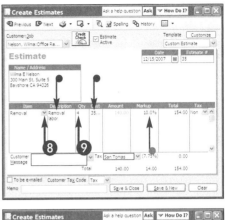

11 Click here to select a customer message.

- You can change the sales tax authority here.

  You can e-mail the estimate as part of a batch by clicking the To be e-mailed option (☐ changes to ☑).

- You can click here to change the customer tax code.

- You can type a memo here.

12 Click Save & Close.

QuickBooks saves the estimate and closes the window.

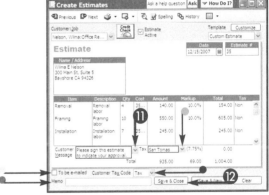

How do I memorize an estimate?

▼ Fill out the estimate using the steps in this section, but do not save the estimate. Instead, after step 11, click Edit and then click Memorize Estimate. QuickBooks removes the Customer:Job for the estimate so that you can use it for any Customer:Job. When you are ready to use the memorized estimate, double-click it in the Memorized Transaction List. For details on memorizing a transaction and using a memorized transaction, see Chapter 18.

Can I create a change order in QuickBooks?

▼ Only if you are using the Contractor's Edition of QuickBooks. Users of other versions can make changes to estimates, but they cannot track change orders. If you plan to make a change to an estimate, display the estimate in the Create Estimates window, print it, and then make changes. Your printed copy is the only record of the original estimate.

How do I make sure that the markup information does not appear on the customer's copy of the estimate?

▼ By default, QuickBooks does not print the markup when you print the estimate. If you want the customer to see the markup, you need to customize the estimate form and select the markup column for printing. See Chapter 24 for details on customizing a form.

Convert an Estimate
to an Invoice

Y ou can convert any estimate you create in QuickBooks to an invoice. Converting an estimate to an invoice saves you time and work and helps ensure accuracy because you do not need to enter the data twice.

You can convert an estimate to an invoice, a sales order, or a purchase order. You convert an estimate to an invoice when you want to prepare an invoice for a customer. You convert an estimate to a sales order when a customer accepts the estimate, but you do not have everything in

stock. You convert an estimate to a purchase order when a customer accepts the estimate and you need to order items to fulfill the estimate.

When you convert an estimate to an invoice, you can convert all or only part of the estimate. If you choose to convert only part of an estimate, you can specify a percentage of the estimate to invoice, or you can create a progress invoice by selecting specific items and their quantities for the invoice. This section shows you how to convert the entire estimate to an invoice. To create a progress invoice, see the section "Create a Progress Invoice."

Convert an Estimate to an Invoice

① Click Customers.

② Click Create Estimates.

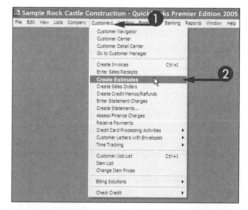

The Create Estimates window appears.

③ Click Previous to display the estimate you want to convert.

④ Click here.

⑤ Click Invoice.

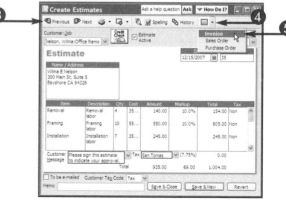

The Create Progress Invoice Based On Estimate box appears.

Note: This box appears only if you selected Progress Invoicing in the Preferences dialog box. See Chapter 5 for details.

6 Click an option to include estimates on your invoice (○ changes to ◉).

- You can create an invoice for a percentage of the estimate if you click the "Create invoice for a percentage of the entire estimate" option and type the percentage.

Note: For details on the last option, see the seciton "Create a Progress Invoice."

7 Click OK.

QuickBooks closes the Create Estimates window and opens the Create Invoices window, showing an invoice for all or just a percentage of the estimate.

- You can print the invoice immediately by clicking the Print button ( ).

- You can mark the invoice and print it later in a batch by clicking the To be printed option (☐ changes to ☑).

8 Click Save & Close.

QuickBooks saves the invoice.

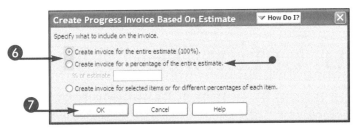

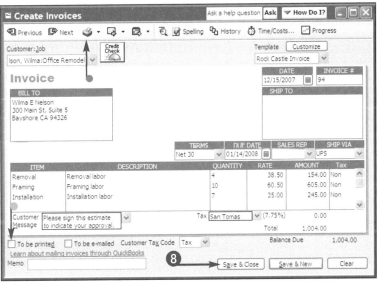

Is there an easy way to find the estimate?

▼ Instead of performing steps 1 to 3, see Chapter 18 for steps to find a transaction, and then double-click the transaction in the Find window; QuickBooks opens the transaction in the Create Estimates window. Then begin with step 4 of "Convert an Estimate to an Invoice."

Do I do anything differently if I create a sales order or purchase order from an estimate?

▼ When you create a purchase order, you choose to create a purchase order for all items or selected items on the estimate. You make no special selections when creating a sales order; QuickBooks simply displays a message, telling you that it has copied the estimate to a sales order. QuickBooks then displays the sales order.

Can I invoice for more than the amount shown on the estimate?

▼ Yes, you can. When you click OK in step 7 in this section, QuickBooks creates the invoice; you can change any amount on this newly created invoice. Note that, if you invoice for more than the amount shown on the estimate, the Transaction History will indicate that the estimate has been billed for more than 100%. To avoid confusion, you may want to edit the estimate or create an additional estimate.

Duplicate an Estimate

I n businesses that use estimates, the work performed is often the same or very close to the same from one customer to another. If you create the perfect estimate for one customer, and another customer comes along needing very similar or the same work performed, you can duplicate the estimate in QuickBooks to use it for the new customer, saving yourself the work of recreating it. You may also want to create several estimates for the same customer, where the estimates are very close but not exactly the same; again, duplicating the original estimate and then modifying the duplicate to differentiate the estimates saves you time and keystrokes.

When duplicating an estimate, QuickBooks makes an exact copy of the estimate, with one exception: The estimate number changes, which initially may be your only visual clue that the duplicated estimate is not the same as the original estimate.

After you duplicate an estimate, you can make changes on the duplicate as appropriate. You do not need to change the customer:job unless you duplicated the estimate to use for a different customer:job than the one listed on the original estimate.

Duplicate an Estimate

① Click Customers.

② Click Create Estimates.

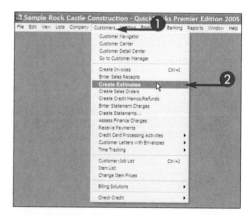

The Create Estimates window appears.

③ Click Previous to display the estimate you want to convert.

● The estimate appears in the window.

④ Click Edit.

⑤ Click Duplicate Estimate.

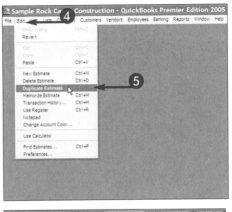

● QuickBooks creates a new estimate exactly like the original except for the estimate number.

⑥ Click Save & Close.

QuickBooks saves the estimate.

What does the Estimate Active option in the Create Estimates window do?

▼ By default, QuickBooks marks all estimates active. After a customer accepts an estimate, if you have created other estimates for the same customer and job, you may want to mark those estimates inactive by deselecting the Estimate Active option (☑ changes to ☐). When you mark an estimate inactive, QuickBooks keeps a record of the estimate but does not use the estimate numbers in reports.

When should I memorize an estimate and when should I duplicate an estimate?

▼ Memorize an estimate when you include the same information again and again for many different customers. Duplicate an estimate when you have already created an estimate, and another job comes along that is so similar to the first that you can simply make a few changes to the duplicate for it to suit your needs. For more information on memorizing an estimate, see the section "Create a Job Estimate."

Must I accept the estimate number QuickBooks assigns?

▼ No, you can change the estimate number by replacing the existing number in the Estimate # box. If you set your Job & Estimate preferences to have QuickBooks warn you about duplicate estimate numbers and you type a number you have already used, QuickBooks permits you to use the number. However, QuickBooks warns you that you have used the number before and gives you the option to change the number.

Create a Progress Invoice

Y ou can create a progress invoice if you are using QuickBooks Pro, QuickBooks Premier, or QuickBooks Enterprise. You create a progress invoice when you need to invoice a customer for part of a job; many companies have agreements with their customers to present an invoice for a portion of a job even though the job is not yet complete. The agreement may be to invoice for a percentage of the job or for specific portions of the job that are complete.

If you know that you will create progress invoices, try to create estimates that contain subtotals for each portion of the job that you intend to invoice separately, because creating the progress invoice from a section of an estimate is easier.

The section "Convert an Estimate to an Invoice" showed how to convert an entire estimate into an invoice. This section shows how to convert only portions of an estimate to an invoice. You transfer lines of the estimate and indicate either the quantity or the estimated percentage completed for the line.

Create a Progress Invoice

① Click Customers.

② Click Create Invoices.

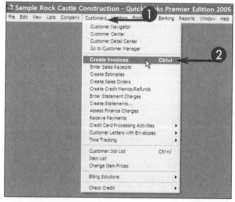

The Create Invoices window appears.

③ Click here and select a Customer:Job.

The Available Estimates window appears.

④ Click the estimate you want to use to create a progress invoice.

⑤ Click OK.

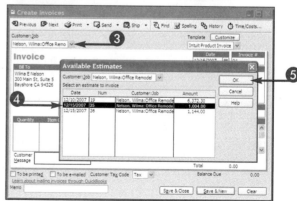

The Create Progress Invoice Based On Estimate dialog box appears.

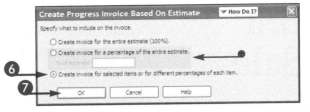

6 Click the "Create invoice for selected items or for different percentages of each item" option (○ changes to ◉).

● You can create a progress invoice based on a percentage of the entire invoice by clicking here and supplying a percentage.

7 Click OK.

The Specify Invoice Amounts for Items on Estimate dialog box appears.

8 Click a line.

9 Type the quantity for which you want to bill.

● You can type an estimated percent complete here.

● The billing amount appears here.

10 Repeat steps 8 to 9 as needed.

11 Click OK.

The lines and amounts you selected appear on the invoice.

You can print the invoice, or click To be printed to print it later.

12 Click Save & Close.

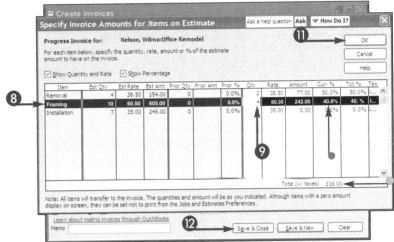

PART III

Can I delete lines that I do not want to bill yet from the invoice?

▼ You should *not* delete $0 amount lines from the invoice. Instead, click Edit and then click Preferences. In the Preferences dialog box that appears, click the Jobs & Estimates icon, and then make sure that you select the "Don't print items that have zero amount" option (☐ changes to ☑). The line appears on the invoice on-screen, but it does not print.

What do the Show Quantity and Rate and the Show Percentage options (☐ changes to ☑) do?

▼ They make visible the Qty, Rate, Curr %, and Tot % columns so that you can specify completion using either quantities or percentages. If you deselect both of these options (☑ changes to ☐), you can specify completion only as a dollar amount per line of the estimate.

When I follow steps 1 to 5, the Create Progress Invoice Based On Estimate dialog box does not appear. What have I done wrong?

▼ You did not turn on the preference to prepare progress invoices. Click Edit and then click Preferences. In the Preferences dialog box that appears, click Jobs & Estimates, and then click the Company Preferences tab. Click Yes in the Do You Do Progress Invoicing section (○ changes to ◉) and click OK. Then retry steps 1 to 5.

Record a Cash Sale

Acustomer may make a purchase and pay for the items immediately. To record this transaction, enter a Sales Receipt. The method the customer uses to pay is not particularly important; the important fact is that the customer pays for the merchandise at the time of sale and does not owe you any money.

When you record a sales receipt, you select a method to record the cash receipt; you can have QuickBooks deposit the money directly to an account, or you can group cash receipts into an account called Undeposited Funds. The Undeposited Funds account is an other current asset account that QuickBooks adds to your Chart of Accounts the first time you record a payment from a sales receipt or invoice; you can think of the Undeposited Funds account as a suspense account where QuickBooks holds your money until you decide the account to which you want to deposit it. The Undeposited Funds account is useful because you can use it to make your deposits match your bank statement, which makes bank statement reconciliation much easier.

Using the QuickBooks Merchant Account Service, a fee-based service, you can process and record credit card sales while creating a sales receipt.

Record a Cash Sale

① Click Customers.

② Click Enter Sales Receipts.

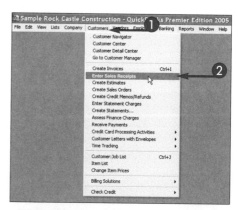

The Enter Sales Receipts window appears.

③ Click here to select a Customer:Job.

You can record noncustomer cash sales to a customer called Cash Sale or leave the Customer:Job field blank.

④ Click here to select a different sales receipt form.

⑤ Click here to select a date for the sale.

● You can click here to change the sales receipt number.

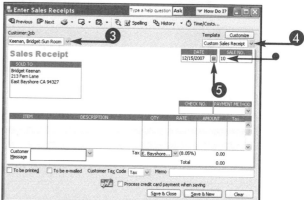

6 Click here to select an item.

- QuickBooks fills in the description and rate.

7 Type a quantity.

- QuickBooks fills in the amount.

8 Repeat steps 7 to 8 for additional items.

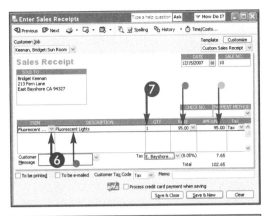

9 Click here to select a customer message.

You can click here to change the sales tax authority and the customer tax code.

- You can type a memo here.

10 Click Save & Close.

QuickBooks saves the cash receipt and closes the window.

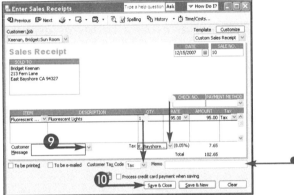

How do I handle cash sales from one-time customers?

▼ In retail shops where customers walk in and make a purchase and may never return, you have no need to track any information about the customer; instead, you need to track the merchandise bought and the money received. To handle these situations, set up a customer called Cash Sale in the Customer:Job list and assign all casual customer sales to the Cash Sale customer.

When should I use a Sales Receipt and when should I use an invoice?

▼ Use a Sales Receipt when you receive payment in full for the service or merchandise at the time of purchase. Use an invoice when the customer does not pay at the time of purchasing the merchandise or receiving the service because the invoice in QuickBooks creates the receivable that you can track.

How can I use Undeposited Funds to make deposits match the bank statement?

▼ If you record cash receipts directly to a bank account, QuickBooks lists each individual check as a bank deposit. However, you typically do not deposit each check individually; instead, you create a deposit ticket that sums the checks. QuickBooks uses the Undeposited Funds account to enable you to accumulate checks and then select the ones that you intend to group on a deposit ticket. See the section "Make Bank Deposits" for details.

Receive a Payment

When a customer sends you a payment for an invoice you issued, you need to record it in QuickBooks to update your cash account and reduce the customer's debt to you. You record payments for invoices using the Receive Payments window.

When you select a customer, QuickBooks automatically displays all unpaid invoices for that customer. You select a payment method — cash, check, or a credit card — along with a payment date and amount. If the customer pays by credit card, you supply the credit card number and expiration date. If the customer pays by check, you can type a check number. The payment method plays a role in

making bank deposits that will match your bank statement and make bank account reconciliation easier. For more on bank reconciliation, see Chapter 17.

When you enter an amount, QuickBooks automatically applies the amount to the oldest open invoice. If the amount paid is greater than the invoice amount, QuickBooks applies the remainder to the next oldest invoice, repeating this process until the entire payment amount is accounted for. However, if an open invoice exists for the exact amount of the payment, QuickBooks applies the payment to that invoice, even if it is not the oldest. If a customer overpays, QuickBooks automatically creates a credit.

Receive a Payment

① Click Customers.

② Click Receive Payments.

   The Receive Payments window appears.

③ Click here to select a Customer:Job.

④ Click here to select a payment method.

   ● If the payment method is a credit card, type the card number and expiration date in the spaces provided.

⑤ Click the calendar button (📅) to select a date for the payment.

   ● You can type a check number here.

⑥ Type the amount of the payment.

   ● QuickBooks marks invoices paid and displays the paid portion of the invoice here; you can change the payment distribution by changing these numbers.

   ● QuickBooks displays under- and over-payment amounts here.

⑦ Click an option (○ changes to ◉) to handle under- or over-payments.

   ● Available discount or credit information appears here.

⑧ Click Discount & Credits.

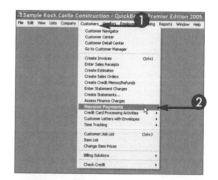

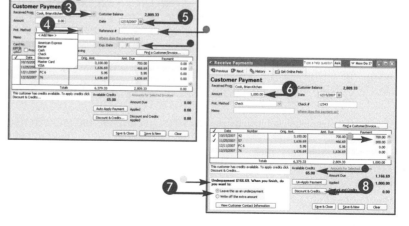

The Discount and Credits dialog box appears.

9 Click beside any credits or discounts you want to apply (☐ changes to ☑).

● QuickBooks updates the Balance Due information.

10 Click Done.

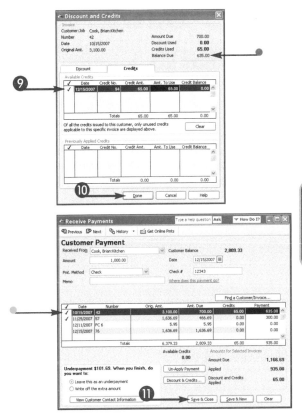

● The Receive Payments window reappears.

QuickBooks updates the Amt. Due, Credits, and Payment lines of the oldest invoice.

11 Click Save & Close.

QuickBooks saves the payment and closes the window.

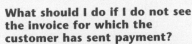

What should I do if I do not see the invoice for which the customer has sent payment?

▼ The chances are good that you have set up more than one job for the customer and the invoice belongs to a different job than the one you selected. To see all outstanding invoices for the customer, select the customer instead of the Customer:Job. You can then create the payment as described in this section.

What should I do if my customer overpays?

▼ Record the entire payment amount; notice that QuickBooks marks all available invoices paid and lists the overpayment amount as an unused payment. You can click Print Credit Memo to print a credit memo that you can send to the customer. Then, save the payment; when you save, QuickBooks indicates that it will create a credit memo for the overpayment amount.

Can I pick a particular invoice to pay if I do not want to pay off the oldest open invoice?

▼ Yes. Remove the check mark (☑) beside the oldest open invoice and click the invoice you want to pay.

What does the Go To button do?

▼ When you highlight an invoice and click Go To QuickBooks displays the invoice you highlighted.

Make Bank Deposits

W hen you receive cash or checks from customers, you record sales receipts or payments in QuickBooks and then you deposit them in the bank. Using the bank deposit feature in QuickBooks, you can group the cash or checks in QuickBooks to match the deposits that your bank records on your bank statement, making the bank statement reconciliation process much easier.

When you record your cash receipts and payments into the Undeposited Funds account, QuickBooks lets you select the QuickBooks transactions that you intend to group on your

bank deposit slip. Because credit card financial institutions summarize your transactions into daily amounts that appear on your bank statement, you also can use the bank deposit feature in QuickBooks to group your credit card transactions for each day. Again, this grouping helps make it easy to reconcile your bank statement. For details on reconciling a bank statement, see Chapter 17.

When you record a bank deposit, you can select the transactions to include in the deposit by payment type, and you can add other payments that did not come from customers to the deposit. You also can receive cash back from the deposit.

Make Bank Deposits

① Click Banking.

② Click Make Deposits.

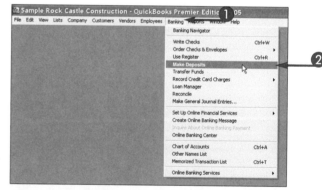

The Payments to Deposit window appears. Behind it, the Make Deposits window appears.

③ Click here to select the types of payments you want to deposit.

Note: If you click Selected types, QuickBooks displays a window where you can select multiple types of payments.

④ Click next to each payment you want to include in the deposit (☐ changes to ☑).

● QuickBooks displays the subtotal for the deposit here.

⑤ Click OK.

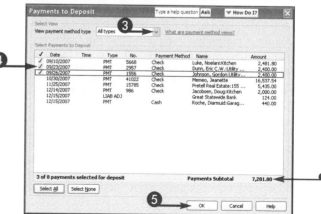

The Make Deposits window appears.

6 Click here to select the account into which you are depositing.

7 Click 🔲 to select the deposit date.

● You can type a memo here.

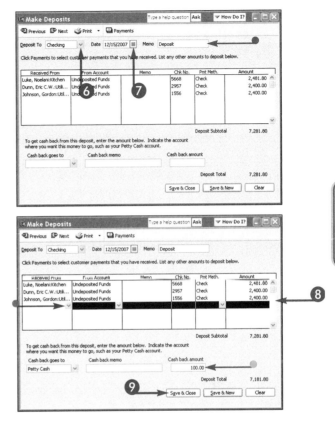

8 Review the list of payments to be deposited.

● You can click here to enter additional deposit amounts.

You can type an amount of cash you want back from the deposit here; you must also type an account.

9 Click Save & Close.

QuickBooks moves the deposit amount from the Undeposited Funds account to the account you selected.

Can I print a deposit ticket that my bank will use or must I hand-write the deposit ticket?

▼ Yes. You can print a deposit slip that your bank will accept as long as the deposit you create contains transactions with a Payment Method of cash, checks, or a combination of cash and checks. Click the Print button (🖨 ▾) in the Make Deposits window and then click Print. QuickBooks offers you the option of printing a deposit slip and summary or just a deposit summary. After you make a selection, click OK. QuickBooks saves the bank deposit and prints your selection.

Do I need to order special forms for bank deposits?

▼ The deposit slip QuickBooks prints is designed for a special form. For ordering information, click 🖨 ▾ on the Make Deposits window and then click Order Deposit Slips.

Can I change the deposits I selected after I click OK on the Payments to Deposit window and while I am viewing the Make Deposits window?

▼ Yes. Click the Payments button in the Make Deposits window. QuickBooks redisplays the Payments to Deposit window, where you can change your selection. Then, continue with steps 5 to 9.

Write Collection Letters

You may find it necessary to send letters to customers who do not pay in a timely fashion in an attempt to collect the money owed to you. Writing collection letters is a difficult task, but QuickBooks makes it easier. QuickBooks comes with a variety of prewritten collection letters that suit most occasions, and the Write Letters feature makes sending the right letter to the right customer easy. To use this feature, you must also be using Microsoft Word 97 or later.

You can make temporary changes to a letter in Microsoft Word after you create it by simply editing the document; QuickBooks supplies a special version of the Merge toolbar to help you. If you are using QuickBooks Pro, QuickBooks Premier, or QuickBooks Enterprise, you can make permanent changes to a letter to better suit your business's needs or add a letter that does not come with QuickBooks.

As you walk through the wizard, you identify the customers you want to consider for a collection letter and select the specific letter you want to use. The wizard also gives you the opportunity to modify the selected list of recipients.

Write Collection Letters

① Click Company.

② Click Prepare Letters with Envelopes.

③ Click Collection Letters.

The Letters and Envelopes Wizard begins, displaying the Choose the Recipients screen.

④ Click the Active, Inactive, or Both option (○ changes to ◉).

⑤ Click an option to create letters for each customer or each job (○ changes to ◉).

⑥ Click an option for number of days past due (○ changes to ◉).

⑦ Click Next.

The Review and Edit Recipients screen appears.

⑧ Click next to the names of customers to whom you do not want to write (☐ changes to ☑).

● You can click an option to sort the list by customer or by amount overdue (○ changes to ◉).

⑨ Click Next.

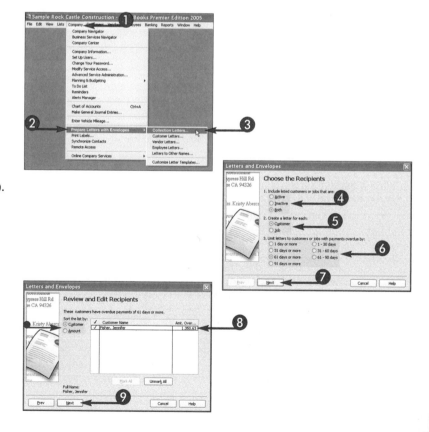

The Choose a Letter Template screen appears.

⑩ Select a letter.

⑪ Click Next.

The Enter a Name and Title screen appears.

⑫ Type the name that will appear as a signature.

⑬ Type the signatory's title.

⑭ Click Next.

Note: *If appropriate, the Information Needed for Letters Is Missing dialog box appears; click OK to continue.*

The letter(s) appears in Microsoft Word.

● If necessary, supply missing information or use the QuickBooks toolbar to edit the letter.

⑮ Click the Print button (🖨).

⑯ Click the Close button (❌) to close Word and return to QuickBooks.

Note: *A window appears that explains how to print envelopes for the letters from QuickBooks.*

⑰ Follow the on-screen instructions if you want to print envelopes.

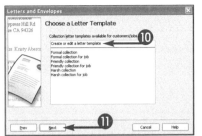

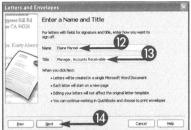

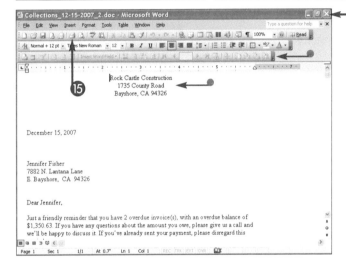

PART III

What do I need to do to print envelopes for the letters?

▼ In the screen that appears after step 16, click Next. QuickBooks displays the Envelope Options dialog box. Select an enveloped size and, if you are using preprinted envelopes, unselect the Print return address option (☐ changes to ☑). You can add a delivery point bar code to the envelopes for letters mailed to addresses in the United States; click the Delivery Point Barcode option (☐ changes to ☑). Click OK, and Word reopens, displaying the Envelope Options dialog box. Place envelopes in the printer and click OK, and Word prints the envelopes, closes, and QuickBooks reappears. Click Finish to close the wizard.

Does supplying missing information in the collection letter in Word update my QuickBooks file with that information?

▼ No. To permanently fix the problem, edit the customers's record in QuickBooks and supply the missing information there.

How can I save an electronic copy of the modified collection letter?

▼ In Microsoft Word, after you make changes, click File and then click Save As and type a new name for the letter.

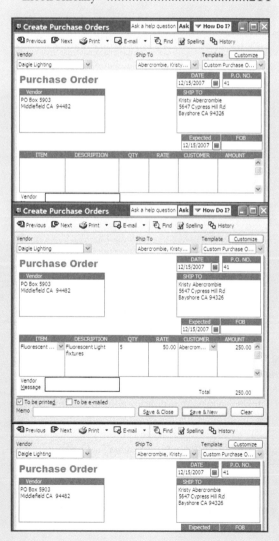

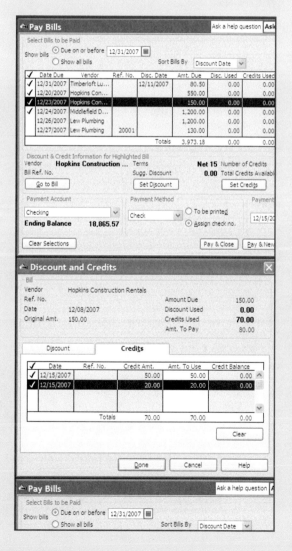

16 — Track Items

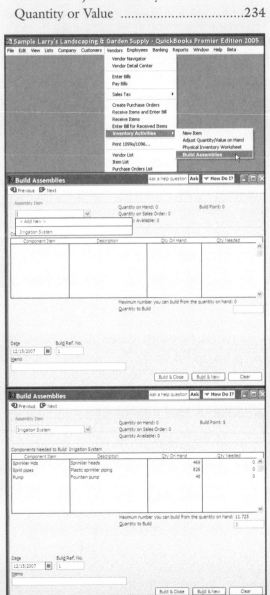

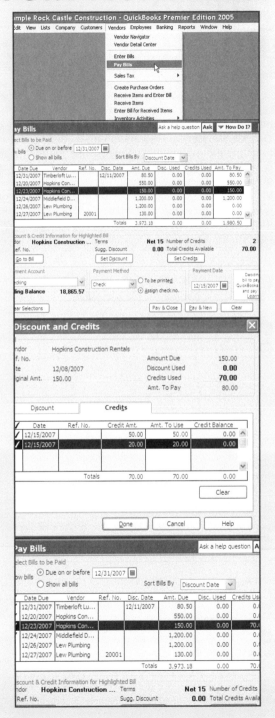

Create Purchase Orders

Y ou can use purchase orders to tell vendors what goods you want to order. Using purchase orders helps you track goods on order before the vendor bills you; when you receive goods against a purchase order, QuickBooks uses the information from your purchase order to create a bill, a check, or a credit card charge for the vendor. You do not need to use purchase orders to order goods from a vendor, but using purchase orders makes tracking items on order easier. You also can use a purchase order to create a drop shipment — that is, order goods from a vendor and have the goods shipped directly to a customer.

To use purchase orders, you must enable them; see Chapter 6 for details on setting preferences in QuickBooks to enable purchase orders.

Purchase orders contain a vendor message box that prints when you print the purchase order form, and a memo that does not print. You can print purchase orders as you create them or in a batch. See Chapter 11 for details on printing in a batch.

Create Purchase Orders

❶ Click Vendors.

❷ Click Create Purchase Orders.

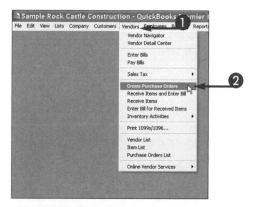

The Create Purchase Orders window appears.

❸ Click here to select a vendor; QuickBooks fills in the vendor's address.

● You can click here to select a drop-ship customer.

● You can click here to select a template.

❹ Click the calendar button (▣) to change the expected date.

● You can click here to type an FOB location.

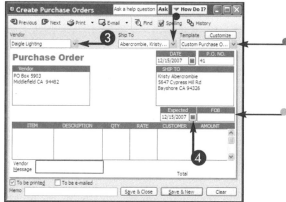

5 Click here to select an item.

QuickBooks fills in the description and rate.

6 Type a quantity.

● QuickBooks calculates the line amount.

7 Click here to assign the line to a customer.

If you selected a customer in step 3, QuickBooks fills in the customer name.

8 Repeat steps 5 to 7 for additional items.

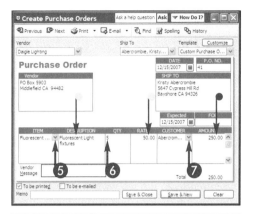

● You can type a message to the vendor here.

● You can click this option to mark the purchase order for batch printing (☐ changes to ☑).

You can click this option to mark the purchase order for e-mailing (☐ changes to ☑).

● You can type a memo here.

9 Click Save & Close.

QuickBooks creates the purchase order.

What does FOB mean?

▼ FOB stands for *Free On Board* and, in accounting terms, refers to the terms between you and a vendor concerning shipping costs and when you, the buyer, assume ownership of the goods. When a vendor ships an item and does not charge the buyer for the shipping, the item is *free on board* the shipping carrier. You can use the FOB field to indicate to your vendor how you want to handle shipping charges by entering a location where shipping charges begin. If you expect to pay shipping, type the vendor's location in the FOB field. However, if you expect the vendor to pay the shipping, type the final destination of the goods in the FOB field.

What is the expected date?

▼ Enter the date you expect the merchandise you are ordering to be delivered. The date you enter here appears on the Inventory Stock Status reports to help you track the delivery of merchandise.

Is there a way to identify both what items I have on hand and what items I ordered on purchase orders?

▼ You can print the Inventory Stock Status by Item report or the Inventory Stock Status by Vendor report; both reports show both the quantity on hand and the quantity on purchase orders. For details on printing these reports, see Chapters 22 and 23.

Enter Bills

When you receive a bill from a vendor, you can enter it into QuickBooks to track it and pay it on time. In this section, you see how to record a bill for both an expense, such as a telephone bill, and for inventory items, using the Enter Bills window. When you use the Enter Bills window for a purchase that involves inventory items, you record both the bill, which updates accounts payable, and the receipt of the items, which updates inventory. However, it is possible that you may receive the items separately from the bill; in this case, use the Create Item Receipts window, which looks like the Enter Bills window but only updates inventory quantities. If you entered a purchase order for the items, QuickBooks prompts you to select the purchase order when you select the vendor as you enter a bill or item receipt.

When you enter a bill or an item receipt, you can assign one or more lines of the document to a customer to create a reimbursable expense that you can bill back to a customer on an invoice. See Chapter 11 for details on invoicing reimbursable expenses.

Enter Bills

Record an Expense

1 Click Vendors.

2 Click Enter Bills.

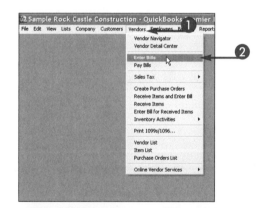

The Enter Bills window appears.

3 Click ▦ to select the bill date.

4 Click here to select a vendor.

- QuickBooks fills in the vendor terms and Bill Due date.

- You can type the vendor's bill number here.

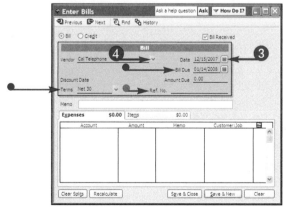

5 Click the Expenses tab.

6 Click here to select an account.

7 Type an amount to charge the account here.

● You can type a memo here.

○ You can click here and assign the expense to a Customer:Job.

8 Repeat steps 6 to 7 to assign the bill to additional accounts.

● QuickBooks fills in the amount of the bill.

9 Click Save & Close.

The expense is recorded.

Enter a Bill for Items

1 Perform steps 1 to 5 clicking the Items tab instead of the Expenses tab in step 5.

2 Click here to select an item.

QuickBooks fills in the description and cost.

3 Type a quantity.

QuickBooks calculates the line amount.

● You can click here to assign the line to a customer.

4 Repeat steps 2 to 3 for additional items.

○ QuickBooks fills in the amount of the bill.

5 Click Save & Close.

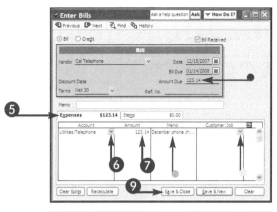

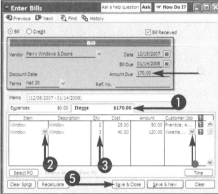

What does the Time button on the Items tab do?

▼ You can use it to pay the selected vendor for time recorded in QuickBooks; see Chapter 10 for details on entering time. When you click Time, QuickBooks enables you to select a time period. Then, QuickBooks fills in the time entered on the bill. If the Items tab does not appear in either the Enter Bills window or the Create Item Receipts window, you must enable inventory in QuickBooks. To enable inventory, see Chapter 6.

Do I need to enter separate bills for the same vendor if I purchase items and also need to record an expense?

▼ No. You can follow the steps in this section and enter information on both tabs of the window. The amount of the bill is the sum of the amounts on both tabs.

Can I assign a line of a bill to a customer and not create a reimbursable expense?

▼ Yes. Click the Reimbursable Expense icon (▦) that appears in the column next to the customer name; QuickBooks places an X through the icon and does not create the reimbursable expense.

How do I display the Create Item Receipts window?

▼ Click Vendors and then click Receive Items.

Handle Recurring Bills

I f you pay the same amount to the same vendor on some regular basis, you can use the Memorize feature to make QuickBooks "remember" the bill and help reduce the amount of time it takes you to meet repetitive obligations. For example, you always pay rent monthly and typically you pay the same amount each month to the same landlord. You also can memorize bills if the amount changes. For example, suppose that you own several buildings for which you must pay the electric bill, and the electric company sends you only one bill for all the buildings. When you enter the bill, you distribute each building's portion to that building's Electricity expense account. You can memorize a bill in QuickBooks even if the amount changes each month; for these types of transactions, memorize the bill for $0 and supply the amount at the time you enter the memorized bill.

QuickBooks records memorized transactions without affecting accounts and, when you enter a memorized transaction, QuickBooks affects accounts using the date you specify when you set up the transaction. Also, be aware that you can memorize other types of transactions; for example, if you invoice customers monthly for a service, you can memorize the invoice and then enter it using the steps in this section.

Handle Recurring Bills

Memorize a Bill

1 Perform the steps in the section "Enter Bills" to record a cost or to enter a bill for items but do not click Save & Close.

2 Click Edit.

3 Click Memorize Bill.

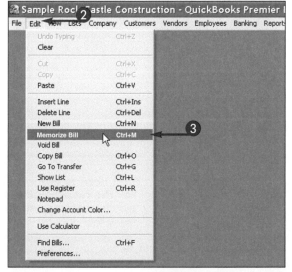

The Memorize Transaction dialog box appears.

4 Click the Remind Me option (○ changes to ◉).

5 Click here to select a frequency.

6 Click ▦ to select the next date for the transaction.

7 Click OK.

QuickBooks memorizes the transaction and redisplays the bill.

8 Click Save & Close.

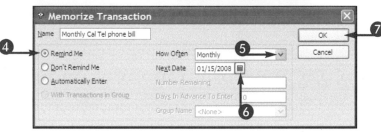

Enter a Memorized Transaction

1 Click Lists.

2 Click Memorized Transaction List.

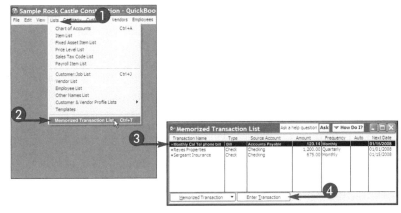

The Memorized Transaction List window appears.

3 Click the transaction you want to enter.

4 Click Enter Transaction.

● The transaction appears in the window where you created it.

5 Click Save & Close.

The transaction is recorded.

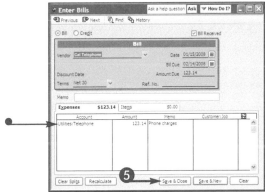

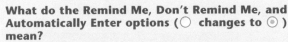

What do the Remind Me, Don't Remind Me, and Automatically Enter options (○ changes to ⊙) mean?

▼ If you choose Remind Me, QuickBooks displays a reminder on the date that you should enter the bill using Reminders; see Chapter 24 for more on Reminders. If you choose Don't Remind Me, you must remember to open the Memorized Transaction List and enter the bill. If you choose Automatically Enter, QuickBooks automatically enters the bill on the selected date and displays a message when you open QuickBooks on or after the scheduled date of the transaction telling you that QuickBooks has entered the transaction. You also set the Number Remaining and Days In Advance To Enter boxes to specify how many transactions to create.

Is there an easy way to pay a monthly bill that distributes amounts among accounts based on percentages?

▼ Yes. You can create a memorized bill that sums to a dollar — and enter the percentage for each line on the bill as a decimal to remind you of the percentage breakdown. For example, if you distribute the bill between three accounts, applying 70 percent to Account 1, 20 percent to Account 2, and 10 percent to Account 3, set up three lines on the memorized bill, assigning $.70 to Account 1, $.20 to Account 2, and $.10 to Account 3.

Create a Memorized Bill Group

I f you have several transactions that you enter weekly or monthly, and you typically enter them around the same time each week or month, you can create a memorized transaction group for these transactions so that you can enter all of them simultaneously instead of entering them one at a time.

You create a memorized transaction group from the Memorized Transaction List window; once a transaction group exists, you place memorized transactions in the group. The transactions in the group do not have to be the same type of transaction. For example, in one memorized

transaction group, you can place your rent bill, your electric bill, any number of memorized invoices to customers, and a memorized check that records an automatic debit from your checking account for insurance premiums.

When you create a memorized transaction group, you supply much of the same information that you supply when you create a memorized transaction; see the section "Handle Recurring Bills" for details on creating a memorized transaction. You then edit existing memorized transactions or create new memorized transactions to add them to the group.

Create a Memorized Bill Group

① Click Lists.

② Click Memorized Transaction List.

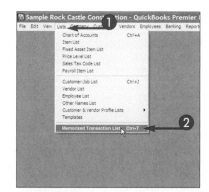

The Memorized Transaction List window appears.

③ Click Memorized Transaction.

④ Click New Group.

The New Memorized Transaction Group dialog box appears.

⑤ Type a name for the group.

⑥ Click the Remind Me option (○ changes to ◉).

⑦ Click here to select a frequency.

⑧ Click ▦ to select the next date for the transaction.

⑨ Click OK.

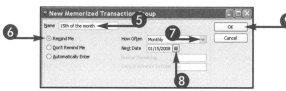

- The Memorized Transaction List window reappears containing the new group.

10 Click a transaction to include in the group.

11 Click Memorized Transaction.

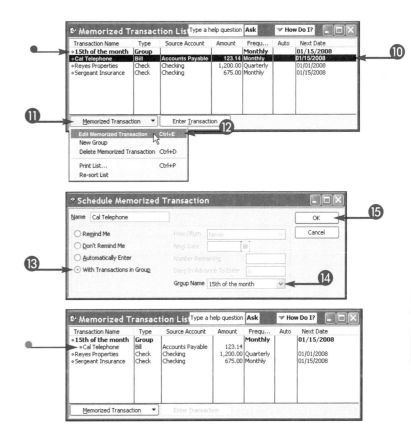

12 Click Edit Memorized Transaction.

The Schedule Memorized Transaction dialog box appears.

13 Click the With Transactions in Group option (○ changes to ◉).

14 Click here to select a group.

15 Click OK.

- The transaction appears in the Memorized Transaction List window indented under the group name.

How do I remove a memorized transaction from a memorized transaction group?

▼ Follow steps 1 to 2 in this section and highlight the transaction you want to remove from the group. Then, click Memorized Transaction and click Edit Memorized Transaction. QuickBooks displays the Scheduled Memorized Transaction dialog box. Click any option other than With Transactions in Group and click OK. QuickBooks updates both the transaction and the group; the memorized transaction still exists but it is no longer part of the group.

When will I see the effects of entering memorized transactions in a memorized transaction group?

▼ If the group contains a memorized bill, the difference appears in your accounts payable account on the date of the memorized bill. If the group contains a memorized check, the difference appears in your bank account on the date of the memorized check — even if you have not yet printed the check. If the group enters a memorized invoice, the accounts receivable account changes on the date of the memorized invoice.

How do I change the amounts on a memorized bill included in a memorized transaction group?

▼ Rememorize the bill. Follow steps 1 to 2 to open the Memorized Transaction List window and then double-click the transaction. When the transaction appears in the Enter Bills window, change the amounts and memorize the bill again by clicking Edit and then clicking Memorize Bill. QuickBooks displays a message, asking if you want to add the transaction to the Memorized Transaction List or replace the existing transaction. Click Replace.

Enter Credit Card Charges

You can enter credit card slips into QuickBooks so that you know, at any point in time, exactly how much is outstanding on your credit card. You can record credit card charges for expenses and for fixed asset, service, Other Charge, and noninventory part items, and, if you order inventory parts, you can enter charges for inventory parts.

You set up credit card accounts for each credit card; see Chapter 2 for details on setting up accounts. When you enter a credit card slip, you select the appropriate credit card, and then you select the vendor from whom you made

the purchase. You identify the date of the purchase and, if you want, you supply a reference number for the transaction. Then, if the charge is an expense — for example, you bought some office supplies — you select an account and record an amount. If you charge a fixed asset, service, Other Charge, noninventory part, or inventory item, you select the item and record an amount. You also can assign the charge to a Customer:Job so that the charge becomes a reimbursable expense that you can bill back to the customer; see Chapter 11 for details on invoicing reimbursable expenses.

Enter Credit Card Charges

Record an Expense

1 Click Banking.

2 Click Record Credit Card Charges.

3 Click Enter Credit Card Charges.

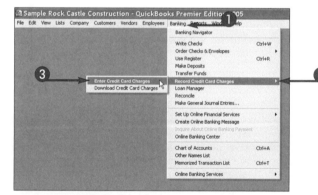

The Enter Credit Card Charges window appears.

4 Click here to select a credit card.

● The balance on the card appears here.

5 Click here to select a vendor for the charge.

● You can click an option to record either a charge or a credit (○ changes to ⦿).

6 Click ▦ to select the charge date.

● You can type a transaction number here.

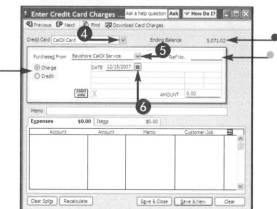

7 Click the Expenses tab.

8 Click here to select an account.

9 Type an amount to charge the account here.

QuickBooks fills in the amount of the charge.

● You can type a memo here.

● You can click here and assign the expense to a Customer:Job.

10 Repeat steps 8 to 9 to assign the charge to additional accounts.

11 Click Save & Close.

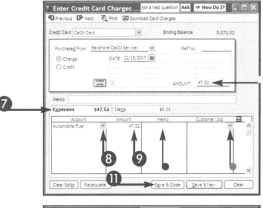

Enter a Charge for Items

1 Perform steps 1 to 6 on the previous page and click the Items tab.

2 Click here to select an item.

QuickBooks fills in the description and, if possible, the cost; you change the cost by typing a value.

● You can type a quantity and click ☑ to assign the line to a customer.

QuickBooks calculates the line amount.

3 Repeat step 2 for additional items.

QuickBooks fills in the amount of the charge.

4 Click Save & Close.

QuickBooks saves your changes.

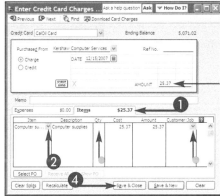

PART IV

How do I record the return of a credit card purchase?

▼ You perform all the steps in this section, with one additional step. After you select the vendor from whom you made the original purchase, click the Credit option (○ changes to ◉). The resulting transaction reduces the balance of your credit card account.

How do I pay my credit card bill when it arrives?

▼ If you write a check each month for your credit card, reconcile the credit card account; at the end of the reconciliation process, QuickBooks prompts you to write the check. You can make a partial or full payment. Reconciling a credit card account is the same as reconciling a bank account; see Chapter 17 for details.

If I make a mistake on a credit card transaction, how do I edit it?

▼ You can use the Previous and Next buttons in the Enter Credit Card Charges window to find and change the transaction, or you can open the Chart of Accounts window and double-click the credit card account. QuickBooks opens the register for the account, where you can find the transaction and make changes to it. You should not make amount changes to a reconciled transaction.

Track Credit Card Charges Electronically

I f your credit card financial institution supports QuickBooks, you can download credit card transactions directly into QuickBooks so that you know your credit card balance at all times without manually entering credit card slips. Downloading credit card transactions is typically a free service at most financial institutions.

QuickBooks contains a list of financial institutions that offer credit cards that support QuickBooks; you need to obtain a card from one of these institutions or, if you already have a card from one of these institutions, contact it to set up the account for online access and obtain a personal

identification number (PIN). Information needed to contact the financial institution and, in many cases, to apply online for the credit card, appears in the list.

Once you have your PIN, you can download transactions; each time you download, QuickBooks refers to a set of downloaded transactions as a QuickStatement. View the QuickStatement and match downloaded transactions to transactions that already exist in the account. When you match transactions, you can edit them if necessary to supply or change account information. QuickBooks remembers accounts you assign and assigns the same account to all future transactions from the same vendor.

Track Credit Card Charges Electronically

① Click Banking.

② Click Record Credit Card Charges.

③ Click Download Credit Card Charges.

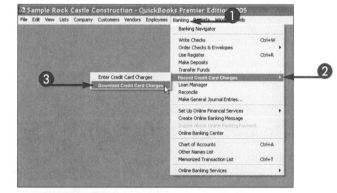

The Online Banking Center window appears.

④ Click here to select a credit card.

⑤ Click next to each item you want to send (☐ changes to ☑).

- Requests to download transactions and send online payments appear here.

⑥ Click Go Online.

QuickBooks asks for your PIN and then downloads the selected items.

⑦ Click a downloaded QuickStatement.

⑧ Click View.

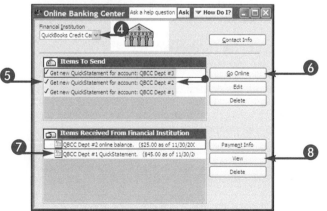

The Match Transactions window appears.

9 Click a transaction in the bottom of the window.

10 Click anywhere on the transaction at the top of the window that matches the selected transaction in the bottom of the window.

11 Click Match.

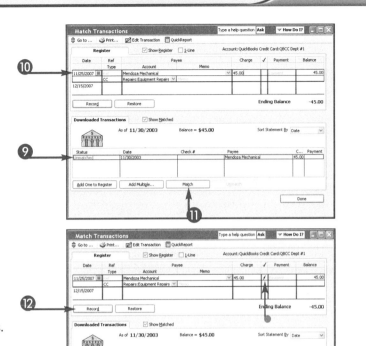

QuickBooks updates the Match Transactions window.

● A lightning bolt (⚡) appears in the Cleared column of the transaction in the top of the window.

● The status of the transaction in the bottom of the window changes to Matched along with the time you matched the transactions.

12 Click Record.

13 Repeat steps 9 to 12 for each transaction in the bottom of the window.

14 Click Done.

All transactions are matched and the Online Banking Center window reappears.

15 Click the Close button (☒) to close the window.

How can I find out if I can download transactions for my existing credit card into QuickBooks?

▼ You can view the list of financial institutions that offer credit cards that support QuickBooks and contact the number listed for your financial institution. To view the list, connect to the Internet while using QuickBooks. Then, in QuickBooks, click Banking, click Set Up Online Financial Services, and then click Online List of Available Financial Institutions. QuickBooks opens a browser window and displays the Financial Institutions Directory. Click the Credit/charge card access button and select your financial institution from the list on the left. Contact information appears in the window on the right.

Can I pay my credit card bill electronically?

▼ Yes. For details on paying electronically, see Chapter 15.

QuickBooks seems to assign downloaded transactions to only one account; what should I do to assign a transaction to multiple accounts?

▼ While viewing a QuickStatement, add the transaction in question to the register. If the Unmatched Transaction dialog box appears, click the Enter Credit Card Charges option (○ changes to ◉). If the transaction already appears in the register, click the Edit Transaction button. In both cases, QuickBooks opens the transaction in the Enter Credit Card Charges window, where you can assign multiple accounts to the transactions.

Pay Bills

When you enter bills into QuickBooks, you can use the Pay Bills window to pay many bills at one time, saving you time and effort. You set up criteria to specify how to display the unpaid bills. You can then sort the bills by Due Date, Discount Date, Vendor, or Amount Due. Many people sort the available bills to be paid by Discount Date to ensure that these bills are paid in time to take the offered discount.

As you click a bill, any credits available from the bill's vendor appear, and you can apply them. QuickBooks applies credits to the selected bill so if you want to apply the credit to a particular bill from a vendor, highlight that bill before you apply the credit.

When you pay bills, you can print checks, use credit cards to pay bills, or set up an online payment; this section describes how to print checks. QuickBooks prints one check per vendor, even if you pay multiple bills from the same vendor. You can also assign check numbers as you create checks or you can create checks to print in a batch. For details on printing checks in a batch, see the section "Print Checks in a Batch."

Pay Bills

① Click Vendors.

② Click Pay Bills.

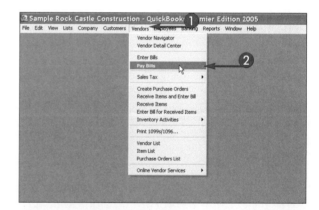

The Pay Bills window appears.

③ Click this option to select bills due on or before a date (○ changes to ⊙).

④ Click the calendar button (▦) to select the date.

⑤ Click here to sort the bills, remembering to select Discount Date to avoid losing discounts.

⑥ Click here to select a bill to pay (☐ changes to ☑).

As you select bills, QuickBooks updates your checking account ending balance and displays vendor credits.

⑦ Click Set Credits.

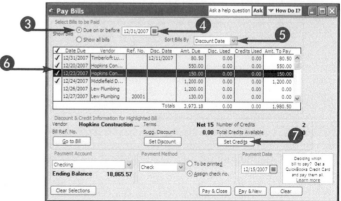

The Discount and Credits window appears.

8 Click here to select a credit to apply (☐ changes to ☑).

9 Repeat step 8 to apply additional credits.

10 Click Done.

The Pay Bills window reappears; QuickBooks adjusts the amount to pay and the total credits available.

11 Click here to select an account from which to pay.

12 Click here to select a payment method.

13 Click ▦ to select a payment date.

14 Click Pay & Close.

QuickBooks pays the bills and reduces your Accounts Payable.

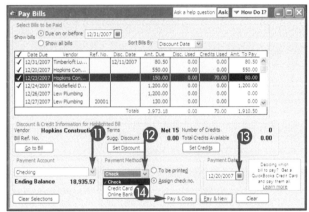

Can I print the vendor's account number on the check?

▼ Yes. You can print it in the Memo field on the check. First, make sure that you have entered the vendor's account number; click Lists, and then click Vendor. In the Vendor List, double-click the vendor to edit information. Then, click the Additional Info tab and make sure the vendor's account number appears in the Account No. field and click OK. Click Edit and then Preferences. In the Preferences dialog box that appears, click the Checking icon. On the Company Preferences tab, select the "Autofill payee account number in the check memo box" option (☐ changes to ☑).

What does the Set Discount button do?

▼ When you click this button, QuickBooks displays the Discount tab of the Discount and Credits window. Use this window only if a vendor offers you a one-time discount, perhaps because shipment was delayed. Do not use this window to enter discounts that apply to vendor terms unless you need to adjust the amount of the discount. If you set up terms properly, those discounts already appear. For more on setting up vendor terms, see Chapter 5. If you enter a discount for an unusual situation, you must also supply an account for the discount. You can apply the discount to an expense account that appears on the bill, or you can set up a separate income account to track discounts.

Pay an Online Credit Card Bill

You can pay the bill for credit cards supported by QuickBooks by printing or handwriting a check or by scheduling an online payment. You can pay the credit card bill from any bank account you want. You pay online credit card bills differently than you pay other credit card bills; see Chapter 17 for details on paying other credit card bills.

When you pay an online credit card bill, QuickBooks displays the statement closing date for the credit card, the minimum payment amount, and the balance due. You can specify an amount to pay — the entire bill, a minimum payment, or some other amount. Regardless of the type of payment you create — a printed or handwritten check or an electronic payment — QuickBooks creates a check for the payment. On the check, you confirm the payee, the amount, the date, and the account on the Expenses tab of the Write Checks window. Checks for credit card bills should always use the credit card account you set up in the Chart of Accounts on the Expenses tab to reduce the balance you owe for the credit card account.

Pay an Online Credit Card Bill

① Click Banking.

② Click Record Credit Card Charges.

③ Click Download Credit Card Charges.

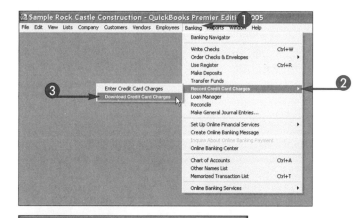

The Online Banking Center window appears.

④ Click Payment Info.

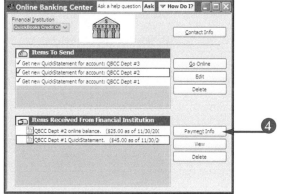

The Credit Card Payment Information dialog box appears.

5 Click Make Payment.

The Make Credit Card Payment dialog box appears.

6 Click an Amount to Pay option (○ changes to ◉).

7 Click a Payment Will Be option (○ changes to ◉).

8 Click here to select an account from which to pay.

9 Click OK.

The Write Checks window appears.

10 Click here to select a payee name.

11 Click here to assign an account.

12 Click Save & Close.

QuickBooks records the payment.

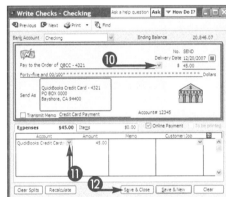

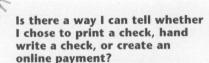

Is there a way I can tell whether I chose to print a check, hand write a check, or create an online payment?

▼ Yes. In the Write Checks window, look at the No. field. If you chose to print a check, "To Print" appears in the No. field. If you chose to hand write a check, the check number appears in the No. field. If you chose to create an online payment, SEND appears in the No. field.

Can I assign the credit card payment to more than one account?

▼ You can, but you should not. The credit card payment debits the account you select and credits a bank account. You want to debit the credit card account to reduce its balance. You may be tempted to distribute the credit card payment to the expenses or items charged to the card, but for online credit cards, you distribute the individual charges when you download them. See Chapter 14 for details.

If "To Print" appears in the No. field, how do I print the check?

▼ Click the Print button, or see the section "Print Checks in Batch" later in this chapter.

If I make an online payment, how do I get the online payment to the financial institution?

▼ You send the payment electronically in the same way that you download credit card transactions for the account. For details on downloading credit card charges, see Chapter 14.

Write Checks

Y ou can use the Write Checks window to write a check for an expense or for service, other charge, fixed asset, inventory, or noninventory items. You should not use the Write Checks window if you want to pay a bill that you entered or if you want to write a paycheck, pay payroll liabilities, or pay sales tax liabilities. In all these cases, you need to use the QuickBooks feature specifically designed for the tasks. For details on paying bills and paying sales tax liabilities, see the sections "Pay Bills" and "Pay the Sales Tax Liability." For details on paying payroll liabilities, see Chapter 9.

When you write a check, you select the account from which to draw the money; if you have more than one checking account, you can have QuickBooks display the checking account of your choice when you open the window.

You also select the payee and the check date, and you can supply a check memo. At the bottom of the Write Checks window, you select expense accounts or items that represent what you purchased.

Write Checks

Record an Expense

① Click Banking.

② Click Write Checks.

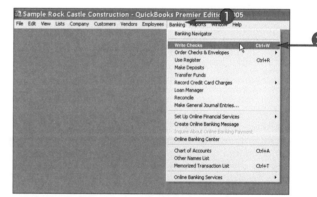

The Write Checks window appears.

③ Click ▦ to select the check date.

④ Click here to select a vendor.

- QuickBooks fills in the vendor's address information.

- You can type a memo for the check face here.

⑤ Click the Expenses tab.

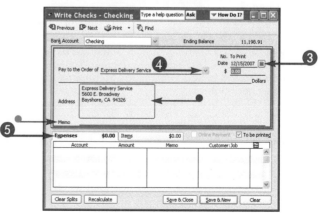

6 Click here to select an account.

7 Type an amount to charge the account.

- You can type a memo here and you can click ☑ and assign the expense to a Customer:Job.

8 Repeat steps 6 to 7 to assign the check to additional accounts.

QuickBooks fills in the amount of the check.

9 Click the To be printed option (○ changes to ◉) to print checks in a batch.

10 Click Save & Close.

Enter a Bill for Items

1 Perform steps 1 to 4 on the previous page, clicking the Items tab.

2 Click here to select an item.

3 Type a quantity.

- QuickBooks fills in the description and cost and calculates the line amount.

- You can click here to assign the line to a customer.

4 Repeat steps 2 to 3 for additional items.

- QuickBooks fills in the amount of the check.

5 Click the To be printed option to print the check later as part of a batch (☐ changes to ☑).

6 Click Save & Close.

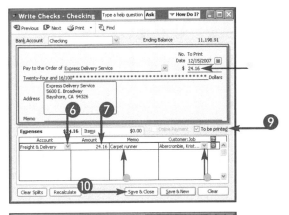

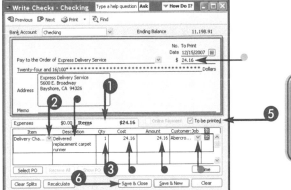

PART IV

When I select a vendor in the Write Checks window, QuickBooks fills in the window with the information from the last check I wrote to that vendor. Why is QuickBooks doing this and how do I stop it?

▼ You have selected the Automatically recall last transaction for this name option. This feature works for bills, checks, and credit card charges. You can stop QuickBooks from automatically filling in these windows by turning off the preference. Click Edit and then Preferences. Click the General icon and, on the My Preferences tab, deselect the Automatically recall last transaction for this name option (☑ changes to ☐).

How do I tell QuickBooks to display a specific bank account each time I open the Write Checks window?

▼ Click Edit and then Preferences. Click the Checking icon, and on the My Preferences tab, click the Open the Write Checks form with option (☐ changes to ☑). Then, click ☑ to select the account you want to use.

Do I need to set up a vendor if I only purchase occasionally?

▼ Set up a vendor only if you want to track purchasing history with that vendor. For checks to occasional vendors, set up the payee on the Other Names list or print the check with no vendor selected at all and hand write the vendor's name on the printed check.

Print Checks
in a Batch

You may find it most efficient to print all checks at the same time — in a batch — instead of printing them as you create them. This approach works particularly well if you have a lot of checks to print; you can create the checks in either the Pay Bills window or the Write Checks window and then, toward the end of the day, you can print the day's checks and mail them. To print a batch of checks, you need to ensure that you select the To be printed option as you pay bills or create checks in the Write Checks window.

After QuickBooks finishes printing a batch of checks, you have the opportunity to identify the first check that did not print correctly, perhaps because the paper jammed in the printer. If necessary, supply the number of the first check that did not print correctly, and QuickBooks does not mark that check and the ones that follow as printed, enabling you to reprint the batch. If all checks print correctly and you do not supply a check number, QuickBooks marks the checks as printed so that they do not reappear when you print the next batch of checks.

Print Checks in a Batch

① Click File.

② Click Print Forms.

③ Click Checks.

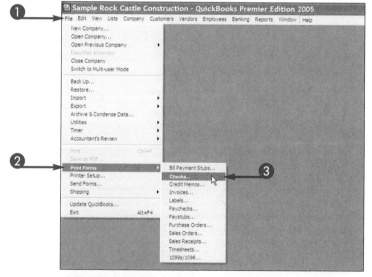

The Select Checks to Print dialog box appears.

QuickBooks selects all checks by default.

④ Click here to select an account from which to print.

⑤ Confirm the first check number.

● You can click here to deselect a check (☑ changes to ☐).

⑥ Click OK.

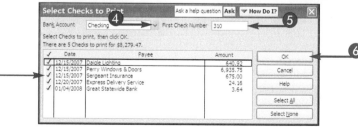

The Settings tab of the Print Checks window appears.

7 Click here to select a printer.

8 Click here to select the printer type.

9 Click a Check Style option (○ changes to ⦿).

10 Click Print.

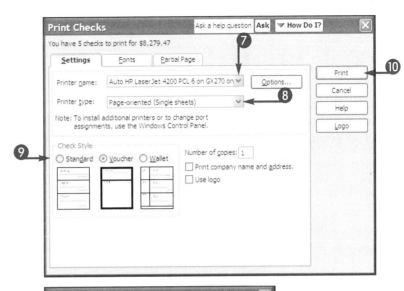

QuickBooks prints the checks and displays the Did check(s) print OK? dialog box.

● If any checks failed to print properly, you can type the number of the first incorrect check here.

11 Click OK.

For all checks that printed correctly, QuickBooks saves the check number.

What style checks can I print from QuickBooks and where can I get them?

▼ QuickBooks supports three check styles, all designed around 8½-x-11-inch paper. Standard checks are 8½ inches wide and come three to a page, with no voucher or stub. Voucher checks are also 8½ inches wide but come only one to a page; QuickBooks prints stub information twice on the remaining portion of the page, providing you with two vouchers. Wallet checks come three to a page but are not 8½ inches wide because the left edge of each check is the stub. You can purchase checks through your bank, directly from Intuit, or from a variety of forms providers that you can locate on the Internet.

If I use Standard checks, do I need to always print checks in multiples of three to avoid wasting checks?

▼ No. When you select either the Standard or Wallet check style, the Checks on 1st Page option appears on the Settings tab of the Print Checks window.

What does the Logo button do?

▼ You can print a bitmap file (BMP) of your company logo on your check. Click Logo and then File. Navigate to the location on your hard drive where you store the logo file and click OK twice.

PART IV

Pay the Sales Tax Liability

Periodically, you must remit sales tax you collect from customers to a state taxing authority. Most states require, by law, that you charge sales tax when you sell goods and, in some states, when you sell services. In many states, you collect sales tax not only for the state but also for cities, counties, and other localities.

Various states have different requirements concerning how often you must remit sales tax; in some states, for example, the dollar amount you collect determines whether you remit monthly, quarterly, or annually. In addition, many states offer you an allowance for handling the collection and record keeping associated with collecting sales tax; you are permitted to keep a small percentage to cover your expenses, so you must adjust the amount due as you create the sales tax liability check.

When you remit sales tax in QuickBooks, you use the Pay Sales Tax window. You typically create one check for each taxing authority; in some states, you remit all sales tax to the state and the state then passes along amounts due to cities, counties, and other taxing authorities.

Pay the Sales Tax Liability

Pay the Liability

① Click Vendors.

② Click Sales Tax.

③ Click Pay Sales Tax.

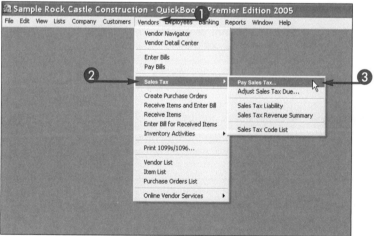

④ In the Pay Sales Tax window, click here to select an account from which to pay sales tax.

⑤ Click 🔲 to select the check date.

⑥ Click 🔲 to select the date through which you want to pay the sales tax liability.

⑦ Click the To be printed option (🔲 changes to ☑) to create a check you want to print later in a batch.

⑧ Click here to select sales tax items to pay (🔲 changes to ☑).

● QuickBooks updates the Amt. Paid column.

⑨ Click OK.

QuickBooks creates the check.

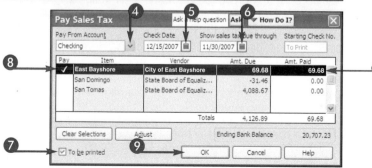

Adjust the Liability Before Paying

1 Complete steps 1 to 7 on the previous page.

2 Click Adjust.

3 In the Sales Tax Adjustment dialog box, click ▦ to select a date for the adjustment.

4 Click here to select the sales tax vendor.

5 Click here to select an account.

6 Click an option to increase or decrease sales tax (○ changes to ◉).

7 Type the amount of the adjustment here.

● You can type a memo here.

8 Click OK.

The Pay Sales Tax window reappears, showing the adjustment transaction.

9 Click here to select sales tax items and adjustments.

● QuickBooks updates the Amt. Paid column.

10 Click OK.

QuickBooks creates the check.

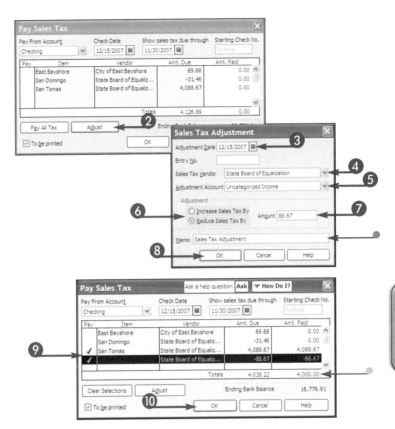

▼ Either delete or void the liability check and then re-create it. To delete or void the check, you must display it in the Write Checks window. You can search for the check — see Chapter 18 for details — or you can open the register of your bank account by double-clicking it in the Chart of Accounts window. Then, click the transaction and then the Edit Transaction button. Once QuickBooks displays the transaction in the Write Checks window, click Edit and then Delete Liability Check or Void Liability Check.

How do I know what account to select for an adjustment, and what is the Entry No. field?

▼ QuickBooks records sales tax adjustments as journal entries; you can supply a number for the adjustment in the Entry No. field. Select an income account if you are decreasing the amount of sales tax due; select an expense account if you are increasing the amount of sales tax due.

How do I print the sales tax liability check?

▼ You can view it in the Write Checks window and click the Print button (🖨) or you can print it as part of a batch of checks. See the section "Print Checks in Batch" for details.

PART IV

Print 1099s and 1096s

Tax laws require that you provide Form 1099 to certain independent contractors, and you can set up QuickBooks to track payments to 1099 vendors for you and produce the 1099s you need. You must send 1099s to all independent subcontractors with whom you did business during the previous year and to whom you paid more than the threshold amount of $600.00. To process 1099s in QuickBooks, you must turn on the feature, and you must identify 1099 vendors and provide their Tax ID numbers in the Vendor List. You must also ensure that a ZIP code appears in the 1099 vendor's address. See Chapter 6 for details.

You also should use the 1099 Summary Report in QuickBooks to verify that the information that appears on the 1099s is correct. The report shows only vendors set up as 1099 vendors to whom you made payments posted against designated 1099 accounts and the payments exceeded the 1099 threshold requirement. After viewing the default version of the report, verify accounts and vendors by changing the report to display first all accounts and then all vendors; if new 1099 payments appear, that may mean that you paid a 1099 vendor using an account you did not establish as a 1099 account, or you may have paid a vendor using a 1099 account, but the vendor does not qualify as a 1099 vendor.

Print 1099s and 1096s

① Load 1099 forms in your printer.

② Click Vendors.

③ Click Print 1099s/1096.

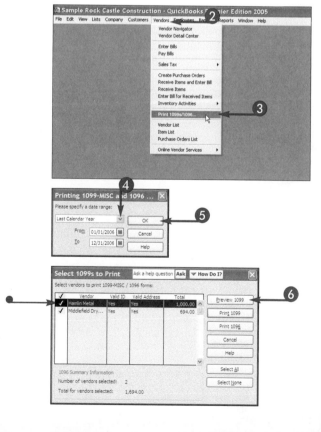

The Printing 1099-MISC and 1096 dialog box appears.

④ Click here to select Last Calendar Year.

⑤ Click OK.

The Select 1099s to Print window appears.

QuickBooks selects all vendors by default.

● You can click here to deselect a vendor (☑ changes to ☐).

⑥ Click Preview 1099.

The 1099 appears on-screen.

● You can click here to enlarge the image.

7 Click Print.

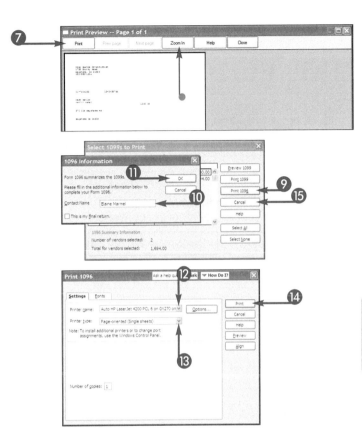

QuickBooks prints the 1099s and the Select 1099s to Print window reappears.

8 Load Form 1096 into your printer.

9 Click Print 1096.

The 1096 Information dialog box appears.

10 Type your contact name here.

11 Click OK.

The Print 1096 window appears.

12 Click here to select a printer.

13 Click here to select a printer type.

14 Click Print.

QuickBooks prints the form and the Select 1099s to Print window reappears.

15 Click Cancel to close the Select 1099s to Print window.

Because QuickBooks prints 1099 information that goes onto the 1099 form but does not print a complete form, can I print a sample to see how things align?

▼ Yes. Load blank paper in your printer. Click File and then click Printer Setup. From the Form Name list of the Printer Setup dialog box, click 1099s/1096. Click Preview and click Print when the preview appears on-screen. QuickBooks prints a sample and redisplays the Printer Setup box. Take the 1099 that you printed onto blank paper and place it in front of a 1099 form. Then, hold the pair of pages up to the light to see if everything aligns properly.

If information does not line up properly, how do I align it?

▼ In the Printer Setup dialog box, click the Align button. QuickBooks displays the Fine Alignment box where you can type the amount of vertical or horizontal adjustments you want to make in $\frac{1}{100}$-inch increments. If you have a dot-matrix printer, you can align the paper by manually adjusting the tractor feed. Print the preview again to check your settings.

How do I print the 1099 Summary Report?

▼ Click Reports and then Vendors & Payables. Last, click 1099 Summary. For details on customizing a report, see Chapter 22.

Write a Letter to a Vendor

QuickBooks makes it easy to correspond with vendors on a variety of matters using the Prepare Letters and Envelopes Wizard and Microsoft Word 97 or higher.

QuickBooks comes with its own selection of preformatted, ready-to-use business letters, grouped by the type of recipient to whom you usually send the letter. You can make temporary changes to a letter in Microsoft Word after you create it by simply editing the document; QuickBooks supplies a special version of the Merge toolbar to help you.

If you are using QuickBooks Pro, QuickBooks Premier, or QuickBooks Enterprise, you can make permanent changes to a letter to better suit your business's needs or add a letter that does not come with QuickBooks. You also can duplicate a letter, delete it, rename it, or move it to another group.

As you walk through the wizard, you select the letter you want to use and the recipients of the letter — you can send the letter to only one vendor, to any selection of vendors, or to all vendors. You also supply the name and title of the person who will sign the letter.

Write a Letter to a Vendor

① Click Company.

② Click Prepare Letters with Envelopes.

③ Click Vendor Letters.

The Prepare Letters and Envelopes Wizard begins showing the Review and Edit Recipients screen.

● You can click an option to view active, inactive, or both types of vendors (○ changes to ◉).

④ Click next to the names of vendors to whom you want to write (☐ changes to ☑).

⑤ Click Next.

The Choose a Letter Template screen appears.

⑥ Click a letter.

⑦ Click Next.

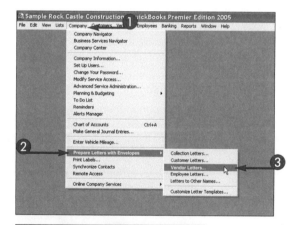

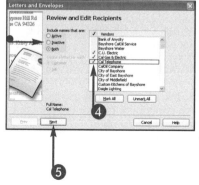

The Enter a Name and Title screen appears.

8 Type the name that will appear as a signature.

9 Type the signatory's title.

10 Click Next.

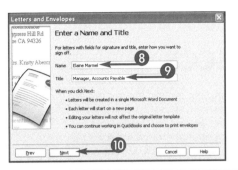

Note: If appropriate, the Information Needed for Letters Is Missing dialog box appears; click OK to exit this dialog box.

The letter(s) appears in Microsoft Word.

● If necessary, supply missing information or use the QuickBooks toolbar to edit the letter.

11 Click the Print button (■).

12 Click the Close button (■) to close Word to return to QuickBooks.

Note: A window appears that explains how to print envelopes for the letters from QuickBooks.

13 Follow the on-screen instructions if you want to print envelopes.

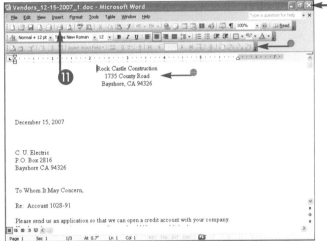

How can I create a new letter and send it to vendors?

▼ Follow steps 1 to 2 in this section. Then, click Customize Letter Templates, and the Choose What You Want to Do screen appears. Click Create a New Letter Template From Scratch (○ changes to ◉) and click Next. Select Vendors as the list of names who will receive the letter (○ changes to ◉), type a name for the letter, and click Create Letter. Microsoft Word opens and you can type your letter; use the QuickBooks toolbar in Word to include company and vendor fields. When you save the letter, it subsequently appears when you run the Prepare Letters and Envelopes Wizard for vendors.

How can I convert an existing Microsoft Word document into a QuickBooks letter for vendors?

▼ Follow steps 1 to 2 in this section and click Customize Letter Templates. On the Choose What You Want to Do screen, click Convert an Existing Microsoft Word Document to a Letter Template (○ changes to ◉) and click Next. Browse to select the Microsoft Word document, select Vendors as the list of names to receive the letter (○ changes to ◉), and click Next. Type a name for the letter that will appear in QuickBooks and click OK. Microsoft Word opens; use the QuickBooks toolbar to add vendor fields and type your letter. When you save the letter, it appears when you run the Prepare Letters and Envelopes Wizard for vendors.

Change Item Prices

You can change the price of service, inventory part, Inventory assembly, non-inventory part, and other charge items whenever you want. QuickBooks enables you to change the prices of one or more items by manually modifying the price; or, you can increase or decrease the price of selected items by a uniform amount or percentage. Typically, you change prices manually when the change you need to make varies from one item to the next. But if you want to increase the price of all service items by 10%, for example, you can make that change uniformly.

When you change item prices, QuickBooks displays current prices for all items within the selected group of items. You can base dollar or percentage increases or decreases on the selected item's current price or unit cost.

You can change item prices within similar groups of items simultaneously, but you cannot simultaneously update prices across groups of items; that is, you can update prices for any or all service items simultaneously, but you cannot simultaneously update both service and inventory part items.

Change Item Prices

Change Prices Individually

① Click Lists.

② Click Item List.

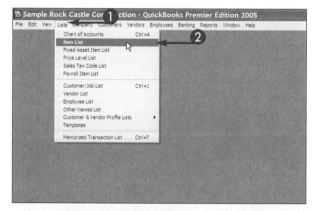

The Item List window appears.

③ Click Activities.

④ Click Change Item Prices.

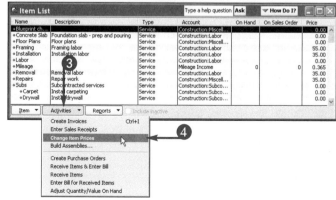

The Change Item Prices window appears.

5 Click here and select an item type for which to view and change prices.

6 Click here to select an item to change.

7 Type a new price here.

8 Repeat steps 6 to 7 to change additional prices.

9 Click OK.

QuickBooks updates the prices.

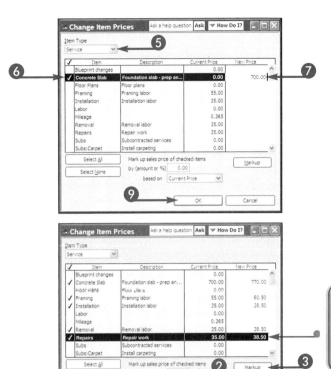

Change Prices Uniformly

1 Complete steps 1 to 6 on the previous page.

2 Click here to type a percentage or amount of price change.

Note: *Include a percent sign (%) to change price by a percentage.*

- You can click here to select a basis for the new price.

3 Click Markup.

- QuickBooks displays the new prices here.

4 Click OK.

QuickBooks saves the new prices.

When I update prices, where do I see the effects?

▼ First, the new price appears in the Edit Item window as the sales price of the item. Click Lists and Item List, and then edit the item in question to view the new price. In addition, the new price appears on all new transactions, but QuickBooks does not update any prices on existing purchase orders, invoices, sales receipts, or memorized transactions. To update memorized transactions, you need to edit and rememorize those transactions. For details on memorizing transactions, see Chapter 18.

How do I record a price decrease?

▼ You can type a lower number in the New Price column, or, if you are updating a group of prices uniformly, you can type either a negative number or a negative percentage in the box labeled "Mark up sales price of checked items by (amount or %)."

How does QuickBooks know the unit cost of an item?

▼ QuickBooks uses the amount that appears in the Cost field of the item's record; you can check the amount by clicking Lists and Item List, and then double-clicking the item.

Build Assemblies

I f you use QuickBooks Premier or QuickBooks Enterprise, you can assemble items from component parts you keep in inventory. You can read about defining inventory assembly items in Chapter 7. When you define an inventory assembly item, you identify its component parts. After you define an inventory assembly item, you must build it to create the finished product from the component parts. When you build an assembly, QuickBooks reduces the number on hand of the component parts and increases the number on hand of the assembled item.

You cannot delete inventory assembly items after you build them, so consider assemblies carefully beforehand. If you are uncertain about whether you need to build a particular assembly, or you do not have enough components to complete a build, you can mark the build as "pending." Later, when you make your decision or have enough components in inventory, you can either complete or delete the build transaction.

You can have QuickBooks remind you to build assembly items when their inventory quantity reaches or falls below the build point. For details on setting a reminder, see Chapter 24.

Build Assemblies

1 Click Vendors.

2 Click Inventory Activities.

3 Click Build Assemblies.

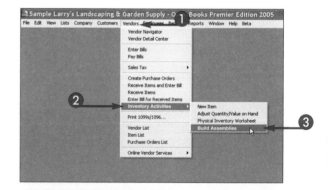

The Build Assemblies window appears.

4 Click here and select an assembly item.

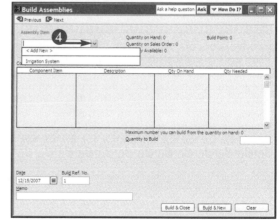

QuickBooks updates the window.

● Quantity information for the assembly appears here.

● Quantity information for the components appears here.

● The maximum you can build based on components appears here.

⑤ Type the quantity to build here.

You can type a memo here.

⑥ Click Build & Close.

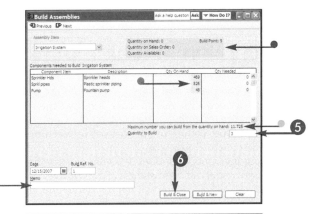

QuickBooks saves the transaction and clears the window.

● You can select the assembly again from the Assembly Item List to see the updated quantities.

Can I simply adjust the quantity on hand of an inventory assembly instead of building it?

▼ No. If you enter an inventory adjustment to increase the quantity on hand of an assembly, QuickBooks increases the quantity on hand of the assembly, but does *not* reduce the quantity on hand of the component parts. Attempting to create assemblies by using inventory adjustments results in erroneous inventory quantities and misstated inventory value.

Instead of building an assembly, can I change the quantity on hand for the assembled item when I create it?

▼ No. Changing the quantity on hand when you create an assembly item results in QuickBooks creating an inventory adjustment. The adjustment increases the number of assemblies, but does not decrease the number of components. Again, you end up with erroneous inventory quantities and misstated inventory value.

How do I mark a build as pending?

▼ Complete all steps in this section but do not save the build transaction. Instead, click Edit and then click Mark Build As Pending. QuickBooks creates a pending transaction instead of building the assembly. You can view pending build transactions on the Pending Builds report. Click Reports, Inventory, and then Pending Builds. Double-click any build on the report to view it in the Build Assemblies window, and then either complete or delete it.

Count and Adjust Inventory Quantity or Value

Most companies that carry inventory count it at least once each year to make sure that the physical quantity on hand matches inventory records. At that time, you make adjustments to inventory records to reflect actual quantities. You may also make adjustments to inventory quantities or values at other times of the year under special circumstances. For example, suppose that you sell fragile items such as crystal, and an accident occurs, breaking several pieces. You may adjust inventory — both quantity and value — at the time of the breakage.

When you make an inventory adjustment, you increase or decrease the value or quantity of items in your inventory account. As double-entry bookkeeping requires, you must assign another account to the transaction to keep the transaction in balance. If you are tracking inventory shortages separately from inventory overages, you need two adjustment accounts. You assign shortages or reductions in inventory to an expense account, and you assign overages or increases in inventory to an income account. In this scenario, you should not mix overage adjustments with shortage adjustments. You can, however, assign all adjustments to one account — either an income or an expense account — and simply track the net overage/shortage based on inventory adjustments.

If appropriate, you can assign an inventory adjustment to a customer.

Count and Adjust Inventory Quantity or Value

Adjust Inventory Quantities

① Click Vendors.

② Click Inventory Activities.

③ Click Adjust Quantity/Value on Hand.

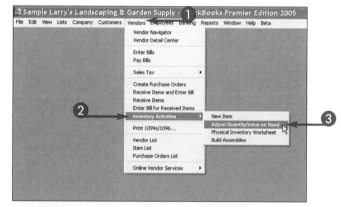

The Adjust Quantity/Value on Hand window appears.

④ Click the calendar button (▦) to select a date for the adjustment.

⑤ Click here to select an account for the adjustment.

● You can click here to assign the adjustment to a Customer:Job.

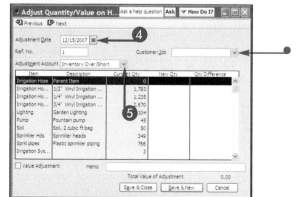

6 Click an item.

7 Type the new quantity here.

QuickBooks fills in the Qty Difference column and the total value of the adjustment.

Note: You can, instead, type the Qty Difference and QuickBooks will adjust the New Qty column.

8 Repeat steps 6 to 7 for each quantity you want to adjust.

- You can type a memo for the adjustment here.

9 Click Save & Close.

QuickBooks saves the adjustment.

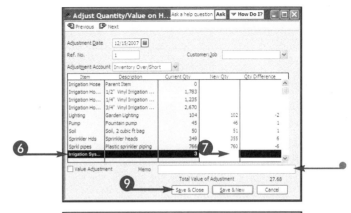

Adjust the Value of Inventory

1 Complete steps 1 to 5 on the previous page.

2 Click the Value Adjustment option (□ changes to ☑).

The window changes to display the Current Value and New Value columns.

3 Click an item.

4 Type the new value of the item here.

5 Repeat steps 3 to 4 for each value you want to adjust.

- You can type a memo for the adjustment here.

6 Click Save & Close.

QuickBooks adjusts the value of the inventory.

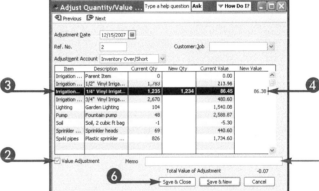

When should I assign an inventory adjustment to a Customer:Job?

▼ You assign the adjustment to a Customer:Job if you did not invoice the customer directly for the items. For example, if you created a summarized invoice for the customer that did not list items sold, but you did actually sell inventory items to the customer, you need to adjust inventory quantities to reduce the quantity on hand for the items you sold. You also need to make sure that the inventory items appear on job profitability reports as a job-related cost.

Is there a report that I can print that helps me perform the physical inventory count?

▼ Yes. The Physical Inventory Worksheet in QuickBooks lists each inventory item, the quantity on hand, and a line where you can write in the physical count. Click Reports, Inventory, and then click Physical Inventory Worksheet.

Is there a way to see all inventory adjustment transactions?

▼ Yes. If you use the Find feature in QuickBooks, you can search for Inventory Adjustment transactions; then you can click the Report button to generate a report of the transactions. For details on finding transactions, see Chapter 18.

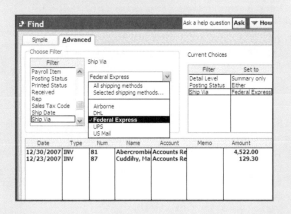

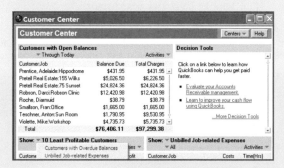

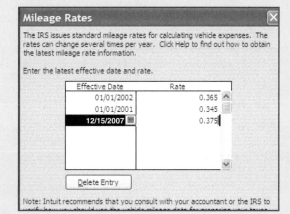

21

Shipping Packages

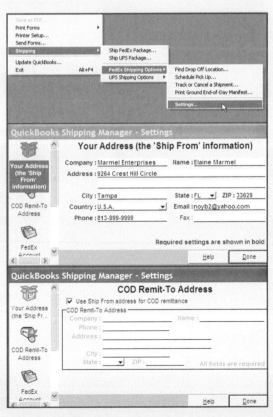

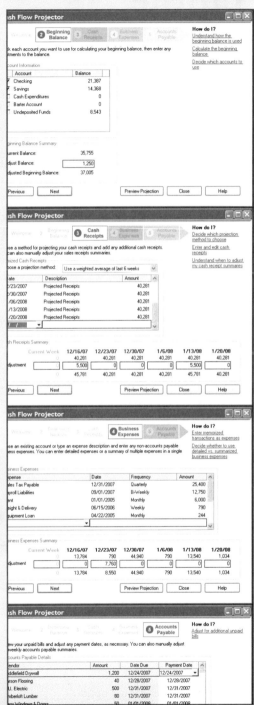

Handle
NSF Checks

Occasionally, you may deposit a customer check drawn against a bank account that does not contain sufficient funds to cover the check. When you deposit a nonsufficient funds (NSF) check, your bank deducts a processing fee for the check from your bank account. In QuickBooks, you need to account for the extra bank charge as well as for the reduction to your bank account that the NSF check caused. You also must decide if you are going to attempt to collect the debt.

To account for the bad check, create an income account where you can record the reduction to income and a taxable other charge item called Bad Check that you tie to the income account you create. You use this item to reduce

both income and your sales tax liability without affecting inventory because your merchandise was not returned. If you want to try to collect the NSF check and you expect to charge your customer a penalty for issuing a bad check, create another other charge item called Bad Check Charge that is not taxable. See Chapter 2 for help setting up an account and Chapter 7 for help setting up an other charge item.

To properly account for an NSF check, you use a credit memo coupled with a refund check. The combination of the two transactions decreases sales and sales tax payable for the customer in question as well as reduces your bank balance.

Handle NSF Checks

Record an NSF Check

① Click Customers.

② Click Create Credit Memos/Refunds.

The Credit Memos/Refunds window appears.

③ Click here to select the customer.

④ Click here to select the Bad Check item.

● QuickBooks fills in the description.

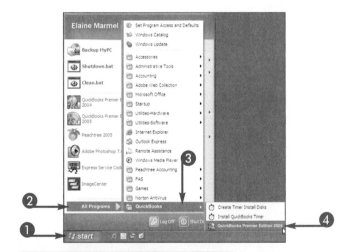

⑤ Type an amount excluding sales tax.

⑥ Click the ⊡ beside the Use Credit to button and click Give refund.

QuickBooks records the credit memo and the Issue a Refund window appears.

⑦ Click here to select an account.

⑧ Deselect the To be printed option (☑ changes to ☐).

⑨ Click here to type a check number.

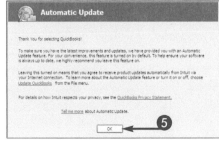

Consider typing NSF followed by the customer's check number to easily identify the returned check during reconciliation.

10 Click OK.

QuickBooks records the transaction.

The Create Credit Memos/Refunds window reappears.

11 Click Save & Close.

QuickBooks records the NSF check.

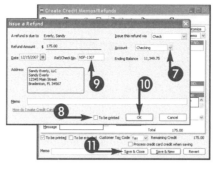

Record a Processing Fee

1 Click Banking.

2 Click Write Checks.

The Write Checks window appears.

3 Type a check number here.

4 Click here to select a vendor.

5 Click the Expenses tab.

6 Click here to select your bank account.

7 Type the amount your bank charged you here.

● You can type a memo here.

8 Click Save & Close.

The processing fee is recorded.

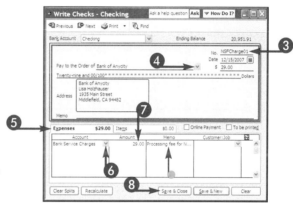

Why do a credit memo and a refund check account for an NSF check?

▼ The original invoice increases Accounts Receivable, your sales tax liability, and an income account. Depositing the NSF check reduces Accounts Receivable and increases your bank account. The credit memo reduces Accounts Receivable, your sales tax liability, and your income. At this point, Accounts Receivable has been reduced too many times and your bank account still contains the deposit; the Refund Check increases Accounts Receivable and reduces your bank account.

How can I rebill my customer to collect the debt?

▼ Invoice your customer for the original amount of the NSF check and any service charge you incurred for processing the check. Assign the sale amount to the Bad Check item you use on the Credit Memo. On a second line, you also may add a penalty charge using the other charge item you establish for bad check processing fees.

Can I just delete the receipt that recorded the NSF check?

▼ To maintain an accurate audit trail that describes the events as they happen, you should not delete the receipt. When you reconcile your bank account, your deposit attempt does not appear, nor does any transaction representing the uncollected check that reduces your cash balance. Also, the processing fee imposed by your bank appears on your bank statement, but not in QuickBooks.

Reconcile a Bank Statement or a Credit Card

Each month, as you write checks and make bank deposits, both you and your bank track your account activity; you need to reconcile your account activities with the bank's version of your account activities once each month when the bank sends you a statement to ensure that you and the bank agree on your account balance.

The statement you receive summarizes the checks you write, deposits you make, and actions the bank takes, such as charging your account for checks you order or adding interest to your account during the month. When you compare the balance on the statement with the balance in QuickBooks, they should match. If they do not match, you need to figure out why and then take some action. See the section "Resolve Discrepancies" later in this chapter.

Transactions that appear on the bank statement are *cleared* transactions. The difference between your QuickBooks balance and the bank statement's balance should be the total of the *uncleared* transactions, which include any checks written or deposits made that the bank has not cleared as of the statement date. To reconcile your account, you add uncleared deposits to the bank statement balance and subtract uncleared checks from the bank statement balance. QuickBooks automates this process.

Reconcile a Bank Statement or a Credit Card

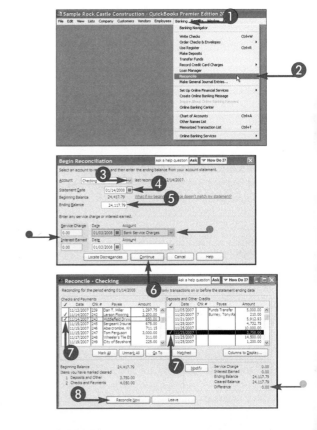

① Click Banking.

② Click Reconcile.

   The Begin Reconciliation window appears.

③ Click here to select an account.

④ Click the calendar button (▣) to select a statement date.

⑤ Type the ending balance listed on the statement here.

   ● You can type any service charges here and interest earned here.

   ● You can click here to select dates and accounts for service charges or interest earned.

⑥ Click Continue.

   The Reconcile window appears.

⑦ Click next to each deposit and check that appears on the bank statement (☐ changes to ☑).

   ● After you check off all deposits and checks that appear on the bank statement, the Difference should equal zero.

Note: *If this value is not zero, see the section "Resolve Discrepancies."*

⑧ Click Reconcile Now.

QuickBooks marks the selected transactions as reconciled and displays the Selection Reconciliation Report window.

9 Click a report type option (○ changes to ⊙).

Note: This example shows Both selected.

10 Click Display.

The Reconciliation Summary report appears.

11 Review the report.

12 Click Print.

13 Click the Close button ([x]) to close the report.

The Reconciliation Detail report appears.

14 Review the report.

15 Click Print.

16 Click [x] to close the report.

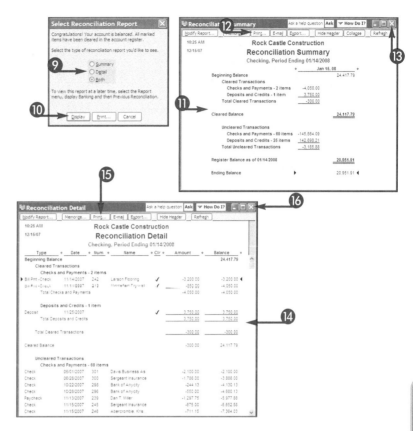

PART V

What do the Columns to Display and the Go To buttons in the Reconcile window do?

▼ Click Columns to Display to select the columns you want to see in the Reconcile window. In addition to the Date, Chk #, Payee, and Amount columns, you can display the Memo column for both the Checks and Payments side of the window and the Deposits and Other Credits side of the window. When you select a transaction and click Go To, QuickBooks displays the transaction in the window where you originally created the transaction.

What do the Matched and Modify buttons in the Reconcile window do?

▼ If you are reconciling an online banking account, click Matched to mark as cleared all transactions you previously downloaded and matched. See Chapter 14 for more on matching transactions for online accounts. The Modify button redisplays the Begin Reconciliation window so that you can change the account, statement date, ending balance, service charge, or interest earned amounts, dates, and accounts.

Can I reconcile a credit card?

▼ Yes. Follow the steps in this section, but select your credit card account in step 3. When you finish reconciling, QuickBooks prompts you to write a check to pay the credit card vendor for the outstanding balance.

Resolve Discrepancies

When you match all the transactions in QuickBooks to the transactions on your bank statement, as illustrated in the section "Reconcile a Bank Statement or a Credit Card," and the difference is something other than 0, you must figure out why and resolve the problem. The difference may not equal 0 for several reasons. First, the bank may have recorded a transaction that you have not recorded in QuickBooks. Look for bank charges such as check reorder charges, service charges, or if your account is interest bearing, interest payments.

Or, the bank may have recorded a transaction for a different amount than you recorded in QuickBooks. Compare the amounts of checks and deposits recorded

in QuickBooks to the amount the bank cleared. It is also possible that you cleared a transaction that did not clear the bank. Review the transactions you checked as cleared. Or, you may have recorded the Statement Ending Balance incorrectly. Make sure you typed the amount correctly.

Or, the beginning balance in QuickBooks may not match the beginning balance on the bank statement. Typically, this problem occurs when you change the amount or cleared status of a reconciled transaction, or delete a reconciled transaction. You can use the Discrepancy report in QuickBooks to help you find transactions that may be causing the problem.

Resolve Discrepancies

① Click Banking.

② Click Reconcile.

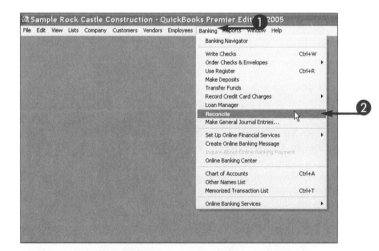

The Begin Reconciliation window appears.

③ Click Locate Discrepancies.

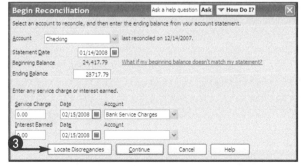

The Locate Discrepancies window appears.

④ Click here to select an account.

⑤ Click Discrepancy Report.

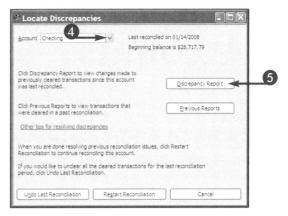

● The Discrepancy Report appears, showing transactions modified since they were reconciled.

You can double-click a transaction to display it in the window where you created it and modify it.

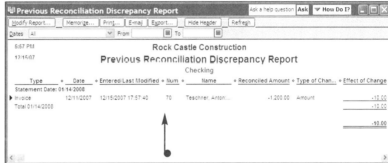

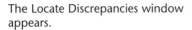

Does the Discrepancy Report show only those transactions that help resolve reconciliation problems?

▼ No. All cleared transactions that have changed appear on the report. If you change the date of a cleared transaction, it appears on the report. You may want to compare previous reconciliation reports to the current report to ensure that previously cleared transactions are still cleared. You can print previous reconciliation reports from the Locate Discrepancies window. Follow steps 1 to 3 in this section, then click Previous Reports. QuickBooks displays a window where you can select reports from previous reconciliations to print; you also can have QuickBooks print those reports showing cleared transactions plus changes made since reconciliation.

Is there an easy way to determine what is causing the difference to be something other than 0?

▼ You can eliminate one of the potential reasons if you use the Sum of the Digits rule. Add the digits of the difference to see if they equal 9 or a multiple of 9. If so, you probably have recorded one or more checks or deposits and transposed digits.

How can I find a deleted transaction?

▼ If you turn on the Audit Trail in QuickBooks, use the Audit Trail report. See Chapter 23 for details. If you have not turned on the Audit Trail report, use the Missing Checks report or create a report of deposits.

Move Funds between Accounts

You can move funds between accounts in QuickBooks using two different methods: You can use the Transfer Funds window or the Make General Journal Entries window.

If you need to move money between balance sheet accounts, the Transfer Funds window makes the task easy. For example, use the Transfer Funds window to move money between your operating bank account and your payroll bank account. If you make an ATM withdrawal or take a cash advance on a business credit card, you can use this window to transfer the funds from the credit card account into a petty cash account.

When you need to transfer funds between two accounts that are not balance sheet accounts, you cannot use the Transfer Funds window; instead, you must create a journal entry. For example, to record a depreciation expense, use a journal entry. If you prepay insurance, you can use a journal entry to record each month's portion of the prepayment to the insurance expense account when you incur the expense.

Journal entries can consist of many lines of debits summing to one or more credits, or many lines of credits summing to one or more debits; the only rule for journal entries is that total debits must equal total credits.

Move Funds Between Accounts

Transfer Funds

① Click Banking.

② Click Transfer Funds.

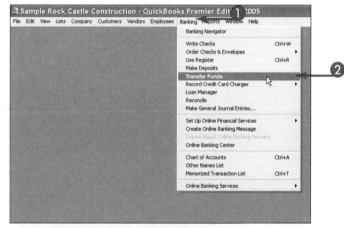

The Transfer Funds window appears.

③ Click ▦ to select a date for the transfer.

④ Click here to select the account from which to transfer funds.

⑤ Click here to select the account to which you want to transfer funds.

⑥ Type the transfer amount here.

● You can type a memo here.

⑦ Click Save & Close.

QuickBooks transfers the funds.

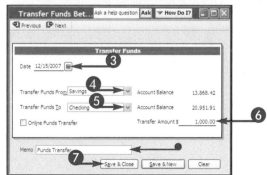

Make a Journal Entry

1 Click Banking.

2 Click Make General Journal Entries.

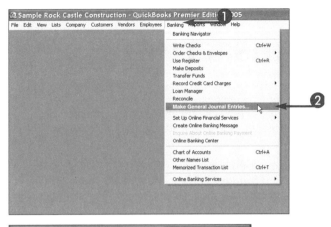

The Make General Journal Entries window appears.

3 Click ▣ to select a date for the entry.

● You can type a number for the entry here.

4 Click here to select an account.

5 Type a debit amount here.

6 Repeat steps 4 to 5, typing an amount in the Credit column when you repeat step 5.

7 Repeat steps 4 to 6 for additional lines on the entry.

8 Click Save & Close.

QuickBooks records the journal entry.

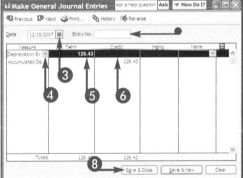

Can I only use the Transfer Funds window when transferring funds between bank accounts?

▼ No. You can use the Transfer Funds window to move money between bank, Other Current Asset, Fixed Asset, Other Asset, Credit Card, Other Current Liability, Long Term Liability, and Equity accounts. For example, if you have a line of credit, you can use this window to move money from the line of credit account into your bank account. Or, if the business owner takes a draw from the business and the money is transferred electronically into the business owner's account, you can use this window to transfer the money in QuickBooks from the business checking account to the owner's draw account.

Can I use a journal entry to move money between classes?

▼ Yes. Typically, you debit and credit the same account but assign different classes to each line of the entry.

How do I know whether to debit or credit an account?

▼ In general, debits increase asset accounts and expense accounts and decrease liability accounts, equity accounts, and income accounts. Credits increase liability accounts, equity accounts, and income accounts, and decrease asset accounts and expense accounts. There are some unusual accounts, such as contra-asset accounts. If you need to make a journal entry using one of these accounts, consult your accountant.

Find a
Transaction

Y ou need to find transactions you entered if you want to double-check, examine the history of, or perhaps correct a transaction. You can search in a variety of ways, but the Find feature is undoubtedly the most robust.

QuickBooks contains both a Simple Find feature and an Advanced Find feature. The Simple Find feature enables you to specify a limited number of search criteria; for example, you can select the type of transaction for which you want to search, set a date range, select a specific name, and specify a transaction number or amount. Often, these criteria are sufficient to help you quickly find the transaction you need.

However, in some cases, you need to use the Advanced Find feature, which enables you to select from many more criteria to narrow your search. Bear in mind that the more search criteria parameters you set, the fewer results QuickBooks finds. You may use an advanced find when searching for transactions that updated a particular account, transactions that have not yet been reconciled, transactions with a particular FOB destination; the possibilities are endless. In this section, you see an example using Advanced Find to search for transactions shipped via Federal Express.

Find a Transaction

Perform a Simple Search

① Click Edit.

② Click Find.

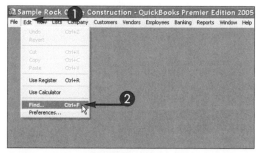

QuickBooks displays the Simple tab of the Find window.

③ Click here and select a transaction type.

④ Click here to select a name.

Note: *The type of name changes depending on the transaction type selected.*

- You can click 🔲 to select starting and ending dates.

- You can type a transaction number to search for a specific transaction or type an amount QuickBooks should search for.

⑤ Click Find.

- QuickBooks displays the results of the search and you can double-click to display the transaction in the window where it was created.

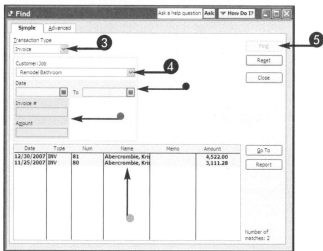

Perform an Advanced Search

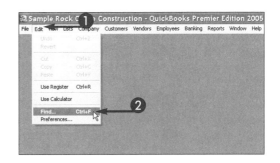

1 Click Edit.

2 Click Find.

QuickBooks displays the Find window.

3 Click the Advanced tab.

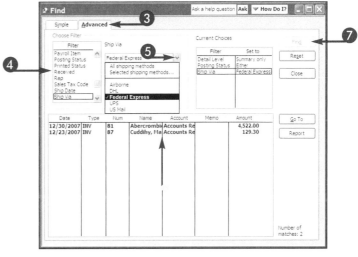

4 Click a filter.

5 Click here and select criteria for the filter.

Note: The available criteria and the method you use to select change, depending on the selected filter.

6 Repeat steps 4 to 5 to add additional filters.

7 Click Find.

QuickBooks displays the results of the search here and you can double-click to display the transaction in the window where it was created.

What are some of the other ways I can search for transactions?

▼ You can open the window where you created the transaction and click the Next and Previous buttons until you find the transaction; you can open the register for an account affected by a transaction and scroll to find the transaction; or you can create a custom report that includes the transaction. See Chapter 22 for more information on creating custom reports.

My search turned up no results. What did I do wrong?

▼ Either no transactions exist with the criteria you specified, or you specified too many criteria. To see more transactions, try eliminating some of the filter criteria you specified; for example, eliminate a transaction number or a date range on a simple find, and remove a filter from an advanced find.

How do I remove a filter I set?

▼ You can click Reset to start the search over, or you can click the filter in the Current Choices box and set its criteria so that you do not filter for it. For example, select all vendors instead of one.

Can I print the results of a search?

▼ Yes. On either tab of the Find window, click Report. QuickBooks does not print the search criteria.

View Transaction Details

S ometimes, viewing the actual transaction is not sufficient. Instead, you need to know what other transactions are tied to the transaction in question. For example, you may want to see payments associated with a customer invoice or checks tied to a vendor bill. In QuickBooks, you view transaction history to obtain this information. If, instead, you need to know the accounts affected by a transaction and the associated debits and credits, use the Transaction Journal. For example, you or your accountant may want to know all the income accounts updated by a particular invoice and the amounts by which those accounts were updated.

Why do I see the message "no history exists for a transaction" when I click the Transaction History button?

▼ You will see a message like this when no related transactions exist for the transaction you are viewing. For example, unpaid bills and open customer invoices have no transaction history. If a customer partially pays an invoice, QuickBooks considers the partial payment as history. If you pay a vendor bill, the check becomes transaction history.

Can I print a list of the transactions that appear in the Transaction History window?

▼ Yes. From the Transaction History window, click Print.

View Transaction Details

1 Display a transaction.

Note: *See the section "Find a Transaction" or use the Next and Previous arrows in the appropriate transaction window to display a transaction.*

2 Click the History button.

QuickBooks displays the Transaction History window.

You can click a transaction and then click the Go To button to view the selected transaction.

3 Click Edit Invoice.

4 Press Ctrl+Y.

QuickBooks displays the Transaction Journal report.

● This report shows the amounts and accounts that QuickBooks debited and credited when you created the transaction.

5 Click the Close button (⊠) to close the report and the transaction window.

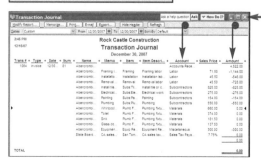

Delete or Void a Transaction

O ccasionally, you need to eliminate the effects of the transaction. In most cases, you have three choices: You can enter a transaction that reverses the original transaction, you can delete the transaction, or you can void the transaction.

Entering a transaction to reverse the original transaction can be difficult and confusing, so most users avoid this option. Many users delete transactions, but this approach does not present a complete picture of your company data; further, unless you use the Audit Trail feature, you have no record of the action. You can read about the Audit Trail feature in Chapter 23. Whenever possible, you should void transactions instead of deleting them.

Why should I void a transaction rather than delete it?

▼ Deleting a transaction removes all traces of the transaction from your QuickBooks company file, but voiding leaves the skeleton of the transaction and sets all the amounts to $0 so that the transaction has no effect on your company's books. When you delete a transaction, you leave no audit trail; so if you mistakenly delete a transaction, reconstructing the transaction is extremely difficult. Voiding a transaction solves this problem by leaving an audit trail.

Delete or Void a Transaction

① Display a transaction.

Note: See the section "Find a Transaction" or use the Next and Previous arrows in the appropriate transaction window to display a transaction.

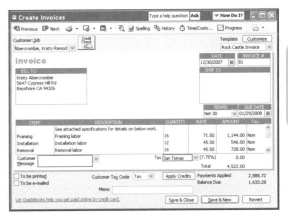

② Click Edit.

③ Click Delete Invoice or Void Invoice.

If you click Delete Invoice, QuickBooks removes the transaction from your company data file.

If you click Void Invoice, QuickBooks removes the effects of the transaction from your company file.

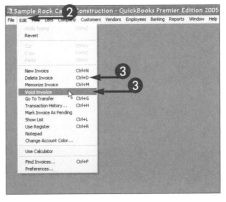

PART V

Memorize a Transaction

I f you prepare any type of transaction on a repetitive basis, you can use the memorize feature to make QuickBooks "remember" the information you enter during the data-entry process to help save time. Suppose, for example, that you run a pest control business and issue an invoice for the same amount each month to a particular customer. As long as you do not increase prices, there are no changes to the invoice each month.

You can memorize almost any type of transaction using the steps in this section. For example, you can memorize sales orders, sales receipts, credit memos, statement charges, purchase orders, bills, checks, and credit card transactions. You cannot memorize time tracking transactions, customer receipts, employee paychecks, inventory adjustments, or assembly builds.

Can you give an example of when to memorize an invoice?

▼ If you issue an invoice for the same amount repeatedly to one or more customers, or if you invoice all your customers for the same item but for different amounts every month, memorize the invoice. You can memorize an invoice with no dollar amounts and fill them in when you enter the memorized transaction. You also can memorize an invoice that you need to distribute to more than one account. For example, suppose that you own a landscaping company and you distribute your invoice partially to a landscaping income account and partially to a lawn treatment income account.

Memorize a Transaction

① Display a transaction.

Note: See the section "Find a Transaction" or use the Next and Previous arrows in the appropriate transaction window to display a transaction.

② Click Edit.

③ Click Memorize Invoice.

Note: If you are memorizing a different transaction type, click the Memorize command for that transaction type.

The Memorize Transaction dialog box appears.

④ Type a name for the transaction here.

⑤ Click the Remind Me option (○ changes to ◉).

⑥ Click here to select a frequency.

⑦ Click ▦ to select the next date for the transaction.

⑧ Click OK.

QuickBooks memorizes and redisplays the transaction.

⑨ Click Save & Close.

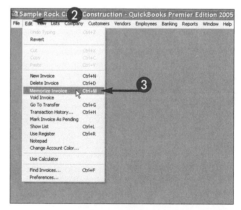

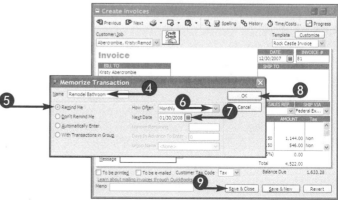

Enter a Memorized Transaction

When you create a memorized transaction, you establish a date on which QuickBooks affects accounts. But QuickBooks does not affect accounts until you enter — or "use," as QuickBooks refers to the process — a memorized transaction that you previously created. The process, therefore, is two-part: You first create a memorized transaction and, when you are ready to affect your accounts with the transaction, you use the memorized transaction. You can tell QuickBooks to automatically use a memorized transaction on a specified date, or you can use the transaction yourself. For details on creating memorized transactions, see the section "Memorize a Transaction"; this section shows you how to use a previously memorized transaction that you did not tell QuickBooks to enter automatically.

Can QuickBooks help me remember to use a memorized transaction that I must change each time I enter it?

▼ Because you must change the transaction each time you use it, you cannot set it up for automatic entry, but you can tell QuickBooks to use a reminder to jog your memory to enter memorized transactions. Reminders appear in a list of their own, but you also can set up QuickBooks to display the Reminders List when you open your company. See Chapter 24 for more on reminders.

Enter a Memorized Transaction

1. Click Lists.
2. Click Memorized Transaction List.

The Memorized Transaction List window appears.

3. Click the transaction you want to enter, noting the date of the transaction.

4. Click Enter Transaction.

The transaction appears in the window where you created it.

● The date of the transaction matches the next date based on the memorized criteria.

You can change this date if you want.

5. Click Save & Close to record the transaction.

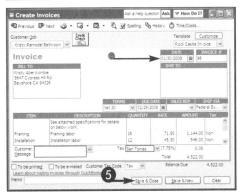

Work with a List Window

Although you use list windows to edit or view the information about the records for that list, you can make the list window itself work for you. For example, you can sort the records listed in the window by any column displayed in the window. Instead of viewing your customers in alphabetical order, you can quickly find out which customer has the highest total estimate if you sort the window in Estimate Total order, from highest to lowest. Or, you may want to view your vendors in the order of the amount of money you owe them, from lowest to

highest. You may also want to view items in the order of quantity on hand, or to view employees in Social Security number order.

You can arrange lists in addition to sorting them. By default, QuickBooks displays list information in a hierarchical view. For example, all jobs for a customer appear indented under the customer's name. All subitems appear indented under the parent item's name, and all subaccounts appear indented under the parent account's name. If you prefer, you can switch to a flat view, where no record appears indented in the window. The flat view is useful when sorting long lists.

Work with a List Window

Sort a List

① Click List.

② Click Customer:Job List.

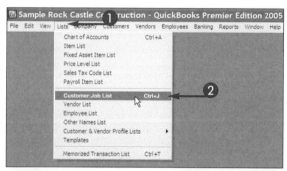

The list window appears, sorted alphabetically by Name.

③ Click any column heading.

● QuickBooks sorts the list in the order of the selected column heading.

Note: *This section shows the Balance Total column after the second click, to sort the column in descending balance order.*

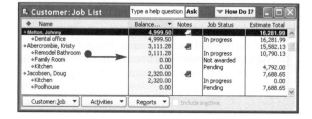

Switch Views

1. Perform steps 1 to 2 on the previous page.

2. Click Customer:Job.

3. Click Flat View.

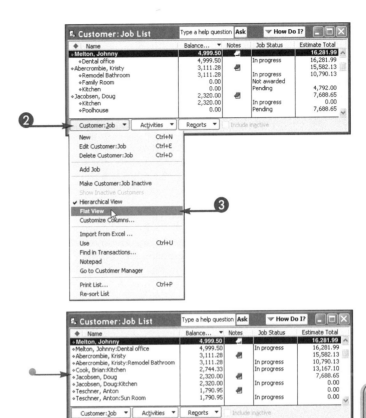

● QuickBooks changes the look of the list from a hierarchical presentation to a flat presentation.

If I no longer need a list entry, can I delete it?

▼ Only if you did not use the entry in any transactions. You can hide entries you used in transactions. Right-click the entry and click Make Inactive. You can display hidden entries if you click the leftmost button in the window and then click Include Inactive. QuickBooks displays hidden entries with an X beside them. To use a hidden item again, right-click it and click Make Active.

Is there a way to identify how the list is currently sorted?

▼ Yes. Next to one column heading, you see a carat (▼) pointing either up or down. If the carat is pointing up, QuickBooks is sorting the list by that column heading in ascending order. An upward-pointing carat results in alphabetical sorting from A to Z or numerical sorting from lowest to highest. A downward-pointing carat indicates the opposite alphabetical and numerical sorting.

Can I get the window back to the way it appeared before I sorted?

▼ Yes. Whenever the list is sorted in any order other than the default order, a diamond (◆) appears in the upper-left corner of the window. Click the diamond (◆) to redisplay the window in hierarchical format, using the default sort order for the window.

Work in the Customer Centers

The Customer Center provides you with overview information concerning customer balances and accounts receivable. The upper-left portion of the window shows you total accounts receivable and the balance due through today; you can change the time frame to view the balance due through, say, the end of the month.

In the bottom of the Customer Center, you can view information that you select from a list; for example, you can view customers with overdue balances — and the overdue balance amount. You also can view unbilled job-related expenses, or you can view the net profit from your ten most — or least — profitable customers, jobs, products, or services. When you double-click one of these amounts, QuickBooks displays a report showing the details behind the amount. You also can click links to read about customer-related decision tools.

You also can zero in on the details for one customer using the Customer Detail Center. The Customer Detail Center shows basic billing and contact information along with credit limit information. In the bottom of the window, you can display two of the following three kinds of information: open invoices and charges for the customer, outstanding items on order, and payments received and credits issued.

Work in the Customer Centers

Work in the Customer Center

① Click Customers.

② Click Customer Center.

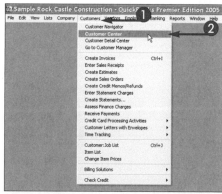

The Customer Center window appears.

● You can scroll through the list of customers with open balances here.

● Use these two sections to display selected information about customers or jobs.

● You can click links in this section to read about fee-based decision tools.

You can double-click most amounts to display a report that comprises the details of that amount.

③ Click the Close button (⊠) to close the window.

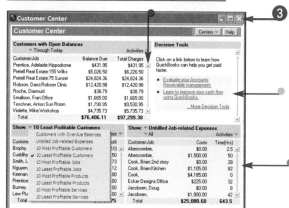

Work in the Customer Detail Center

1 Click Customers.

2 Click Customer Detail Center.

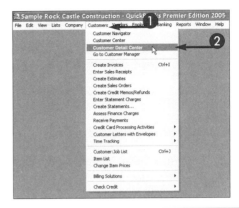

The Customer Detail Center window appears.

3 Click here to select a customer.

○ You can use these two sections to display selected information about the customer.

● You can click links in this section to read about fee-based decision tools.

You can double-click any row in the lower section of the window to display that transaction in the window where you created it.

4 Click ⊠ to close the window.

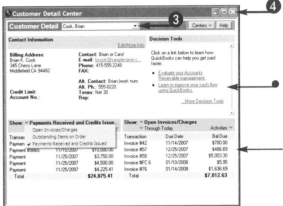

What report do I see when I double-click a dollar amount in the Customer Center?

▼ The report you see when double-clicking a dollar amount depends on the information being displayed in the Customer Center at the time. For example, if you double-click an amount in the Customers with Open Balances section, QuickBooks displays the Open Invoices report for that customer. If you double-click an amount while viewing the ten most or least profitable customers, QuickBooks displays the Job Profitability Detail report for that customer. If you double-click an amount while viewing unbilled job-related expenses, QuickBooks displays the Unbilled Costs by Job report for that customer.

What does the Centers button do?

▼ You can open the Company Center, the Customer Center, the Customer Detail Center, or the Vendor Detail Center from the menu QuickBooks displays when you click Centers.

What decision tools are available?

▼ Intuit makes available Accounts Receivable tools that analyze your accounts receivable, tools to help you improve your cash flow by reducing your collection period, and a tool to help you select the right sales form — an invoice, a sales receipt, or a statement — for your business. Some decision tools are fee-based.

Work in the Vendor Detail Center

Although QuickBooks does not contain an overview center for vendors and accounts payable like it does for customers and accounts receivable, you find a Vendor Detail Center. Like the Customer Detail Center, you can use the Vendor Detail Center to zero in on the details of one vendor. The Vendor Detail Center shows basic contact information along with credit limit information. In the bottom of the window, you can display two of the following three kinds of information: unpaid bills, outstanding purchase orders, and payments issued. You can double-click any entry in these sections to view that entry in the window where you created it.

What decision-making tools are available for accounts payable?

▼ Only the one listed in the Vendor Detail Center window — the tool that helps you evaluate your level of borrowing to determine if you are borrowing too much or too little. This tool uses and explains the Debt to Equity ratio, one of many ratios you can use to evaluate your business. The Debt to Equity ratio uses your balance sheet to evaluate your level of debt. You and your accountant should decide on an appropriate level of debt for your business and then use this tool to compare where your debt is with where you want it to be.

Work in the Vendor Detail Center

① Click Vendors.

② Click Vendor Detail Center.

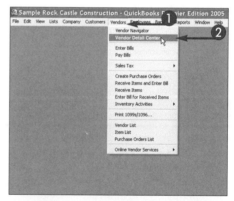

The Vendor Detail Center window appears.

③ Click here to select a vendor.

● You can use these two sections to display selected information about the vendor.

● You can click links in this section to read about fee-based decision tools.

You can double-click anywhere on a row to display that transaction in the window where you created it.

④ Click ☒ to close the window.

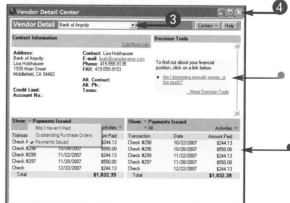

Work in the Company Center

Q uickBooks contains a Company Center with an overview of your company's financial position. At the top of the Company Center, the balances of your accounts receivable, accounts payable, bank, credit card, and current liability accounts appear. You can view an account or an amount in this section to see either a register or a report of details for the amount. At the bottom of the Company Center, the Income and Expense Trend bar graph appears; you can open the graph to see a QuickInsight combination bar and pie chart, and you can drill down the bars and pie slices that appear to see more details.

MASTER IT

What report appears when I double-click an amount in the Account Balances section of the Company Center? If I click Activities?

▼ For the Account Balances section, the report that appears depends on the amount you double-click. If you double-click Amt Due for an accounts receivable or accounts payable account, the Open Invoices report or the Unpaid Bills report appears. For other accounts, QuickBooks displays a QuickReport of transactions for the selected account.

Click Activities in the Account Balances section to display a menu of windows you can open and reports related to the accounts that appear in the section. Click Activities in the Income and Expense Trend section to print one of three versions of the Profit & Loss report.

Work in the Company Center

1 Click Company.

2 Click Company Center.

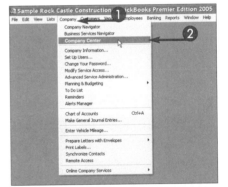

The Company Center window appears and contains balances, graphs, and links that you can double-click to view details.

● This section displays account balances for important accounts.

● This section displays an income and expense graph.

● Links in this section lead to fee-based decision tools.

○ These links open the Customer Center.

3 Click ☒ to close the window.

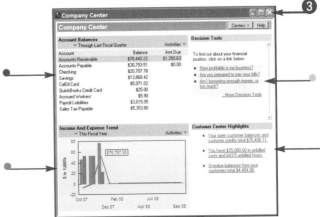

Make a Loan Payment

I n Chapter 2, you see how to set up loans in the Loan Manager. The Loan Manager helps you view payment schedules, set up loan payments, and analyze different loan scenarios. When you set up a loan in the Loan Manager, you also make payments against the loan from the Loan Manager. The Loan Manager calculates the principal and interest portions of the loan payment as well as any escrow or other fees and splits the loan payment for you into the correct accounts, based on the way you set up the loan.

When you make a loan payment, you can either enter a bill that you subsequently pay using the Pay Bills window, or you can write a check that you can print immediately or later. Or, if your loan payment is made electronically, you can write a check from the Loan Manager and assign a number without printing the check. This section shows you how to make a loan payment by writing a check that you can print later.

When you use the Loan Manager to make a loan payment, you can make a regular payment or an extra payment.

Make a Loan Payment

① Click Banking.

② Click Loan Manager.

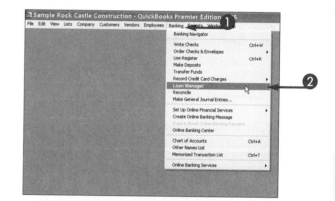

The Loan Manager window appears.

③ Click a loan to pay.

④ Click Set Up Payment.

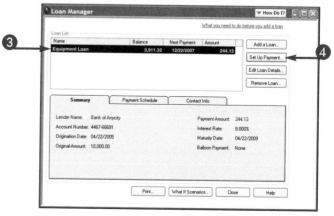

The Set Up Payment window appears.

5 Click here to select a payment type.

6 Double-check the payment information amounts.

7 Click OK.

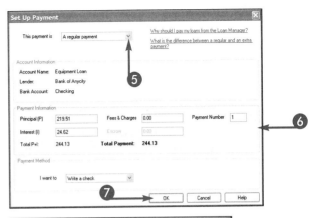

The Write Checks window appears.

8 Click the To be printed option to print your checks in a batch (☐ changes to ☑).

9 Click Save & Close.

The Loan Manager window reappears.

10 Click Close in the Loan Manager window.

The Loan Manager makes the loan payment.

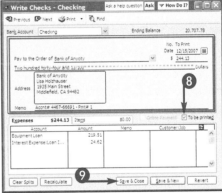

What is an extra loan payment and why would I want to make one?

▼ Your loan has terms that involve you paying interest — a fee the lender charges for loaning you the money. Each regular loan payment pays back some of the actual loan and some of the interest due. When you make an extra loan payment, you can specify how you want the lender to account for that money. If you apply the extra loan payment to the principal of the loan, you pay back the loan faster and therefore pay less interest. Making extra loan payments can reduce the premium you pay for borrowing the money.

Can I change the amount I pay on a regular loan payment?

▼ Yes. You can change any portion of your loan payment — the principal, interest, escrow, or fees and charges amount. You can, for example, pay additional principal to pay off the loan faster and reduce the amount of interest you pay on the loan. Any changes you make to any facet of the payment apply only to the particular payment you are setting up; the next time you set up a payment for the loan, all the information you see will be the original information.

Using the Cash Flow Projector

The flow of cash through your business can make or break it, so projecting cash flows is crucial. You may be selling products or services at phenomenal rates, but if your customers do not pay you, you cannot pay your own bills. Excess cash flowing into your business can be a lost opportunity. If you can project the receipt of that cash and the time period for which you do not need it to run your business, you can invest it, using it to make more money for your business.

QuickBooks contains two Cash Flow reports. The Statement of Cash Flows report shows you cash flow from a historical perspective, and the Cash Flow Forecast report uses your QuickBooks data to project future cash flows for a specified period of time. See Chapter 22 for help printing a report.

The Cash Flow Projector is a wizard that walks you through preparing a six-week projection of cash inflows and outflows using current QuickBooks data and additional projected cash receipts or expenses. None of the data you enter in the wizard updates your QuickBooks data. To use the tool effectively, make sure that you have entered all transactions before you run the tool. Be aware of any adjustments not represented by transactions that you may need to make.

Using the Cash Flow Projector

① Click Company.

② Click Planning & Budgeting.

③ Click Cash Flow Projector.

The first screen of the Cash Flow Projector Wizard appears.

④ Click Next.

The Beginning Balance screen appears.

⑤ Select accounts you want to include when calculating the beginning cash balance (☐ changes to ☑).

● You can adjust the cash balance here.

⑥ Click Next.

The Cash Receipts screen appears.

⑦ Click here to select a projection method.

● You can manually add expected receipts by clicking here to select a date and typing in the Description column next to the date.

● You can adjust the next six weeks' expected cash receipts here.

⑧ Click Next.

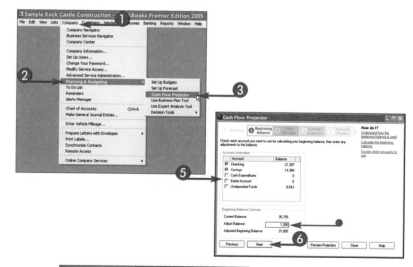

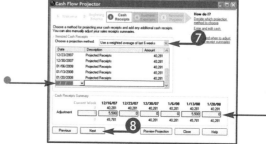

The Business Expenses screen appears.

You can manually add expected expenses by clicking here and selecting an account and typing here.

● You can adjust the next six weeks' expected expenses here.

⑨ Click Next.

The Accounts Payable screen appears.

● You can manually adjust payment dates by clicking here to select a date.

● You can adjust the next six weeks' expected accounts payable here.

⑩ Click Finish Projection.

The Weekly Cash Flow Projection window appears, showing projected cash flow for the next six weeks.

⑪ Click Print to print the report.

⑫ Click Close twice to close the Cash Flow Projector.

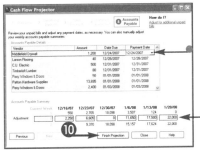

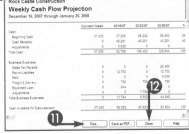

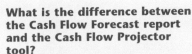

What is the difference between the Cash Flow Forecast report and the Cash Flow Projector tool?

▼ Both the Cash Flow Forecast report and the Cash Flow Projector tool use your QuickBooks data to project future cash flows for a specified period of time, but the Cash Flow Projector tool gives you more flexibility in creating an accurate cash flow picture by permitting you to select and adjust the QuickBooks data that you include in the cash flow and to include other cash flow information.

What appears on the first screen of the Cash Flow Projector tool?

▼ The Welcome screen of the Cash Flow Projector Wizard explains that the tool uses your QuickBooks data to project your cash flows and creates a summary of your cash flow requirements for the next six weeks by calculating cash on hand, incoming cash, and expenses and bills. From the Welcome screen, you also can view a sample cash flow projection produced by the tool.

Why would I want to save the projection produced by the Cash Flow Projector tool as a PDF?

▼ If you save the projection and print it, you can then prepare a different projection using different data to compare different potential situations. For example, you may want to see what your cash flow will look like both with and without an expected deposit in Week 3.

Sell a Fixed Asset

As you learn in Chapter 2, fixed assets are things that you own and use in a way that benefits your business for longer than one year and generates revenue, either directly or indirectly, for your business. If you own the printing presses you use, those presses are fixed assets. The ovens in a restaurant used to prepare food are fixed assets. Buildings, office furniture, computers, cash registers, and vehicles are all considered fixed assets.

Because fixed assets last longer than one year, generally accepted accounting principles permit you to allocate the expense of a fixed asset purchase over the fixed asset's

useful life rather than recognizing the entire expense in the year you make the purchase. This process of spreading an expense over the life of the asset is called *depreciation*.

Eventually, you may have no use for a particular fixed asset; for example, you may decide to replace a computer. You may sell a fixed asset, give it away, or even throw it away. At that point, you need to remove it from your books. This section shows you how to sell a fixed asset for cash to one of your customers.

Sell a Fixed Asset

① Click Customers.

② Click Enter Sales Receipts.

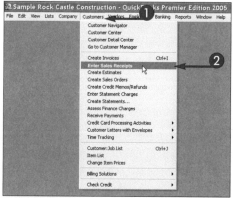

The Enter Sales Receipts window appears.

③ Click here to select a Customer:Job.

④ Fill in the top of the Sales Receipt form.

Note: *See Chapter 13 for more information on Sales Receipts.*

⑤ Click here to select the fixed asset item.

● QuickBooks fills in the description.

⑥ Type the amount.

QuickBooks displays a message about the sale price of the fixed asset item.

⑦ Click Yes.

⑧ Click Save & Close.

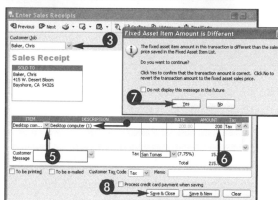

QuickBooks displays a message about updating fixed asset sales information.

9 Click Yes.

QuickBooks records the transaction, closes the window, and updates the fixed asset information.

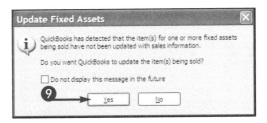

10 To view the sales information about the fixed asset, open the Fixed Asset Item List and double-click the item.

Note: See Chapter 2 for details on opening the Fixed Asset Item List.

- The sale information appears here.

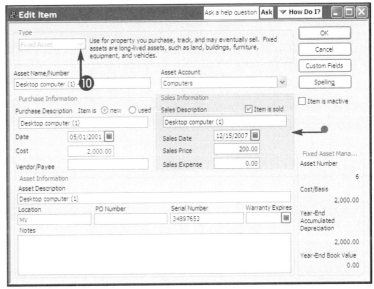

PART V

What should I enter in QuickBooks if I do not sell a fixed asset but, instead, give it away or throw it away?

▼ You need to enter a journal entry. Because each fixed asset is associated with a fixed asset account, you credit the fixed asset account and you debit an expense account where you track gains or losses on assets. If you track the fixed asset's depreciation in a separate account, you need to credit the fixed asset account and debit both the accumulated depreciation account and the expense account where you track gains or losses on assets. When you see the message asking if you want to track the sale of this fixed asset, click Yes. Note that this does not update the Fixed asset item. You need to edit the item to mark it as sold.

Will a fixed asset item still appear in the list after I sell it?

▼ Yes, but you can mark the fixed asset item as inactive; in the Fixed Asset Item List, highlight the item, click the Item button, and click Make Inactive.

If my customer plans to pay me later for the asset, how do I handle the transaction?

▼ Do everything described in this section except use the Create Invoices window, which you can display if you click Customers and then click Create Invoices. QuickBooks creates a receivable, and when you receive payment, QuickBooks reduces the receivable and increases your cash account.

Set Up
Forecasts

You can set up both budgets and forecasts in QuickBooks. Budgets and forecasts are estimates you make for account values. In QuickBooks, you can create a budget for profit and loss accounts and for balance sheet accounts, although most people do not try to budget for balance sheet accounts, because their amounts represent the value of the account at a specific point in time. You can create forecasts for profit and loss accounts only and you can create either a budget or a forecast for a uniquely identified period of time; you also can create budgets or forecasts for Customer:Jobs and classes.

While there is no definitive explanation of the difference between a budget and a forecast, typically, budget amounts remain the same for the duration of the budget period, while people tend to revise forecast amounts as time passes using actual information to obtain more accurate forecasts.

The method you use to create a budget or a forecast in QuickBooks is almost identical, so this section provides an example of creating a forecast.

Set Up Forecasts

1 Click Company.

2 Click Planning & Budgeting.

3 Click Set Up Forecast.

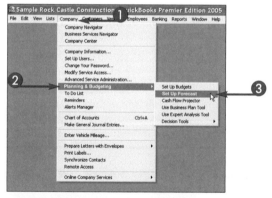

The Create New Forecast Wizard begins.

4 Click here to select a year for the forecast.

5 Click Next.

The Additional Forecast Criteria screen appears.

6 Click a forecast criteria option
(○ changes to ⦿).

Note: *If you have turned on class tracking, an option appears here to create a forecast for a class.*

7 Click Next.

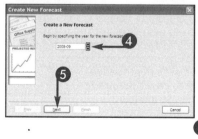

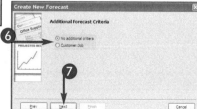

The Choose how you want to create a forecast screen appears.

8 Click this option to create the forecast using last year's data (○ changes to ⊙).

9 Click Finish.

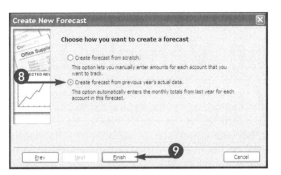

The forecast appears on-screen.

● You can change any amount by selecting it and typing.

● You can click Save to save changes without closing the window.

10 Click OK.

QuickBooks saves the budget and closes the window.

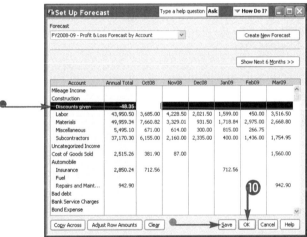

What does the Adjust Row Amounts button do?

▼ This button enables you to increase or decrease all months or selected months of a particular forecast row by a dollar amount or a percentage. To increase all months, simply click the button. To increase a particular month and all future months of a row, click in the month where you want the increase or decrease to begin, and then click the button. When the Adjust Row Amounts dialog box appears, choose to increase starting from the first month of the forecast or the selected month of the forecast. Then, specify the amount or percentage to increase or decrease and click OK.

What does the Show Next 6 Months button do?

▼ This button appears only if your screen resolution is set to less than 1024 x 768; under these conditions, QuickBooks displays only six months of your forecast at a time and you use the Show Next 6 Months button to display the subsequent six months.

What does the Copy Across button do?

▼ Use it to assign the same amount to every month of a particular row. Type the amount for the row in the first month that the amount should appear. Then, click Copy Across, and QuickBooks fills the amount into all subsequent months for that row.

Add Vehicles to the Vehicle List

You can use the Vehicle Tracking feature in QuickBooks to track the mileage you use on your vehicles, assign a cost to the mileage, and, if you want, bill your customers for the mileage. The mileage incurred on your vehicles may be tax deductible; you are permitted to deduct either the actual vehicle expenses or a standard mileage rate, but you cannot deduct both. With the vehicle mileage tracking information you collect in QuickBooks, your accountant can decide which deduction most benefits you.

To track mileage, start by adding vehicles to the Vehicle List. After you have added a vehicle to the Vehicle List, drivers of the vehicle need to monitor the vehicle's odometer and provide you with odometer readings that you can record in QuickBooks. You should create a form that you give to each driver; the form should contain the vehicle's name — preferably the same name you supply in QuickBooks — as well as columns for the trip starting and ending dates, the vehicle's starting and ending odometer readings, and the customer's name if the trip applies to a customer. Drivers should complete the log at the beginning and end of each trip and provide you with the information you need to record in QuickBooks.

Add Vehicles to the Vehicle List

① Click Lists.

② Click Customer & Vendor Profile Lists

③ Click Vehicle List.

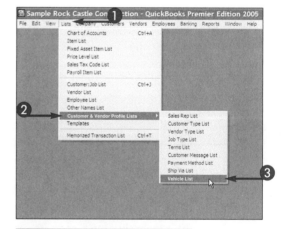

The Vehicle List window appears.

④ Click Vehicle.

⑤ Click New.

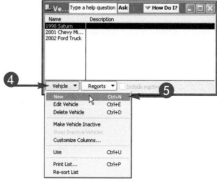

The New Vehicle dialog box appears.

6 Type the name of the vehicle here.

7 Type a description of the vehicle here.

8 Click OK.

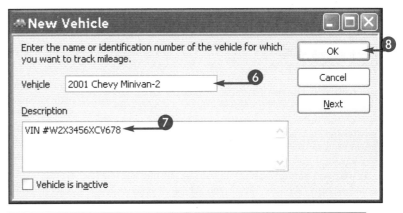

● QuickBooks saves the vehicle in the Vehicle List.

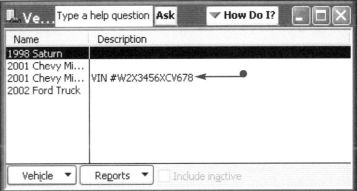

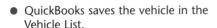

If my employees use their own cars for business purposes, should I set up their cars in the Vehicle List?

▼ Your employees are entitled to mileage reimbursement for business use of a personal vehicle. Because the vehicles you set up in the list do not affect your company data, you can set up vehicles you do not own so that you can record and track mileage. At the end of the year, you can use vehicle mileage reports to help determine the amount of reimbursement, which is included on the employee's last paycheck of the year. See the section "Reimbursing Employees for Mileage Expense" for details on creating the reimbursement.

How can I change vehicle information?

▼ Follow steps 1 to 3 in this section to open the Vehicle List window. Click a vehicle to select it, click Vehicle, and then click Edit. QuickBooks displays the Edit Vehicle dialog box, which looks just like the New Vehicle dialog box. Make your changes and click OK.

Can I print a list of my vehicles?

▼ Yes. Follow steps 1 to 3 in this section to open the Vehicle List window. Next click Vehicle, and then Print List.

Track Vehicle Mileage

To track mileage for a vehicle, you enter mileage slips that identify the vehicle driven, the trip start and end date, the odometer start and end date, and the total miles driven. The slip also contains a place where you can type a description of the trip. You can also assign the mileage slip to a Customer:Job and make the slip billable so that you can charge the customer for the mileage. When you fill in the slip, if you supply the starting and ending odometer readings, QuickBooks calculates the total mileage.

If you intend to bill your customers for mileage used on your vehicles, you need to set up a service item or an other charge item in QuickBooks to assign the mileage income to the proper account. At the same time, you establish a billing rate for the mileage that QuickBooks uses to calculate the mileage charge. See Chapter 7 for details on creating a service item and an other charge item.

You can adjust the rates QuickBooks uses to calculate vehicle expenses. Typically you use the IRS-issued rates for vehicle expense, which usually changes at the beginning of each year, but can change several times during a year. Check with your accountant for the latest IRS rates.

Track Vehicle Mileage

Record Mileage

① Click Company.

② Click Enter Vehicle Mileage.

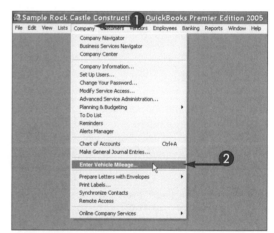

The Enter Vehicle Mileage window appears.

③ Click here and select a vehicle.

④ Click the calendar buttons (▦) to select trip starting and ending dates.

- You can type the odometer starting and ending values here.

⑤ Type the miles traveled here.

- You can bill the mileage to a customer by clicking here (☐ changes to ☑) and then clicking ☑ to select the customer and the item.

- You can type a description of the trip here.

⑥ Click Save & Close.

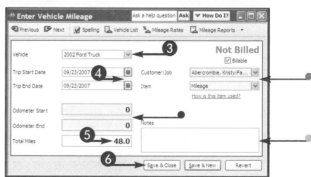

Change Mileage Rates

1 Perform steps 1 to 2 on the previous page.

2 Click Mileage Rates.

3 In the Mileage Rates window, click ▦ to select an effective date.

4 Type the mileage rate.

5 Click Close.

QuickBooks redisplays the Enter Vehicle Mileage window.

6 Click the Close button (▣) to close the window.

View Vehicle Mileage Summary

1 Perform steps 1 to 2 on the previous page.

2 Click Mileage Reports.

QuickBooks displays the Mileage by Vehicle Summary report.

You can double-click any value to see the details behind it.

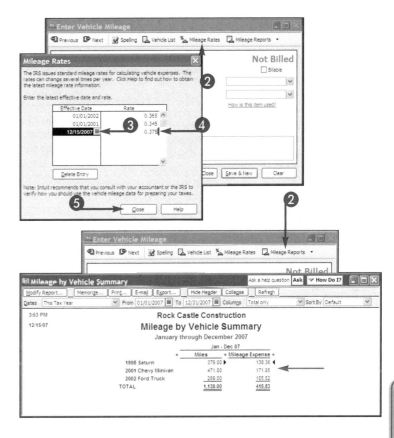

Can you explain the difference between the mileage rates I enter from the Enter Vehicle Mileage window and the mileage rate I establish on the service or other charge item?

▼ The mileage rates you enter through the Enter Vehicle Mileage window help establish the cost of mileage that can be tax deductible. You should use the rates that are the most current IRS-established rates for deducting vehicle mileage. QuickBooks uses the rate you establish on the Service or Other Charge item, which you create to assign a billing value to mileage and that appears when you include mileage on an invoice to a customer.

What other reports are available about the Vehicle Tracking feature?

▼ The Mileage by Vehicle Detail, the Mileage by Job Summary, and the Mileage by Job Detail reports are available. The Mileage by Vehicle Summary report appears in this section and shows the miles and billable amounts associated with each vehicle. Double-click an amount to view the Mileage by Vehicle Detail report, which lists the individual mileage entries for a particular vehicle. The Mileage by Job Summary shows miles and billable amounts assigned to each job; double-click an amount to view the Mileage by Job Detail report, which lists individual mileage records assigned to the job.

Invoicing Customers for Mileage

You can charge customers for the mileage applied to your vehicles. When you create a mileage slip — see the section "Track Vehicle Mileage" for details — you mark the slip as billable and supply the name of the Customer:Job and the service or other charge item you created to invoice mileage. As you create mileage slips, you can supply a description of the trip that you can transfer to the customer's invoice. When you prepare an invoice for the customer, these mileage charges are available for invoicing. Essentially, QuickBooks treats these billable time entries as reimbursable expenses.

Mileage charges billed to customers appear as line items on an invoice. For the description column on the invoice, you can choose to use the description typed in the Notes field of a mileage entry, or the description you supplied when you created the service or other charge item assigned to the mileage entry. Or, QuickBooks can include both descriptions on the customer's invoice.

If you have many mileage entries for a particular customer, you can also choose to combine the mileage entries into one line-item entry on the customer's invoice. If you combine entries, QuickBooks prints no information from the Notes fields of the mileage entries.

Invoicing Customers for Mileage

① Click Customers.

② Click Create Invoices.

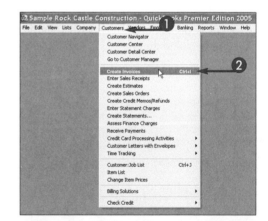

QuickBooks displays the Create Invoices window.

③ Click here to select the customer.

Note: *Click OK if QuickBooks displays a message indicating that you have outstanding billable time or costs.*

④ Fill in any charges for the customer besides the mileage charges.

Note: *See Chapter 11 for details.*

⑤ Click Time/Costs.

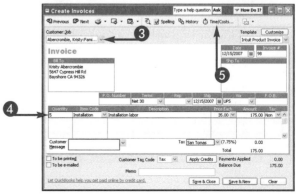

The Choose Billable Time and Costs dialog box appears.

⑥ Click the Mileage tab.

⑦ Click next to each mileage charge you want to include on the invoice.

● You can click here (☐ changes to ☑) to print only one line for mileage on the invoice.

⑧ Click OK.

● QuickBooks adds the mileage charges to the invoice.

⑨ Click Save & Close.

What happens when I click Options on the Choose Billabe Time and Costs dialog box?

▼ The Options for Transferring Billable Mileage dialog box appears, enabling you to include each mileage entry as a separate line on the invoice, or to print one line for all mileage entries with the same service or other charge item. If you choose to print one line for all mileage entries that use the same service or other charge item, QuickBooks prints the description from the service or other charge item on the invoice. If you choose to include separate lines for each mileage entry, then you can print, in place of the Description on the invoice, the information stored in the Notes field of the entry, the service or other charge item description, or service or other charge both.

Although I selected the "Print selected mileage and costs as one invoice item" option, the mileage entries I included on a customer bill appear separately. Why?

▼ On-screen, the entries appear separately, but, when you print the invoice, one line with a description of "Total Reimbursable Expenses" appears. Descriptions from mileage entries do not appear.

Is there a report that I can print to view unbilled mileage charges?

▼ Yes. You can print the Mileage by Job Detail report. Click Reports, click Jobs, Time & Mileage, and then Mileage by Job Detail. The Billing Status identifies whether an entry has been billed or remains billable.

Reimbursing Employees for Mileage Expense

I f your employees use their personal vehicles for business, they are entitled to reimbursement for the mileage expense. You typically reimburse employees for mileage expense on some regular basis, such as monthly. To create the reimbursement, you can write a separate check using the Write Checks window or you can use a nontaxable payroll addition item for mileage expense. For details on creating a payroll addition item, see Chapter 4. This section provides an example using a nontaxable addition called Mileage Reimb.

Although you can cut a separate paycheck for mileage reimbursement, you are less likely to make mistakes if you include the mileage reimbursement on a regular paycheck.

If you use a separate check, you must remember to eliminate regular paycheck additions and deductions, such as 401k contributions and medical insurance deductions.

To make the reimbursement, each employee should report the total business miles traveled. Mileage expense reimbursements cover gas, repairs, and depreciation as well as miles traveled while the employee was performing work for your business. You may also want to reimburse the employee for tolls. You then use the employee's mileage report and the current year's IRS guidelines for the mileage reimbursement rate to calculate the reimbursement. The mileage report should become an important part of the papers you keep as supporting documentation.

Reimbursing Employees for Mileage Expense

① Click Employees.

② Click Pay Employees.

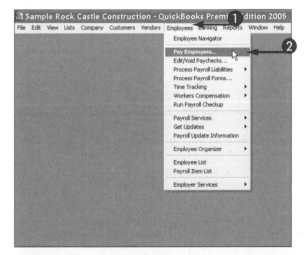

The Select Employees To Pay window appears.

③ Click here and select a bank account.

④ Click here to mark checks for printing in a batch (○ changes to ◉).

⑤ Click next to each employee you intend to pay (☐ changes to ☑).

⑥ Click here to preview the paycheck (○ changes to ◉).

⑦ Click Create.

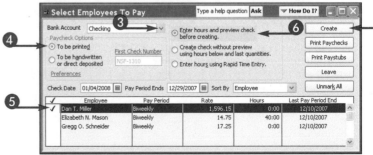

The Preview Paycheck window appears.

8 If you are creating a mileage reimbursement check only, delete items in these sections by highlighting them and pressing Ctlr-Delete on the keyboard.

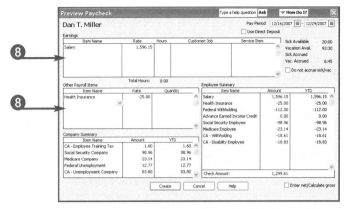

9 Click here to select the mileage reimbursement item.

● QuickBooks supplies the rate.

10 Click here and type the number of miles to reimburse.

● QuickBooks adds the mileage reimbursement total to the paycheck and adjusts payroll taxes.

11 Click Create.

QuickBooks creates the paycheck and displays the next employee's paycheck.

12 Repeat steps 8 to 11 for each employee you selected in step 5.

After paying all employees, QuickBooks redisplays the Select Employees To Pay window.

13 Click Print Paychecks.

Note: Follow the steps in Chapter 8 for details on printing checks.

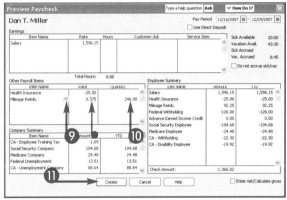

PART V

Can I use the Vehicle Mileage Tracking feature in QuickBooks to calculate and reimburse employee mileage?

▼ If an employee uses his own car predominantly for business, you can set up the employee's vehicle in the Vehicle List — use the employee's name as the name of the car — and enter mileage for the car. At the end of the month, you can print the Mileage by Vehicle Summary or Detail report to view the mileage associated with the employee's car, and you can then reimburse the employee on a paycheck as described in this section. To print either report, click Reports, click Jobs, click Time & Mileage, and then click the report.

Will I be misstating my company's financial position if I track an employee's car using the Vehicle Mileage Tracking feature?

▼ First, understand that the Vehicle Mileage Tracking feature was intended to track miles traveled on vehicles owned by your business so that you can deduct the vehicle usage on your business tax return; also, you make mileage expense reimbursements to employees when your employees use their own cars for business purposes. With that said, cars that appear on the Vehicle List do not affect any of your company's accounts, so you can include an employee's vehicle on the list. However, do not set up an asset account for an employee's car because you do not own the car.

Print Mailing Labels

When you need to correspond with customers, vendors, employees, or anyone whose name and address appear on the Other Names List, you can have QuickBooks print a mailing label for you to avoid addressing an envelope.

QuickBooks enables you to select from a wide variety of Avery Label styles, and you can print one label or a group of labels. You can select any or all customers, vendors, employees, or other names, or you can select by Customer Type or Vendor Type. Suppose, for example, that you run a pest control business and you want to prepare a special

mailing to your residential customers. Because you set up "Residential" as a Customer Type, you can print mailing labels by selecting the "Residential" Customer Type and then you can use the Write Letters feature in QuickBooks to prepare the letter. See Chapter 13 for details on the Write Letters feature for customers, Chapter 15 for details on the Write Letters feature for vendors, and Chapter 8 for details on the Write Letters feature for employees.

When you print labels, you can sort them alphabetically by name or numerically by ZIP code; sorting by ZIP code is handy if you are preparing bulk mailings.

Print Mailing Labels

1. Click File.

2. Click Print Forms.

3. Click Labels.

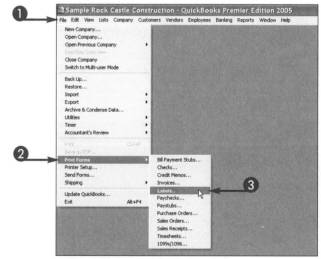

The Select Labels to Print dialog box appears.

4. Click options to select for whom you want to print labels (○ changes to ◉).

   ● You can click here to select names from specific ZIP codes (☐ changes to ☑) and supply a ZIP code.

5. Click here to select a sort method.

   ● You can click this option (☐ changes to ☑) to print shipping addresses where available.

6. Click OK.

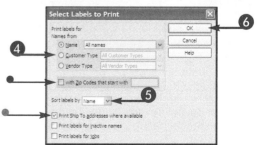

The Print Labels window appears.

7 Click here to select a printer and printer type.

8 Click here to select a label style.

9 Click a printing direction option (○ changes to ⊙).

10 Click Preview.

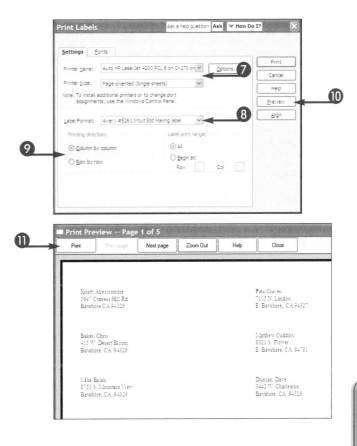

The labels appear on-screen formatted for the label style you selected.

11 Click Print.

QuickBooks prints the labels.

How do I select only certain customers when I print labels?

▼ In the first section of the Select Labels to Print dialog box, click the Name option (○ changes to ⊙). Then click 🔽, and from the list that appears, click Selected names. The Select Name dialog box appears. Click the Manual option (○ changes to ⊙) and then click each name you want to select from the list on the right side of the dialog box. This technique works whether you want to print labels for selected customers, vendors, employees, or people on the Other Names List. You also can use this technique to print labels for a mix of customers, vendors, employees, and names on the Other Names List.

Do I need to align the labels?

▼ You can align labels if necessary. To test, print a page of labels on blank paper instead of a sheet of labels. Then, place the printed page in front of a sheet of labels and hold both up to the light. If you need to adjust the printing, click Align in the Print Labels window. The Fine Alignment dialog box appears, where you can move text up, down, to the left, or to the right in $\frac{1}{100}$-inch increments. To move text down, type a negative number in the Vertical box. To move text to the left, type a negative number in the Horizontal box.

Review Shipping Manager Settings

Y ou can use the Shipping Manager feature in QuickBooks to ship packages via Federal Express without leaving QuickBooks. When you start the Shipping Manager for the first time, you connect to the Internet and walk through a wizard that helps you sign up for a FedEx account. If you already have an account, you can supply the account number while walking through the wizard to associate the account number with QuickBooks to receive discounts FedEx offers to QuickBooks users. During the setup process, you establish a user ID and password so that you can log onto the FedEx site.

During the on-screen interview, you establish your company's shipping address and phone and e-mail contact information, your FedEx account number, the default printer you use to print FedEx shipping labels, defaults for the package types you ship most often, and a COD Remit-To Address. For the COD Remit-To Address, you can use your company's shipping address or another address. After completing the wizard, you can review the shipping options established for you and, if necessary, change any options you set while completing the on-screen interview. This section shows you how to review settings and make changes.

Review Shipping Manager Settings

① Click File.

② Click Shipping.

③ Click FedEx Shipping Options.

④ Click Settings.

The QuickBooks Shipping Manager - Settings window appears.

⑤ Click the Your Address icon.

The Ship From information appears.

- You can change any information by typing in the appropriate field.

⑥ Click the COD Remit-To Address icon.

The COD Remit-To Address screen appears.

By default, the COD Remit-To Address uses the Ship From address.

- To use a separate address for COD shipments, click here (☑ changes to ☐) and then type an address.

⑦ Click the FedEx Account icon.

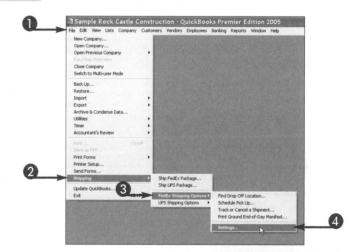

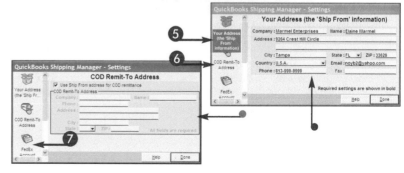

The Your FedEx Account Information screen appears.

● You can change your account number or signature release authorization number.

You can click the Re-Register link to re-register with Federal Express.

⑧ Click the Your Printer icon.

The Your Printer screen appears.

● You can click here to select a different default printer.

● You can select a different printer for each shipment if you click this option (☐ changes to ☑).

● You can click this option to print two copies of each shipment manifest (☐ changes to ☑).

⑨ Click the Defaults icon.

The Defaults screen appears.

You can click here to select the default FedEx package QuickBooks should use.

● You can click here to select the default FedEx service.

● For boxes and tubes, you can type a default weight here.

● You can click here to establish default ground package dimensions, service, weight, and declared value.

⑩ Click Done.

QuickBooks saves your shipping settings.

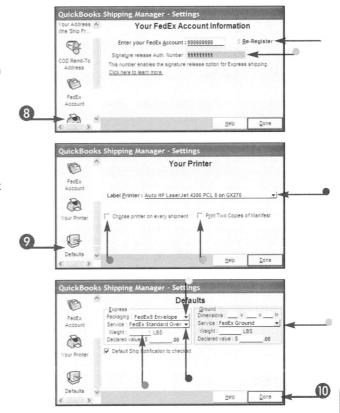

PART V

What is a COD Remit-To Address?

▼ When you ship a package COD, you send a shipment to one location and you receive funds for the shipping cost, as well as for the goods, from the package recipient. To process a COD package, FedEx prints two labels — one for the outbound shipment and one for the returning shipment containing the funds to pay for the shipment. Your company may ship and receive packages using a warehouse, but you may not want funds for COD packages to be delivered to the warehouse. Instead, you may prefer that COD funds be delivered to your accounting department. Using the COD Remit-To Address, you can specify one location for making shipments and another for receiving funds for COD shipments.

After I associate an existing FedEx account number with QuickBooks, am I restricted to using QuickBooks to ship packages via FedEx?

▼ No. If you decide that you do not want to use the Shipping Manager feature in QuickBooks, you can still ship packages from the FedEx Web site or using other FedEx shipping methods.

How can I set default dimensions when the dimensions of every package are different?

▼ You only need shipping dimensions on a package if the size is larger or heavier than the average package. Otherwise, you can leave the dimensions blank.

Ship a Package

You can use the Shipping Manager feature in QuickBooks to ship packages via Federal Express without leaving QuickBooks. You can make FedEx Express or FedEx Ground shipments, and you complete an on-screen version of the FedEx shipping label. You specify the recipient's name, address, and phone number. For FedEx Express packages, you specify the type of Federal Express service you want to use — First Overnight, Priority Overnight, Standard Overnight, 2Day, or Express Saver. First Overnight gets the package there fastest and costs the most, while Express Saver is the slowest and least expensive delivery method. You also identify the type of packaging used, the weight and declared value of the shipment, and

you can specify any special handling options necessary. You can pay for the cost of the shipment or bill the shipment to the recipient or to a third party.

For FedEx Ground shipments, you specify the type of Federal Express Service you want to use — Ground or Home Delivery — and you identify the weight and declared value of the shipment. You can pay for the cost of the shipment or bill the shipment to the recipient or to a third party.

You can also request a rate quote prior to shipping FedEx Express or FedEx Ground.

Ship a Package

① Click File.

② Click Shipping.

③ Click Ship FedEx Package.

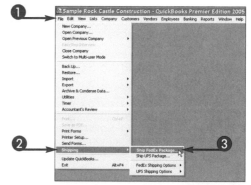

The Shipping Form window appears.

④ Click here to select a service.

● You can type a shipment reference here.

⑤ Type the recipient's name and address.

⑥ Click a service option (○ changes to ◉).

⑦ Click a packaging option (○ changes to ◉), and if appropriate, supply a weight.

● You can declare a value here.

⑧ Click a payment option (○ changes to ◉).

⑨ Click Rate Quote.

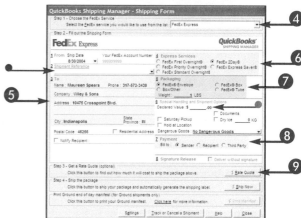

After connecting to the Internet, a FedEx rate quote for the proposed shipment appears.

⑩ Click OK.

⑪ Click Ship Now.

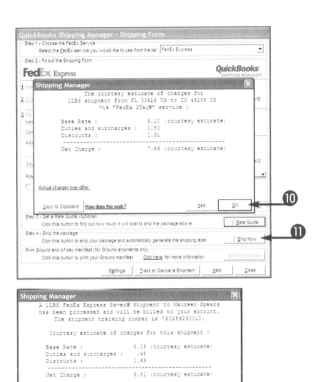

After processing the shipment, a label prints and the confirmation with the tracking number appears on-screen.

⑫ Click OK.

The Shipping Manager windows close.

What is the Ground Manifest and how do I print it?

▼ For FedEx Ground shipments, you should print a daily manifest that closes shipping for the day. Click File, Shipping, FedEx Shipping Options, then Print Ground End-of-Day Manifest. Typically, you print this report after you complete all ground shipping for the day, but you can process additional ground packages after printing the manifest; simply print the manifest again. It is acceptable to print the manifest more than once on a given day. If you have not printed a manifest by midnight, FedEx closes the day for you, and you can print the manifest using Notepad. With a typical QuickBooks installation, manifest files will appear in C:\Program Files\Common Files\Intuit\QuickBooks.

Can I use address information from the Customer:Job List to fill in FedEx shipping labels in the Shipping Manager?

▼ Yes. Initiate the shipment from the Create Invoices window by clicking the Ship button on the toolbar. QuickBooks prefills the FedEx shipping form with the customer's address information.

Where will I see information that I supply in the Shipping Reference field.

▼ The Shipping Reference information prints on the shipping label. For FedEx Express shipments, the information also appears on the bill you receive from Federal Express.

PART V

Find a Drop-Off Location

I f your business does not pay for a Federal Express courier to make a regular stop at your location, you can drop off your packages at a Federal Express location for shipping. You can use the Shipping Manager to get a list of locations near you. You can specify any combination of staffed locations, self-service locations, or FedEx Authorized ShipCenter locations.

When you search for a drop-off location, you make the search on the Federal Express Web site. You need to connect to the Internet before you start the steps described in this section.

You search for drop-off locations by specifying your address, including the city, state, and ZIP code, or your phone number. You can specify additional search criteria, such as the location with the latest express drop-off in your area, locations with Express drop-off after a specified time, locations with Saturday service, locations that hold Express packages, locations that accept dangerous goods, and locations that have packaging supplies. When you search for locations, you can specify that a map be displayed. The Federal Express Web site returns the locations that meet the criteria you specify.

Find a Drop-Off Location

① Click File.

② Click Shipping.

③ Click FedEx Shipping Options

④ Click Find Drop Off Location.

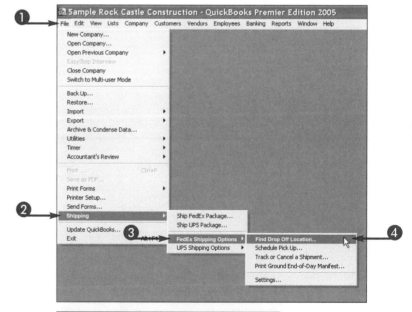

The Launch Web Browser? dialog box appears.

⑤ Click OK.

The FedEx Web site appears.

6 Type your address or intersection here.

7 Type your city here.

8 Click here to select your state.

9 Type your ZIP code here.

● You can type your phone number instead of all address information.

● You can click options for the types of locations to see here (☐ changes to ☑).

10 Click Find locations.

The results of the search appear.

11 Scroll down and find the location nearest you.

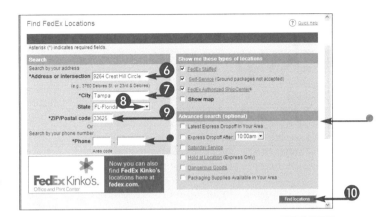

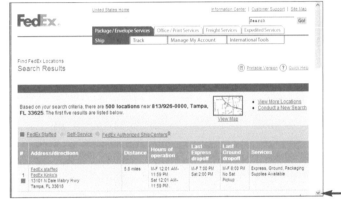

The search returned over 500 sites; how can I narrow the search to return fewer locations?

▼ First, in the Show me these types of locations section, deselect one or more options (☑ changes to ☐) to search only for FedEx Staffed sites, for Self-Service sites, or only for FedEx Authorized Ship Center sites. Then, use the criteria in the Advanced search to eliminate more sites. For example, you can click Saturday Service to rule out a large number of locations.

What does Saturday Service mean?

▼ Typically, FedEx does not pick up or deliver on Saturdays. However, Saturday delivery is available in the majority of U.S. cities that have Priority Overnight and 2Day service. Pickup or drop-off must occur on Friday for Overnight service and Thursday for 2Day service. Most Saturday deliveries occur by either 1:30 p.m. or 4:30 p.m., depending on the destination location. Saturday pickup is available for certain areas, and both Saturday drop-off and pickup cost extra.

What happens when I click a link for one of the sites returned in the search?

▼ The FedEx site displays driving directions to the site.

Does it matter whether I search by address or by phone number?

▼ If you search using address information rather than using your phone number, the distance between the FedEx location and your site and the driving directions will be more accurate.

PART V

Schedule a Pickup

I f your business does not pay for a Federal Express courier to make a regular stop at your location, you can schedule a pickup at your location. You pay an extra fee for this service on a per pickup basis. You can use the Shipping Manager to visit the FedEx Web site and schedule the pickup. Because you schedule pickups at the FedEx Web site, your computer must have an Internet connection; if necessary, you should log on to the Internet before you start the steps in this section.

You can schedule a pickup for either a FedEx Express shipment or a FedEx Ground shipment; depending on the time of day you schedule the pickup, FedEx Express

shipments can be picked up the same day or the next business day. For FedEx Ground shipments, you can schedule a pickup for the next business day or any business day up to two weeks in the future.

To schedule a pickup, you must log on to the FedEx Web site using the User ID and password that you created when you signed up for your FedEx account. The type of information you provide is basically the same, regardless of whether you schedule a FedEx Express pickup or a FedEx Ground pickup. This section demonstrates scheduling a FedEx Express pickup.

Schedule a PickUp

① Click File.

② Click Shipping.

③ Click FedEx Shipping Options.

④ Click Schedule Pick Up.

The Launch Web Browser? dialog box appears.

⑤ Click OK.

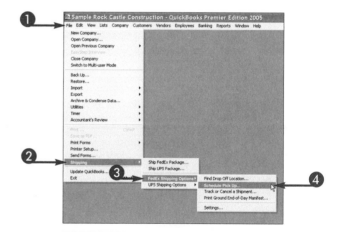

The Schedule a Pickup page of the FedEx Web site appears.

⑥ Click the link for the type of service you want.

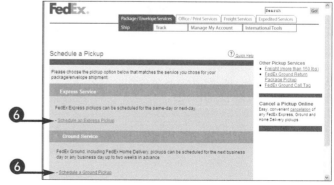

The fedex.com Login screen appears.

7 Type your User ID and password.

Note: *You established your User ID and Password when you set up your FedEx account.*

8 Click Login.

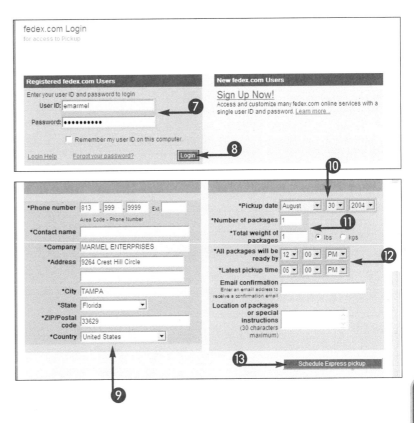

fedex.com Login
for access to Pickup

Registered fedex.com Users
Enter your user ID and password to login
User ID: emarmel
Password: ●●●●●●●●●●
☐ Remember my user ID on this computer.
Login Help   Forgot your password?   Login

New fedex.com Users
Sign Up Now!
Access and customize many fedex.com online services with a single user ID and password. Learn more...

The FedEx Pickup Information window appears.

9 Confirm your company name, address, and phone number.

10 Click ▾ and select a pickup date.

11 Type the number of packages and total weight here.

12 Type the time the package will be ready and the latest pickup time here.

13 Click Schedule Express pickup.

FedEx schedules the pickup and provides a confirmation number.

*Phone number 813 - 999 - 9999 Ext
Area Code - Phone Number
*Contact name
*Company MARMEL ENTERPRISES
*Address 9264 Crest Hill Circle
*City TAMPA
*State Florida
*ZIP/Postal code 33629
*Country United States

*Pickup date August ▾ 30 ▾ 2004 ▾
*Number of packages 1
*Total weight of packages 1 ● lbs ○ kgs
*All packages will be ready by 12 ▾ 00 ▾ PM ▾
*Latest pickup time 05 ▾ 00 ▾ PM ▾
Email confirmation
Enter an email address to receive a confirmation email
Location of packages or special instructions (30 characters maximum)

Schedule Express pickup

Can I make changes to a pickup that I scheduled?

▼ No. You must cancel the pickup you scheduled and then schedule the pickup again, making the changes that you need to make. To cancel a pickup, follow steps 1 to 4. On the Schedule a Pickup page, in the lower-right corner, click the Cancellation link. The Cancel a Pickup page appears. You must supply your account number, your pickup confirmation number, and the scheduled pickup date. Then click Cancel the pickup.

What is a FedEx Ground Call Tag?

▼ The FedEx Ground Call Tag service enables you to notify FedEx Ground to pick up packages your customers are returning to you at your customers' locations and then ship them to you. This service is available in the United States and Canada for nonhazardous materials. You can schedule a FedEx Ground Call Tag pickup for the next business day.

Do I need to schedule separate pickups for FedEx Express and FedEx Ground shipments?

▼ Yes. Different drivers collect packages for FedEx Express and FedEx Ground. If you need separate pickups, schedule one first and then schedule the other using the steps in this section.

Are there weight limitations for pickups?

▼ Yes. To schedule a pickup of more than 150 pounds, use FedEx Express Freight. Click the link on the right side of the Schedule a Pickup page.

Track a Shipment

Once you ship a package and it enters the FedEx system, you can track the package's movements using the Shipping Manager. Essentially, you can identify where the package is at any point in time. This feature is particularly useful if your customer wants to know where the package is.

To track a package, you need the package's tracking number or reference number, both of which are assigned to the package at the time you ship the package. Then, you can use the Shipping Manager to take you to the Track

Shipments page of the FedEx Web site, where you supply the tracking number or the reference number. FedEx then provides location information for the shipment.

You can track multiple packages simultaneously by entering multiple tracking numbers or door tag numbers at the same time. Door tag numbers are 14-digit numbers that begin with the letters "DT" and are followed by 12 numbers.

Because you obtain tracking information from the FedEx Web site, you need to be logged on to the Internet when you perform the steps in this section.

Track a Shipment

① Click File.

② Click Shipping.

③ Click FedEx Shipping Options.

④ Click Track or Cancel a Shipment.

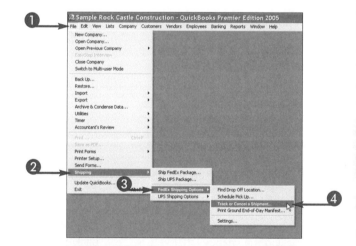

The Recent Shipments window appears.

⑤ Click the shipment you want to track.

⑥ Scroll to the right.

⑦ Write down the tracking number.

⑧ Click Track.

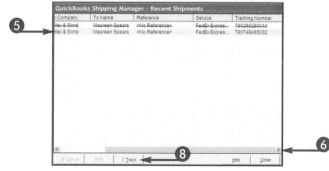

The Track Shipments page of the FedEx Web site appears.

9 Type the tracking number here.

10 Click Track.

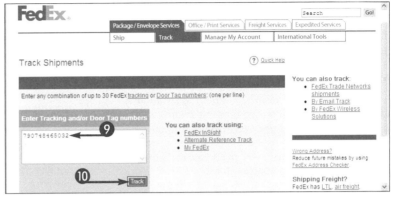

The Detailed Results page of the FedEx Web site appears.

● Shipment tracking information appears here.

● You can click here to track additional shipments.

11 Click the Close button (⊠) to close the window and return to QuickBooks.

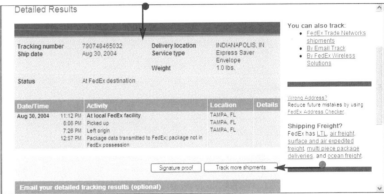

Where and how do I enter multiple tracking numbers to track more than one package?

▼ Enter multiple tracking numbers on individual lines on the Track Shipments page. If you enter more than one tracking number, FedEx returns the Summary Results page, which shows the delivery status, destination, date, and time for each tracking number. Click a tracking number link to display the Detailed Results page — shown in this section — for that shipment.

Can I track packages without tracking or reference numbers?

▼ Yes. You can register for FedEx InSight, a free tracking management tool that is available on the FedEx Web site. It lets you monitor the status of all your shipments based on your FedEx account number. It also alerts you of any events that may have affected the status of your shipment. To register and use InSight, click the FedEx InSight link on the Track Shipments page.

Is there a limit to the number of tracking numbers I can enter at one time?

▼ You can enter up to 25 tracking numbers or door tag numbers at one time, one number to a line on the Track Shipments page.

When does FedEx remove tracking information from its Web site?

▼ You can view tracking information for a package up to 120 days after you ship the package. If the shipment is older than 120 days, you can call FedEx to obtain tracking information.

Cancel a Shipment

Occasionally, you may need to cancel a scheduled shipment. For example, after you schedule a shipment, you realize that the shipment is incomplete. Or you may discover that an employee is traveling to the location of the shipment and can deliver the package. In either case, you need to cancel the shipment to avoid being charged for it.

You can cancel a shipment through QuickBooks using the Shipping Manager. The Shipping Manager connects to the FedEx Web site and cancels the selected package. Although

you do not see any Web pages when you cancel a shipment, you must be logged on to the Internet to cancel the shipment.

You select the shipment that you want to cancel from the Shipping Manager's Recent Shipments window. When you cancel the shipment, the Shipping Manager asks you to confirm cancellation of the selected shipment. Once you confirm cancellation, the Shipping Manager connects to the FedEx Web site and cancels the shipment. After the shipment is canceled, the Shipping Manager notifies you that you successfully canceled the shipment.

Cancel a Shipment

① Click File.

② Click Shipping.

③ Click FedEx Shipping Options.

④ Click Track or Cancel a Shipment.

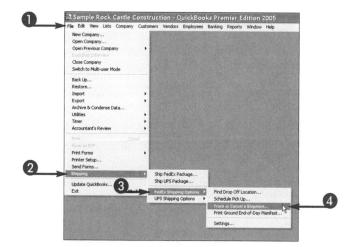

The Recent Shipments window appears.

⑤ Click the shipment that you want to cancel.

⑥ Click Cancel.

QuickBooks asks you to confirm that you want to cancel the shipment.

⑦ Click Yes.

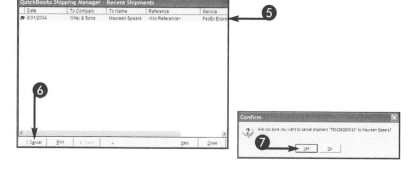

A message appears indicating that QuickBooks is canceling the shipment.

The Recent Shipments window reappears.

● Canceled shipments appear with a line drawn through them.

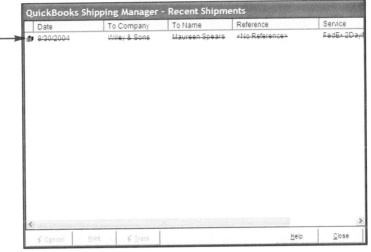

How long do shipments appear in the Recent Shipments window?

▼ Canceled shipments appear with a line drawn through them until the day after you cancel them. Shipments that you do not cancel remain visible in the Recent Shipments window up to 10 days after you ship them.

Are there any restrictions on shipments that can be canceled?

▼ You can cancel a FedEx Express shipment scheduled to ship today that you have not shipped and then reschedule it on the same day without any trouble. FedEx assigns a new number to the shipment and so does not assume that the two shipments are actually the same shipment. You cannot cancel FedEx Ground shipments after you print the Ground End-of-Day Manifest.

Can I cancel a shipment from the FedEx Web site?

▼ Yes you can, but using the Shipping Manager is easier because you do not need to navigate a Web site. If you log on to the FedEx Web site, www.fedex.com, and then navigate to the Track/History page, you see a list of shipments scheduled to ship today. Select a shipment and click the Cancel shipment button.

Review UPS Shipping Manager Settings

Y ou can use the UPS Shipping Manager feature in QuickBooks to ship packages via United Parcel Service without leaving QuickBooks. When you start the UPS Shipping Manager for the first time, you connect to the Internet and walk through a wizard that helps you connect an existing UPS account to QuickBooks or sign up for a UPS account if you do not already have one.

During the setup process, you establish a user ID and password so that you can log onto the UPS site. You then establish your company's shipping address, phone number,

e-mail address, and your UPS account number. You also specify your typical pickup frequency, review and agree to the UPS End User License Agreement, and select a default printer to use when printing UPS labels.

After you complete the interview, you can adjust some of the settings you selected; for example, you can change the default printer you use to print UPS shipping labels, and you can establish defaults for the package types you ship most often. This section shows you how to review settings and make changes.

Review UPS Shipping Manager Settings

① Click File.

② Click Shipping.

③ Click UPS Shipping Options.

④ Click Settings.

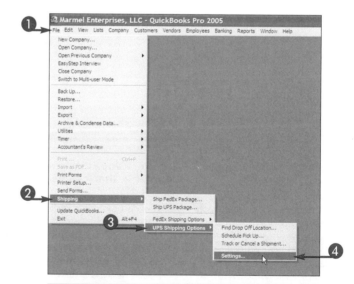

The QuickBooks Shipping Manager Settings window appears.

⑤ Click Printers.

The Printer Setup information appears.

● You can click here to select a different default printer.

● You can select a different printer for each shipment if you click here (☐ changes to ☑).

● You can print a test label by clicking here.

⑥ Click Shipment Defaults.

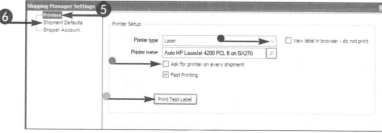

The screen where you set defaults appears.

You can click to set default shipping preferences options (☐ changes to ☑).

● You can establish default package dimensions, weight, declared value, and delivery confirmation information here.

⑦ Click Shipper Account.

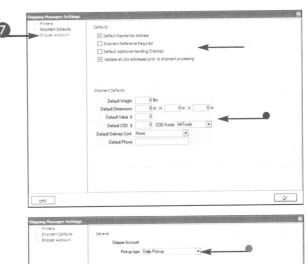

The information about your UPS account appears.

● You can change your pickup type by clicking here and selecting a different one.

● You can change company profile information here.

⑧ Click OK.

QuickBooks saves your shipping settings.

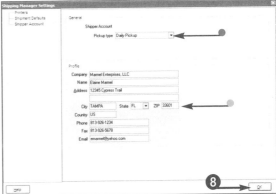

After I associate an existing UPS account number with QuickBooks, am I restricted to using QuickBooks to ship packages via UPS?

▼ No. If you decide that you do not want to use the Shipping Manager feature in QuickBooks, you can still ship packages from the UPS Web site or using other UPS shipping methods.

On the Printer Setup window, what happens if I select the View label in browser – do not print option (☐ changes to ☑)?

▼ When you print a UPS label, the label appears in your Web browser, where you can review it and then print it using the Print command in your Web browser. Only half of the page contains the UPS label; the other portion contains instructions for using the label and for getting the package to UPS.

In the Shiptment Defaults section, what choices do I have for COD Funds?

▼ When you ship a package COD, you need to identify the type of funds you are willing to accept as payment. Your choices are All Funds, Personal or Company Check, Check, or Cashiers Check or Money Order. When setting defaults, select the type of COD funds you accept most often.

Ship a Package via UPS

Ysou can use the Shipping Manager feature in QuickBooks to ship packages via United Parcel Service without leaving QuickBooks. You can make UPS Ground, 3 Day Select, 2nd Day Air, and Next Day Air shipments. To create a shipment, you complete an on-screen version of the UPS shipping label. You specify the recipient's name, address, and phone number. You can select up to three types of e-mail notifications. A Ship notification informs the recipient that a package is on the way; the Ship notification also contains the package tracking number. An Exception notification comes from the

shipping carrier when something goes wrong; for example, the shipping carrier generates an e-mail if a delivery attempt fails. A Delivery notification comes from the shipping carrier to the shipper when a package is delivered.

You also identify the type of packaging used and the weight and declared value of the shipment, and you can specify any special handling options necessary. You can pay for the cost of the shipment or bill the shipment to the recipient or to a third party. You can also request a rate quote prior to shipping UPS Express or UPS Ground.

Ship a Package VIA UPS

① Click File.

② Click Shipping.

③ Click Ship UPS Package.

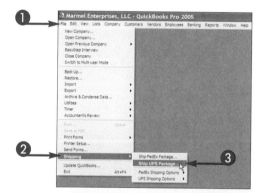

The QuickBooks Shipping Manager for UPS window appears.

④ Type the recipient's name and address.

⑤ Click any or all notification options (☐ changes to ☑).

⑥ Click ☑ and select a service, then select the type of service (☐ changes to ☑).

⑦ Identify the packaging here; if appropriate, typing a weight.

● You can declare a value and type a shipping reference here.

● You can click here and select a delivery confirmation option.

⑧ Click Rate quote.

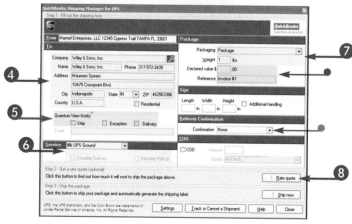

After connecting to the Internet, UPS displays a rate quote for the proposed shipment.

9 Click Close.

10 Click Ship now.

After processing the shipment, a label prints and the confirmation with the tracking number appears on-screen.

11 Click Close.

The Shipping Manager windows close.

Can you describe my shipping service options?

▼ Services you can select appear in order from least expensive to most expensive: Ground, 3 Day Select, 2nd Day Air, 2nd Day Air A.M., Next Day Air Saver, Next Day Air, andNext Day Air Early A.M. As you would expect, the least expensive service, Ground, provides the slowest delivery time. UPS distinguishes its services based on guaranteed delivery time at the destination location of the package. Next Day Air Early A.M., the fastest available service, guarantees delivery by 8 A.M. the next day in the contiguous 48 states and 8:30 A.M. in the rest of the United States. For complete details, visit www.ups.com.

What can I do if I damage the label and cannot use it?

▼ You can reprint the label. Follow steps 1 to 3 in the section "Track a UPS Shipment" to open the Shipments for Today window and click the shipment for which you want to reprint a label. Then click Reprint Label.

Is there a way to use address information from the Customer:Job list to fill in UPS shipping labels in the Shipping Manager?

▼ Yes. Initiate the shipment from the Create Invoices window by clicking the Ship button on the toolbar. QuickBooks prompts you to select shipping vis UPS or via Federal Express. After you select UPS, QuickBooks prefills the UPS shipping form with the customer's address information.

PART V

Find a UPS Drop-Off Location

I f your business does not pay for a UPS courier to make a regular stop at your location, you can prepare your packages using the Shipping Manager and then drop off your packages at a UPS location for shipping. You can use the Shipping Manager to get a list of locations near you. You can specify any combination of staffed UPS Customer Centers, UPS Stores, UPS drop boxes, or independently owned and operated shipping service centers that handle UPS packages.

When you search for a drop-off location, you make the search on the UPS Web site. You need to connect to the Internet before you start the steps described in this section.

You search for drop-off locations by specifying your address, including the city and state or the ZIP code, or your phone number. You can specify additional search criteria, such as locations with air or ground services and pickup times later than a time you specify. Or, you can search for locations with Saturday air service that pick up packages after a time you specify. When you search for locations, you can specify that a map be displayed. The UPS Web site returns the locations that meet the criteria you specify.

Find a UPS Drop Off Location

① Click File.

② Click Shipping.

③ Click UPS Shipping Options.

④ Click Find Drop Off Location.

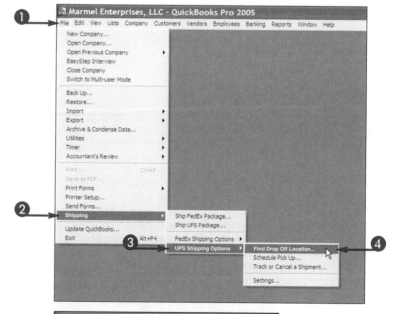

The Launch Web Browser? dialog box appears.

⑤ Click OK.

The UPS site appears.

6 Type your ZIP code here.

- You can type your phone number instead of address information.

- You can click these options (☐ changes to ☑) to select the location types you want to see.

7 Click Find.

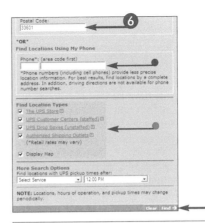

The results of the search appear.

8 Scroll down and find the location nearest to you.

When I search, not enough locations appear to give me a choice when dropping off my packages. What should I do?

▼ The search returns all the locations within 20 miles of the address you provide. The number of drop-off locations that appears depends on whether you are in a metropolitan area or a rural area. To increase or decrease your choices, make changes to the types of locations that you include in the search. To find more locations, include all location types; similarly, eliminate location types to reduce the number of locations found. Then, use the More Search Options criteria to eliminate more sites. For example, you can click Saturday Service to rule out a large number of locations.

How does Saturday Service work?

▼ Saturday pick up is available in most U.S. locations for overnight and two-day air packages. Saturday delivery is available at all locations where Next Day Air Early A.M. service is available Monday through Friday, and in all locations where the guaranteed delivery time for Next Day Air service is either 10:30 A.M. or 12:00 P.M. Next Day Air Early A.M. packages will arrive one hour later on Saturday than they arrive on a weekday. Next Day Air packages will arrive one to one-and-one-half hours later on Saturday than they do on a weekday.

Schedule a UPS Pickup

If your business does not pay for a UPS courier to make a regular stop at your location, you can schedule a pickup at your location. You pay an extra fee for this service on a per pickup basis. You can use the Shipping Manager or visit the UPS Web site and schedule the pickup. Because you schedule pickups at the UPS Web site, your computer must have an Internet connection; if necessary, you should log onto the Internet before you start the steps in this section.

You can schedule a pickup for the same day or a future date, depending on the time of day you schedule the pickup. If you schedule a pickup for a future date, you can schedule the pickup for any of the next four business days. When you schedule a pickup, you receive a pickup request number so that you check the status of a pickup as needed. You check the status of a pickup at the UPS Web site using a link on the Schedule a Pickup page that you see in this section. When you click the link, you see a box in which to enter your pickup request number.

Schedule a UPS Pickup

1. Click File.

2. Click Shipping.

3. Click UPS Shipping Options.

4. Click Schedule Pick Up.

   ● The Launch Web Browser? dialog box appears.

5. Click OK.

   The Schedule a Pickup page of the UPS site appears.

6. Type your User ID here.

7. Type your password here.

Note: *You established your User ID and Password when you set up your UPS account.*

8. Click the Login button (➡).

   The UPS Pickup Information window appears.

9. Click here and select a pickup date.

10. Type the earliest and latest pickup times here.

11. Select a UPS Account Number.

12. Scroll down to confirm your company name, address, and phone number.

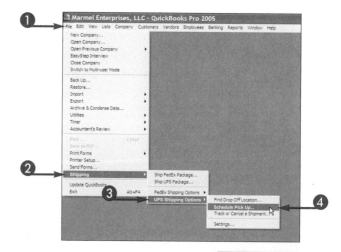

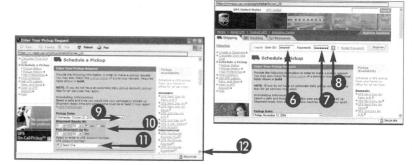

⑬ Scroll down further to type the total weight.

⑭ Type the number of letters and packages.

⑮ Scroll down to select notifications.

⑯ Click Continue.

The Enter Your Pickup Request page appears.

● If you are shipping a UPS Ground or 3 Day Select package, type the package's tracking number.

⑰ Scroll down to select a billing method (○ changes to ◉) for the pickup; you can use the same method you select for the package.

⑱ Scroll down and click Continue.

The Verify Pickup Request Details screen appears.

You can click Edit in any section to change information.

⑲ Scroll down and click Request Pickup.

● UPS schedules the pickup and provides a pickup request number.

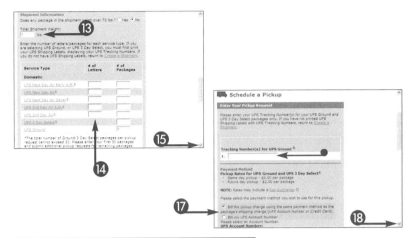

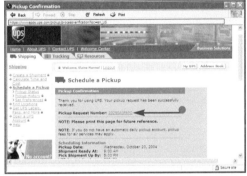

How much advance notice must I provide for a pickup and how much advance notice must I provide to cancel a pickup?

▼ When you create a pickup request at the UPS Web site, you type both a pickup time and a shipment ready time. The pickup time must be at least one hour later than the shipment ready time. You can change or cancel a pickup at any time before the driver arrives.

Is there a limit on the number of packages I can include in a pickup?

▼ For UPS Ground and 3 Day Select packages, you cannot include more than 30 packages in a single pickup. You can, however, schedule additional pickups for additional Ground or 3 Day Select packages. There is no maximum number of packages that UPS will pick up.

How does UPS bill me for the pickup charge?

▼ You can bill the pickup charge to any UPS account or credit card that you previously set up at the UPS Web site. If you have not yet set up alternate UPS accounts or a credit card, click the My UPS button when you first log into the UPS Web site. You can then click a link in the Manage My UPS section that enables you to add UPS accounts and credit cards.

Track a UPS Shipment

Once you ship a package and it enters the UPS system, you can track the package's movements using the Shipping Manager. Essentially, you can identify where the package is at any point in time. This feature is particularly useful if your customer wants to know where the package is. For more on shipping a package using UPS, see the section "Ship a Package via UPS."

To track a package, you need the package's tracking number or reference information so that you can identify the package in the Shipments window. You assign the reference number when you set up the package label, and

UPS assigns the tracking number when you print the label. You use the Shipments window to take you to the Track by Tracking Number page of the UPS Web site, where UPS then provides summary location information for the shipment. You also can view details that list, by day and time, the location of the package and the activity performed on the package. For example, each package has an origin scan that identifies the location from which the shipment originated. Each package also has a departure scan that indicates when the package left that location.

Because you obtain tracking information from the UPS Web site, you need to log onto the Internet when you perform the steps in this section.

Track a UPS Shipment

① Click File.

② Click Shipping.

③ Click UPS Shipping Options.

④ Click Track or Cancel a Shipment.

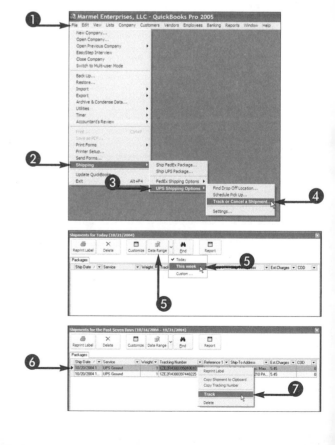

The Shipments window appears.

⑤ Click Date Range and select a shipment date.

You can click Custom to select a specific date range.

The shipments shipped during the selected date range appear.

⑥ Right-click the shipment you want to track.

⑦ Click Track.

The UPS Package Tracking page of the UPS Web site appears.

● Shipment tracking information appears here.

⑧ Click the Detail link.

● Additional shipment details appear.

⑨ Click ⊠ to close the window and return to QuickBooks.

Can I track more than one package at a time?

▼ Yes, but you cannot initiate multiple package tracking from within QuickBooks. Log onto the UPS Web site and click the Tracking tab at the top of the page. Then, click the Track by Tracking Number link on the left side of the page. You can then enter and track up to 25 tracking numbers.

Can I track packages without using tracking numbers?

▼ Yes. On the UPS Web site, you can use the reference information you assign to a package when you create the label. Because the reference information may not be unique — you may have assigned a generic description like "Books" to more than one package sent to different customers — you can narrow a search by reference by including a date range, UPS account number, destination ZIP code, and destination country information.

How can I receive e-mail notices of package status?

▼ Using Quantum View Notify, a free service, you can receive e-mail alerts for Ship, Exception, and Delivery package events on up to 25 tracking numbers. A Ship alert tells you when a package enters the UPS system, and a Delivery alert tells you when the package has been delivered. An Exception alert, which is only available within the U.S., tells you when a package delivery date has been rescheduled.

Cancel a
UPS Shipment

O ccasionally, you may need to cancel a scheduled shipment. After you create a shipment, you realize that the shipment is incomplete. Or you may discover that an employee is traveling to the location of the shipment and can deliver the package. In either case, you need to cancel the shipment to avoid being charged for it.

You can cancel a shipment through QuickBooks using the Shipments window after waiting 24 hours from the time you created the shipment. The Shipping Manager connects to the UPS Web site and cancels the selected package.

Although you do not see any Web pages when you cancel a shipment, you must be logged onto the Internet to cancel the shipment.

You select the shipment that you want to cancel from the Shipments window. When you cancel the shipment, the Shipping Manager asks you to confirm cancellation of the selected shipment. Once you confirm cancellation, the Shipping Manager connects to the UPS Web site and cancels the shipment. After the shipment is canceled, the Shipping Manager notifies you that you successfully canceled the shipment and reminds you to discard any labels that you will not use.

Cancel a UPS Shipment

① Click File.

② Click Shipping.

③ Click UPS Shipping Options.

④ Click Track or Cancel a Shipment.

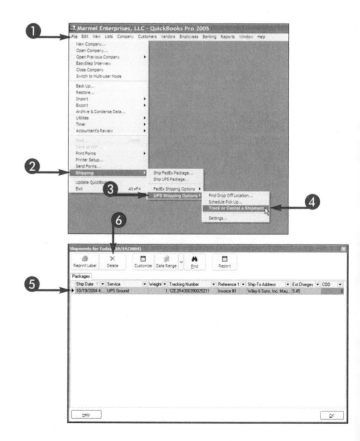

The Shipments window appears.

⑤ Click the shipment that you want to cancel.

⑥ Click Delete.

QuickBooks asks you to confirm that you want to delete the shipment.

7 Click Yes.

A message appears reminding you to discard the label for the shipment.

8 Click OK.

The Shipments window reappears.

● Canceled shipments no longer appear in the window.

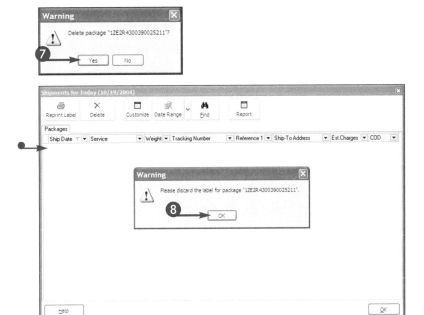

Are there any restrictions on cancelling packages?

▼ You may cancel a shipment when the shipment is under a UPS customer account associated with your MYUPS account, but not an account billed directly to a credit card. In addition, UPS has to have received information about the shipment, but not yet taken possession of the shipment. Also, the request to void the shipment must be made more than 24 hours after UPS receives the shipment's information if you process the shipment through the UPS Web site.

Can I cancel a shipment from the UPS Web site?

▼ Yes, you can. To cancel a shipment from the UPS Web site, note the shipment's tracking number, log onto www.UPS.com, and click the Tracking tab at the top of the page. Then click the Void Shipment link on the left side of the page and type the package's tracking number in the space provided. When you click Continue, UPS cancels the shipment.

What is the longest time I can wait to cancel a shipment before UPS insists that I pay for the shipment?

▼ You must wait at least 24 hours from the time you create a shipment before you can cancel it. After that initial 24 hour period elapses, you have 28 days to cancel a shipment before UPS charges you for the unshipped package.

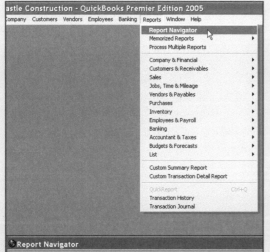

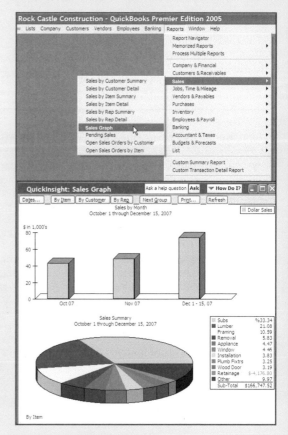

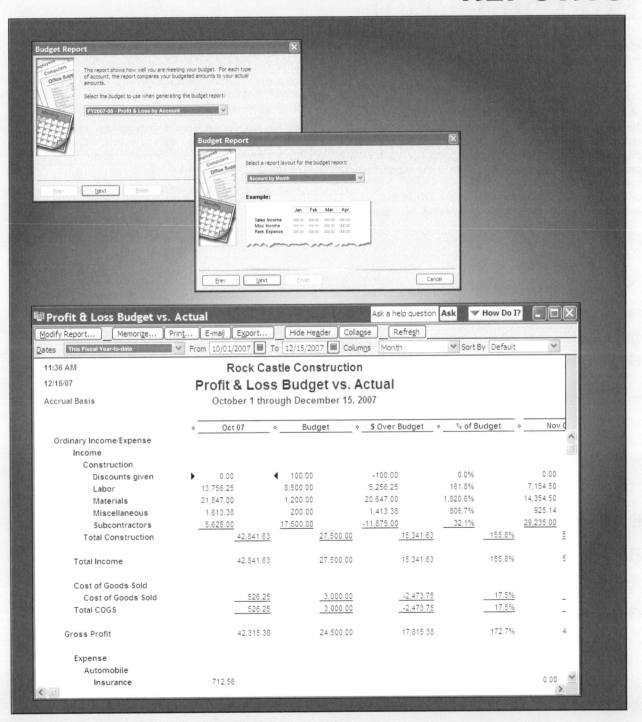

Find and Print a Report

After entering data into your QuickBooks company file for a while, you may eventually want to find and print reports. QuickBooks contains the Report Navigator feature that you can use to help you identify the report you want to print. The Report Navigator feature provides a brief description of the information each report provides and can show you a sample of the report before you print it. You can view samples and descriptions of many different reports so you can identify the report that is appropriate for your needs. Once you find the report, you

can preview it on-screen, and then you can set basic date range criteria and any other criteria you need to display the information you want to see.

The Report Navigator window organizes reports into major categories; these same major categories appear on the Reports menu, so you can print the report without using the Report Navigator window.

Once you display a report on-screen using either the Report Navigator window or the Reports menu, you can print the report.

Find and Print a Report

Find a Report

① Click Reports.

② Click Report Navigator.

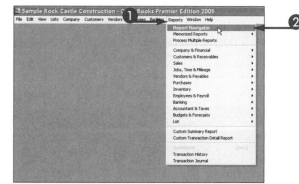

The Report Navigator window appears.

③ Click one of the categories along the side of the window to select a report type.

④ Point to an icon in a report.

● A sample of the report appears along with the report's description.

⑤ Click the report name link.

The report appears on-screen.

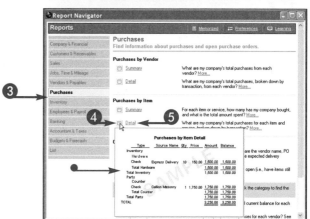

Print a Report

1 Complete steps 1-5 in Find a Report.

2 Click Print.

The Print Reports dialog box appears.

3 Click here to select a printer.

4 Click an orientation option and a page range option (○ changes to ⊙).

- You can click options (☐ changes to ☑) to break or fit reports per your specifications, as well as specify the number of copies you want.

- You can click the Margins tab to change the report margins from the default of ½ inch on all sides.

5 Click Print.

QuickBooks prints the report.

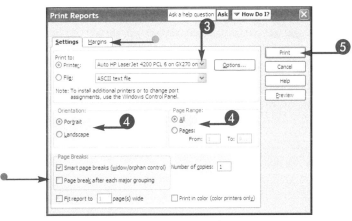

What happens if I click Modify Report?

▼ QuickBooks displays the Modify Reports dialog box, which contains four tabs. On the Display tab, you can select a date range for the report and a sorting order for the report. You also can typically select the columns that appear on the report; in some cases you can also select rows. On the Filters tab, you can reduce the amount of data on your report by filtering to show only certain data. On the Header/Footer tab, you can specify which header and footer fields print and how the fields read. On the Fonts tab, you can click a report element and then change its font.

What happens if I click Export?

▼ QuickBooks displays the Export Report dialog box, from which you can export the selected report to a comma-separated values file or to a new or existing Excel workbook. When exporting to Excel, QuickBooks can include a worksheet that explains how to link Excel worksheets so that updating one worksheet updates another.

What does the Smart page breaks option do?

▼ By clicking this option (☐ changes to ☑), you avoid printing the first line of a section at the bottom of a page by itself or the last line of a section at the top of a page by itself.

Memorize
a Report

Y ou can save time in the future when you memorize reports that you print on a regular basis or for which you create customized settings to display the information you need. When you memorize a report, QuickBooks stores the settings you used to create the report, and each time you print the memorized version of the report, QuickBooks uses those settings, saving you time because you do not need to manually re-create those settings.

Memorizing a report has another benefit; you can include the memorized report in a memorized report group — a collection of reports. Typically, most people group reports

by subject. For example, you may create a memorized group of reports that you print at the end of the month. Memorized report groups also save you time, because QuickBooks enables you to simultaneously print all reports in a memorized report group instead of creating each report individually and then printing it.

This section demonstrates how to memorize a version of the Profit & Loss Standard report and include it in an existing report group. You can memorize any report and you can choose to include it in any report group or simply memorize it without including it in a group.

Memorize a report

① Click Reports.

② Click Company & Financial

③ Click Profit & Loss Standard.

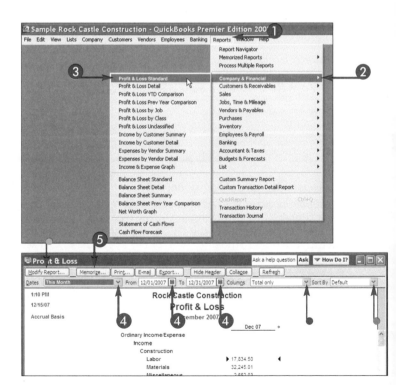

The report appears on-screen.

④ Click either ☑ or the calendar button (▦) to change the report dates.

- You can click here to change the columns displayed.

- You can click here to sort the report in another order.

- You can click Modify Report to change or filter the report.

⑤ Click Memorize.

The Memorize Report dialog box appears.

You can type a new report name.

● You can save the report in a memorized report group if you click this option (☐ changes to ☑) and then click here to select the group.

6 Click OK.

QuickBooks memorizes the report.

● The report appears on the Memorized Report menu in the group you selected.

You can click the report to print it.

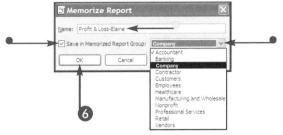

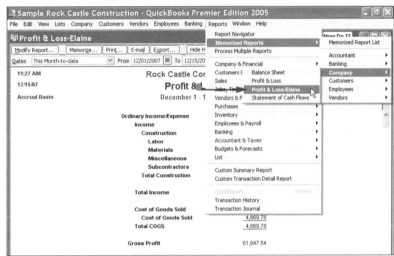

Why does my memorized report show different data when I print it at different times?

▼ When QuickBooks memorizes a report, it memorizes the report settings, not the report data. That is, QuickBooks memorizes the rows and columns that should appear on the report as well as the filters that eliminate data from the report. QuickBooks does not memorize the actual data on the report. To save the data that appears on a report, do not memorize the report; export it to Excel and save the Excel file. To export the report data to Excel, click the Export button at the top of the report window and follow the on-screen instructions. Exporting to Excel is not available in QuickBooks Basic.

After I memorize a report, can I change the name I assigned to it?

▼ Yes. Click Reports, click Memorized Reports, and then click Memorized Report List. In the Memorized Report List window, click the report you want to rename, click Memorized Report, and then click Edit. In the Edit Memorized Report dialog box — it looks just like the Memorize Report dialog box shown in this section — type a new name for the report.

Can I delete a memorized report?

▼ Yes. Click Reports, click Memorized Reports, and then click Memorized Report List. In the Memorized Report List window, click the report you want to delete, click Memorized Report, and then click Delete.

Print a Group of Memorized Reports

If you place your memorized reports in groups, you can print the entire group at one time instead of selecting each report and then printing it. For more information on memorizing a report, see the section "Memorize a Report."

Most people create memorized report groups to organize reports by subject. For example, you may create a memorized report group that you print at the end of the month. Or, you may create a memorized report group that contains reports pertinent to contractors. You may also want to create a memorized report group that contains reports related to billing customers for hours or expenses.

Once you create a memorized report group, you can include reports in the group as you memorize the reports, as shown in the section "Memorize a Report." Or, you can move existing memorized reports into a group by clicking and dragging. When you click and drag a memorized report from one group to another, QuickBooks removes the report from the first group and places it in the second.

And, while you can print an entire group of reports as described in this section, you also can print an individual memorized report without printing other reports in the group.

Print a group of Memorized Reports

1 Click Reports.

2 Click Memorized Reports.

3 Click Memorized Report List.

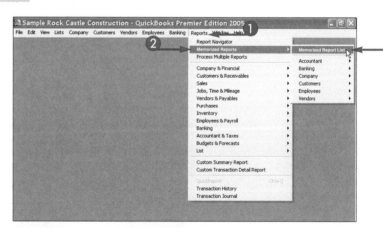

The Memorized Report List window appears.

4 Click a report group heading.

Note: *Report group headings appear in bold type.*

5 Click Display.

The Process Multiple Reports window appears.

- You can click next to any report to exclude it from printing (☑ changes to ☐).

6 Click Display.

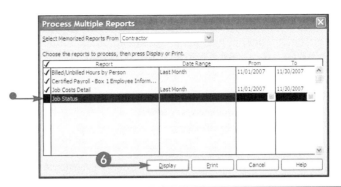

QuickBooks displays all the selected reports.

7 Click any report title bar to view that report.

- You can click Print to print any report.

Note: See the section "Find and Print a Report" for more details.

8 Click the Close button (☒) to close a report.

Can I print an individual memorized report without printing the whole group?

▼ Yes. There are two ways to print a single memorized report. You can deselect all other reports in the group; use this technique when you want to print just a few reports in a memorized report group. To print a single report, follow steps 1 to 3 and then highlight the report you want to print. Click Display, and the report appears on-screen. Or, instead of clicking Display, you can click Print; if you click Print, QuickBooks displays the Print Reports dialog box, where you can establish printer and report format settings. See the section "Find and Print a Report" for details on printing.

Can I make changes to a memorized report once it appears on-screen?

▼ Yes. Use the list boxes at the top of the report screen or click Modify Report to make changes, which remain in effect only while the report appears on-screen. You can make the changes permanent by rememorizing the report; click the Memorize button while viewing the report, and QuickBooks displays a message asking if you want to replace the existing memorized report or create a new memorized report. Click Replace.

Can I create a new report group?

▼ Yes. See the section "Create a Memorized Report Group" for details.

Create a Memorized Report Group

You can create a group of memorized reports so that you can print several memorized reports simultaneously instead of printing them one at a time. Memorizing reports saves you time because you do not need to set up the report each time you print it — QuickBooks saves the report settings when you memorize the report. Grouping memorized reports, perhaps by subject, saves you time when you need to print the group of reports, because you can print them all simultaneously instead of printing them individually. See the section "Memorize a Report" for details on creating a

memorized report, and see the section "Print a Group of Memorized Reports" for details on printing a group of memorized reports.

Most people create memorized report groups that include reports that are related in some way. For example, many people create a memorized report group for the payroll reports they print each payday. Once you create a memorized report group, you can include reports in the group as you memorize the reports, as shown in "Memorize a Report." Or, you can move existing memorized reports into a group by clicking and dragging. When you click and drag a memorized report from one group to another, QuickBooks removes the report from the first group and places it in the second.

Create a memorized report group

① Click Reports.

② Click Memorized Reports.

③ Click Memorized Report List.

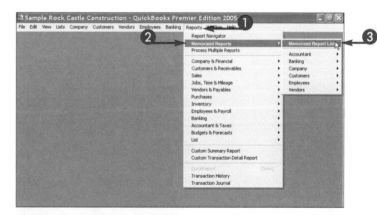

The Memorized Report List window appears.

④ Click Memorized Report.

⑤ Click New Group.

The New Memorized Report Group dialog box appears.

6 Type a name for the group here.

7 Click OK.

The new group appears in the Memorized Report List window.

8 Click over a diamond (◈) beside a report title and drag the report into the new group.

As you drag, a dotted line marks the current location if you release the mouse button.

The report moves into the new group.

Can I change the name of an existing report group?

▼ Yes. Follow steps 1 to 3 to open the Memorized Report List window. Then, click the name of the group you want to change and click Memorized Report. From the menu that appears, click Edit. In the Edit Memorized Report Group dialog box that appears, type the new name and click OK.

Can I delete a report group?

▼ Yes, but you must first delete all reports in the group or move the reports out of the group you want to delete. You can delete a report by clicking it and then clicking Memorized Report and then clicking Delete. You can move a report out of the group by clicking and dragging it as described in step 8.

What are some other memorized report groups that I may want to create?

▼ You may create a memorized report group that contains reports pertinent to contractors. Or, you may create a memorized report group that contains reports related to billing customers for hours or expenses. You also may want to create a memorized report group that you print at the end of the month.

Create a Custom Summary Report

On occasion, you cannot find the report you want to print listed among the reports in the Report Finder window or on the Reports menu. In these cases, you can create custom reports; QuickBooks enables you to create a Custom Summary report or a Custom Transaction Detail report. The Custom Summary report shows sums of numbers rather than the details behind the sums that make up the number.

Most people create variations of the Balance Sheet or the Profit & Loss statement using the Custom Summary report, but the report gives you such great flexibility that you can

create many other types of reports. Down the left side of standard reports, you can print only accounts, but down the sides of a custom report, you can have just about any field. This section shows an example of a report that shows Income by Class and Customer Type.

When you create a Custom Summary report, you use the Modify Report dialog box to select rows and columns for the report, to filter the report, to select header and footer options to display, and to select fonts for various sections of the report. The report shown in this section is not filtered by any criteria.

Custom summary report

① Click Reports.

② Click Custom Summary Report.

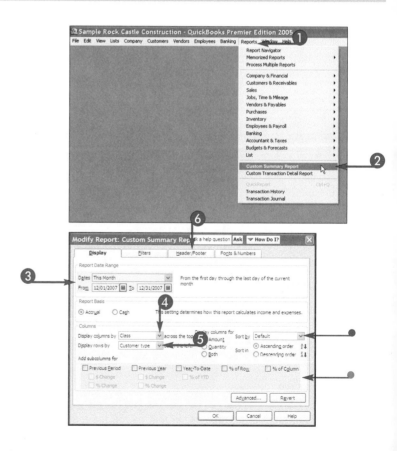

The Custom Summary report appears in the background and the Modify Report dialog box appears in the foreground.

③ Click these options to set a reporting time frame.

④ Click here to select columns to display; for this example, select Class.

⑤ Click here to select rows to display; for this example, select Customer type.

- ● You can click here to select a specific sort order.

- ● You can add comparison columns by clicking these options (☐ changes to ☑).

⑥ Click the Header/Footer tab.

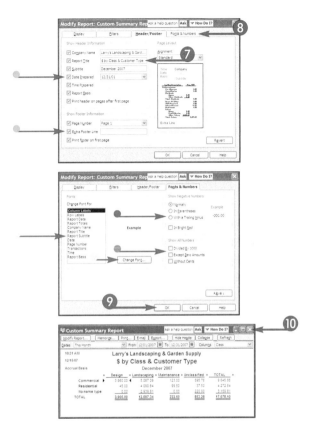

7 Click here, delete the current title, and type a new title.

● You can remove any header or footer information from the report by clicking these options (☑ changes to ☐).

8 Click the Fonts & Numbers tab.

You can click a report element and then click Change Font to select a different font for that report element.

● You can control the appearance of negative numbers by clicking one of these options (○ changes to ◉).

● You can click these options to control the appearance of all numbers (☐ changes to ☑).

9 Click OK.

The report appears on-screen.

Note: You can memorize this report to avoid setting it up in the future; see the section "Memorize a Report" for details.

10 Click ☒ to close the report.

Because the Custom Summary report does not show the transactions that are included in a number, what report can I use to see transactions?

▼ When you want to see the details that that make up a summary number and you cannot find the report you want, you can create a Custom Transaction Detail report. See the next section for more about creating this type of report.

Should I select Cash or Accrual as the Report Basis?

▼ The answer depends on whether you want to see money you have spent or collected or money you owe to vendors or are owed by customers. Accrual-basis reports include unpaid invoices and bills, while cash-basis reports include only cash spent or collected. For example, a cash-basis report on vendor-related information includes checks, credit card transactions, and bill-pmt checks; the same report on an accrual basis also includes bills but will *not* include bill-pmt checks.

How do I know what columns or rows to display?

▼ Selecting the correct columns and rows is a matter of trial and error. You simply need to experiment.

Why are the numbers on my report negative?

▼ Probably because the numbers represent income amounts. Typically, increases to income are credits, and credits are often represented by negative numbers.

Create a Custom Transaction Detail Report

W hen you cannot find a report that provides you with transaction detail, you can create a Custom Transaction Detail report. QuickBooks also enables you to create a Custom Summary report, which shows sums of numbers rather than the details behind the sums that make up the number. The Custom Transaction Detail report shows the details behind numbers on a Summary report. While you can create a Custom Transaction Detail report for almost anything you want, this section shows an example of payments made during a specific time frame to each vendor type.

When you create a Custom Transaction Detail report, you use the Modify Report dialog box, which contains four tabs: Display, Filters, Header/Footer, and Fonts & Numbers. The rows on a Custom Transaction Detail report are the transactions; you use the Display tab to determine the columns that will appear on the report, the date range of the report, the field by which you want to total the report, the field by which you sort the report, and whether you sort the report in ascending or descending order. Also on the Display tab, you can choose to produce a cash-basis or accrual-basis report.

Create a Custom Transaction Detail Report

① Click Reports.

② Click Custom Transaction Detail Report.

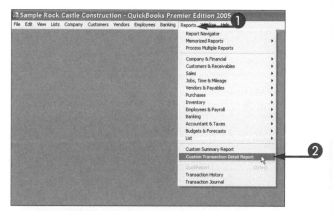

The Custom Transaction Detail report appears in the background and the Modify Report dialog box appears in the foreground.

③ Click ▼ or ▦ to select a report date range.

④ Click here to remove or add report columns; for this example, remove Clr and Split.

The check mark (☑) beside the field disappears.

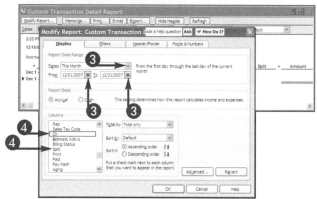

⑤ Click here to select a field by which to total; for this example, select Vendor Type.

● You can click here to change the sort order.

⑥ Click the Filters tab.

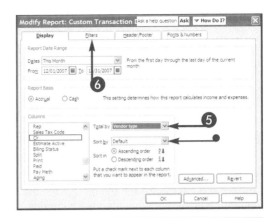

● You set a filter by selecting the field on which you want to filter and then setting the parameters for that field.

● Existing filters appear here.

You can remove a filter by clicking it and then clicking Remove Selected Filter.

How does the report basis determine how the report calculates income and expenses?

▼ When you report on a cash basis, you report only money that has come into or gone out of your business. You do not report money owed to you or money you owe. Money owed to you appears on your A/R Aging report and includes invoices to your customers that have not yet been paid. Money you owe appears on your A/P Aging report and includes bills you have entered but not yet paid. When you report on an accrual basis, you show unpaid invoices and bills as well as money collected and paid out during the time period.

What happens when I click Advanced on the Display tab?

▼ QuickBooks displays the Advanced Options dialog box where you can set two options. First, you can choose to include all accounts even if no transactions affected the account during the report time frame, or you can choose to include only accounts affected by transactions during the report time frame. Second, you can select the method for showing balances. If you choose Current, QuickBooks shows balances as of today. If you choose Report Date, QuickBooks calculates balances through the report date. The Current option is the faster method.

continued

PART VI

Create a Custom Transaction Detail Report *(Continued)*

When you create a Custom Transaction Detail report, you often want to limit the transactions that appear on the report. You can limit transactions by setting a report date range on the Display tab or by using the Filters tab.

On the Filters tab, the fields available to limit the report appear on the left side. As you select a field, QuickBooks displays criteria for that field that you can use to reduce the report size; the criteria changes depending on the field you select. For example, you can filter a report to include only

certain customers or accounts. Or, you can select only certain items or classes to appear on a report. You can display only cleared transactions or only uncleared transactions on the report. Filters you create appear on the right side of the Filters tab; if a particular field does *not* appear on the right, you have not limited the report using any criteria for that particular field.

On the Header/Footer tab, you can select the information that appears in the header and footer area of the report. On the Fonts & Numbering tab, you can select any report element and change its font.

Create a Custom Transaction Detail Report *(continued)*

⑦ Click a field.

⑧ Click ☑ or a split option (○ changes to ◉) to set the criteria for the field.

   ● The filter appears here.

⑨ Click the Header/Footer tab.

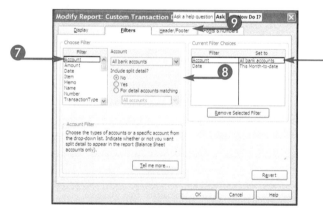

⑩ Click here, delete the current title, and type a new title.

   ● You can remove any header or footer information from the report by clicking an option (☑ changes to ☐).

⑪ Click the Fonts & Numbers tab.

- You can click a report element and then click Change Font to select a different font for that report element.

  You can click an option to control the appearance of negative numbers (○ changes to ◉).

- You can click an option to control the appearance of all numbers (☐ changes to ☑).

⑫ Click OK.

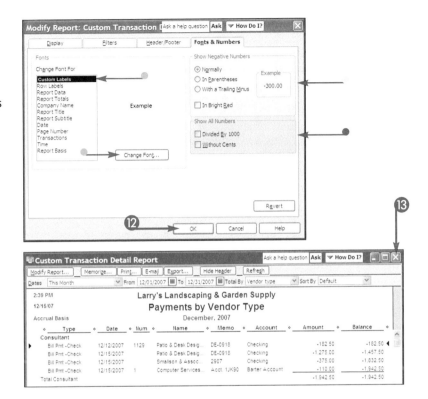

The report appears on-screen.

Note: *You can memorize this report to avoid setting it up in the future; see "Memorize a Report" for details.*

⑬ Click ⊠ to close the report.

Can I filter a Customer Transaction Detail report for an amount and, if so, how?

▼ Yes, but you may prefer to use the Find window to search for an amount. To use the Find window, click Edit and then Simple Find. Type the amount in the Amount box and click Find. QuickBooks displays all transactions with the amount you supplied. For more information on using the Find box, see Chapter 18. To filter for an amount, click Amount in the Filter List and type the amount. Using the Filters tab, you can also filter for transactions with amounts greater than or equal to, less than or equal to, or simply equal to the amount.

How do I select a filter for a report?

▼ Selecting filters is really a matter of trial and error. To effectively use filters, select them individually and display the report; that way, you can see the effect each filter has on the report and you are more likely to build the report you really want to build than if you try multiple filters at the same time.

What happens if I remove the check (☑ changes to ☐) from Report Basis on the Header/Footer tab?

▼ QuickBooks does not specify on the report whether you produced the report on a cash or accrual basis.

Export a Report to Excel

O ccasions may arise where you want to manipulate report information, perhaps to see what would happen if you took some particular action. To manipulate data, you can export report information from QuickBooks to a comma-separate file — a file with a .csv extension — or you can export the information to Excel.

When you export to Excel, you can choose to export to a new Excel workbook or to an existing workbook; this section shows an example of exporting to a new Excel workbook. You also can tell QuickBooks to send a worksheet page of frequently asked questions and answers about

exporting report information to Excel. When you export to an existing workbook, you can select the workbook and specify whether QuickBooks should place the report on a new worksheet page within the workbook or place it on an existing page.

Before you export, you can identify a variety of formatting options to preserve in Excel. You also can select Excel features to use such as AutoFit, which automatically sizes columns in Excel so that all your data appears on-screen. And, you can select printing options that affect the way the report prints from Excel.

Export a Report to Excel

① Click Reports.

② Click Company & Financial.

③ Click Expenses by Vendor Summary.

The report appears on-screen.

- If necessary, click Modify Report to make changes to the report using the techniques described in "Create a Custom Summary Report" and "Create a Custom Transaction Detail Report."

④ Click Export.

The Basic tab of the Export Report dialog box appears.

⑤ Click an option to select a file for the report (○ changes to ◉).

If you select a comma-separated values (.csv) file, skip to Step 9.

If you select An existing Excel workbook, you can click Browse to select the workbook and you can specify the sheet within the workbook where the report should appear.

- You can select this option to also export a worksheet of commonly asked questions and answers.

⑥ Click the Advanced tab.

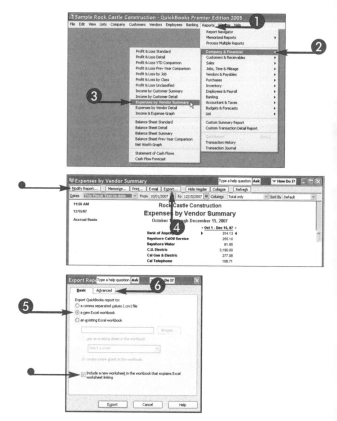

● You can click these options
(☐ changes to ☑) to identify the
formatting you want to preserve
when you export.

7 Click these options (☐ changes
to ☑) to select Excel features to use.

8 Click these options (○ changes
to ◉ and ☐ changes to ☑) to
select printing options when printing
the report from Excel.

9 Click Export.

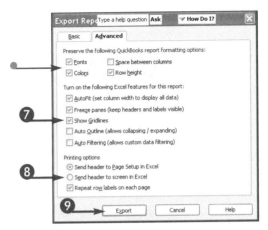

QuickBooks exports the file to Excel,
which opens, showing the report.

You can use any feature in Excel to
modify the report information.

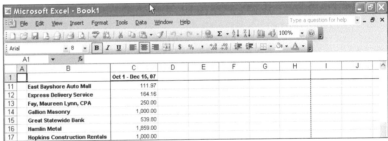

What happens if I deselect the AutoFit option?

▼ The AutoFit option on the Advanced tab
automatically sizes the columns in Excel to fit
the data you export. If you deselect this option
(☑ changes to ☐), the information in a cell
exceeds the viewing area of the cell, and some of
your data in Excel will appear cut off. You will
need to size the column manually to view all the
data in the cell. To resize the column manually in
Excel, move the mouse pointer onto the line that
marks the right edge of the column containing
the truncated information and double-click. Excel
resizes the column to accommodate the cell
containing the longest line of information.

What happens when I select the Auto Filtering option (☐ changes to ☑) on the Advanced tab?

▼ When you view the report in Excel, you will notice
▾ appearing just below the column letter of each
column. When you click the ▾, Excel displays a list
of options you can select to sort or filter the
information. For example, in a multicolumn report,
you can sort all the information in the report in
ascending order based on the values in one column.
Or, you can filter the information to view only lines
containing a particular value. You can also set up a
custom filter that enables you to select multiple
criteria; setting multiple criteria usually means you
view less information, because fewer lines of the
report can meet all the criteria.

Company and Financial Reports

You can obtain an overview picture of your business's status by evaluating financial statements. For example, you can identify potential problems, such as out-of-control spending, or opportunities, such as income sources, on which you should concentrate to increase your profits.

Your Profit & Loss statement helps you evaluate your business's performance. The Income section identifies revenue sources that bring money into your business. The Cost of Goods Sold section shows the costs directly related to producing the goods or services you sell. The Expenses section shows the overhead costs related to running your business, not producing goods or services. To increase profit, consider increasing income while reducing overhead costs or the costs related to producing goods or services.

The Balance Sheet Lists the balances for asset, liability, and equity accounts as of the date of the report. The report name comes from the accounting equation:

Total Assets = Total Liabilities + Total Equity

Assets are things you own. Liabilities represent the claims of others against the assets of your business. Equity is the amount of money remaining if you sell all your assets and pay off all your liabilities.

The Statement of Cash Flows summarizes financing and investing activities and can help you manage the flow of cash in and out of your business by showing you the sources of cash, the uses of cash, and the net increase or decrease in cash in your business.

Company & Financial Reports

Profit & Loss

① Click Reports.

② Click Company & Financial.

③ Click Profit & Loss Standard.

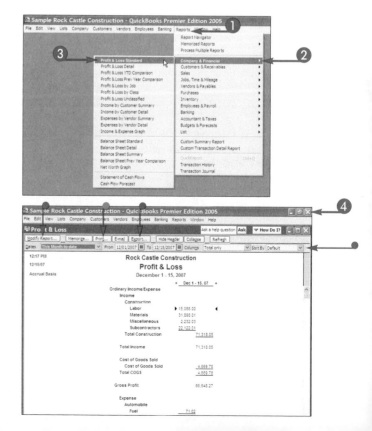

The Profit & Loss Standard report appears.

● You can click Modify Report or use these fields to change report settings or click Export to send the report to Excel.

Note: See Chapter 22 for more on these options.

● You can click Print to print the report.

④ Click the Close button (⊠) to close the report.

Balance Sheet

1 Repeat steps 1 to 2 on the previous page.

2 Click Balance Sheet Standard to open the Balance Sheet Standard report.

- You can click Modify Report or use these fields to change report settings or click Export to send the report to Excel.

Note: See Chapter 22 for more on these options.

You can click Print to print the report.

3 Click ☒ to close the report.

Statement of Cash Flows

1 Repeat steps 1 to 2 on the previous page.

2 Click Statement of Cash Flows to open the Statement of Cash Flows report.

- You can click Modify Report or use these fields to change report settings or click Export to send the report to Excel.

Note: See Chapter 22 for more on these options.

- You can click Print to print the report.

- You can click Classify Cash to assign accounts to different sections of the report.

3 Click ☒ to close the report.

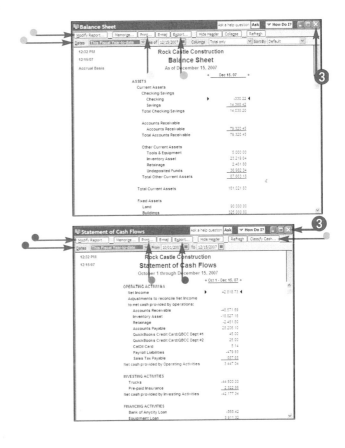

Is there a way to check the Statement of Cash Flows?

▼ The sum of the net cash numbers for operations, investing, and financial activities equals the amount shown on the *Net cash increase for period line* of the report. At the bottom of the report, values appear for cash at the beginning of the period and at the end of the period; these numbers are *not* the result of any other numbers on the report. If you subtract *Cash at end of period* from *Cash at beginning of period*, the amount you get will equal the amount shown on the *Net cash increase for period* line of the report.

Can you give examples of reducing cost of goods sold expenses?

▼ Try buying materials from different vendors or negotiating better costs with current vendors perhaps based on the volume of business you do with your vendors.

What is Retained Earnings and how does it differ from Net Income?

▼ Retained Earnings represents the combined profit or loss of the business since the inception of the business. The figure that appears on the Net Income line comes directly from your Profit & Loss statement and represents the combined profit or loss of the business for the current year.

PART VI

Customer Reports

Customers are people or organizations that pay you for the goods you produce or the services you perform. As such, they are an integral part of your business and you can answer questions such as "How much does Smith, Inc. owe me?" or "What invoices remain unpaid?" using customer reports.

The A/R Aging report comes in two versions — a summary and a detail. The summary version shows you the total owed to you buy each customer and how much of the customer's balance is overdue; the report divides the customer's balance into aging periods, showing the amount that is not yet past due, the amount that is 1–30 days past

due, the amount that is 31–60 days past due, the amount that is 61–90 days past due, and the amount that is greater than 90 days past due. The detail report uses the same aging periods and shows each individual transaction in the period.

The Open Invoices report shows, by customer, which invoices have not yet been paid, the date due, terms, and amount, and the customer's total balance.

The Collections report helps you identify customers with overdue invoices and provides the information you need to contact these customers so that you can try to collect the money owed to you.

Customer Reports

A/R Aging Detail

① Click Reports.

② Click Customers & Receivables.

③ Click A/R Aging Detail.

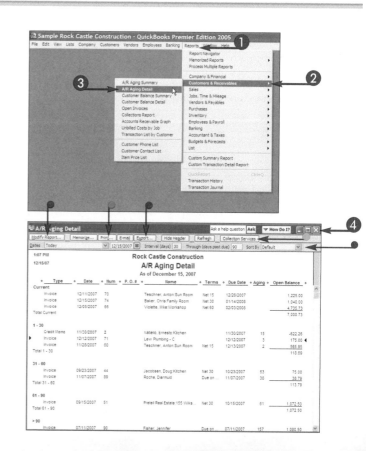

The A/R Aging Detail report appears.

- You can click Modify Report or use these fields to change report settings or click Export to send the report to Excel.

Note: *See Chapter 22 for more on these options.*

- You can click Print to print the report.

- You can click Collection Services to learn about fee-based collection services offered by Intuit.

④ Click ☒ to close the report.

Open Invoices

1️⃣ Repeat steps 1 to 2 on the previous page.

2️⃣ Click Open Invoices to open the Open Invoices report.

　　You can click Modify Report or use these fields to change report settings or click Export to send the report to Excel.

Note: See Chapter 22 for more on these options.

● You can click Print to print the report.

● You can click Collection Services to learn about fee-based collection services offered by Intuit.

3️⃣ Click ⊠ to close the report.

Collections Report

1️⃣ Repeat steps 1 to 2 on the previous page.

2️⃣ Click Collections Report to open the Collections Report report.

　　You can click Modify Report or use these fields to change report settings or click Export to send the report to Excel.

Note: See Chapter 22 for more on these options.

　　You can click Print to print the report.

● You can click Collection Services to learn about fee-based collection services offered by Intuit.

3️⃣ Click ⊠ to close the report.

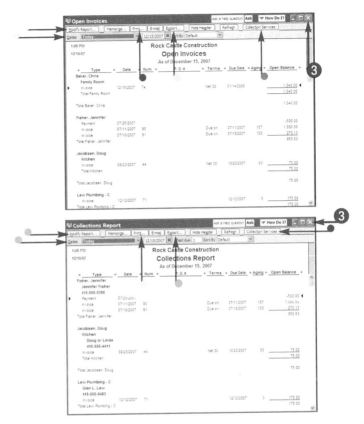

What does the Accounts Receivable graph show?

▼ This combination graph presents a visual representation of the money owed to you. The bar chart at the top of the report displays the dollars owed, with each bar representing an aging period; you can see, at a glance, the dollars that are current, the dollars that are 1 to 30 days past due, the dollars that are 31–60 days past due, the dollars that are 61–90 days past due, and the dollars that are more than 90 days past due. The slices in the pie chart at the bottom of the report represent each customer's share of the total due to you. You can easily identify who owes you the most money.

What does the Customer Balance Summary report show?

▼ This report shows you, as of the report date, the amount each customer:job owes. The report does not use any aging periods but shows, instead, totals due from the customer. The detail version of this report includes the invoices that make up each customer:job's balance — again, using no aging periods.

Is there a report that shows how profitable each customer is to me?

▼ Yes. You can use the Income by Customer Summary or Detail report to see this information. To print either report, click Reports and then click Company & Financial.

Sales Graph

T he visual image presented by the Sales Graph report helps draw your attention quickly to information that may be obscure in a report of numbers. The Sales Graph report consists of two graphs: the Sales by Month bar chart and the Sales Summary pie chart. The Sales by Month bar chart shows sales for the three-month reporting period. QuickBooks uses the data it collects from your invoices, sales receipts, and credit memos.

The slices of the Sales Summary pie chart represent sales by item; you can use the buttons at the top of the report window to change the slices to display sales by customer or sales by sales rep.

Master It

Can I view the transactions included in a bar or pie slice?

▼ Yes. When you double-click a Sales by Month bar and QuickBooks displays the pie chart summary for that month, double-click a pie slice to view transactions. Also, when you double-click a pie slice in the three-month Sales Summary on the Sales Graph report, QuickBooks displays a bar chart for that income category. Double-click an income category bar on that chart, and QuickBooks displays the transactions included in that bar.

Sales Graph

① Click Reports.

② Click Sales.

③ Click Sales Graph.

Both graphs of the Sales Graph report show a sales summary for the last three months; the bar chart breaks down sales by month, and the pie chart breaks down sales by item, customer, or sales rep.

● You can use these buttons to change report settings.

● You can click Next Group to see the charts for the next group of items, customers, or sales reps.

● You can double-click any bar or pie slice to display details for that bar or pie slice.

④ Click ☒ to close the report.

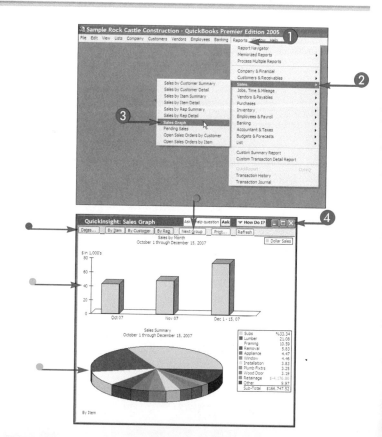

Profit and Loss by Job

You can use the Profit & Loss by Job report to evaluate how much or little money your company is making on each job. The report is formatted like a standard Profit & Loss report but contains columns for each job. The Income section identifies revenue sources that brought in money for each job. The Cost of Goods Sold section shows the costs directly related to producing the goods or services for each job. The Expenses section shows the overhead costs related to each job. To increase profit, consider increasing income while reducing overhead costs or the costs related to producing goods or services.

MASTER IT

Is there another report that provides profit and loss information about each job without all the details?

▼ You can print the Job Profitability Summary, which lists jobs down the side and displays three columns of information for each job: Actual Cost, Actual Revenue, and Difference, in dollars. If the difference is positive, you are making money on the job; if the difference is negative, you are losing money on the job. You can double-click any cost or revenue number on the report to drill down and view a list of transactions included in that number. If you drill down on one of the Difference values, QuickBooks displays the transactions that make up both the cost and the revenue numbers.

Profit & Loss by Job

1 Click Reports.

2 Click Jobs, Time & Mileage.

3 Click Profit & Loss by Job.

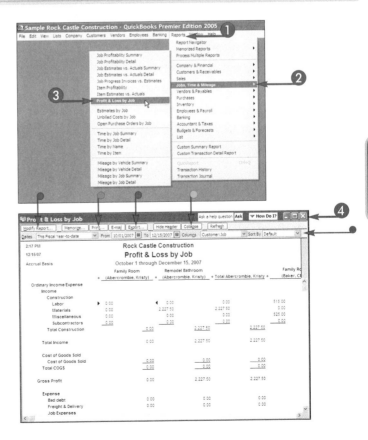

The Profit & Loss by Job report appears.

● You can click Modify Report or use these fields to change report settings or click Export to send the report to Excel.

Note: *See Chapter 22 for more on these options.*

● You can click Print to print the report.

● You can click Collapse to hide subaccounts.

4 Click ☒ to close the report.

Vendor and Payables Reports

Vendors are people other than employees or organizations that you pay for goods or services you need to operate your business. As such, they are an integral part of your business and you can answer questions such as "How much money do I owe Jones, Inc.?" or "What bills remain unpaid?" using vendor reports.

The A/P Aging report comes in two versions — a summary and a detail. The summary version shows you the total you owe to each vendor and how much of the owed balance is overdue; the report divides the balance due into aging periods, showing the amount that is not yet past due, the

amount that is 1–30 days past due, the amount that is 31–60 days past due, the amount that is 61-90 days past due, and the amount that is greater than 90 days past due. The detail report uses the same aging periods and shows each individual transaction in the period.

The Unpaid Bills Detail report lists, by vendor, each outstanding bill, its due date, how many days old it is, and the amount due.

The Vendor Balance Summary report lists each vendor and the amount you owe, providing you with an at-a-glance overview of money owed to each vendor.

Vendor & Payables Reports

A/P Aging Detail

1. Click Reports.

2. Click Vendor & Payables.

3. Click A/P Aging Detail.

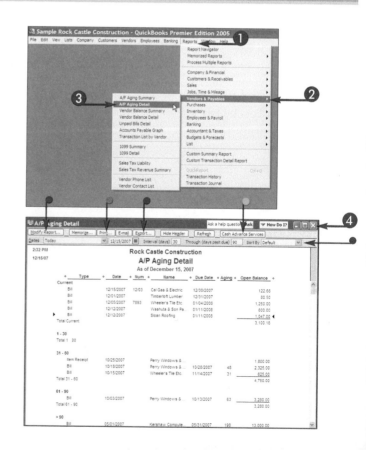

The A/P Aging Detail report appears.

● You can click Modify Report or use these fields to change report settings or click Export to send the report to Excel.

Note: *See Chapter 22 for more on these options.*

● You can click Print to print the report.

● You can click Cash Advance Services to learn about fee-based collection services offered by Intuit.

4. Click ☒ to close the report.

Unpaid Bills Detail

1. Repeat steps 1 to 2 on the previous page.
2. Click Unpaid Bills Detail to open the Unpaid Bills Detail report.
3. Click ⊠ to close the report.

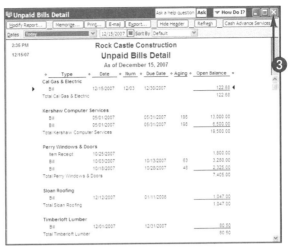

Vendor Balance Summary

1. Repeat steps 1 to 2 on the previous page.
2. Click Vendor Balance Summary to open the Vendor Balance Summary report.

   You can double-click an amount to view the transactions included in it.
3. Click ⊠ to close the report.

What do I see if I double-click an amount on the Vendor Balance Summary report?

▼ QuickBooks displays the Vendor Balance Detail report for the vendor whose amount you double-clicked. On the Vendor Balance Detail report, you see all the transactions that make up the balance you owe the vendor. You can double-click any transaction to view it in the window where you created it.

What happens when I click Cash Advance Services?

▼ QuickBooks displays information you can use to obtain the QuickBooks Platinum Plus for Business MasterCard, which is designed to work with QuickBooks. In addition to downloading credit card transactions directly into QuickBooks so that you always know your account balance, this particular credit card also enables you to see the details as well as the total of a credit card purchase.

Are there reports that provide me with sales tax information?

▼ You can print the Sales Tax Liability report and the Sales Tax Revenue Summary report. The first report shows, for each sales tax item, total sales, taxable sales, nontaxable sales, tax rate, tax collected, and tax payable as of the report date. The second report shows, for each sales tax item, taxable sales, nontaxable sales, and total sales.

Open Purchase Orders Report

Y
ou can use the Open Purchase Orders report to help you track unfilled purchase orders. The report shows you the vendor, the date you entered the purchase order, the purchase order number, the expected delivery date, and the amount. If you drill down on any transaction listed on the report, you see it in the Create Purchase Orders window, where you can view the items on the purchase order, identifying the original quantity and the quantity already received. QuickBooks also contains a variation of the Open Purchase Orders report called the Open Purchase Orders by Job report that organizes the same information by job rather than by vendor.

Are there reports that shows me how much money I have spent with a vendor and on a particular item?

▼ To determine how much money you have spent with a vendor, you can print either the Purchases by Vendor Summary report or the Purchases by Vendor Detail report. You can print either report on a cash or an accrual basis. Use the cash basis to include income and expenses based on the date cash changed hands. Use the accrual basis to include income and expenses based on the date you incurred the liability. To find out how much you have spent on a particular item, print either the Purchases by Item Summary report or Purchases by Item Detail report.

Open Purchase Orders Report

1 Click Reports.

2 Click Purchases.

3 Click Open Purchase Orders.

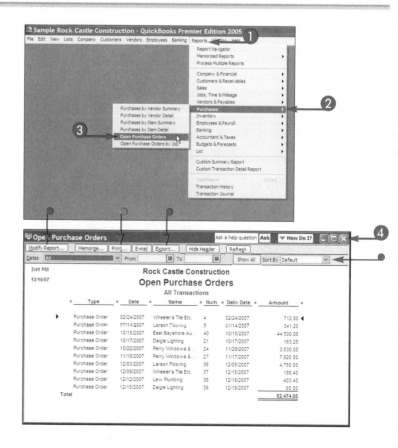

The Open Purchase Orders report appears.

● You can click Modify Report or use these fields to change report settings or click Export to send the report to Excel.

Note: See Chapter 22 for more on these options.

● You can click Print to print the report.

You can double-click a transaction to see it in the window where you entered it.

4 Click ☒ to close the report.

Customer Phone List

Y「ou can use the Customer Phone List report to print a list of each customer's phone number. You can customize this report to include additional information for each customer, such as the customer's alternate phone number, fax number, address, e-mail address, balance, sales tax code and item, and custom field information. QuickBooks contains a phone list report for customers, vendors, employees, and for the Other Names List. List reports in general are useful whenever you want to view information you stored for any entry on any list that appears on the List menu. Think of list reports as a way to customize and print information that appears in List windows.

What is the difference between the Customer Phone List and the Customer Contact List?

▼ The Customer Phone List displays only the customer's name and primary phone number. The Customer Contact List displays the customer's name, billing address, contact name, and primary phone number. These differences also apply to the Employee Phone List and the Employee Contact List, the Vendor Phone List and the Vendor Contact List, and the Other Names Phone List and the Other Names Contact List.

What information appears on the Item Price List?

▼ The item name, description, price, and preferred vendor.

Customer Phone List

① Click Reports.

② Click List.

③ Click Customer Phone List.

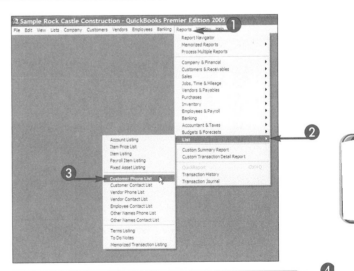

The Customer Phone List report appears.

● You can click Modify Report or click Export to send the report to Excel.

Note: See Chapter 22 for more on these options.

● You can click Print to print the report.

You can double-click a line to see the customer in the Edit Customer window.

④ Click ⊠ to close the report.

Inventory Reports

Inventory represents, for the most part, things you sell or buy to resell. In QuickBooks, you use items to represent inventory. QuickBooks also uses items for other things such as noninventory parts, services, and sales taxes, but the reports in this section focus on inventory. You can use inventory reports to identify how much you have on hand and what your inventory is worth in dollars.

The Inventory Valuation Summary report shows you, for each inventory and assembly item, the item description, the quantity on hand, the average cost, the value, the percent of total inventory that the item represents, the sales price, the retail value, and the percent of total retail value that the item represents.

Use the Physical Inventory Worksheet when you manually count your inventory items, a task most businesses complete annually. Print copies of this report and hand them out to the employees who do the counting; you can update inventory in QuickBooks from the counts on these sheets.

The Inventory Stock Status by Item report lists each item's description, preferred vendor, reorder point, quantity on hand, quantity on sales and purchase orders, next scheduled delivery date, amount sold per week, and quantity available for sale. The report also identifies items you should order.

Inventory Reports

Inventory Valuation Summary

① Click Reports.

② Click Inventory.

③ Click Inventory Valuation Summary.

The Inventory Valuation Summary report appears.

● You can click Modify Report or use these fields to change report settings or click Export to send the report to Excel.

Note: See Chapter 22 for more on these options.

● You can click Print to print the report.

You can double-click a line in the report to see the list of transactions included in the summary number.

④ Click ☒ to close the report.

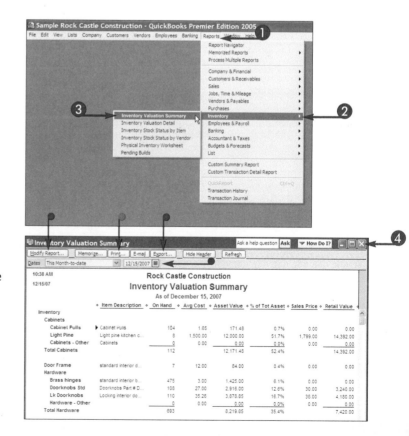

Physical Inventory Worksheet

1 Repeat steps 1 to 2 on the previous page.

2 Click Physical Inventory Worksheet to open the Physical Inventory Worksheet report.

● You can click Modify Report or click Export to send the report to Excel.

Note: *See Chapter 22 for more on these options.*

You can click Print to print the report.

You can double-click a line in the report to see a QuickReport for the item.

3 Click ☒ to close the report.

Stock Status by Item

1 Repeat steps 1 to 2 on the previous page.

2 Click Inventory Stock Status by Item to open the Inventory Stock Status by Item report.

● You can click Modify Report or use these fields to change report settings or click Export to send the report to Excel.

Note: *See Chapter 22 for more on these options.*

● You can click Print to print the report.

You can double-click a line in the report to see a QuickReport for the item.

3 Click ☒ to close the report.

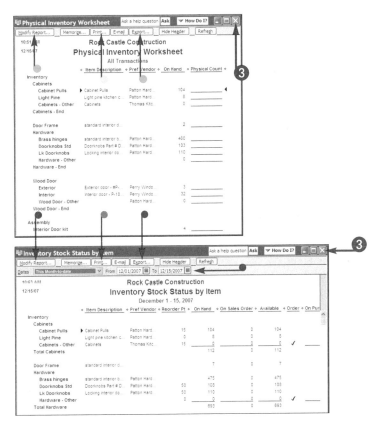

What does the Inventory Valuation Detail report show?

▼ This report lists each item and all the transactions that include the item. For each transaction, you see the date, name, number, quantity, cost if the transaction is a bill, quantity on hand, average cost, and item value. The quantity on hand, average cost, and item value have no connection with the transaction. QuickBooks lists the quantity on hand and the average cost, and calculates the item value.

Is there a report I can use to help me manage inventory by vendor?

▼ Yes. Print the Inventory Stock Status by Vendor report. This report lists each vendor and the items you typically buy from that vendor. For each item, the report displays the description, reorder point, quantity on hand, quantity on sales and purchase orders, next scheduled delivery date, amount sold per week, and quantity available for sale. The report also identifies items you should order.

Is there a report that I can print to provide information about assemblies I need to build?

▼ Yes. You can print the Pending Builds report, which lists the assembly items you have marked for building along with the transaction number, the quantity, and any memo you may have included when you created the pending build. For more information on pending builds, see Chapter 16.

Employees and Payroll Reports

You can use reports about employees and payroll in QuickBooks to help you track payroll information and ensure that you pay all payroll taxes in a timely and accurate manner.

The Payroll Summary report displays, for the report period, the total amount paid to each employee for each assigned payroll item. The report displays hours and rates if the payroll item is based on hours or includes a rate. The Gross Pay section includes wages, commissions, bonuses, and tips. Adjusted Gross Pay is Gross Pay less pretax deductions. Net Pay is the amount the employee receives. The Employer Taxes and Contributions section shows amounts accrued during the report period regardless of whether you pay the amounts.

The Payroll Item Listing report lists, for each payroll item, the type, amount, annual limit, expense account, liability account, and tax tracking value. When a payroll item does not seem to calculate properly, this report can help you determine why.

The Employee Earnings Summary report lists the same kind of information you find on the Payroll Summary report, but using a different format. On the Payroll Summary report, payroll items appear down the side of the report while employees appear across the top. On the Employee Earnings Summary report, the rows and columns are flipped.

Employees & Payroll Reports

Payroll Summary

1. Click Reports.
2. Click Employees & Payroll.
3. Click Payroll Summary.

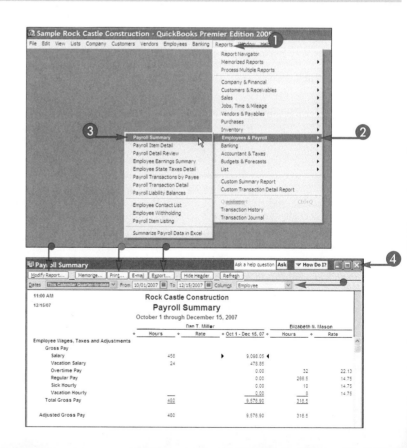

The Payroll Summary report appears.

- You can click Modify Report or use these fields to change report settings or click Export to send the report to Excel.

Note: See Chapter 22 for more on these options.

- You can click Print to print the report.

You can double-click a line in the report to see the list of transactions included in the summary number.

4. Click ☒ to close the report.

Payroll Item Listing

1. Repeat steps 1 to 2 on the previous page.

2. Click Payroll Item Listing to open the Payroll Item Listing report.

   - You can click Modify Report or use these fields to change report settings or click Export to send the report to Excel.

Note: *See Chapter 22 for more on these options.*

   You can click Print to print the report.

   You can double-click a line in the report to edit the payroll item's setup.

3. Click ✕ to close the report.

Employee Earnings Summary

1. Repeat steps 1 to 2 on the previous page.

2. Click Employee Earnings Summary to open the Employee Earnings Summary report.

   - You can click Modify Report or use these fields to change report settings or click Export to send the report to Excel.

Note: *See Chapter 22 for more on these options.*

   You can click Print to print the report.

   You can double-click a value on the report to see the list of transactions included in the summary number.

3. Click ✕ to close the report.

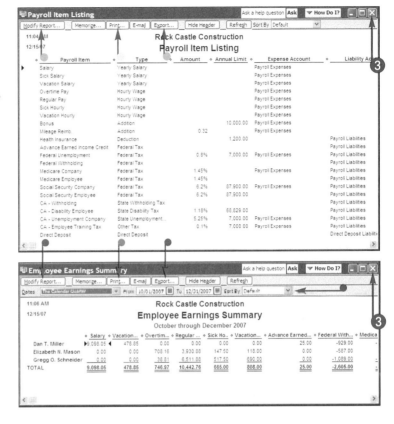

Is there a report that can help me fill out state payroll tax forms?

▼ Most state reports require the employee's name, social security number, taxable wages for a specified period, and the amount of tax withheld. You can use the Employee Contact list to get each employee's name and social security number, and you can customize the Employee Earnings Summary to include only state payroll items. With the Employee Earnings Summary on-screen, click Modify Reports, and then click the Filters tab. Click Payroll Item in the Current Filter Choices list. Click the Payroll Item down arrow and select All State.

Is there a report that I can print to tell me what payroll liabilities I need to pay?

▼ Yes. You can print the Payroll Liability Balances report, which lists each payroll liability down the side and each month across the top of the report. The numbers in the report show the amounts you owe for a given liability and given month.

Is there a report that will show me payments I have made and to whom?

▼ Yes. You can print the Payroll Transactions by Payee report. The report lists liability checks, paychecks, and adjustments made during the report period.

Banking Reports

You will find most banking reports useful when reconciling bank accounts. The Missing Checks report lists, for a particular bank account, the checks that you have written. The report includes each check number, date, payee, memo, amount, and account debited. Because the report sorts in check number order, you can easily identify missing or duplicate check numbers.

The Deposit Detail report lists all payments, regardless of whether you have deposited them. The report includes payment number if assigned, the date, the payee, the account, and the amount. QuickBooks subtotals payments by deposit to help you match the deposits to your bank statement.

The Previous Reconciliation report identifies the cleared and uncleared status of transactions for the report period. The report lists the transaction type, date, number, name, amount, and balance for transactions that existed at the time of the reconciliation and new transactions. QuickBooks groups transactions on the report so that all cleared transactions appear first, then uncleared transactions, and then new transactions. Within the group of cleared transactions, QuickBooks groups checks and payments together, followed by deposits and credits.

Banking Reports

Missing Checks

1. Click Reports.

2. Click Banking

3. Click Missing Checks.

   The Missing Checks dialog box appears.

4. Click here and select an account.

5. Click OK.

   The Missing Checks report appears.

   ● You can click Modify Report or use these fields to change report settings or click Export to send the report to Excel.

   Note: *See Chapter 22 for more on these options.*

   ● You can click Print to print the report.

   You can double-click a value to see the transaction in the window where you created it.

6. Click ⊠ to close the report.

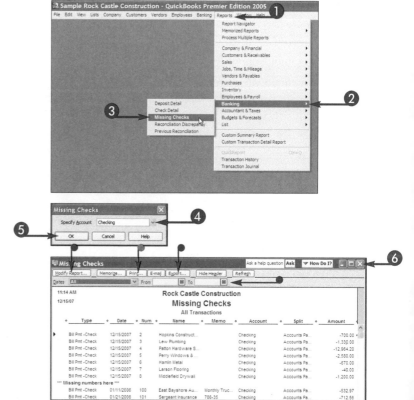

Deposit Detail

1 Repeat steps 1 to 2 on the previous page.

2 Click Deposit Detail to open the Deposit Detail report.

You can double-click a value to see the transaction in the window where you created it.

3 Click ▣ to close the report.

Previous Reconciliation

1 Repeat steps 1 to 2 on the previous page.

2 Click Previous Reconciliation to open the Select Previous Reconciliation Report dialog box.

3 Click here to select an account.

4 Click here to select a statement ending date.

5 Click a Type of Report option (○ changes to ◉).

6 Click Display.

7 Click OK to dismiss an information message that appears.

The Reconciliation Detail report appears.

You can double-click a value to see the transaction in the window where you created it.

8 Click ▣ to close the report.

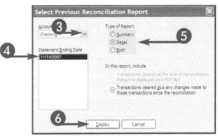

Is there a way that I can view all transactions that affect an account?

▼ There are several ways. You can print the Transaction Detail by Account report or the General Ledger report, both found by clicking Reports and then Accountant & Taxes. Both reports print all accounts by default, but you can filter them to print the accounts you need. For balance sheet accounts, you can open the account's register. Click Lists and then click Chart of Accounts. Then, double-click the account and QuickBooks displays the account register. If you double-click an income or expense account, QuickBooks displays an account QuickReport, which lists all transactions within the report period that affects the account.

Why can I select Accounts Receivable or an asset account when creating the Missing Checks report?

▼ You can select Accounts Receivable when creating the Missing Checks report because you can use the Missing Checks report in accounts receivable to check for missing or duplicate invoice numbers. Similarly, you can use the report in asset accounts to look for missing or duplicate payments.

What does the Reconciliation Discrepancy report show?

▼ This report shows reconciled transactions that have changed since you reconciled the account. The report lists the transaction type, date, modification date, number, name, reconciled amount, type of change, and the effect of the change. For details on this report, see Chapter 17.

Accountant and Taxes Reports

While most Accountant & Taxes reports are used primarily by your accountant, you may find several of them useful when you are trying to track down a problem.

The Trial Balance report shows you the account balance total as of the report date for all accounts. It lists the balances as either a debit or credit; if you follow the account rules that assets and expenses usually have debit balances while liabilities, equity, and income usually have credit balances, you can use the report to identify potential posting problems.

The Audit Trail report is useful if you have turned on the Audit Trail feature; see Chapter 1 for details. When the Audit Trail feature is on, the Audit Trail report shows each transaction that was modified or deleted. For each transaction, the report displays information such as the transaction's number, type, date, and time entered or modified; the name of the user who modified the transaction; and accounts affected by the transaction.

The General Ledger report is organized by account and lists each transaction that affects the account. For each transaction, the report displays the transaction type, date, number, name, memo, and amount. Because every transaction affects at least two accounts, the report also shows you the other accounts affected by the transaction.

Accountant & Taxes Reports

Trial Balance

1 Click Reports.

2 Click Accountant & Taxes.

3 Click Trial Balance.

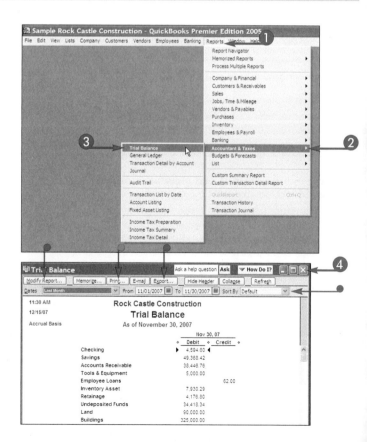

The Trial Balance report appears.

- You can click Modify Report or use these fields to change report settings or click Export to send the report to Excel.

Note: *See Chapter 22 for more on these options.*

- You can click Print to print the report.

You can double-click a value to see the transactions included in the value.

4 Click ⊠ to close the report.

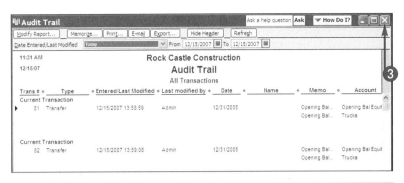

Audit Trail

1 Repeat steps 1 to 2 on the previous page.

2 Click Audit Trail to open the Audit Trail report.

You can double-click a field to see the transaction in the window where you created it.

3 Click ⊠ to close the report.

General Ledger

1 Repeat steps 1 to 2 on the previous page.

2 Click General Ledger to open the General Ledger report.

You can double-click a value to see the transaction in the window where you created it.

3 Click ⊠ to close the report.

What does the Journal report show?

▼ The Journal report lists every transaction that you entered during the report period and shows, for each transaction, the number, the type, the date, the name, the memo, and the accounts that the transaction debited and credited. This report is useful when you want to track down and correct errors associated with selecting the wrong account when saving transactions.

What does the Transaction Detail by Account report show?

▼ The Transaction Detail by Account report shows much of the same information as the General Ledger report. The major differences are the Transaction Detail by Account report shows whether a transaction has cleared, and does not display the account's balance; instead, it displays the total of the transactions that affect the account during the report period.

What does the Income Tax Preparation report show?

▼ The Income Tax Preparation report shows each account, the account type, and the tax line to which you assigned the account. This report is most useful if you intend to use QuickBooks in conjunction with TurboTax, Intuit's tax preparation software. To assign a tax line to an account, double-click the account on the report to display the Edit Account dialog box. Then, click the Tax Line down arrow and select a tax line.

Budget vs. Actual Report

You can print the Budget vs. Actual report only if you have previously prepared a budget; Chapter 19 discusses setting up forecasts, and the process for setting up budgets is nearly identical to the process of setting up forecasts.

The Budget vs. Actual report enables you to compare actual income and expenses to the amounts you estimated in your budget for the report period. Making this comparison helps you evaluate whether you are operating within budget constraints. The report lists income and expense accounts down the side. Across the top of the report you see the

actual amount of income or expenses for a particular month, the budgeted amount for that month, the dollars over or under budget, and the percentage of the budget that account represents. In the $ Over Budget column, where you see the dollar over or under budget amount, QuickBooks displays either a positive or negative number. A positive number represents dollars by which you have exceeded the budgeted amount. A negative number represents dollars below the budgeted amount.

To print this report, you walk through a wizard that prompts you to select a budget to use for comparison and a report layout.

Budget vs. Actual Report

① Click Reports.

② Click Budgets & Forecasts.

③ Click Budget vs. Actual.

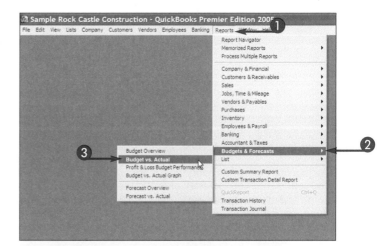

The Budget Report Wizard begins.

④ Click here to select a budget to use for the report.

⑤ Click Next.

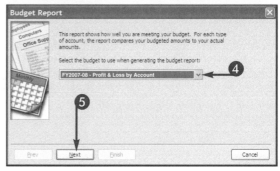

The second screen of the wizard appears.

6 Click here to select a report layout.

7 Click Next.

The last screen of the wizard appears.

8 Click Finish.

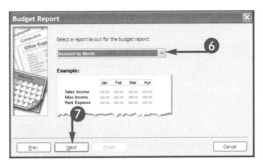

The report appears.

- You can click Modify Report or use these fields to change report settings or click Export to send the report to Excel.

Note: See Chapter 22 for more on these options.

- You can click Print to print the report.

You can double-click a nonbudget value to view the transactions that make up the summary value.

9 Click ☒ to close the report.

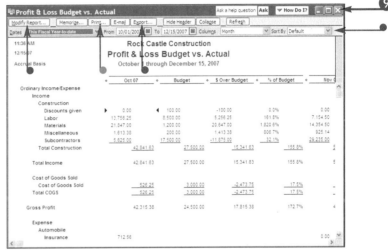

What does the Budget Overview report show?

▼ This report lists the amounts you entered when you prepared your budget. A wizard walks you through the preparation of this report, where you select the budget on which you want to report and a report layout. The report itself looks very much like the Profit & Loss Budget vs. Actual report shown in this section; income and expense accounts appear down the side of the report, while the report columns are budget months that show bugeted dollars for an income or expense account for that month. This report does not show any actual dollars or make comparisons.

What does the Profit & Loss Budget Performance report show?

▼ This report compares budgeted to actual income and expenses for the current month and quarter to the current month's budget, the year-to-date budget, and the annual budget. A wizard also walks you through preparation of this report, where you select the budget on which you want to report and a report layout. The report itself looks very much like the Profit & Loss Budget vs. Actual report shown in this section; income and expense accounts appear down the side of the report, while the report columns are this month's actual amounts, this month's budget, the quarter's actual amounts, the year-to-date budget, and the annual budget.

QuickBooks Backu Ask a help question | Ask | ▼ How Do I?   ☒

| Back Up Company File | Schedule a Backup |

Automatic backup:

☑ Automatically back up when closing data file every   3   times

Your file will be backed up to the Autobackup folder located in your QuickBooks program directory.

Schedule backup:

Click New to schedule a regular backup of your data file even while you are away from your computer.

Description	Backup Location	Status	Next Backup

New...   Edit...   Delete

OK   Cancel   Help

Schedule a Backup   ☒

Enter a description of the backup task you want to schedule.

Backup:

Description   My Backup

Location   E:\   Browse...

☑ Number of backups to keep   3

Select the time and day you want to back up this data file:

StartTime   01 ▼ : 00 ▼   AM ▼

Run this task every   1 ▼   weeks on:

☑ Monday   ☑ Tuesday   ☑ Wednesday

Ask a help

| My Preferences | **Company Preferences** |

	Show Summary	Show List	Don't Remind Me	
Checks to Print	⦿	○	○	5
Paychecks to Print	⦿	○	○	5
Invoices/Credit Memos to Print	⦿	○	○	5
Overdue Invoices	⦿	○	○	5
Sales Receipts to Print	⦿	○	○	
Sales Orders to Print	⦿	○	○	
Inventory to Reorder	⦿	○	○	
Assembly Items to Build	⦿	○	○	
Bills to Pay	⦿	○	○	10
Memorized Transactions Due	⦿	○	○	5
Money to Deposit	⦿	○	○	
Purchase Orders to Print	⦿	○	○	
To Do Notes	⦿	○	○	

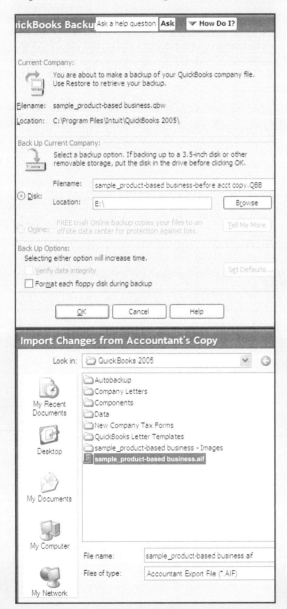

Work with Reminders

Y ou can use the Reminders feature in QuickBooks to remind you of almost any event. For example, QuickBooks can remind you to pay bills or print forms such as invoices, sales orders, and purchase orders. You can have QuickBooks remind you to print checks or deposit money in the bank. If you use memorized transactions that QuickBooks does not automatically enter, you can have QuickBooks remind you to enter memorized transactions. When you set up a reminder, it appears on the Reminders List.

Alerts, generated by QuickBooks, also appear on the Reminders List. Alerts are messages about QuickBooks; for example, you might see an alert that an update to

QuickBooks is available for you to download. You can dismiss an alert by marking it as completed in the Reminders List window.

QuickBooks displays reminders and alerts in the Reminders window in three formats: a custom format that you define in the Preferences dialog box, a format that shows a summarized list of reminder categories, and a detailed list that includes the categories as well as all reminders within each category.

To enable the Reminders feature, you establish preferences that identify the reminders that you want to create. To view reminders, you open the Reminders window. You can remove reminders from the list when you no longer need them.

Work with Reminders

Create Reminders

① Click Edit.

② Click Preferences.

The Preferences dialog box appears.

③ Click the Reminders icon.

The My Preferences tab appears.

- You can click here (☐ changes to ☑) to display the Reminders List when you open QuickBooks.

④ Click the Company Preferences tab.

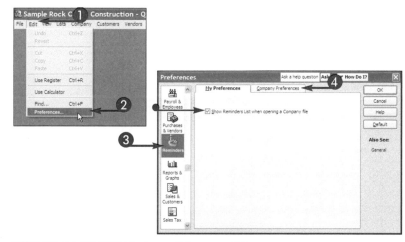

⑤ Click an option for each type of reminder (○ changes to ◉).

⑥ As appropriate, type the number of days QuickBooks should remind you prior to the event.

⑦ Click OK.

QuickBooks saves your settings.

View Reminders

1 Click Company.

2 Click Reminders.

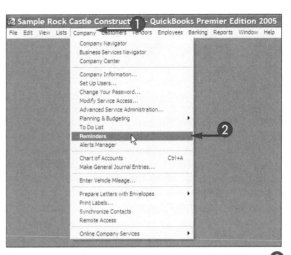

The Reminders window appears, displaying the Custom View.

- You can click Expand All to view all details of all reminder categories.

- You can click Collapse All to display only reminder categories.

3 Click the Close button (⊠) to close the window.

Can I print reminders?

▼ Yes. Follow steps 1 to 2 in the "View Reminders" subsection to display the Reminders window. Then, set up the list in the organization that you want to print by clicking Expand All, Custom View, or Collapse All. While viewing the list using the organization you want to print, click File and then Print List. QuickBooks displays the Print Lists dialog box, where you select a printer and then click Print to print the list.

What is the difference between an alert and a reminder?

▼ Alerts, generated by QuickBooks, are important business events often external to your day-to-day operation of QuickBooks. For example, QuickBooks generates an alert if an update to QuickBooks exists that you need to download. Reminders, created by you, focus more on tasks you perform within QuickBooks, such as making loan payments, paying bills, or making deposits.

How do I remove a reminder I no longer need?

▼ In general, you do not remove reminders; when the date for the reminder passes or you take the action specified by the reminder, QuickBooks removes it from the Reminders List. You can mark To Do notes as done; see the section "Create a To Do Note" for details.

Create a
To Do Note

When you have a task you need to do that does not appear as one of the tasks about which QuickBooks reminds you, you can use a To Do note. These notes are free-form notes that are not tied to any particular event in QuickBooks. For example, you may need to print checks for an upcoming company function. You can think of To Do notes the same way that you would think of tasks you place on a To Do list in your contact management or calendar program.

You can tie To Do notes to calendar dates when you create them; when you complete an action associated with a To Do note, you can mark it completed. You also can delete To Do notes or mark them inactive. You also can print individual To Do notes or print a report of To Do notes that appear in the list.

To Do notes appear in their own list, but you can choose to include them in the Reminders List. QuickBooks typically displays the entire To Do note in the To Do Note window, but you can display only a portion of the note that summarizes it if you set up the note properly.

Create a To Do Note

① Click Company.

② Click To Do List.

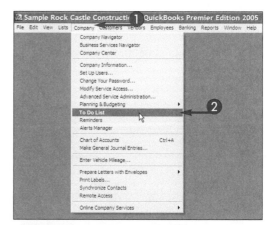

The To Do List window appears.

③ Click To Do.

④ Click New.

The New To Do dialog box appears.

5 Type the To Do message here.

6 Click the calendar button (▦) to select a reminder date.

7 Click OK.

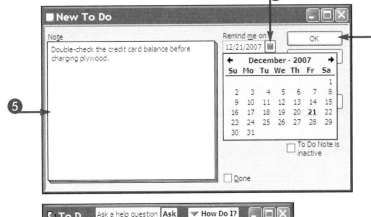

The To Do List window reappears.

● The new To Do note appears in the window.

How do I get rid of a To Do note?

▼ You can mark a To Do note as completed by right-clicking it in the To Do List window and clicking Mark As Done. The note remains in the To Do List window, but QuickBooks displays a check mark (☑) beside it. You can hide a To Do note by right-clicking it and then clicking Make Inactive. The To Do note still exists in your data file but disappears from the To Do List window. You can delete a To Do note by clicking it in the To Do List window, clicking To Do, and clicking Delete. In this case, QuickBooks removes the To Do note from your company data file.

How can I display only a summary of a lengthy To Do note?

▼ Type a summary of the note on the first line, press Enter, and type the rest of the note. QuickBooks displays only the first line of the entry in the To Do List window.

How do I print To Do notes?

▼ You print a particular To Do note by clicking the note in the To Do List window, clicking To Do, and then clicking Print Note. Print the list of To Do notes by clicking To Do and then clicking Print List. Print the To Do Note report from the To Do List window by clicking the Reports button and clicking Detail List. Print the same report from the Reports menu by clicking Reports, Lists, and then To Do Notes.

Set Desktop View Preferences

You can set Desktop preferences to enable QuickBooks to display the desktop of your choice, and you can save those settings when you create them or when you close a QuickBooks company, or you can keep a previously saved desktop.

You can choose to have QuickBooks maximize every window you open or you can have QuickBooks display each window you open so that you can see some portion of it, no matter how many windows you open. You can choose to display QuickBooks navigators, which help you find your way around QuickBooks, and you can select the navigator you want to see by default when you open your company. For more information on navigators, see Chapter 1.

What happens if I click Display or Sounds in the Preferences dialog box?

▼ Clicking Display opens the Windows Display Properties dialog box, where you can change your screen resolution, define a Windows color scheme, or select a background wallpaper for your Windows desktop. You also can select a screen saver, set the time before the screen saver appears, and set a password for the screen saver so that only those who know the password can dismiss it. Clicking Sounds displays the Windows Sounds and Audio Devices Properties dialog box, where you can control the volume of sounds and assign sounds to events in QuickBooks.

Set Desktop View Preferences

① Click Edit.

② Click Preferences.

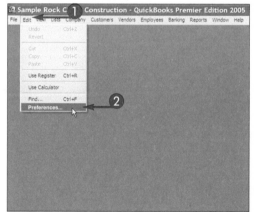

The Preferences dialog box appears.

③ Click the Desktop View icon.

④ Click the My Preferences tab.

⑤ Click an option to control window behavior in QuickBooks (○ changes to ◉).

⑥ Click here to select the default navigator QuickBooks opens when you start the program.

⑦ Click an option to control saving the QuickBooks desktop (○ changes to ◉).

⑧ Click here to select a different color scheme.

⑨ Click OK.

QuickBooks saves your settings.

Set Spelling Preferences

QuickBooks comes with a spelling checker that you can use to ensure that documents you send to customers and vendors contain accurate spelling. In the Preferences dialog box, you can turn off the spelling checker or control the behavior of the spelling checker. For example, you can specify that the spelling checker ignore Internet addresses rather than highlight them as incorrectly spelled words. You also can tell the spelling checker to ignore numbers, words with the first letter capitalized, words spelled in all uppercase letters, and words with capital letters appearing in the middle of the word.

MASTER IT

If I turn off the spelling checker, is there still a way to use it?

▼ Yes. By turning off the spelling checker in the Preferences dialog box, QuickBooks does not automatically check spelling in forms. However, while working in any form window, you can click the Spelling icon at the top of the form to make QuickBooks check the spelling in the form. Using this approach, you do not need to check every form before saving or printing it; instead, you can spell-check selectively.

Set Spelling Preferences

1 Click Edit.

2 Click Preferences.

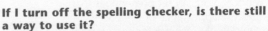
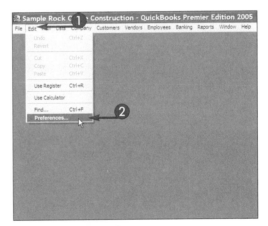

The Preferences dialog box appears.

3 Click the Spelling icon.

4 Click the My Preferences tab.

● You can click this option to turn off spell-checking (☑ changes to ☐).

5 Click these options to identify the kinds of words QuickBooks should ignore when checking spelling (☐ changes to ☑).

6 Click OK.

QuickBooks saves your settings.

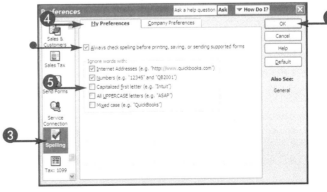

Set E-mail Preferences

I f you intend to e-mail forms to customers or vendors, you can set preferences that control the appearance of the cover message QuickBooks includes for each form you e-mail. When you e-mail a form, QuickBooks creates a PDF (portable document format) file of the form that the recipient can read using the free Adobe Reader program. You can attach the PDF file to an e-mail message. The preferences you set for e-mail relate to the text that appears in the e-mail message QuickBooks automatically generates when you e-mail a form. You can control the salutation of the message, the subject, and the message text.

What happens if I click Spelling?

▼ QuickBooks checks the spelling of the text on-screen in the Preferences dialog box; if it finds errors, QuickBooks displays a dialog box that enables you to correct the errors.

How do I send a form to a customer in e-mail?

▼ You must fill in the customer's e-mail information in the customer's entry in the Customer List window. Then, while displaying the completed form on-screen, you can click the Send button or the E-mail button, depending on the window you are viewing. QuickBooks displays a screen that you can use to preview the message, and you can click Send Now or Send Later.

Set E-mail Preferences

① Click Edit.

② Click Preferences.

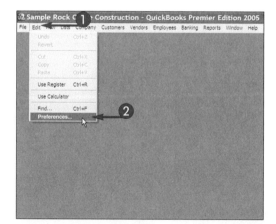

The Preferences dialog box appears.

③ Click the Send Forms icon.

④ Click the Company Preferences tab.

⑤ Click here to select the type of form for which to set defaults.

● You can click here to change "Dear" to "To."

⑥ Click here to select a salutation format.

⑦ Type a standard subject here and type standard text to appear in the cover message for the selected form here.

⑧ Click OK.

QuickBooks saves your settings.

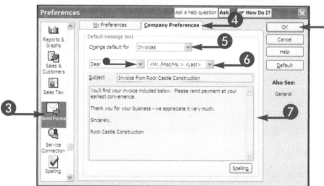

Set Preferences for Integrated Applications

QuickBooks integrates with a variety of software that perform functions related to accounting but are not part of QuickBooks, and you can set preferences to control the behavior of these applications that integrate with QuickBooks.

In many cases, the integrating software enhances a function available in QuickBooks or provides a more intense solution than QuickBooks. For example, Timeslips, a time and billing software package, contains extensive functions needed by people who bill primarily by the hour. However, these same people need their billing information in QuickBooks to maintain a complete general ledger. Timeslips can integrate with QuickBooks to send billing information to QuickBooks.

What happens if I click Properties?

▼ QuickBooks displays the Properties dialog box for the highlighted application. On the Details tab, you see the program's name, developer, and the date last accessed. On the Access Rights tab, you can control whether the application can access QuickBooks and if so, whether you should be prompted to allow access for the application or whether the application can have automatic access to QuickBooks. You also can control whether the application has access to social security numbers, customer credit card numbers, and other personal information.

What happens if I click Remove?

▼ QuickBooks removes the application from the list of applications that can access the company data file.

Set Preferences for Integrated Applications

① Click Edit.

② Click Preferences.

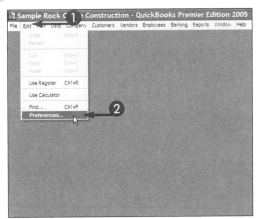

The Preferences dialog box appears.

③ Click the Integrated Applications icon.

④ Click the Company Preferences tab.

- You can click these options to deny access to your company file to all programs or to have QuickBooks notify you before a program accesses your company data file (☐ changes to ☑).

- You can click here to allow or deny access to individual applications.

⑤ Click OK.

QuickBooks saves your settings.

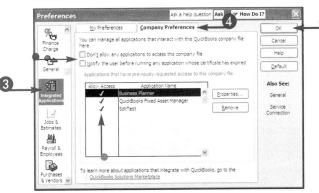

Set Preferences for Reports and Graphs

Y ou can set preferences for the way QuickBooks handles reports and graphs. For example, if you know that you are going to modify most reports every time you print them, you can have QuickBooks automatically display the Modify Report dialog box before it actually prepares the report, saving you the time QuickBooks uses to prepare a report that you know you will not use.

You also can specify whether QuickBooks should display summary reports on a cash or an accrual basis. The accrual basis generally provides a more accurate picture of where your company stands financially because the accrual basis

recognizes revenues and expenses when they occur rather than when you receive payment or pay bills.

Using the Aging Reports options, you can set the starting point for counting the number of overdue days on aging reports, which show, for each unpaid invoice or bill, how much is currently due and how much is past due. Choose to age from the due date if you want the overdue days to start from the due date that appears on an invoice, statement, or bill. Choose to age from the transaction date if you want the overdue days to start from the date you entered on an invoice or a bill or the date you created a statement.

Set Preferences for Reports and Graphs

① Click Edit.

② Click Preferences.

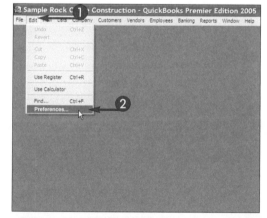

The Preferences dialog box appears.

③ Click the Reports & Graphs icon.

④ Click the My Preferences tab.

- You can click this option to display the Modify Report dialog box each time before you open a report (☐ changes to ☑).

⑤ Click here to select a refresh option (○ changes to ◉).

- You can click these options to speed up graph presentation and use patterns instead of colors on graphs (☐ changes to ☑).

⑥ Click the Company Preferences tab.

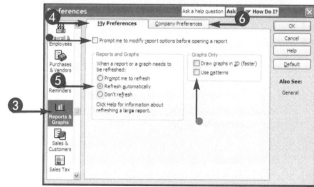

7 Click an option to select the default basis for reports (○ changes to ⦿).

8 Click an Aging Reports option (○ changes to ⦿).

9 Click an option for the appearance of accounts on reports (○ changes to ⦿).

10 Click Format.

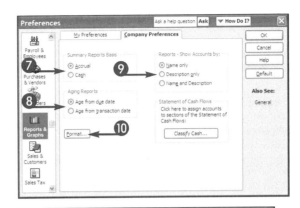

The Report Format Preferences dialog box appears.

11 Deselect these options so that the corresponding information does not appear on reports (☑ changes to ☐).

12 Click here to select a report alignment.

- You can click the Fonts & Numbers tab to control the appearance of numbers and establish default fonts for selected report sections.

13 Click OK to close the Report Format Preferences dialog box.

14 Click OK.

QuickBooks saves your settings.

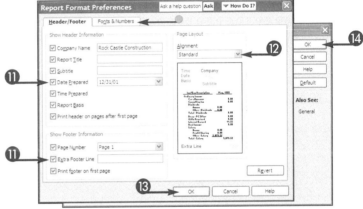

Why does QuickBooks includes refresh options?

▼ Generally, QuickBooks updates reports that you are viewing if you make changes that affect the data on the report. Sometimes, however, you may make changes that QuickBooks cannot automatically incorporate in the report. In these cases, QuickBooks needs to refresh the report, which means regenerating it from scratch. Because re-creating a report can be a lengthy process if your company data file is large, QuickBooks enables you to set options to automatically refresh, prompt you before refreshing, or not refresh at all. Select the option that works best with the amount of data in your company data file.

What happens when I click Classify Cash?

▼ The Classify Cash dialog box appears. Using this dialog box, you can assign accounts to various sections of the Statement of Cash Flows Report. For details on this report, see Chapter 23.

What happens if I click Format on the Company Preferences tab?

▼ QuickBooks displays the Report Format Preferences dialog box, which contains the options you see in the Modify Reports dialog box on the Header/Footer tab and the Fonts & Numbers tab. Any options you set in this dialog box become defaults for all reports, so you can control header and footer information and font and number formats for all reports.

Customize the Icon Bar

QuickBooks contains an Icon Bar that enables you to quickly open a variety of windows in QuickBooks. The Icon Bar appears on-screen immediately below the menu bar, and you can customize the icons that appear on the Icon Bar to make sure that the icons you use most often are available. For example, you can place icons on the Icon Bar that open the Create Invoices window, the Write Checks window, the Enter Bills window, and the Receive Payments window. You also can control the appearance of the icons by displaying a picture only or a picture combined with a text description of the icon's purpose.

QuickBooks also enables you to select the pictures you want to assign to each task and change the descriptive text if the default meaning does not work well for you. Be aware that the length of the Icon Bar cannot exceed the width of your screen; if you add too many icons to display on the bar or if you use a long text description for an icon, some icons may seem to disappear from the Icon Bar. In reality, you see a small carat at the right end of the Icon Bar; if you click the carat, QuickBooks displays any hidden icons.

Customize the Icon Bar

Display the Icon Bar

1 Click View.

2 Click Icon Bar.

- The Icon bar appears at the top of the screen.

3 Click View.

4 Click Customize Icon Bar.

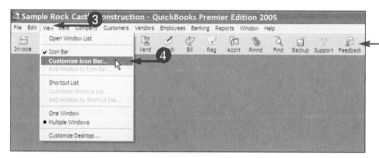

Customize the Icon Bar

The Customize Icon Bar dialog box appears.

5 Click a Display Option to control the appearance of icons on the Icon bar (○ changes to ⊙).

- You can add a line to the right of an icon if you click that icon in the list and then click Add Separator; in the list, the separator appears as "(space)".

350

Add an Icon to the Bar

① Complete steps 1 to 4 on the previous page, clicking the icon you want to appear to the left of the new icon.

② Click Add.

③ In the Add Icon Bar Item dialog box, click the icon you want to add.

● To change the icon picture click here.

You can type a label and description for the icon.

④ Click OK.

The new icon appears in the Icon Bar Content list and on the Icon bar.

Edit an Icon on the Bar

① Complete steps 1 to 4 on the preceding page, clicking the icon you want to edit.

② Click Edit to open the Edit Icon Bar Item dialog box.

● To change the icon picture click here.

● You can type a label and description here.

③ Click OK.

④ Click OK.

QuickBooks saves the changes.

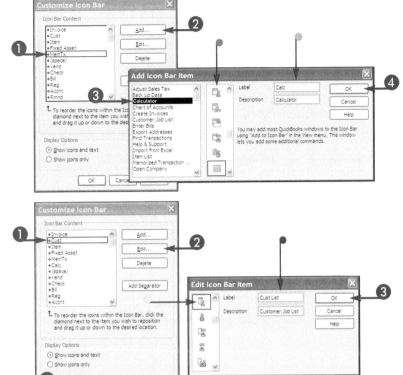

How can I change the order of the icons on the Icon Bar?

▼ Complete the steps in this section so that you have all the icons on the Icon bar that you want. Then, while viewing the Customize Icon Bar dialog box, click and drag ◆ beside an icon you want to move to the location where you want it to appear. As you position the mouse pointer over the ◆ that appears next to an icon, the mouse pointer changes to a four-headed arrow. As you drag, a dotted line appears attached to the mouse pointer to help you identify the mouse pointer's current location.

Is there any limit to the length of the name I can assign to an icon?

▼ You can type up to 30 characters for an icon's name, but remember that long names will expand the space that an icon occupies on the Icon bar, causing QuickBooks to hide icons on the right edge of the Icon bar.

Is there a way to add the Pay Bills window to the Icon Bar?

▼ You can add most QuickBooks windows to the Icon bar. Open the window that you want to add to the Icon bar. Then click View and click Add to Icon Bar.

Create a Custom Template Form

I f you find that the invoice and statement template forms — and purchase order forms if you turn on the inventory feature — that QuickBooks creates for you do not fully meet your needs, you can easily create your own form. In this section, you define the fields that appear on an invoice template form. To adjust the appearance and location of fields on forms, you use the Layout Designer in QuickBooks; see the section "Modify the Appearance of a Template Form" for details.

You can create templates for all printable forms including Invoices, Sales Receipts, Estimates, Sales Orders, Credit Memos/Refunds, Statements, and Purchase Orders. You cannot create templates for checks.

If an existing template form closely matches the form you want to use, you can edit the existing form. In some cases, you cannot make many changes to the default form, but you can duplicate the form and modify the duplicate; see "Edit a Predefined Template" for details on duplicating a form.

When you define a form, you select the fields that appear on-screen; you also can choose to print any field that appears on-screen, and you can choose to print a field that you do not display on-screen. For example, Intuit's default packing slip form prints the project name but does not display the information on the form on-screen.

Create a Custom Template Form

1 Click Lists.

2 Click Templates.

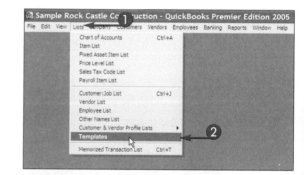

The Templates window appears.

3 Click Templates.

4 Click New.

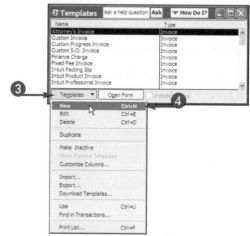

The Select Template Type window appears.

5 Click an option for the type of form you want to create (○ changes to ◉).

The example in these steps uses Invoice.

6 Click OK.

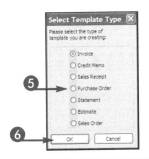

The Header tab of the Customize Invoice dialog box appears.

7 Type a name for the template here.

8 Click the options to select the lines that you want to appear on-screen (☐ changes to ☑).

9 Click the options to select the lines that you want to appear on the printed form (☐ changes to ☑).

10 Type the information that should appear on-screen and when you print the form.

11 Click the Fields tab.

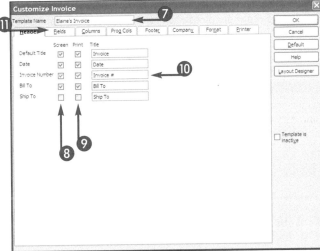

How do I edit a custom template form?

▼ Follow steps 1 to 3 and then click Edit. For most forms, you see the Customize dialog box that appears in this section. You use the same techniques described in this section to change the fields that appear on a template form as you do to add fields to the form, selecting or deselecting options and changing descriptive information. If you select a predefined QuickBooks template form, you see only the Company tab and the Format tab. To change other information on a predefined form, you can duplicate the form and then edit the duplicate. See the section "Edit a Predefined Template" for details on duplicating a form.

Is there a way to change the name of the form that appears on-screen when I open the window?

▼ Yes. For example, if you do not use the word "invoice" in your business, but instead, you and your employees refer to the document as a "customer bill," you can change the form title. Follow steps 1 to 6 or edit an existing template that is not a predefined template. On the Header tab, click in the Title column next to Default Title and change the description from Invoice to Customer Bill. Click OK and QuickBooks saves the change. When you display the form in the Create Invoices window, the new title appears; it will also print.

Create a Custom Template Form *(Continued)*

During the process of creating a custom template form, you define header fields that include the form title, date, number, and shipping and billing information. You also define other fields that typically appear near the header information but are optional to the form; for example, you may include a customer's purchase order number on an invoice form.

On the Columns tab, you define the fields that appear in the section of the form where you list the individual items involved in the transaction, such as item number, quantity, rate, and description.

All invoice-based templates have a Prog Cols tab that you do not see when creating a Receipts form or a Sales Orders form. Using the fields on the Prog Cols tab, you can display

rates, quantities, and amounts stored on estimates as well as information about previously billed quantities and amounts. Fewer options appear on this tab if progress invoicing is turned off. See Chapter 12 for more information on progress invoicing.

Using the fields on the Footer tab, you can print or display total information and messages.

The Company tab controls information about your company that appears on the form. For example, you can print your company name and address along with phone and fax numbers as well as e-mail and Web site addresses. If, however, you use a preprinted form, you will not want to include any of this information.

Create a Custom Template Form *(continued)*

The Fields tab appears.

⑫ Click the options to select the fields that you want to appear on-screen (☐ changes to ☑).

⑬ Click the options to select the fields that you want to appear on the printed form (☐ changes to ☑).

⑭ Type the information that should appear on-screen and when you print the form.

Note: *You make changes to the Columns, Prog Cols, and Footer tabs using steps 12 to 14.*

⑮ Click the Company tab.

⑯ Click the options to select company information to include when printing the form (☐ changes to ☑).

● You can click the Use Logo option (○ changes to ◉) to assign your company logo to the form, then click Specify to navigate to the location where you store your logo.

⑰ Click the Format tab.

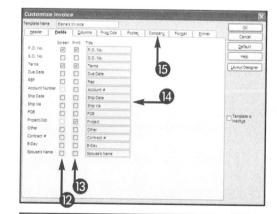

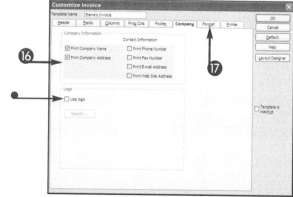

Note: As you click in this list, the word "Example" changes to display the element's font.

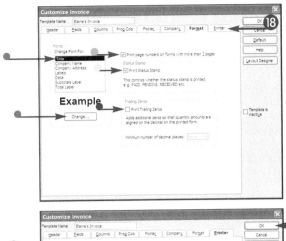

- You can click here and then click Change to change the element's font.

- You can click this option to eliminate page numbers (☑ changes to ☐).

  You can click this option to print the stamp QuickBooks displays while viewing the form window on-screen (☐ changes to ☑).

- You can click this option to print zeros to align numbers on the decimal point (☐ changes to ☑).

⑱ Click the Printer tab.

⑲ Click a printer settings option (○ changes to ◉).

⑳ Click OK.

The Templates window reappears, showing the template you just created.

Can I arrange columns in a specific order?

▼ Yes. Follow steps 1 to 3, highlight a template to edit, then click Templates, and Edit. Click the Columns tab, which contains the same columns that appear on the Fields tab. The Columns tab, however, contains one additional column called Order. In the Order column next to each field, type a number that specifies the order in which you want the fields to appear in the details section of the form. For example, to display and print the item in the leftmost column, type 1 in the Order column next to Item.

How do I use the template I just created?

▼ Open the window for the form type. For example, if you created an invoice, click Customers and then Create Invoices. Click ☑ in the upper-right corner of the window, immediately below the Customize button. From the list, select the template you created. QuickBooks changes the appearance of the window to display your template with its fields. You do not need to select your template every time you open the window; QuickBooks continues to use the selected template until you select a different template from the list, even after you close QuickBooks.

Modify the Appearance of a Template Form

The section "Create a Custom Template Form" shows you how to add or remove fields from a template form. If you need to move fields or resize them or add a text box or data field that does not appear in the Customize dialog box, you can use the Layout Designer to make the change.

The Layout Designer controls the physical placement and appearance of the information on template forms. You can add text boxes, data fields, and even graphic images to a template form; QuickBooks can place a border around any

text box, data field, or graphic image. You can control the appearance of the border by selecting a pattern and line thickness, and you can round the corners of the border. You also can control the alignment of text within a text box and the font QuickBooks uses for the text in the box. QuickBooks also enables you to fill the background of a box, which can create a very dramatic effect. For example, on an invoice, you can set up a text box for the title of the form where the background of the box is black and the text is white.

Modify the Appearance of a Template Form

Open the Layout designer

① Click Lists.

② Click Templates.

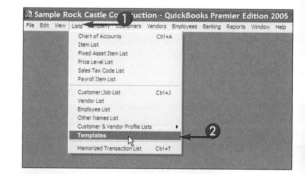

The Templates window appears.

③ Click the template you want to edit.

④ Click Templates.

⑤ Click Edit.

The Customize Invoice dialog box appears.

6 Click Layout Designer.

Add a Text Box

The Layout Designer dialog box appears.

● You can click the outline of any box to select that field to check its properties, copy or remove it, or change its alignment.

7 Click Add.

8 Click Text Box.

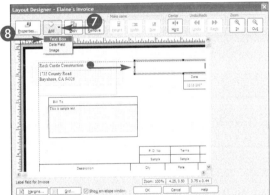

What happens when I click Properties in the Layout Designer dialog box?

▼ The Properties dialog box for the selected field appears. If the selected field is an image, the name and file size of the image appear. If the selected field is a text box or a data field, the Properties dialog box contains three tabs. On the first tab, you can control the vertical and horizontal position of the information within the selected field and the font used to display the field. From the second tab, you can control whether a border appears around the selected field and the appearance and color of that border. From the third tab, you control whether QuickBooks fills the box with color and, if so, the color QuickBooks uses.

What happens when I click Grid in the Layout Designer dialog box?

▼ QuickBooks displays the Grid and Snap Settings dialog box. From this dialog box, you can control whether dots forming a grid appear on-screen and whether objects automatically align to the grid. You can use the grid to help you position and align objects consistently on the form.

Is there a way to identify the selected field?

▼ Yes. The name of the selected field appears in the lower-left corner of the Layout Designer dialog box, just above the Margins button.

PART VII

continued

Modify the Appearance of a Template Form *(Continued)*

Using the Layout Designer, you can center objects horizontally between the left and right margin of the page. Within a text box, you can control the horizontal and vertical placement of text. You can align objects on a template and make two or more objects the same height, width, or size to create a uniform effect. You also can enlarge fields on a template so that all the information in the field appears when you print or display the form.

Intuit sells window envelopes that you can use to send forms to customers or vendors; in the Layout Designer dialog box, you can display a shaded area that represents the windows of the window envelope; using the shaded areas, you can position address information so that it will appear in the window area.

The Layout Designer is available for all templates except predefined templates that QuickBooks creates automatically. If you want to modify the appearance of a predefined template, you must make a copy of the template and then make your changes on the copy. For details on making a copy of a template, see the section "Edit a Predefined Template."

Modify the Appearance of a Template Form *(continued)*

Change Text Appearance

The Properties dialog box appears.

⑨ Type the text that should appear in the box here.

⑩ Click a horizontal justification option (○ changes to ◉).

⑪ Click a vertical justification option (○ changes to ◉).

● You can click here to select a font.

● You can click here to select a text color.

⑫ Click the Border tab.

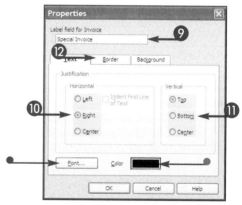

Set Borders

● You can click a border option to add or eliminate a border surrounding the box (○ changes to ◉).

⑬ Click an option for the border corners (○ changes to ◉).

⑭ Click an option for the border pattern (○ changes to ◉).

⑮ Click an option for the border thickness (○ changes to ◉).

● You can click the Background tab to assign a color to fill the background of the box.

⑯ Click OK.

QuickBooks places the text box on the layout.

You can move and resize the text box.

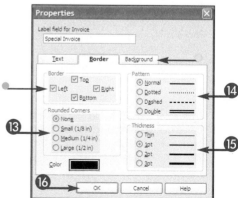

Add a Data Field

⑰ Click Add.

⑱ Click Data Field.

The Add Data Field dialog box appears.

⑲ Click a field to add.

⑳ Click OK.

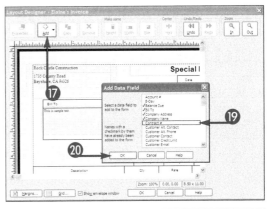

● QuickBooks adds a label and the field.

You can move the data field by clicking and dragging it.

㉑ Click OK twice to save the form.

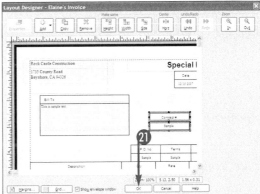

How do I move and resize a text box?

▼ Select the box so that a border containing handles — small black squares (▣) — appears. To move an object, place the mouse pointer over the selection border; the mouse pointer changes to a mouse pointer attached to a four-headed arrow. Once the mouse pointer changes, click and drag the object's selection border. To make an object larger, place the mouse pointer over one of the black handles. As you move the mouse pointer over the handle, the pointer changes to a two-headed arrow. Once the pointer changes, click and drag outward. When you release the mouse button, QuickBooks resizes the field.

What does the Height button do?

▼ It enables you to make two objects the same size vertically. Click the object whose height you want to change. With that object selected, press and hold the Shift key and click the second object you want to align. QuickBooks selects both objects. Once both objects are selected, the Height button becomes available. Click it, and QuickBooks changes the vertical height of the first object to match the height of the second object. You make two objects the same width or size using the same technique.

Edit a Predefined Template

Quick Books creates some templates that are predefined; if you try to edit one of these templates, you can change only the information that appears on the Company tab and on the Format tab of the Customize dialog box. If the predefined template is very close to the template you want to create, you can duplicate it; when QuickBooks duplicates a template, all tabs of the Customize dialog box are available, along with the Layout Designer.

When you duplicate a template, QuickBooks creates a second copy of the original, retaining the original name but placing the letters DUP at the beginning of the template name. Once you duplicate a template, you can edit it in any way described in the sections "Create a Custom Template Form" and "Modify the Appearance of a Template Form." In addition to making changes to the Company tab and the Format tab, you can add or remove header and footer information, fields, and columns. You also can use the Layout Designer to move or resize elements or add text boxes, data fields, or images to the form template. When editing the form, change its name to something more meaningful; you can eliminate the DUP characters QuickBooks inserts in the form template name.

Edit a Predefined Template

① Click Lists.

② Click Templates.

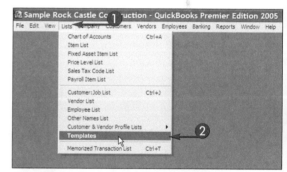

The Templates window appears.

③ Click the template you want to edit.

④ Click Templates.

⑤ Click Duplicate.

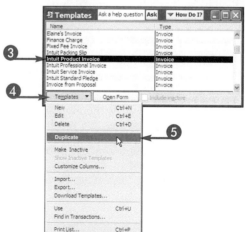

6 In the Select Template Type dialog box that appears, click an option to select the type of form you want to create (○ changes to ◉).

The example in this section uses Invoice.

7 Click OK.

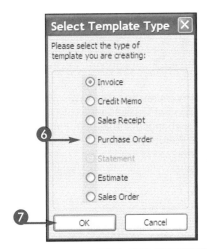

Select Template Type

Please select the type of template you are creating:

- ◉ Invoice
- ○ Credit Memo
- ○ Sales Receipt
- ○ Purchase Order
- Statement
- ○ Estimate
- ○ Sales Order

OK   Cancel

● The duplicated template appears in the Templates window.

You can double-click the template to edit it.

Note: *See the sections "Create a Custom Template Form" and "Modify the Appearance of a Template Form" for details.*

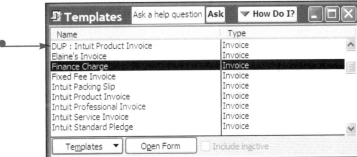

Templates   Ask a help question Ask   ▼ How Do I?

Name	Type
DUP : Intuit Product Invoice	Invoice
Elaine's Invoice	Invoice
Finance Charge	Invoice
Fixed Fee Invoice	Invoice
Intuit Packing Slip	Invoice
Intuit Product Invoice	Invoice
Intuit Professional Invoice	Invoice
Intuit Service Invoice	Invoice
Intuit Standard Pledge	Invoice

Templates ▼   Open Form   ☐ Include inactive

What does the Open Form button do?

▼ If you click a template in the Templates window to select it and then click the Open Form button, QuickBooks opens the window for which the form was created and displays that form in the window. The Open Form button enables you to view the form from the Templates window to help you while modifying the form. Although you can use the form in the window that appears to create a transaction, you can more efficiently display the form for entering transactions by opening the window and using the Template ☑ to select the form.

On the menu that appears when I click Templates in the Templates window, what does the Customize Columns option do?

▼ That option does not affect any of the forms in the Templates window; instead, it affects the appearance of the Templates window itself. QuickBooks displays three columns in the Templates window — Name, Type, and Active Status. The Active Status column only appears if you have made a template inactive. By clicking the Customize Columns choice, you display the Customize Columns dialog box, where you can control the columns that appear in the Templates window. Every list window has a Customize Columns choice that works the same way.

Update QuickBooks

The Automatic Update feature ensures that you have the latest release of your version of QuickBooks; you may want to make some changes to the functioning of the Automatic Update feature to include additional types of updates or to handle updating QuickBooks in a multiuser environment.

Periodically, Intuit releases updates to QuickBooks to address problems or add functionality to the program. These updates are not new versions of the program; they are enhancements to the program to make it function better. When you install QuickBooks, you automatically install an update agent that checks for updates whenever you connect to the Internet.

Some users prefer to check manually for updates rather than let QuickBooks check, but updating automatically is recommended. If you make no changes to the way the Automatic Update feature functions, QuickBooks automatically checks for certain types of updates while your computer is connected to the Internet, downloads updates when they are available, and installs them when you close QuickBooks. The process happens without interrupting you as you work in QuickBooks. If you do not use an "always on" Internet connection and your Internet connection is interrupted while QuickBooks is downloading an update, nothing happens at that time. QuickBooks automatically continues the download process the next time you connect to the Internet.

Update QuickBooks Automatically

① Click File.

② Click Update QuickBooks.

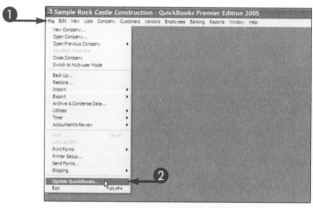

The Update QuickBooks dialog box appears.

● You can click Update Now to update QuickBooks immediately.

③ Click the Options tab.

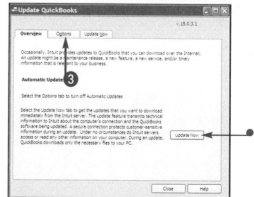

④ Click an option to turn Automatic Update on or off (⚪ changes to ⦿).

⑤ Click an option to share downloaded updates in a multiuser environment (⚪ changes to ⦿).

If you click Yes in step 5, you can select a download location.

⑥ Click next to each type of update you want to download (☐ changes to ☑).

⑦ Click the Update Now tab.

● QuickBooks displays the updates it will download.

⑧ Click Get Updates.

QuickBooks connects to the Internet and downloads any available updates.

⑨ When QuickBooks finishes downloading updates, click Close.

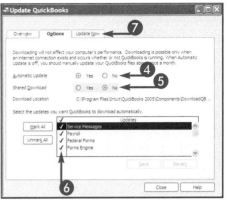

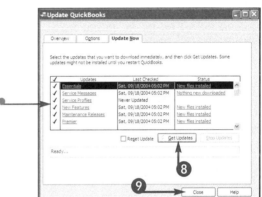

How does the Shared Download option work?

▼ Use this option in multiuser environments where you must update multiple copies of QuickBooks. When you click the Yes option (⚪ changes to ⦿), QuickBooks downloads updates to the location on your network where you store the shared company data file. To make this option work correctly, each workstation on your network must have a unique copy of the same version of QuickBooks, your company data file must reside in a shared folder on your network that all workstations can access, and each workstation must enable this option from within its individual copy of QuickBooks.

Will I hurt anything if I turn off Automatic Update?

▼ QuickBooks continues to function, but you do not automatically receive updates that may fix problems in the software. Turning off Automatic Update is not recommended because QuickBooks searches for updates in the background without interrupting your work. You do not even need to be using QuickBooks for Automatic Update to do its job when you connect to the Internet. If you must turn off Automatic Update, make it a habit to manually check for updates at least once a month. You can set up a reminder in QuickBooks to check for updates; see Chapter 24 for details on creating reminders.

Back Up Your Company

There probably is no task more important than backing up your company data file. Without a backup, recovering from a failed hard drive is a nightmare, because you have to re-create your company data file. With a backup, you can quickly and easily recover by restoring the backup. For details on restoring a backup, see the section "Restore a Backup."

You can back up your company data file manually using your own schedule; for example, you may want to back up QuickBooks every evening before you leave for the day. If you prefer, you can have QuickBooks prompt you to back up after you close QuickBooks a specified number of times. Or, you can set up a backup schedule in QuickBooks that occurs automatically at a specified time on specified days of the week.

When you back up your company data, QuickBooks copies all your company data, exactly as it appears at that moment, into the backup file. You should verify the backup, particularly if you back up to floppy disks, which decay more quickly than any other form of data storage. Verifying a backup makes the process take longer, but it ensures that the backup you create is one that you can use in case of an emergency.

Back Up Your Company

Back Up Manually

① Click File.

② Click Back Up.

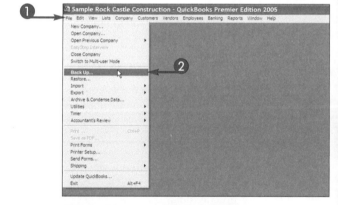

The QuickBooks Backup dialog box appears.

● Information about the company you are backing up appears here.

③ Type a location to store your backup.

● You can click Browse to navigate to the location.

④ Click this option if you want to verify the backup (☐ changes to ☑).

⑤ Click Set Defaults.

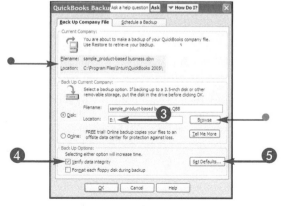

6 In the Set Defaults dialog box, click the options you want (☐ changes to ☑).

QuickBooks can remind you to back up as you close your company; type the number of times to back up.

You can type a default backup location.

You can include the date and time of the backup in the backup filename.

- Windows XP users can use the Windows CD Writing Wizard to help write backups to CD.

7 Click OK.

8 Click OK.

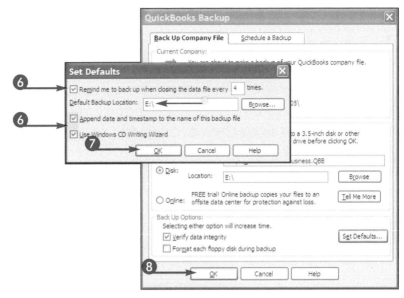

QuickBooks backs up your data, and a message appears when the backup completes successfully.

9 Click OK.

How often should I back up?

▼ The answer is a matter of personal preference that you should decide in conjunction with your risk-taking tolerance. Ask yourself the question, "If I do not back up my data today, how much effort will be required to re-create all the work I did today?" If you think that re-creating your work will take no time at all, you can skip backing up. The more time it takes you to re-create, however, the less willing you should be to skip backing up. Remember, backing up your company file usually takes no more that five minutes. If re-creating your work takes more than five minutes, backing up is worthwhile.

What does the Online option on the Back Up Company File tab do?

▼ Intuit offers a fee-based service that enables you to back up your QuickBooks company file to a remote server. This approach helps you safely store backups away from your office. You can schedule these off-line backups so that you do not need to remember to do them, and the backups are encrypted and transferred across the Internet to the off-site location. You also can store data other than your QuickBooks company file, making the cost of the service more palatable because you protect more data for the fee.

continued

Back Up Your Company *(Continued)*

Y ou can back up your QuickBooks company file to any type disk — floppy disks, CDs, Zip disks, or even a hard drive. You should not back up your company data file to the same hard drive where the company data file resides, but you can safely store a backup on an external hard drive or even on a thumb drive; using any of these media, you can easily remove backups from your office to an off-site location.

Regardless of the media you use, you should not overwrite your last backup with your current backup. You should keep several backups — if you back up daily, keep at least one

week's worth of backup files. That way, if a problem arises, you have several chances to recover before you find yourself in the position of re-creating your company data file from scratch. If you back up to floppy disks, use different sets of disks for each day of the week and mark the backup date on the disk so that you can distinguish one backup set from another. If you back up to a hard drive, CD, or Zip disk, date your backups so that you can easily identify them. As you create your backup, you can add today's date to the filename.

Back Up Your Company *(continued)*

Automatically Back Up on Closing

1. Complete steps 1 to 2 on the previous page.

2. Click the Schedule a Backup tab.

3. Click this option to turn on the automatic backup feature (☐ changes to ☑), typing a number for frequency.

4. Click OK.

    QuickBooks saves your settings.

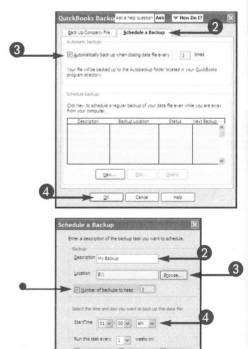

Schedule a Backup

1. Complete steps 1 to 2 in the subsection "Automatically Back Up on Closing," clicking New on the Schedule a Backup tab.

2. In the Schedule a Backup dialog box, type a name for the scheduled backup.

3. Type a location or click Browse to select a location for the backup.

   - You can click here (☐ changes to ☑) to specify a number of backups to keep.

4. Click here to select a backup time.

5. Click a specific day to back up (☐ changes to ☑).

6. Click OK.

The Enter Windows Password dialog box may appear.

● If you see this dialog box, type and retype your Windows password.

● The scheduled backup appears in the Schedule backup section on the Schedule a Backup tab of the QuickBooks Backup dialog box.

⑦ Click OK.

QuickBooks saves your settings.

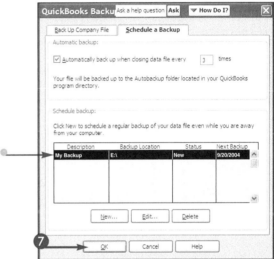

Where should I store my backups?

▼ Although you may think that you need your backups close at hand, you are better off if you store backups in a location other than your office. If you store backups at your office and your office is burglarized or destroyed by fire, all your precautions will have been a waste. Instead, consider storing backups at home or in a bank vault.

What is wrong with backing up to the same hard drive where I store my company data file?

▼ One of the reasons you back up is to protect yourself if your hard drive fails — and hard drives do fail. If you store your backups on the same hard drive where you store your company data file and that hard drive fails, you lose both your company file and your backups.

What is a thumb drive?

▼ A thumb drive, also called a pen drive or a keychain drive, is a fairly inexpensive hard drive about the size of your thumb that attaches to your computer through a USB connection. Using Windows XP or Windows 2000, simply plug in the drive, and the operating system automatically assigns it the next available drive letter. View the drive's contents from My Computer. To back up to the drive, specify its drive letter in the QuickBooks Backup dialog box.

Restore
a Backup

If your data becomes corrupt or your hard drive crashes and must be replaced, you can easily get your company data file back to where it was before the disaster occurred by restoring your latest backup. Restoring a backup is not a difficult process; you only need the location of the backup file to be up and running.

In most cases, when you restore a QuickBooks backup, you restore it over an existing company file. Restoring over an existing company file completely overwrites that file and replaces the information in that company with the

information from the backup. If you are restoring a backup because your company data file became corrupt, it is perfectly acceptable to write over the corrupted data file. If your hard drive failed and you are setting up a new hard drive, you need to install QuickBooks before you can restore your data. When you open QuickBooks for the first time, QuickBooks prompts you to create a new company. You can set up the new company with minimum information because restoring the backup replaces all information in the company with the information stored in the backup. For details on creating a new company, see Chapter 1.

Restore a Backup

① Click File.

② Click Restore.

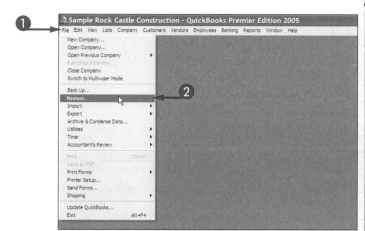

The Restore Company Backup dialog box appears.

● QuickBooks suggests the last backup filename and location you created here.

● If necessary, click Browse to navigate to a different backup file.

● QuickBooks suggests the company filename and location here.

● If necessary, type a different company name or click Browse to navigate to a different location.

③ Click Restore.

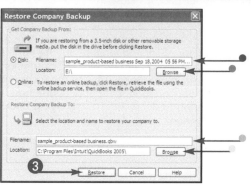

The Backup dialog box appears, asking if you are sure that you want to overwrite an existing company.

④ Click Yes.

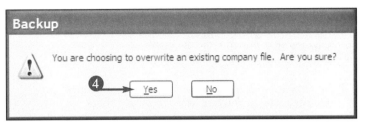

The Delete Entire File dialog box appears.

⑤ Type **YES**.

⑥ Click OK.

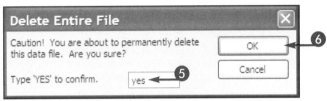

QuickBooks restores your data, and a message appears when the restore process completes successfully.

⑦ Click OK.

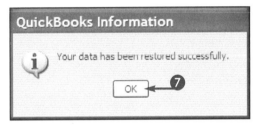

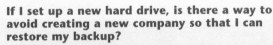

If I set up a new hard drive, is there a way to avoid creating a new company so that I can restore my backup?

▼ Yes. You can open one of the sample companies that comes with QuickBooks. When you follow step 2 in this section to restore your data, change the filename in the Restore Company Backup To section at the bottom of the Restore Company Backup dialog box to the filename you want to assign to your company. Using this technique, you do not need to create a new, blank company and overwrite it, and you also do not overwrite the sample company.

Is there a way to avoid overwriting an existing company when I restore a backup?

▼ Yes. Change the filename in the Restore Company Backup To section at the bottom of the Restore Company Backup dialog box to the filename you want to assign to your company.

If I use the Online Service to back up, do I restore differently?

▼ In the Get Company Backup From section of the Restore Company Backup dialog box, click the online option and click Restore. Then, follow the on-screen instructions. Using this method, you cannot change the filename in the Restore Company Backup To section at the bottom of the Restore Company Backup dialog box.

Verify and Rebuild Data

You may want or need to verify your company data file occasionally. You may want to simply check your data to make sure it is error-free. Or, you may want to verify your data if you receive errors such as Invalid Protection Faults or Fatal Errors, or if strange events begin to occur in your data. For example, you may notice that payments you already deposited reappear in the Payments to Deposit window. Or, you may notice that names do not appear in lists or transactions are missing from reports. Reports may display discrepancies; for example, you may not see all accounts on a Balance Sheet report, making the report appear out of balance.

When you verify data, QuickBooks creates a file and logs any errors it finds in a file named qbwin.log. QuickBooks updates the qbwin.log file every time you verify data, so the file contains information from every time that you verify data. The latest information appears at the end of the log file. You can open the log file while working in QuickBooks to view the information it contains.

You can use the Rebuild feature to attempt to repair damaged data. Be aware that the Rebuild utility can repair data problems, but it also can create data problems; for that reason, you must back up your data before you rebuild it.

Verify and Rebuild Data

Verify Data

① Click File.

② Click Utilities.

③ Click Verify Data.

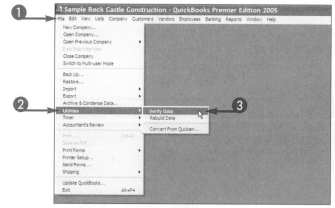

QuickBooks verifies your data and displays a message with the results.

④ Click Close.

Rebuild Data

① Complete steps 1 to 2 in the subsection "Verify Data."

② Click Rebuild Data.

A message appears, explaining that you must back up your data before rebuilding.

③ Click OK.

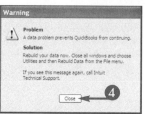

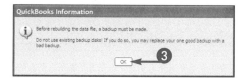

The QuickBooks Backup dialog box appears.

④ Type a filename and location here

● You can click Browse to navigate to a location for the backup.

⑤ Click OK.

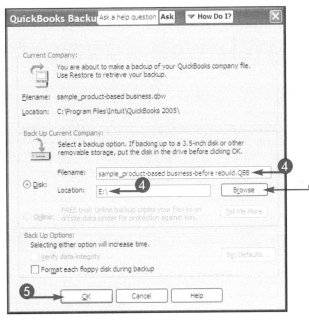

QuickBooks rebuilds your data, and when the process completes, a message appears.

⑥ Click OK.

How do I open the qbwin.log file to read it?

▼ While working in your company, press F2. The Product Information dialog box appears. Press Ctrl+2, and QuickBooks displays the Tech Help window. Click the Open File tab, and in the list of files that appears on the left side of the window, click qbwin.log. On the right side of the window, click Open File.

While looking at the files on the Open File tab, I noticed qbwin.log.old; what is that file?

▼ At some point, another user renamed the qbwin.log file to qbwin.log.old. Using this technique, you can force QuickBooks to create a new log file. When you verify data and QuickBooks does not find a log file, QuickBooks creates a new version of qbwin.log. You may want to create a new log file when the qbwin.log file contains so much information that you find it difficult to find the most current information.

What happens if my data verifies as OK?

▼ QuickBooks displays a message telling you that it found no errors.

What do I do if my data does not rebuild successfully?

▼ You can try restoring a backup. After you restore, verify the data to ensure that the data you backed up is not corrupted. If you cannot find an uncorrupted backup of your data, contact Intuit Technical Support; for a fee, it may be able to repair your company data.

Archive and Condense Data

Because your company data file grows in size over time, you may want to archive and condense data to speed up processing in QuickBooks. When you archive and condense, QuickBooks creates a copy of your original data file, and then QuickBooks removes data from the company file prior to a date you specify — called the ending date — as long as the transactions dated before the ending date do not affect transactions dated after the ending date. QuickBooks replaces the data it removes with transactions that summarize, by month, the detailed information QuickBooks removes. The numbers and

balances in your company file are not affected by archiving and condensing. The only changes are in the size of your company file and the level of detail you can view.

Typically, you can expect QuickBooks to remove transactions that are complete, such as a bill and the bill-payment checks that pay the entire bill or a fully paid invoice and its receipts. However, QuickBooks does not remove the bill-payment check if you have not yet cleared the check on a bank statement. Similarly, QuickBooks does not remove the fully paid invoice and a receipt if you have not yet deposited the receipt and cleared the deposit on the bank statement. You can override some of these constraints.

Archive and Condense Data

1 Click File.

2 Click Archive & Condense Data.

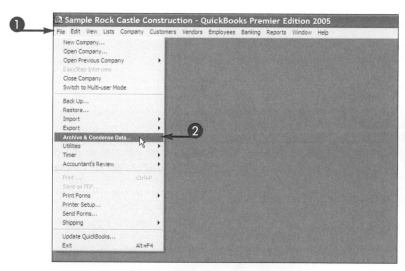

A message box appears warning you that budget data may be affected.

3 Click Yes.

The first page of the Archive & Condense Data Wizard appears.

④ Click an option for removing transactions (○ changes to ◉).

● If you click the first option, you can click the calendar button (▦) to set a date for the earliest transactions to remove.

Note: Click the second option only if you want to start your company over.

⑤ Click Next.

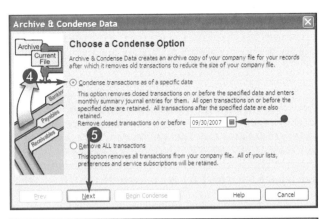

The Select Additional Criteria for Removing Transactions screen appears.

⑥ Click these options to identify the types of transactions to remove (☐ changes to ☑).

⑦ Click Next.

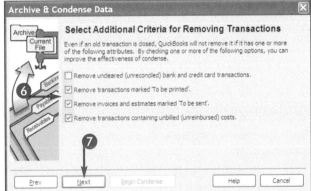

What does the Remove ALL transactions option do?

▼ When you select this option (○ changes to ◉) on the Choose a Condense Option window of the wizard and proceed through the condensing process, QuickBooks removes all transactions from your company but retains all list items. When you finish, all your customers, vendors, employees, items, payroll items, and all other list information still appear in your company. But if you run reports, all dollars display as $0 because no transactions exist. Use this option if you want to start over but do not want to reenter all list information. Right after using this option is a good time to edit lists and delete unwanted entries, because no transactions are tied to the entries.

What constraints can I override?

▼ You can tell QuickBooks to condense uncleared bank and credit card transactions, transactions marked to be printed or sent, and transactions that contain unused reimbursable expenses.

The bar measuring progress on-screen has not changed for a long time; should I try to cancel the condensing process?

▼ Not necessarily. During condensing, QuickBooks scans your company data file three times, so the completion level may seem to be the same for a long time. But, if the light indicating activity on your hard drive remains on or flashes, QuickBooks is still condensing and you should not cancel.

continued

Archive and Condense Data *(Continued)*

Condensing has different effects in different areas of QuickBooks. For example, QuickBooks tends to condense fewer inventory transactions than other types of transactions. And, QuickBooks does not condense payroll transactions dated in the current calendar year. QuickBooks condenses only those estimates associated with jobs designated as closed in the Customer:Job List.

QuickBooks condenses billed time data, time data you mark "not billable," and time data for jobs designated as closed in the Customer:Job List. But QuickBooks does not condense billed time data if you pay employees based on time data and you have not yet paid your employees for the billed time.

The summary transactions that QuickBooks creates for deleted transactions are general journal entries; typically, you find one general journal entry each month for the amount of all deleted transactions. You can easily identify the summary transactions in registers; GENJRNL appears in the Type field.

Your computer's speed, amount of memory, and the size of your company data file determine the length of time QuickBooks needs to condense your data file. Condensing can take just a few minutes or several hours, and you cannot use other applications while QuickBooks condenses your data. So, you may want to condense data just before leaving for the day or weekend.

Archive and Condense Data *(continued)*

The Select Unused List Items To Remove screen appears.

8 Click the options to identify unused list items to remove (☐ changes to ☑).

9 Click Next.

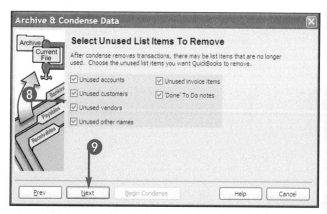

The Proceed with Condense? screen appears.

10 Click Begin Condense.

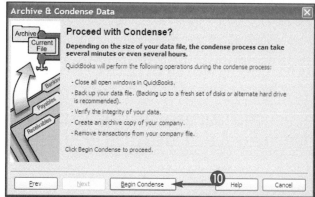

A message appears, telling you that you must back up your data before condensing; click OK.

The QuickBooks Backup dialog box appears.

⑪ Type a filename and location here

- You can click Browse to navigate to a location for the backup.

⑫ Click OK.

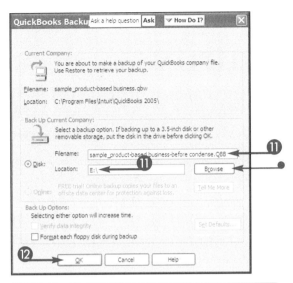

QuickBooks condenses your data, and when the process completes, a message appears.

⑬ Click OK.

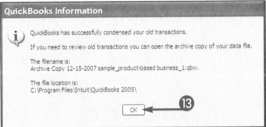

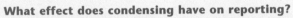

What effect does condensing have on reporting?

▼ Condensing does not affect account balances, so you can still create reports like the Profit & Loss Previous Year Comparison that summarize financial activity for the period of time you condensed. You are not able to create reports that show daily detail or reports that show balances for individual customers or vendors for the condensed time period because QuickBooks deletes the individual transactions that provide the detail. Because QuickBooks retains information about each of your taxable items and your tax vendors, you can get accurate reports about your sales tax liability.

What is archiving?

▼ When you condense, QuickBooks automatically creates a copy of your company file before condensing. You can use the archive copy to run detail reports or reports showing balances for customers and vendors for those periods in which transactions have already been condensed.

Does QuickBooks use the archive copy in any special way?

▼ Yes. QuickBooks uses the archive file to restore your company data file if QuickBooks encounters an error while condensing. If the condense process completes successfully, QuickBooks retains both the archive copy and the condensed data file. If QuickBooks encounters an error and restores your company from the archive file, QuickBooks does not retain the archive copy.

Set Up Security

Y ou can set up security in QuickBooks to protect a QuickBooks data file from unauthorized access. If you are using QuickBooks Pro, Premier, or Enterprise, you can require each user to type a unique user name and password to open the data file. You can limit each user's access to only those areas of the company data file that you specify, and you can identify the types of functions the user can perform. For example, you can permit a user to run reports but not view payroll information.

The first user who sets up security must also set up the QuickBooks Administrator — the Admin user — a special user who has the ability to set up other users. When you start the process of setting up security, QuickBooks automatically prompts you to set up the Admin user and assign a password to that user. Typically, the Admin user has access to all areas of the program; no other user has full access. There is no point in setting up security and then granting full access to any user other than the administrator; granting full access to anyone other than the administrator defeats the purpose of security, which is to control access to your company data file.

Set Up Security

① Click Company.

② Click Set Up Users.

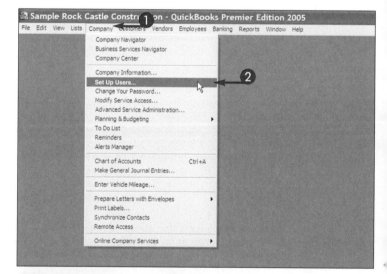

The User List window appears.

Note: If you have not set up a password for the administrator, QuickBooks prompts you to do so; follow steps 5 and 6 to create the administrator's password.

③ Click Add User.

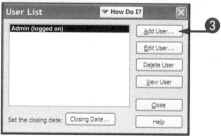

The Set up user password and access Wizard begins.

④ Type the user name here.

⑤ Type a password here.

⑥ Retype the password here.

⑦ Click Next.

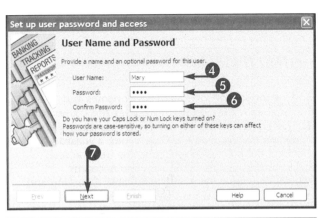

The Access for user screen appears.

⑧ Click the first option to establish security for the selected user (○ changes to ◉).

⑨ Click Next.

Are passwords required for users?

▼ No, but not assigning passwords to users defeats the purpose of security. Without passwords, all users have access to all areas of the program. The only way to limit access for a user is to assign a password to that user and then instruct your employees not to share their passwords. However, you, as the administrator, should make a record of all passwords assigned to all employees. When an employee leaves your company, make it a habit to change the passwords of all remaining employees as a precaution. Changing passwords is similar to changing the locks on the doors of your offices.

How many users can I set up in my QuickBooks data file?

▼ You can set up as many users as you want. However, the number of users that can simultaneously access your company file depends on your QuickBooks licensing agreement.

Can I use the same user names and passwords for QuickBooks that I use for Windows?

▼ You can, but you should consider at least using different passwords to increase the amount of protection you provide to your QuickBooks data. If you use different passwords, getting onto a computer does not automatically guarantee entry into QuickBooks.

continued

Set Up Security
(Continued)

The administrator sets up all user passwords; setting up user nam begins the process of assigning After creating the user name and passw you through the process of specifying t capabilities. You see screens for Sales an Receivable, Purchases and Accounts Pay Credit Cards, Inventory, Time Tracking, Employees, Sensitive Accounting Activit Financial Reporting, and Changing or D For all screens except the last one, you want the user to have no access, full ac access. In most cases, selective access n

transactions, creating and printing transactions and forms, transactions and creating screens present the same nly the screens for Sales and chases and Accounts Payable.

up users and assigns passwords, log on each time you open supply your user name and e-sensitive and must match e administrator creates. If you company, check to ensure that gaged.

[handwritten annotations: USER, Admin, Rooster, USER, USER, Money, Close Date, Rooster]

Set Up Security *(continued)*

⑩ In the Sales and Accounts Receivabl click an option to allow or deny the access to Sales and Accounts Receiv (○ changes to ◉).

- If you click the Selective Access option, click an option for creating and printing transactions and reports (○ changes to ◉).

⑪ Click Next.

⑫ In the Purchases and Accounts Payable screen, repeat steps 10 to 11 for Checking and Credit Cards, Inventory, Time Tracking, Payroll and Employees, Sensitive Accounting Activities, and Sensitive Financial Reporting.

The Changing or Deleting Transactions screen appears.

⑬ Click an option to permit or deny the user the ability to change or delete transactions (○ changes to ◉).

⑭ Click an option to permit or deny the user the ability to change or delete transactions recorded prior to the closing date (○ changes to ◉).

⑮ Click Next.

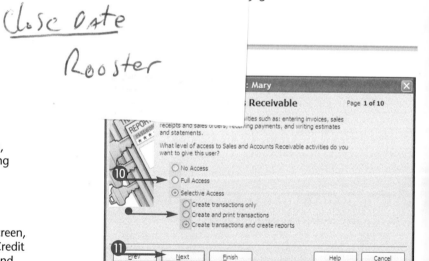

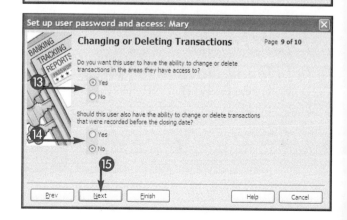

● A summary of permissions for the selected user appears.

⑯ Click Finish.

The User List reappears with the user's name in it.

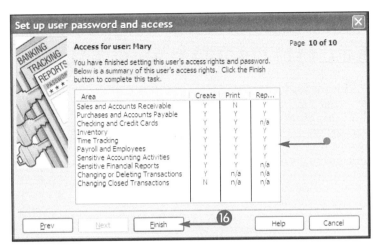

When you open the company, the QuickBooks Login dialog box appears.

⑰ Type your user name here.

⑱ Type your password here.

⑲ Click OK.

QuickBooks opens if you supply the correct user name and password.

What is sensitive financial reporting?

▼ The term "sensitive financial reporting" actually refers to all reports in QuickBooks. You can choose to give a user the ability to create reports, but not print them, or create them and print them. Permissions you assign in this area override restrictions you may have established in other security areas. Be aware, however, that allowing a user to create and print sensitive financial reports does *not* give the user the right to change transactions that appear on the reports. If you want a user to change transactions on a report, you must give the user that capability in the appropriate area.

What are sensitive accounting activities?

▼ Sensitive accounting activities include transferring funds between accounts, making journal entries, and using online banking.

Does setting up security have any impact on backing up my data?

▼ As long as you do not lose your administrator's password, no. If you do lose the administrator's password and you must use Intuit's data recovery services because your backups do not work, you must provide some proof to Intuit that you are the owner of the business before Intuit repairs your data. This added security practice ensures that Intuit repairs data for only authorized parties.

Create an Accountant's Copy

The Accountant's Review feature enables both you and your accountant to easily work with your QuickBooks data at the same time. Your accountant may review your accounting records every month or at the end of your fiscal year, when preparing financial statements, and when preparing your company's tax return. During the review, accountants sometimes generate entries that change your company's information, and your accountant may prefer to record these entries rather than have you record them. Using the Accountant's Review feature, you make a special backup of your company data for your accountant. When the accountant returns your data and you restore it, QuickBooks updates your company instead of overwriting it.

Please note that when your accountant uses the Accountant's Copy, your work in QuickBooks is restricted. You cannot delete from any list, reorganize any list, or rename existing accounts or list items.

MASTER IT

Is my accountant's work restricted while working in the Accountant's Copy?

▼ Yes. Your accountant cannot enter or memorize any transactions except general journal transactions; edit or delete existing transactions; memorize reports; reorganize, make inactive, or delete entries on any list; delete items or accounts; enter or change employee year-to-date payroll setup transactions; add, change, or delete payroll items; send changes made to 941, 940, or W-2s back to your company data file; or send changes made to preferences back to your company data file.

Create an Accountant's Copy

① Click File.

② Click Accountant's Review

③ Click Create Accountant's Copy.

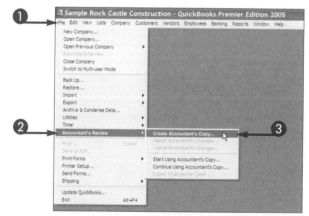

The Save Accountant's Copy to dialog box appears.

QuickBooks suggests using your company's filename with an extension of .QBX.

④ Click Save.

A message appears indicating that the Accountant's Copy was successfully created.

⑤ Click OK.

The title bar changes to include your company's name, followed in parentheses by the phrase Accountant's Copy Exists.

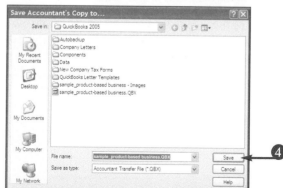

Cancel an Accountant's Copy

You can return QuickBooks to normal working order, without importing any changes from your accountant, by canceling the Accountant's Copy. Suppose that you created an Accountant's Copy as described in the section "Create an Accountant's Copy" and you gave the copy to your accountant. Further suppose that, after a period of time, your accountant informs you that no changes are necessary and you will not be receiving a file to import. You can cancel the Accountant's Copy to re-enable your ability to delete from lists, reorganize lists, and rename existing accounts or items. When you cancel the Accountant's Copy, QuickBooks removes the message about the Accountant's Copy from the title bar.

What does the Start Using Accountant's Copy menu command do?

▼ This command enables the accountant to open and work in the Accountant's Copy you provided. The file name of the copy you created for your accountant ends in .QBA.

What does the Continue Using Accountant's Copy menu command do?

▼ If your accountant needs to switch to another company before he or she finishes working in your company, he or she can reopen your company using this command.

Cancel an Accountant's Copy

1 Click File.

2 Click Accountant's Review.

3 Click Cancel Accountant's Changes.

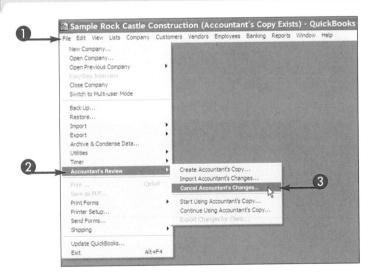

The Invalidate Accountant's Copy dialog box appears.

4 Click OK.

QuickBooks changes the title bar to indicate that you are now working in your own company.

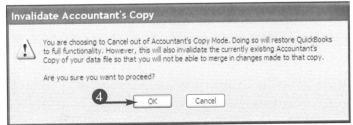

Import Accountant's Changes

In most cases, when you give your accountant an Accountant's Review Copy, he or she returns a file to you that contains changes you need to make in your QuickBooks company file. You import the file into QuickBooks, which updates your company data file with the changes that your accountant made. QuickBooks does not overwrite your company file during this process, but instead combines the data in the file your accountant gives you with the data in your company file. This merging of data is what makes the Accountant's Copy feature valuable: both you and your accountant can work with your data simultaneously, with neither of you experiencing much in the way of inconvenience.

The process of importing your accountant's changes is very similar to restoring a backup. Your accountant provides the file that you need to restore, and then you open your QuickBooks company data file and select the file the accountant provides. QuickBooks merges the information from the accountant's file with the information in your company data file. You lose no data — the accountant's file does not overwrite any of your data — and you lose no time while your accountant works. You lose only some minor functionality while the Accountant's Copy exists.

Import Accountant's Changes

① Click File.

② Click Accountant's Review.

③ Click Import Accountant's Changes.

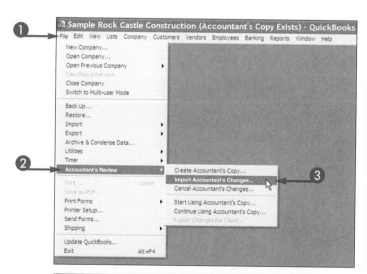

The Accountant Import dialog box displays a message indicating that you must back up before proceeding.

④ Click OK.

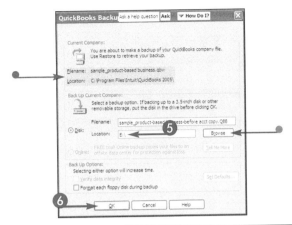

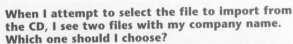

The QuickBooks Backup dialog box appears.

● Information about the company you are backing up appears here.

⑤ Type a location to store your backup.

● You can click Browse to navigate to the location.

⑥ Click OK.

The Import Changes from Accountant's Copy dialog box appears.

⑦ Select the file your accountant provided.

⑧ Click Open.

QuickBooks imports the changes your accountant provided.

QuickBooks removes the reference to the Accountant's Copy from the program title bar.

When I attempt to select the file to import from the CD, I see two files with my company name. Which one should I choose?

▼ The name of the file your accountant created that you should import ends in .AIF. If you use Windows XP and cannot see file extensions while viewing files, open the Tools menu and click Folder Options. The Folder Options dialog box appears; click the View tab, find the Hide Extensions of Known File Types check box, and remove the check that appears in the box (☑ changes to ☐). Click OK to close the box. You should now be able to distinguish files on the CD.

Can you clarify what the various filename extensions signify?

▼ Yes. .QBW represents a regular company data file. .QBB represents a backup of a company data file. .QBX represents the Accountant's Copy file that you create to give to your accountant. When your accountant restores the file you provide, QuickBooks assigns the file an extension of .QBA. When your accountant creates a file of the changes made in the Accountant's Copy — the file that you will merge with your company data — QuickBooks assigns an extension of .AIF. The only other file name extension that you will see associated with QuickBooks is .IIF, which is the extension QuickBooks assigns whenever you export list information.

Track Back Orders Using Pending Invoices

I f you use QuickBooks Premier or Enterprise, you can use sales orders to track back orders. For all other versions of QuickBooks, you can use pending invoices to track back orders.

Because each customer may want you to handle back-order situations differently, you can use the customer's notepad to help you track each customer's preference. Think of the notepad as a sticky note that contains some miscellaneous pieces of information about the customer. The beauty of the customer's notepad is that you can view it while creating an invoice. So, when you create an invoice for a customer and one of the items on the invoice results in a back order, you can view the customer's notepad to identify the way that the customer wants you to handle orders that may contain items you must backorder and then proceed accordingly.

Therefore, tracking back orders requires some setup work on your part. You need to store each customer's back-order preferences on each customer's notepad; the first part of this section shows you how to store these preferences. Then, you can create invoices as usual, and when you encounter an item you must backorder, you can use the rest of the steps in this section to handle it.

Track Back Orders Using Pending Invoices

Define Customer Back-order Preferences

1 Click Lists.

2 Click Customer:Job List.

The Customer:Job List window appears.

3 Double-click the Customer:Job for which you want to set back-order preferences.

The Edit Customer or Edit Job window appears.

4 Click Notes.

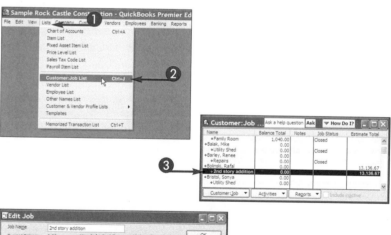

The Notepad dialog box appears.

5 Type the customer's back-order preferences here.

6 Click OK twice to save the choices.

7 Repeat steps 3 to 6 for each customer.

8 Click the Close button (⊠) to close the Customer:Job List window.

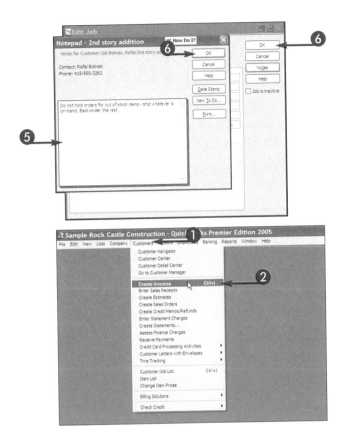

Invoicing for Back Orders

1 Click Customers.

2 Click Create Invoices.

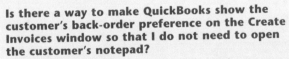

Is there a way to make QuickBooks show the customer's back-order preference on the Create Invoices window so that I do not need to open the customer's notepad?

▼ Yes. You can create a custom field for the customer's back-order preference, fill in each customer's back-order preference in the custom field, and then display the custom field on the template you use in the Create Invoices window. See Chapter 2 for details on creating a custom field, see Chapter 5 for details on storing information in the custom field, and Chapter 24 for details on adding a custom field to an invoice template form.

What makes a pending invoice different from a regular invoice?

▼ Pending invoices do not affect your company's accounts, do not appear in registers, and do not appear on any reports except the Pending Sales report. You can use pending sales for other things besides back orders. For example, if you bill customers only for time, you can create a pending invoice that tracks the time you spend. Or, during the process of placing an order, a customer may hesitate and ask to call you back to finalize the order after getting approval from a supervisor. In this case, mark the sale as pending.

continued

Track Back Orders Using
Pending Invoices *(Continued)*

Each customer may want you to handle back-order situations differently. For example, some customers do not want you to fill any of the items on the order; they may cancel the order if any single item is out of stock. Other customers may not cancel the order but may want you to hold the entire order until you receive the backordered item and ship the entire order at one time. Still other customers may want you to ship immediately whatever you have in stock and ship the balance when you receive it. This task shows you how to handle this last

situation and invoice for the items you have in stock and create a pending invoice for the items you do not have on hand.

Like sales orders, pending invoices do not affect your company's accounts. Instead, they act as placeholders to remind you that you have made a sale but simply cannot fulfill your obligation to deliver the merchandise at the present time. After you receive the goods, you can change the status of the pending invoice to a regular invoice; at that time, QuickBooks does update your company's accounts to reflect the sale.

Track Back Orders Using Pending Invoices *(continued)*

The Create Invoices window appears.

③ Click here to select a Customer:Job.

④ Fill in the window as you usually would complete an invoice.

Note: *See Chapter 11 for details on completing an invoice.*

Note: *If you invoice more of an item than you have on hand, QuickBooks displays a warning; click OK.*

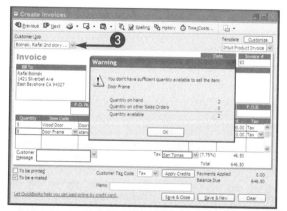

The Create Invoices window reappears.

⑤ Click Edit.

⑥ Notepad.

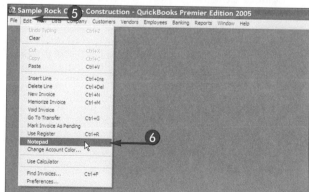

The customer's notes appear.

7 Read the customer's back-order preference.

8 Click OK.

The Create Invoices window reappears.

9 Change the quantity on the invoice to match the customer's preferences.

Note: *See Chapter 11 for details on completing an invoice.*

10 Click Save & New.

11 Repeats steps 1 to 4, selecting the same customer and the item you need to back order.

12 Click Edit.

13 Click Mark Invoice As Pending.

● QuickBooks marks the invoice as pending.

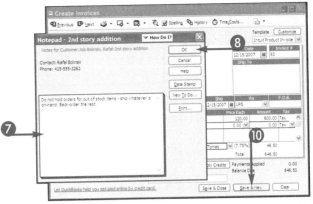

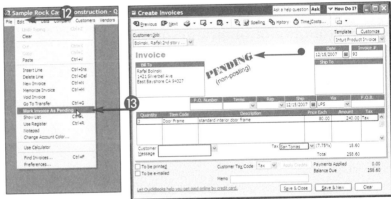

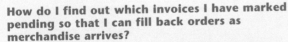

How do I find out which invoices I have marked pending so that I can fill back orders as merchandise arrives?

▼ You can use the Pending Sales report. Click Reports, click Sales, and then click Pending Sales. Set the date range to All so that you do not miss any pending sales, and memorize the report by clicking the Memorize button and assigning a report name and, if appropriate, a memorized report group. On the Pending Sales report, QuickBooks displays the invoice date, number, customer name, memo, account, and amount. You can double-click any entry on the report to display it in the window where you created it.

After I receive the merchandise, do I need to reenter the information from the pending invoice onto a real invoice to fill the order?

▼ No. You can change the status of a pending invoice so that it becomes a regular invoice. Display the pending invoice in the Create Invoices window by double-clicking it while viewing the memorized Pending Sales report referred to in the previous tip. Change the invoice date to the current date. Then, click Edit and then Mark Invoice as Final. QuickBooks removes the Pending stamp from the invoice. When you save the invoice, QuickBooks updates your sales and accounts receivable accounts with the information on the invoice.

Calculate Sales Commissions

If you pay sales commissions on paid invoices only, you need a way to determine the amount of commission to pay your sales representatives.

Many companies offer commissions to employees or independent contractors who act as sales representatives; commissions are usually based on the individual's sales. Most companies pay commissions to sales representatives based on paid invoices only; that way, the company does not pay a commission for a sale that may later become uncollectible. Your company may need a way to assign sales to the appropriate sales representative and then identify each salesperson's paid invoices so that you pay

commissions to the correct sales representative for only paid invoices. QuickBooks cannot calculate the sales commission due to a sales representative directly, but through a combination of QuickBooks and Excel, you can easily determine a sales representative's commission amount.

As a first step, make sure that you assign a sales representative to every sale; you also need to assign the sales representative to credit memos when customers return merchandise. To assign sales representatives to invoices and credit memos, you need to add the Sales Rep field to each invoice and credit memo template that you use.

Calculate Sales Commissions

Add the Sales Rep Field to Templates

① Click Lists.

② Click Templates.

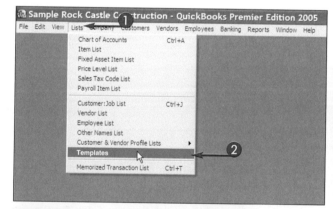

The Templates window appears.

③ Double-click the template you need to edit.

The Customize Invoice dialog box appears.

④ Click Fields.

⑤ Click the REP option to display the Rep field on-screen (☐ changes to ☑).

- You can change the description that appears on-screen here.

⑥ Click OK.

QuickBooks saves the changes to the template, and the Templates window reappears.

⑦ Repeat steps 3 to 6 for each template to which you need to add the sale representative.

⑧ Click ☒ to close the Templates window.

Report on Sales

① Click Reports.

② Click Sales.

③ Click Sales by Rep Summary.

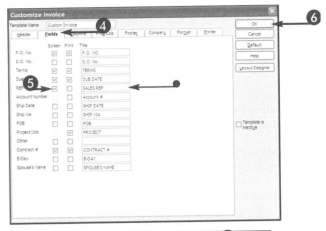

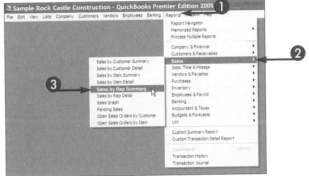

continued

What is the easiest way to add a sales representative to an existing document?

▼ Double-click the amount and QuickBooks displays the Sales by Rep Detail report. You can double-click a transaction to display it in the window where you created it. Add a sales representative and save the document. QuickBooks prompts you to assign the sales representative to the Customer:Job permanently. Click Yes, and QuickBooks makes the assignment and assigns the same rep to future documents for that customer. You must manually assign the sales rep to all existing documents.

What is the easiest way to find the transactions to which I need to add a sales representative?

▼ Print the Sales by Rep Detail report by clicking Reports, Sales, and then Sales by Rep Detail. All the transactions you entered but did not assign to a sales representative appear under the heading "No sales rep."

Do I need to worry about invoices, sales receipts, and credit memos already entered into QuickBooks that do not contain a sales representative's name?

▼ If you have not paid commissions for these transactions and want to include them in your sales commission calculation, then yes, you need to add the correct sales representative to each transaction. See Chapter 11 for details on creating and editing invoices.

Calculate Sales Commissions *(Continued)*

Make sure that you customize each template that you use; if you use one of the predefined templates that QuickBooks creates for you, you need to make a copy of the template that you can use instead of the predefined template. You cannot add the Sales Rep field to a predefined template, but you can add it to a copy of a predefined template. For details on making a copy of a predefined template and editing the template, see Chapter 24.

Using your new customized templates, do business as usual, assigning sales representatives to invoices, sales receipts, and credit memos as appropriate.

When you are ready to pay commissions, you need to produce a report in QuickBooks that contains the amounts your company has collected for each salesperson's sales. You can use the Sales by Rep Summary report to determine these amounts. Unless you have changed your default settings, QuickBooks displays the report on an accrual basis, which includes all sales made by each sales representative. To display only sales your company has collected, you need to modify the report to display on a cash basis.

Calculate Sales Commissions *(continued)*

The report appears on-screen.

④ Click ▾ or click the calendar button (▦) to select the report period.

⑤ Click Modify Report.

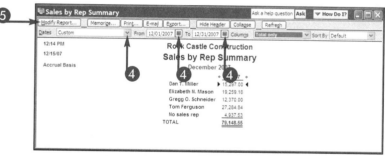

The Display tab of the Modify Report dialog box appears.

⑥ Click the Cash option (○ changes to ◉).

⑦ Click OK.

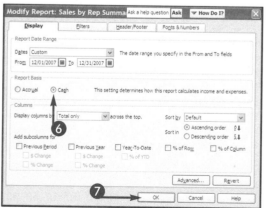

The report reappears on-screen.

⑧ Click Export.

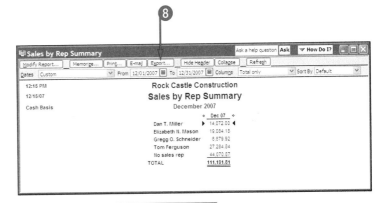

The Export Report dialog box appears.

⑨ Click the "a new Excel workbook" option (○ changes to ⊙).

⑩ Click Export.

Excel opens and displays the report.

How can I add the report to the same Excel workbook each month so that I have copies of the complete report in Excel?

▼ The first time you create the report in Excel, follow the steps in this section, type the report period in the upper-left corner of the workbook, and then save the workbook. When you subsequently export the Sales by Rep Summary report, click the "an existing Excel workbook" option (○ changes to ⊙) in the Export Report dialog box and then click Browse to select the file you saved. To keep things simple, click the "create a new sheet in the workbook" option (○ changes to ⊙) so that each report appears on a separate sheet in the workbook.

How do I ensure that I do not pay a sales representative for the same sale twice?

▼ Select a date range for the report that does not overlap with the date range of a report you produced previously. Most businesses pay commissions once each month for the preceding month. Keep copies of the reports so that you can identify the date range of each report.

What happens if I click the "Include a new worksheet in the workbook that explains Excel worksheet linking" option?

▼ When you click this option (□ changes to ☑) in the Export Report dialog box, Excel adds an explanatory sheet that explains how to create formulas across worksheets. You do not need to check this box.

continued

Calculate Sales Commissions *(Continued)*

After you change the basis of the Sales by Rep Summary report, the report shows you total collected sales but does not show you how much commission you should pay each sales representative. You can use QuickBooks and Excel to determine that amount. You can produce the report in QuickBooks and then export it to Excel, where you can easily calculate the commission amount due to each sales representative for the period using some very basic formulas.

The report lists sales representatives in one column and total collected sales in another column. Once you have the report in Excel, you create two additional columns for the

report. In one column, you enter the sales commission rate for each sales person. In the other column, you store a formula that multiplies the collected sales amount by the commission rate. You then copy the formula down the column so that Excel calculates commission amounts due to each sales representative.

Once you know the commission amounts, you can include them on a paycheck if the sales representative is an employee, or you can simply write a check for the commission amount if the sales representative is an independent contractor.

Calculate Sales Commissions *(continued)*

Calculate Commissions

⑪ Click here and type a title for the percentage column.

⑫ Click here and type a title for the commission amount column.

⑬ Type sales commission rates as decimals in this column.

⑭ Click here and type =.

⑮ Click here and type *.

⑯ Click here.

⑰ Click here or press Enter.

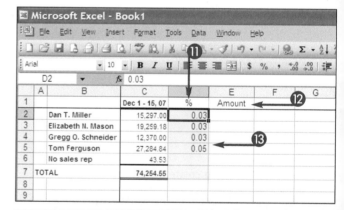

Excel stores the formula and displays the commission amount.

18 Click in the cell containing the formula.

19 Click the Copy button (icon).

20 Click and drag to select the cells in column E that should contain commission amounts.

21 Click the Paste button (icon).

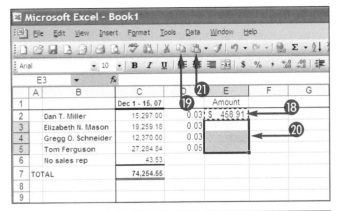

● Excel copies the formula to the selected cells.

22 Click anywhere to finish copying and pasting.

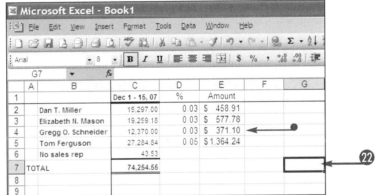

How do I pay sales commissions?

▼ If the sales representative is a 1099 vendor, use the Expenses tab of the Write Checks window, ensuring that you include the Commissions expense account as a 1099 account in the Preferences dialog box. See Chapter 6 for details on setting 1099 preferences. If the sales representative is an employee, create a wages payroll item called Commissions. Then, add that payroll item to the information of each employee/sales representative by editing the employee. When you create a paycheck for the employee, the commissions item appears in the Earnings section, where you fill in the amount you calculated in Excel. For help creating the payroll item, see Chapter 4.

Is it okay to have some amounts not assigned to sales representatives?

▼ Yes. For example, you typically do not assign finance charge transactions, sales tax transactions, or discount transactions to sales representatives.

If the commission rate is different for each sales representative, will the formula for the commission amount be accurate if I copy it?

▼ Yes. By default, Excel uses relative cell addressing when copying formulas. That means that Excel adjusts the formula when you copy it. If you copy a formula in cell E2 that multiplies the contents of D2 by C2 to cell E3, Excel adjusts the formula in E3 to multiply D3 by C3.

PART VII

Track Unpaid Invoices by Salesman

Many companies require their sales representatives to follow up on uncollected sales, and the sales representative needs a method to identify those uncollected sales.

Most companies pay the sales representative only for collected sales, providing an incentive for the representative responsible for the sale to follow up on any uncollected sales. Because the sales representative has a vested interest in collecting the sale, both the sales representative and the company benefit by this arrangement.

In QuickBooks, you can create a report that the sales representative can use to identify and track down uncollected sales. The report is a variation of the Collections report, which shows unpaid invoices for a specified period. The report includes the terms and due date of each open invoice as well as the age and balance of each invoice and excludes other information that usually appears on the report. The report also contains contact information that the sales representative can use to get in touch with the customer to determine if there is a way to expedite payment.

When you create this report, you filter it for one sales representative at a time; that way, you can print separate reports for each sales representative.

Track Unpaid Invoices by Salesman

① Click Reports.

② Click Customers & Receivables.

③ Click Collections Report.

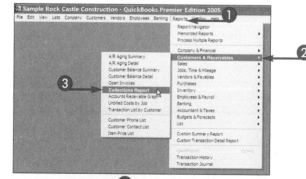

The Collections report appears.

④ Click Modify Report.

The Modify Report dialog box appears.

⑤ Click the Filters tab.

⑥ Click Aging.

⑦ Click Remove Selected Filter.

⑧ Repeat steps 6 to 7 for the Due Date filter.

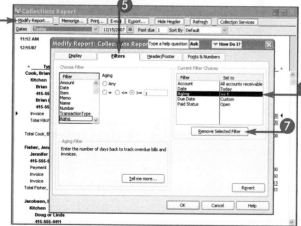

⑨ Click Rep.

⑩ Click here to select a rep.

⑪ Click the Header/Footer tab.

⑫ Click here and type a more significant report title.

⑬ Click OK.

The report for the selected sales representative appears.

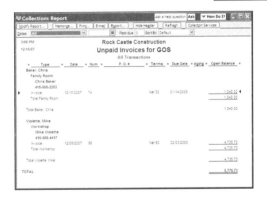

I believe that more unpaid invoices exist than appear on the report; how can I be sure?

▼ You may not have assigned all invoices to a sales representative. If you have not added the Sales Rep field to your invoice and credit memo template forms, complete the steps in the subsection "Add the Sales Rep Field to Templates" in the section "Calculate Sales Commissions." Then, print the Sales by Rep Summary report by completing the steps in the subsection "Report on Sales" in the same section. Double-click each sale listed under No Sales Rep on the report and assign the correct sales representative. After you assign all invoices and credit memos to a sales representative, the report you create in this section should be accurate.

Is there an easy way to modify the existing report for another sales representative or must I re-create it from scratch?

▼ While viewing the current version of the report, you can click Modify Report. In the Modify Report dialog box, click the Filters tab. Click the Rep field in the Current Filter Choices list on the right side of the tab. Click the ⊡ in the middle of the tab and select a different sales representative. Do not forget to change the report title on the Header/Footer tab if you included the sales representative's name in the report title. Once you create these reports, you may want to memorize one report for each sales representative; see Chapter 22.

Make and Track an Employee Loan

O ccasionally, you may loan money to an employee with the understanding that the employee will repay the loan from his or her regular paycheck.

You can assign each loan you make to an employee to an other current asset account called Employee Loans. You can use one main account and set up subaccounts for each employee to whom you loan money. For help creating an account or subaccount, see Chapter 2.

While you can try to include the loan on an employee's payroll check, the easiest way to extend the loan to the employee is using the Write Checks window. On the Expenses tab, select the employee's loan account, supply the amount of the loan, and print the check.

To set up QuickBooks to let the employee repay the loan through payroll deductions, create an employee loan deduction payroll item. For details on creating a deduction payroll item, see Chapter 4.

After you create the loan repayment deduction payroll item, you assign it to the employee so that it appears when you create a paycheck for the employee.

Make and Track an Employee Loan

Write the Loan Check

1 Click Banking.

2 Click Write Checks.

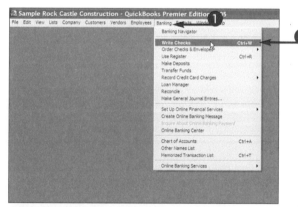

The Write Checks window appears.

3 Click here to select the employee.

Note: *Click OK to dismiss a warning message that appears indicating that you should write paychecks from the Pay Employees window.*

4 Click the Expenses tab.

5 Click the here to select the Employee Loans account.

6 Type the loan amount here.

7 Click Save & Close.

QuickBooks saves the loan check.

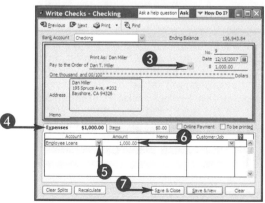

Assign the Loan to the Employee

① Click Lists.

② Click Employee List.

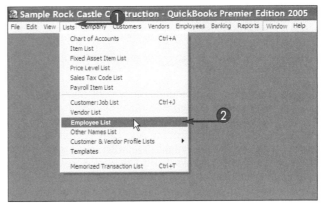

The Employee List window appears.

③ Double-click the employee to whom you loaned money.

The Edit Employee dialog box appears.

How do I handle the employee loan if, instead of loaning the employee money by writing a check, I allow an employee to use my credit card?

▼ If an employee purchases something using your credit card or an instore charge account, record the transaction in the Enter Bills window or the Enter Credit Card Charges window instead of the Write Checks window. Click Vendors and then click Enter Bills, or click Banking, then Record Credit Card Charges, and then Enter Credit Card Charges. Select the vendor who will send you a bill for the purchase. On the Expenses tab, select the employee's loan account and type the charge amount. Handle the loan repayment as described in this section using a payroll item.

What should I do if I loan money a second time to the employee?

▼ If you filled in the loan amount as the limit, create a second payroll item for the new loan. For any individual deduction item, QuickBooks will not deduct any more money from the employee's paycheck once it reaches the limit, and changing the limit on the item does not affect the program's behavior. When you create the new payroll item, you can assign it to the same account you used for the employee's first loan; you do not need another loan account.

PART VII

continued

Make and Track an Employee Loan *(Continued)*

When you create the loan repayment deduction payroll item, assign it to the employee loan account you create when you write the loan check. As you continue through the Add New Payroll Item Wizard, you can accept the defaults QuickBooks suggests for the Tax Tracking Type, Taxes, and Calculate Based on Quantity. On the Gross vs. Net page of the wizard, tell QuickBooks to calculate the payroll item based on net pay. On the Default Rate and Limit page, specify the loan repayment amount as the default rate and fill in the loan amount as the default limit. Filling in the loan amount as the limit ensures that QuickBooks does not exceed the loan amount when it deducts loan repayments.

QuickBooks assumes that each deduction has an annual limit and that calculation of the deduction limit should restart at the beginning of every year; in the case of an employee loan, this is not true, so, be sure to indicate on the Default Rate and Limit page that you do not want QuickBooks to restart the limit calculation at the beginning of each year.

After you assign the loan repayment deduction payroll item to the employee, QuickBooks automatically deducts the repayment amount from the employee's paycheck each time you pay the employee.

Make and Track an Employee Loan *(continued)*

④ Click here to select Payroll and Compensation Info.

⑤ Click in the Item Name column, and click ☑ that appears to select the loan payroll item for the employee.

QuickBooks fills in the loan repayment amount and the loan amount.

⑥ Click OK.

QuickBooks saves the modification.

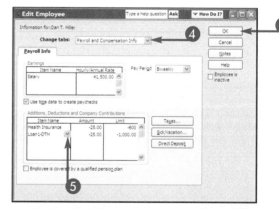

Pay the Employee

① Click Employees.

② Click Pay Employees.

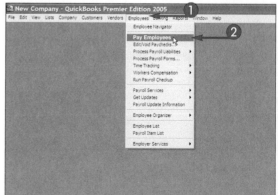

The Select Employees to Pay window appears.

3 Click here to select a bank account.

4 Click the To be printed option to print the check later in a batch (○ changes to ◉).

5 Click next to each employee you intend to pay (☐ changes to ☑).

6 Click the "Enter hours and preview check before creating" option (○ changes to ◉).

7 Click Create.

The Preview Paycheck window appears.

● The loan deduction appears in the Other Payroll Items section.

● The loan repayment amount appears in the Employee Summary section, reducing the employee's paycheck.

8 Click Create.

QuickBooks creates the check.

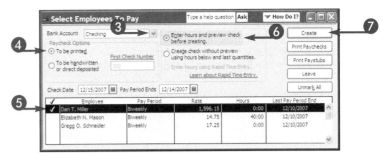

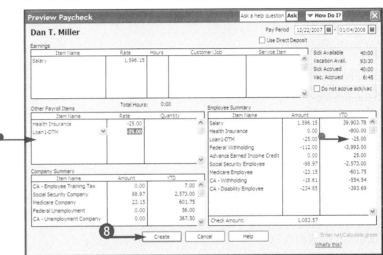

What agency should I specify if I am setting up an employee loan repayment and my business is the payee?

▼ You do not need to set up any agency — the agency is optional. If you do not set up an agency, no liability appears in the Pay Payroll Liabilities window, so QuickBooks does not expect you to make payments to an agency for the money you recollect from an employee's loan.

What should I do if I loan money to more than one employee and the repayment rate is different for each employee?

▼ Set up multiple deduction payroll items to represent each loan you make; consider including the employee's initials in the payroll item name so that you can identify each employee's deduction payroll item. You can then follow the steps in this section to write the loan check and set up the loan for repayment through payroll checks.

What should I do if the employee wants to repay the loan by writing a check to my business?

▼ You do not need to set up a deduction payroll item and assign it to the employee. Instead, use the Make Deposit window to record the repayment. Open the Banking menu and click Make Deposits. In the Make Deposits window, fill in the employee name in the Received From column and the employee's loan account in the From Account column.

Health Savings Accounts

Y ou can set up QuickBooks to record health savings account benefit payments on paychecks and on Federal Form W-2s.

Health savings accounts are tax-sheltered, interest-bearing accounts that employees can use to offset medical expenses. Health savings accounts are the successors of medical savings accounts; the health savings account legislation became law in December 2003.

A health savings account is similar to an IRA, but the money deposited into it is designated for medical expenses. Deposits are 100 percent tax-deductible and employees can easily withdraw money by check or debit card to pay

routine medical bills until the insurance deductible is met. Larger medical expenses are covered by a low-cost, high-deductible health insurance policy that is required by the health savings accounts legislation.

While not a requirement of a health savings account, many employers have found that they can contribute to or fully fund health savings accounts as a benefit to employees. The cost of high-deductible health insurance is significantly less expensive than traditional health insurance plans, and the employer can pass along the savings to employees by contributing to a health savings account. This section demonstrates how to set up QuickBooks for health savings accounts that are fully funded by the company.

Health Savings Accounts

Set Up the HSA Payroll Item

1 Click Lists.

2 Click Payroll Item List.

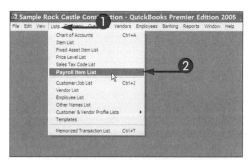

The Payroll Item List window appears.

3 Click Payroll Item.

4 Click New.

The Add new payroll item wizard begins.

5 On the first screen of the wizard, click Custom Setup.

6 Click Next.

7 On the Payroll item type screen that appears, click the Company Contribution option (○ changes to ◉).

8 Click Next.

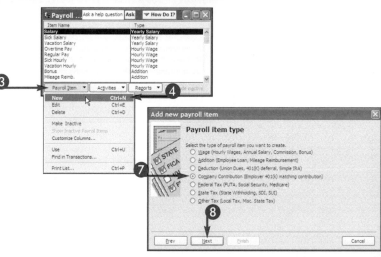

The next wizard screen appears.

9 Type a name for the payroll item.

10 Click Next.

The next wizard screen appears.

11 Select the Health Savings Account Liability account.

12 Click Next.

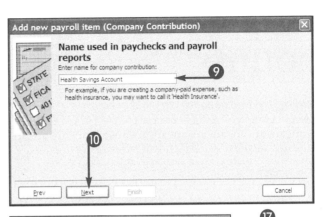

The next wizard screen appears.

13 Click here to select Co. Paid Med Savings for the Tax tracking type.

14 Click Next until you see the Default Rate and Limit page of the wizard.

15 Deselect the This is an annual limit option (☑ changes to ☐).

16 Click Next through all the rest of the wizard screens, accepting the defaults QuickBooks suggests, and on the last screen, click Finish.

17 Click the Close button (☒) to close the Payroll Item List window.

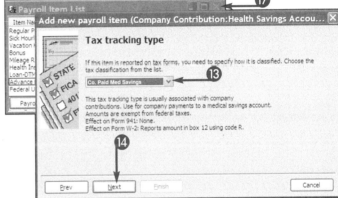

How do I set things up if our company makes contributions to our employees' health savings accounts that match the employees' contributions?

▼ Follow the steps in this section, but also create a health savings account deduction payroll item to handle the employees' share of the health savings account contribution. Set up the deduction with a Tax Tracking Type of None; do not calculate the deduction payroll item based on a quantity, base the calculation on gross pay; and do not supply a default rate or limit. When you assign the deduction to an employee, set the rate and set the limit based on the health savings account's provisions, which you can obtain from the administrator of the health savings account.

How should I set things up if more than one employee wants a health savings account?

▼ You do not need to make any changes. Just assign the health savings account payroll item to each employee. Do not specify an amount when creating the item; specify the amount when you assign it to the employee.

Is every medical insurance policy with a high deductible eligible to use in conjunction with a health savings account?

▼ No. You must double-check with your insurance carrier to determine if the policy you have is eligible. You can also find some very good information about eligible policies at www.ehealthinsurance.com.

PART VII

continued

Health Savings Accounts *(Continued)*

Freedom of choice is another benefit an employee receives by using a health savings account. Typically, the employee can choose a physician from a preferred provider organization (PPO) directory and does not encounter the restrictions that health maintenance organizations (HMOs) impose.

Last, in many cases, the employee can invest the health savings account money in fairly liquid, interest-bearing investments so that the contributions grow. Most health savings accounts are trusts that are administered by an agency, and therefore may be subject to a small annual administration fee. The administrator tracks withdrawals from and deposits to the health savings account so that the

employee can easily identify when deductibles are met and when the medical insurance policy takes over paying medical bills. If the employee does not incur medical expenses, the money remains in the health savings account, accruing interest, and, after age 65, the employee can withdraw money from the account for any reason without penalty.

The health savings account legislation limits annual contributions; the limits vary for individuals and families; generally, the maximum annual nontaxable contribution you can make to a health savings account is equal to the amount of the medical insurance policy deductible, subject to a maximum amount of $2,600 for individuals and $5,150 for families.

Health Savings Accounts *(continued)*

Assign the Item to the Employee

1. Click Lists.

2. Click Employee List.

The Employee List window appears.

3. Double-click the employee for whom you set up a health savings account.

The Edit Employee dialog box appears.

4. Click here to select Payroll and Compensation Info.

5. Click here and click ▾ that appears to select the HSA payroll item.

6. Type the per-paycheck amount.

7. Type the limit.

8. Click OK.

QuickBooks saves the modification.

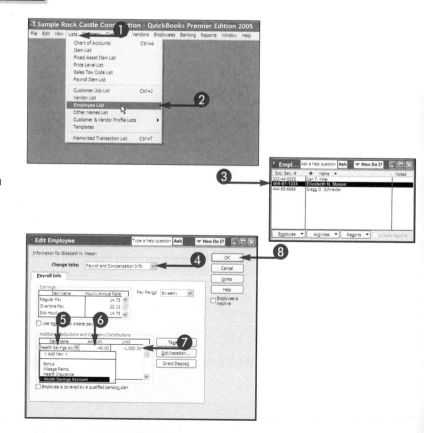

Pay the Employee

① Click Employees.

② Click Pay Employees.

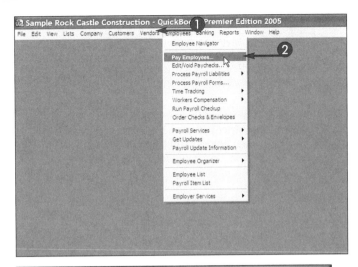

The Select Employees To Pay window appears.

③ Click here to select a bank account.

④ Click the To be printed option to print the check later in a batch (○ changes to ◉).

⑤ Click next to each employee you intend to pay (☐ changes to ☑).

⑥ Click this option to enter hours and preview checks before printing (○ changes to ◉).

⑦ Click Create.

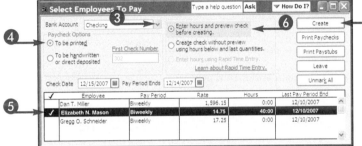

How do I pay the health savings account liability to the administrator?

▼ If you supply the administrator as the agency when you set up the company contribution payroll item for the health savings account, QuickBooks automatically displays any amount due from you to the administrator in the Pay Liabilities window, along with all your other payroll liabilities. You can then select the liability and pay it as appropriate. For details on paying payroll liabilities, see Chapter 9.

Why do I set up a company contribution payroll item instead of any other type of payroll item?

▼ For company contribution payroll items, QuickBooks accrues company money as both a liability and an expense. The liability for a health savings account is owed to the plan administrator, and the company can declare the amount it contributes as a company expense, which is tax-deductible. In addition, the company contribution payroll item does not affect the employee's paycheck.

Can you withdraw money from a health savings account for nonmedical reasons?

▼ Yes, but the withdrawal is taxable and you are subject to a 10 percent withdrawal penalty to discourage such withdrawals. In this respect, health insurance accounts are very similar to IRAs.

Are the contributions to health Insurance accounts subject to social security and Medicare?

▼ No. The contributions — both employer and employee contributions — are completely tax free, making the health savings account even more attractive than an IRA.

PART VII

continued

Health Savings Accounts *(Continued)*

To set up a health savings account in QuickBooks, you can create an other current liabilities account where health savings contributions appear. For details on creating an other current liabilities account, see Chapter 2.

If your company funds employees' health savings accounts, then you need to create a company contribution payroll item for the health savings account. The steps in this section assume that your company funds the health savings account entirely for the employee.

After you create the health savings account payroll item, you assign it to each employee who has a health savings account. At that time, you can specify the amount the company contributes to the account.

When you pay the employee, the contribution appears in the other payroll Items section as a negative number and in the Company Summary section as a positive number. The amount does not affect the employee's taxes or net pay.

Finally, when you produce W-2s in January for the preceding year, contributions to the health savings account appear in Box 12 of the W-2.

Health Savings Accounts *(continued)*

The Preview Paycheck window appears.

● The health savings account contribution appears in the Other Payroll Items section.

● The health savings account contribution also appears in the Company Summary section.

⑧ Click Create.

QuickBooks creates the paycheck.

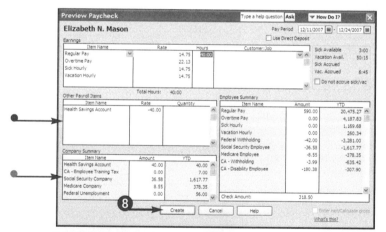

Check W-2s

① Click Employees.

② Click Process Payroll Forms.

The Select Form Type dialog box appears.

③ Click the Federal form option (○ changes to ⊙).

④ Click OK.

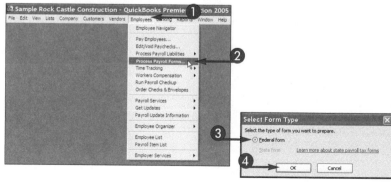

The Select Payroll Form dialog box appears.

5 Click Annual Form W-2.

6 Click OK.

Note: *A message about W-2 adjustments appears; click OK to clear the message.*

The Process W-2s window appears.

7 Click next to the employee for whom you made health savings account contributions (☐ changes to ☑).

8 Click Review W-2.

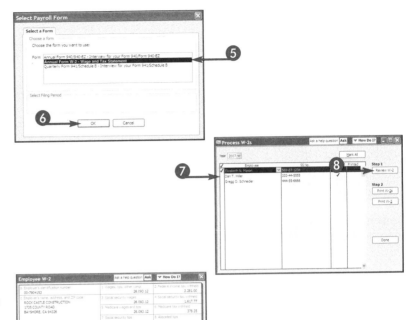

The W-2 appears.

● Health savings account contributions appear in Box 12.

9 Click OK.

QuickBooks processes the W-2.

What makes the amount of the company contribution appear in Box 12 of the W-2?

▼ The Tax Tracking type for a payroll item determines where QuickBooks places the amounts for the payroll item on a W-2. QuickBooks automatically displays amounts for a payroll item with a Tax Tracking Type of Co. Paid Med Savings in Box 12 of the W-2.

Are there rules about the deductible amounts for the insurance policy and how they relate to the annual contribution amount?

▼ Yes. For individuals, the deductible must be at least $1,000, and for families, the deductible must be at least $2,000. Under the health savings account legislation, contributions can equal the amount of the deductible, not to exceed $2,600 for individuals and $5,150 for families.

If an employee leaves the company, what happens to the health savings account?

▼ The health savings account belongs to the employee, not the company. The employee can move to another company or another state, and the health savings account belongs to the employee. Also, the funds in a health savings account do not disappear if not used during a calendar year.

PART VII

Create a Bonus Check

I f you subscribe to the QuickBooks Enhanced Payroll Service, you can easily create bonus checks where you enter the net dollar amount of the bonus check and QuickBooks calculates gross wages, taxes, and, if appropriate, deductions. Accountants often refer to this process as *grossing up* a paycheck. Many companies use this approach to create bonus checks and to create a once-a-year check for a company owner.

These bonus checks in QuickBooks should be handled as separate checks and you should not include them on a regular paycheck. In fact, to create a bonus check by

specifying the net pay amount, you can include only one payroll item in the Earnings section of the paycheck. Create a wage payroll item and designate it as a bonus payroll item; you can name the item Bonus or Annual Salary or anything you want. For details on creating a wage payroll item, see Chapter 4.

When you create a paycheck that grosses up net pay, you must be careful about including other deductions on the paycheck. While QuickBooks takes the deductions into consideration as it grosses up wages and taxes, you typically do not want to include deductions on bonus checks. Instead, you include them on regular paychecks.

Create a Bonus Check

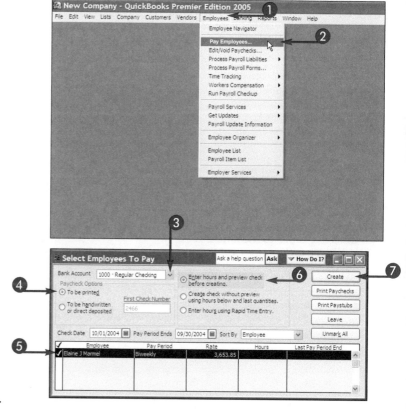

1 Click Employees.

2 Click Pay Employees.

The Select Employees To Pay window appears.

3 Click here to select a bank account.

4 Click the To be printed option to print your check later in a batch (○ changes to ◉).

5 Click next to each employee you intend to pay (☐ changes to ☑).

6 Click the "Enter hours and preview check before creating" option (○ changes to ◉).

7 Click Create.

The Preview Paycheck window appears.

⑧ Click any items that appear in the Earnings and Other Payroll Items sections and press Ctrl-Delete to delete them.

⑨ Click here and select the bonus payroll item.

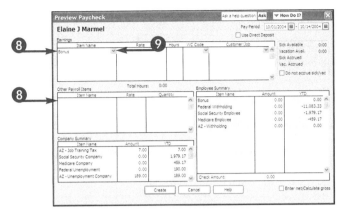

⑩ Click the Enter net/Calculate gross option (☐ changes to ☑).

⑪ Type the bonus pay amount here.

● QuickBooks calculates the gross wages and all appropriate taxes.

⑫ Click Create.

QuickBooks saves the bonus check.

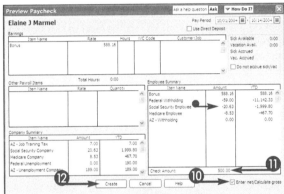

How do I create a bonus check if I do not subscribe to the Enhanced Payroll Service?

▼ You create a wage payroll item for the bonus. You can write a separate check that contains only the bonus payroll item or you can include the bonus payroll item on a regular paycheck along with other earnings, deductions, and additions. QuickBooks does not automatically gross up a net check amount for you. Add the Bonus payroll item to the Other Payroll Items section when you preview the paycheck and type an amount for the bonus. QuickBooks calculates taxes and adjusts the check accordingly. Using this approach, you must manually figure out a gross bonus amount to pay a specific net amount.

If I do not subscribe to the Enhanced Payroll Service, should I create a separate bonus check or include the bonus on a regular paycheck?

▼ Include the bonus on a regular paycheck; otherwise, you may unintentionally underwithhold federal income taxes. Suppose that you have three employees, earning $1,000, $2,500, and $3,500 biweekly, respectively. Because of the government's sliding-scale tax schedule, the federal income taxes for the employee earning $3,500 will be more per paycheck than the combined taxes of the other two employees. Similarly, if you pay an employee $1,000 biweekly and, in a separate bonus check, give him or her $2,500, you do not withhold as much federal income tax as if you paid the employee $3,500 on one paycheck, as required by law.

Set Up for Workers' Compensation

I f you subscribe to the QuickBooks Enhanced Payroll Service, you can set up payroll so that QuickBooks tracks and accrues your workers' compensation liability.

Workers' compensation is a payment that companies make, usually to insurance companies, to provide benefits to workers who are injured on the job. When workers are injured and the injury is deemed work-related, the insurance company pays workers' compensation benefits that typically include medical expenses and possibly wages.

Each state establishes workers' compensation categories and corresponding rates based on the danger level of the work performed by employees in the category. The insurance

company calculates your premium based on the amount of gross pay each employee receives and the workers' compensation category of the employee. For example, the workers' compensation rate for office workers is lower than the rate for construction workers because construction workers are more likely to be injured on the job than office workers are. The rates for workers' compensation categories also depend on the number of accidents that have occurred at your place of business. As the number of accidents increases, the premiums increase.

Set Up for Workers' Compensation

1 Click Employees.

2 Click Workers Compensation.

3 Click Set Up Workers Comp.

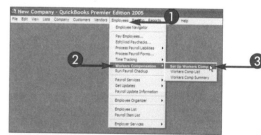

The Workers Compensation Setup Wizard begins.

4 Click Next on the Welcome screen.

The Who is your Workers Compensation Insurance Carrier? page appears.

5 Click here to select your workers' comp insurance carrier.

● You can type your account number here.

6 Click Next.

The Set Employee Default Job Classification Codes screen appears.

7 Click here and then click Add New to add Workers Comp codes.

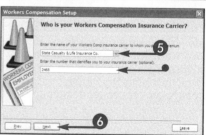

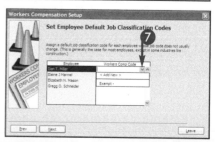

The New Workers Compensation Code dialog box appears.

8 Type the code number here.

9 Type the code description here.

10 Type the rate per $100.00 of gross wages here.

11 Click ▤ to select the starting date for the rate.

12 Click OK.

The Set Employee Default Job Classification Codes Wizard screen reappears.

13 Repeat steps 7 to 12 to add more codes.

The Set Employee Default Job Classification Codes screen reappears.

14 Click here to add a Workers Comp code for the first employee.

15 Repeat step 14 for each employee.

16 Click Next.

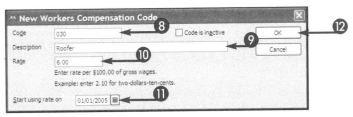

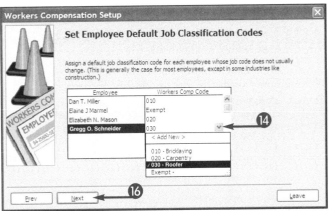

What should I do if my experience factor changes after I have finished setting up the Workers Compensation feature in QuickBooks?

▼ You can change your experience factor — and set an effective date for it — from the Workers Comp Code List. Click Lists and then Workers Comp List. In the Workers Comp Code List window that appears, click Experience Modification, and then Edit. The Edit Experience Modificaton Factor dialog box appears. Type a new factor — type only the number and do not enter a decimal or a percent sign — and select a starting date. Then, click OK to save the change.

What should I do if my insurance company adds workers' compensation codes after I have finished setting up the Workers Compensation feature in QuickBooks?

▼ You can add codes by clicking Lists and then Workers Comp List. In the Workers Comp Code List window that appears, click Workers Comp Code and then New. The New Workers Compensation Code dialog box appears; fill it out using steps 8 to 12 in this section.

How do I set up overtime payroll items?

▼ Follow the steps to create a wage item; see Chapter 4 for details.

PART VII

continued

Set Up for Workers' Compensation *(Continued)*

To use the Workers Compensation feature in QuickBooks effectively, you need to set up workers' compensation before writing paychecks; otherwise, the workers' compensation reports and liability amount will not be accurate. So, plan to start using workers' compensation in QuickBooks on January 1.

To set up workers' compensation, you need to know the codes your insurance company uses and the rates charged for each code, your state's regulations for workers' compensation and overtime, and your experience factor, if assigned by the insurance company. The experience factor increases or reduces your workers' compensation premium.

Most companies pay an overtime premium, such as time-and-a-half, when an employee works more than the specified number of hours in a pay period. Time-and-a-half consists of the employee's regular hourly rate plus half of the regular hourly rate for the hours that exceed 40 hours per week. The extra half of the regular hourly rate — the amount that exceeds the regular rate of pay — is considered overtime premium. In many states, you calculate your workers' compensation liability only on regular wages. If you pay overtime, you should set up overtime payroll items for all types of wages prior to setting up workers' compensation.

The next wizard screen appears.

⑰ Click an Experience Modification Factor option (○ changes to ◉).

- If you click Yes, type a factor here as a whole number, which QuickBooks converts to a percentage; then click ▦ to select a starting date for the experience factor.

⑱ Click Next.

The Overtime Payments screen appears.

⑲ Click Yes or No to specify whether you pay overtime wages (☐ changes to ☑).

Note: *If you click No, you do not see the screen where you describe handling overtime premiums; for this section, click Yes.*

⑳ Click Next.

The Overtime Premiums and Workers Compensation Calculations screen appears.

㉑ Click an option to handle overtime premiums (○ changes to ◉).

㉒ Click Next.

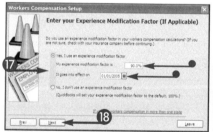

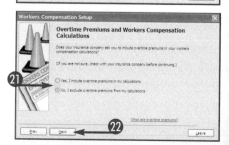

The Name your Workers Compensation Payroll Item screen appears.

㉓ Type a name for the Workers' Compensation payroll item.

㉔ Click Next.

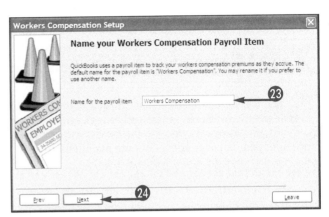

The Completing the Workers Compensation Setup Wizard screen appears.

㉕ Review the summary information.

● To make changes, click Prev.

● You can deselect this option if you do not want to view Help information on workers' compensation (☑ changes to ☐).

㉖ Click Finish.

QuickBooks saves the setup information.

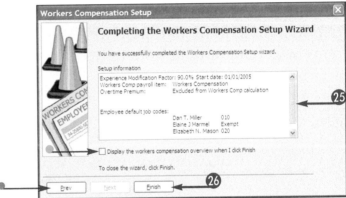

If I do not want to use the Workers Compensation feature, do I need to take any special steps?

▼ Yes. By default, QuickBooks turns the feature on and then prompts you to set up the feature each time you attempt to pay employees or perform some other payroll-related task. To turn off the prompt, click Edit and then Preferences. Click Payroll & Employees and click Set Preferences. In the Workers Comp Preferences dialog box that appears, deselect the Track Workers Comp option (☑ changes to ☐) and click OK twice to save your settings.

Can the QuickBooks Workers Compensation feature handle workers' compensation calculations for more than one state?

▼ Not entirely, but you can use a portion of the feature. Set up separate workers' compensation codes for the same job in different states, enabling QuickBooks to calculate basic workers' compensation amounts accurately for each employee. The Workers Compensation feature supports only one experience factor at a time, however, so if you have different experience factors in different states, set your experience factor to 100 percent. When the experience factor is 100 percent, QuickBooks does not increase or reduce your workers' compensation liability and you can accurately calculate your liability manually.

Payroll and Workers' Compensation

Once you set up the Workers Compensation feature, QuickBooks automatically accrues your workers' compensation liability each time you pay an employee; you do not need to take any additional actions. You can view the amount accrued on each paycheck as you preview paychecks. QuickBooks calculates the workers' compensation amount by dividing gross wages by $100 and then multiplying the result by the rate you set for each workers' compensation code. If you set an experience factor, QuickBooks adjusts the workers' compensation amount by multiplying it by your experience factor. You also can print a series of reports that provide information about workers' compensation. The Workers

Comp Summary report shown in this section organizes information by workers' compensation code and shows gross wages, any overtime premium, workers' compensation wages and hours, the workers' compensation rate, the workers' compensation premium, the experience factor, and the adjusted workers' compensation premium.

The Workers Compensation by Code and Employee report shows the same information as the Workers Comp Summary report, but the Workers Compensation by Code and Employee report breaks the information down further by listing employees that fall into each workers' compensation code category.

Payroll and Workers' Compensation

Workers' Comp and Paychecks

1. Click Employees.

2. Click Pay Employees.

   The Select Employees To Pay window appears.

3. Click here to select a bank account.

4. Click the To be printed option to print the check later in a batch (○ changes to ◉).

5. Click next to each employee you intend to pay (☐ changes to ☑).

6. Click the "Enter hours and preview check before creating" option (○ changes to ◉).

7. Click Create.

   The Preview Paycheck window appears.

8. Review the paycheck for accuracy and make changes as needed.

   - The employee's Workers Compensation Code appears here.

   - The amount accrued for the Workers Compensation liability appears here.

9. Click Create.

   QuickBooks creates the paycheck and stores the Workers Comp liability.

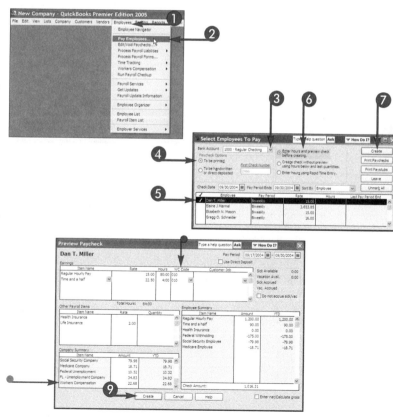

Review Workers Comp Accruals

1 Click Reports.

2 Click Employees & Payroll.

3 Click Workers Comp Summary.

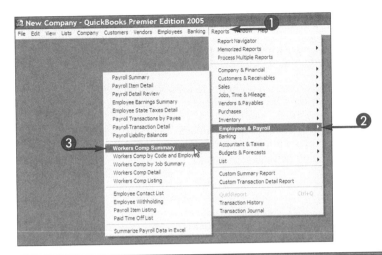

The Workers Comp Summary report appears.

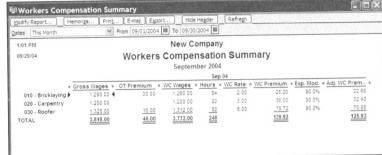

If I pay workers' compensation in more than one state and I have different experience factors in each state, is there an easy way to calculate my workers' compensation liability?

▼ Yes. Make sure that you set up separate workers' compensation codes for the same jobs in each state and that your experience factor is 100 percent. Then, filter the Workers Comp Summary report by selecting workers' compensation codes for only one state. Export the report to Excel, where you can set up a column for your experience factor and multiply the Total WC Premium values by the factor to calculate the amount due. The formula and setup are identical to the one described in the section "Calculate Sales Commissions."

If an employee performs work that falls into a different workers' compensation code than I have assigned to the employee, what should I do?

▼ You can change the workers' compensation code when you preview the employee's paycheck. In the WC Code column in the Earnings section, click and select a different code. QuickBooks recalculates the value that appears in the Company Summary section. You also can split an employee's hours among two or more codes by selecting the wage item multiple times in the Earnings section and selecting a different workers' compensation code on each line.

PART VII

continued

Payroll and Workers' Compensation *(Continued)*

If you assign an employee's hours to jobs, you can use the Workers Comp by Job Summary report to view a breakdown by job for each workers' compensation code category of overtime premium, workers' compensation wages, hours, workers' compensation premium, and adjusted workers' compensation premium.

The Workers Comp Detail report provides information for each paycheck within a workers' compensation code category. On the report, you see the payee's name, the payroll items that appear on the paycheck, the gross wages, overtime premium, workers' compensation wages, hours, workers' compensation code rate, workers' compensation premium, experience modification factor, and adjusted workers' compensation premium. At the bottom of the report, totals appear for the report period.

The Workers Compensation Listing report shows you the same information that appears in the Workers Comp Code window — the workers' compensation code, description, rate, and effective date — along with the next rate and effective date of the next rate.

You pay the workers' compensation insurance bill from the Pay Liabilities window. Because you assigned your workers' compensation insurance carrier in the Workers Compensation Setup Wizard, QuickBooks displays the liability in the Pay Liabilities window. When the bill arrives, pay it from the Pay Liabilities window; if the bill does not match the accrued liability amount, you may need to adjust the liability amount; see Chapter 9 for details.

Payroll and Workers' Compensation *(continued)*

Pay the Workers' Comp Liability

① Click Employees.

② Click Process Payroll Liabilities.

③ Click Pay Payroll Liabilities.

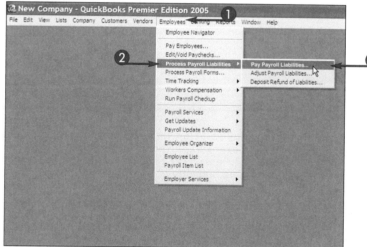

The Select Date Range For Liabilities dialog box appears.

④ Click here to select a time frame.

- You can select specific dates by clicking 🔲.

⑤ Click OK.

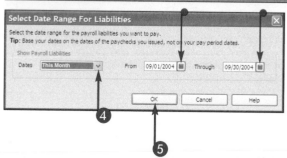

The Pay Liabilities window appears.

6 Click here to select a bank account.

7 Click 🔳 to select a check date.

8 Click the "Review liability check to enter expenses/penalties" option (◯ changes to ◉).

9 Click next to the Workers Compensation liability (☐ changes to ☑).

10 Click Create.

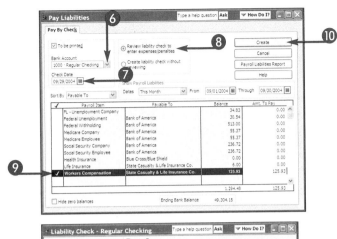

QuickBooks saves the liability check and it appears on-screen.

● You can print the check by clicking the Print button (🖨), or you can wait to print the check with a group of other checks.

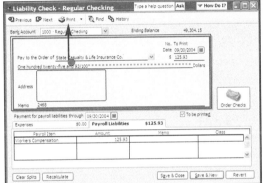

How do I assign a workers' compensation code to a job.

▼ You do not assign the workers' compensation code directly to a job; you assign it indirectly by assigning an employee's hours to a job. By default, you assign workers' compensation codes to employees. Then, you pay employees, which automatically assigns their wages to workers' compensation codes. If you assign an employee's hours to a job at the same time that you pay the employee, you automatically assign the workers' compensation wages associated with those hours to that job. You can use the Workers Comp by Job Summary report to see the breakdown of workers' compensation information for each job.

Where will I see workers' compensation accrue on a paycheck?

▼ The workers' compensation code appears in the WC Code column in the Earnings section next to the Hours column. The amount QuickBooks accrues appears in the Company Summary section, which appears in the lower-left corner of the Preview Paycheck window.

How do I handle employees who are not subject to workers' compensation?

▼ QuickBooks automatically creates an Exempt workers' compensation code; assign this code to all employees not subject to workers' compensation, and QuickBooks does not calculate workers' compensation information or accrue any liability when you pay these employees.

INDEX

continued

continued

INDEX

There's a Visual™ book for every learning level . . .

. . . all designed for visual learners – just like you!

Top 100 Simplified® Tips & Tricks

Tips and techniques to take your skills beyond the basics. Full color.

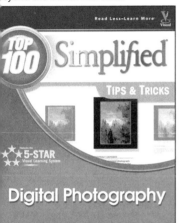

Visual Blueprint™

Where to go for professional level programming instruction. Two-color.

Read Less - Learn More®

For a complete listing of Visual books, go to wiley.com/go/visualtech

Also available:

- **Windows XP: Top 100 Simplified Tips & Tricks, 2nd Edition**
- **Photoshop Elements 3: Top 100 Simplified Tips & Tricks**
- **Mac OS X v.10.3 Panther: Top 100 Simplified Tips & Tricks**
- **eBay: Top 100 Simplified Tips & Tricks**
- **HTML: Top 100 Simplified Tips & Tricks**
- **Office 2003: Top 100 Simplified Tips & Tricks**
- **Excel 2003: Top 100 Simplified Tips & Tricks**
- **Photoshop CS: Top 100 Simplified Tips & Tricks**
- **Internet: Top 100 Simplified Tips & Tricks**

Also available:

- **HTML: Your visual blueprint for designing effective Web pages**
- **Excel Programming: Your visual blueprint for creating interactive spreadsheets**
- **Unix for Mac: Your visual blueprint to maximizing the foundation of Mac OS X**
- **MySQL: Your visual blueprint for creating open-source databases**
- **Active Server Pages 3.0: Your visual blueprint for developing interactive Web sites**

- **Visual Basic .NET: Your visual blueprint for building versatile programs on the .NET Framework**
- **Adobe Scripting: Your visual blueprint for scripting in Photoshop and Illustrator**
- **JavaServer Pages: Your visual blueprint for designing dynamic content with JSP**
- **Access 2003: Your visual blueprint for creating and maintaining real-world databases**

You can master all kinds of topics visually, including these

All designed for visual learners – just like you!

Read Less - Learn More®

eBay® Business Kit
0-7645-6816-7

iPod® and iTunes®
0-7645-7702-6

Creating Web Pages
0-7645-7726-3

For a complete listing of *Master VISUALLY*® titles and other Visual books, go to wiley.com/go/visualtech

Visual An Imprint of ⊕**WILEY** Now you know.